Bernstein's
REVERSE
DICTIONARY

Books by Theodore M. Bernstein

HEADLINES AND DEADLINES (*with Robert E. Garst*)
WATCH YOUR LANGUAGE
MORE LANGUAGE THAT NEEDS WATCHING
THE CAREFUL WRITER
MISS THISTLEBOTTOM'S HOBGOBLINS

Bernstein's
REVERSE
DICTIONARY

Theodore M. Bernstein

with the collaboration of

Jane Wagner

Quadrangle/The New York Times Book Co.

Fourth printing, April 1976.

Designed by Tere LoPrete

Library of Congress Cataloging in Publication Data

Bernstein, Theodore Menline, 1904–
  Bernstein's reverse dictionary.

  Includes index.
  1. English language—Synonyms and antonyms.
  2. English language—Dictionaries. I. Wagner, Jane.
  II. Title.   III. Title: Reverse dictionary.
PE1591.B45   1975   423'.1   75-19178

. . . and this one is for Ethel

Yes, A New Dictionary

A conventional dictionary lists words alphabetically and gives you their meanings. This unconventional dictionary lists an array of meanings alphabetically and gives you the words. That is why it is called a Reverse Dictionary.

The words it discovers for you are those you have momentarily forgotten or those you never knew or those of whose meanings you were not quite certain. If I tell you how the concept originated, it may make the idea more quickly understandable.

One evening a couple of us, in the course of conversation, got onto the subject of Chinese cuisine. My friend said he was especially fond of won ton soup. That led me to remark that the words "won ton" made perhaps even more sense if they were read backward. Whereupon my friend cried out, "Yes, just like that famous sentence, 'Madam, I'm Adam.' What *do* you call that kind of sentence?" I replied, "I know the word you want, but I'm damned if I can think of it at this moment. But anyway, 'won ton' is not what that word refers to, because then 'won ton' would have to read exactly the same backward as forward. And it doesn't."

On and off, between drinks, the two of us struggled for the rest of the evening to recall that word, elusive and yet familiar to both of us.

The next morning I telephoned him in triumph. "You know what we needed?" I said. "A reverse dictionary."

"A what?" said he.

"A reverse dictionary. When we couldn't think of that word last night we would have gone to the reverse dictionary and looked under the *b*'s for 'backward,' and it would have said something like, 'backward—a sentence that reads backward the same as forward: PALINDROME.' Or we could have looked under the *r*'s for 'reverse' and it would have said, 'reverse—a sentence that reads the same in reverse as forward: PALINDROME.' Or if neither of those definitions had occurred to us, we could have tried under the *r*'s for 'right to left—a sentence that reads from right to left just as it does from left to right: PALINDROME.' Get it?"

He got it, all right, and that is how this project began.

It has entailed labor, to be sure, but it was lovable labor. I found it lovable and so did Jane Wagner, who toiled mightily and perceptively as my collaborator. Our labor involved two principal tasks. One was selecting the words to be included in this lexicon; the other was framing the definitions in ways that would make the words readily findable.

In selecting the entries, we had to hit a happy medium between commonplace, everyday words that everyone except a thirteen-month-old infant knows (and would never have to grope for) and words that are so remote from general use that only a specialist in a particular field would have occasion to employ them. Thus you won't find *and* or *the* or *boy* or *box* in this dictionary, nor will you find many words like *bradykinin* or *intratelluric* or *thysanuran*. But you will find *brouhaha* and *cholesterol* and *alliteration* and *danseur*.

Framing the definitions was somewhat more difficult. Let me first set forth two items of terminology that we used and that will be used in this introduction. The word to be defined—that is, the word the user of this dictionary is groping for—we call the *target word*. The first word or words of each definition—that is, the word or phrase that is a synonym for the target word, or at least bears a sense relation to it—we call the *clue word*. It is the clue words that are alphabetized in this vocabulary and it is the clue words that lead into definitions of the target words.

Naturally in most instances these clue words cannot be the first words that ordinarily appear in dictionary definitions, since dictionary definitions often begin with such things as "of or pertaining to" or "the act of" or "any of various substances." Phrases like those would not be helpful here; the first word of each entry must be meaningful. In addition, it must be a word that most likely would occur to the groper for a target word. Let's say the groper was groping for "Adonis"; most probably he would turn to the *h*'s and look for "handsome" or he would turn to the *m*'s and look for "man." Either way he would be rewarded: Under the *h*'s he would find "handsome man: ADONIS" and under the *m*'s he would find "man of great beauty: ADONIS." And he would be at grope's end.

Although we have tried to adhere to dictionary definitions—particularly, although not exclusively, to the concise ones in Funk and Wagnalls Standard College Dictionary—we have sometimes had to modify them so as to begin with meaningful clue words. Moreover, although our definitions give the sense of the target word accurately, their wording on a few occasions does not conform to the part of speech of the target word. For instance, one entry for the noun "agnosticism" is not a noun but rather a phrase: "God's existence questioned." Using that definition provides a helpful clue word—"God's"—and no damage is done to the word's meaning. This book is not, after all, a conventional dictionary.

Still, for a person momentarily lacking any kind of conventional dictionary whatever, this lexicon could help fill the gap. The target words appear alphabetically at the back of the book as an index, accompanied by page numbers that tell where their definitions or synonyms may be found. In other words, this reverse dictionary if used *in reverse* could be a conventional dictionary, though a very abridged one. That puts it one up on a normal dictionary, which can be used in only one direction. Of course, the definitions in this one are not so detailed nor so comprehensive as those in a conventional dictionary, and they are not intended to be. Yet they do give more than a hint of what each target word means.

This reverse dictionary is not a thesaurus either, yet within the limitation of the number of words it contains it can serve a similar purpose. The normal thesaurus throws masses of synonyms and closely or distantly related words at you, often leaving you to find your own way out of the jungle it has created. This lexicon gives you, by means of the clue words, synonyms or closely related expressions ranging from one to five or six for each target word. For the target word ACAUDAL, all that anyone needs for a synonym or a definition is "tailless." For the target word AMBIENCE, however, more is required, and in this vocabulary you will find five entries, as follows:

—atmosphere of a place or situation
—environmental distinctiveness
—feel of a place or situation
—milieu
—surroundings

Thus when using this dictionary for its principal purpose, if you could not recall the word AMBIENCE you could look under any one of those five entries and there the target word would be awaiting you. On the other hand, if you were looking for another way of saying "ambience," you could look in the index and be referred to all of those five entries. In doing that you would be using this work as a thesaurus.

Parenthetically, listing those five entries referring to AMBIENCE brings to mind one of the fascinating difficulties we encountered in devising this dictionary. We found we had to be seers—mind readers for thousands of people. We constantly kept asking ourselves the question, "If Jane Doe Smith couldn't recall Word A, what kindred word or expression to look under would pop into her mind?" We tried to think of as many relevant look-up words as we could and thus the clue words kept multiplying.

That process gave the book a lagniappe that hadn't occurred to us at first: the more entries the wider the opportunity for service to word fiends—vocabulary builders, crossword-puzzle workers and double-crostic solvers. After all, the pattern of this book is not unlike that of a crossword puzzle dictionary, though neither could replace the other. But if the crossword puzzle demanded a six-letter word for a "handsome man," you would find "Adonis" waiting for you in these pages.

If you wanted to get still more fun out of this basically serious book, you could use it to generate new word games in your living room. For instance, after the first round of cocktails, the host, leafing through these pages, could ask Guest A, "What's a word for an ancient adding machine?" If the guest came up with "abacus," the host could reward him with a second cocktail. Then the host could turn to Guest B and say, "Give me any one of a half a dozen definitions of 'abecedarian,' " and if Guest B scratched his head in vain, the host could say, "What you need is another cocktail," and give it to him. And so it could go.

Fundamentally, however, this book is designed with a serious purpose. It is intended to help all users of English, and particularly serious writers, to find words that temporarily are eluding them or words that they did not know even existed. It has as a chief purpose keeping them from settling for a second-best word by making easily available the precise word they require and should have. And needless to say, precision in language is a continuing imperative.

*   *   *

Now for three minor details that should be called to the attention of users of this dictionary:

1. The various kinds of phobias are not entered separately. They appear in a listing under the clue word "phobias."

2. Likewise, the various kinds of manias are not entered separately. They appear in a listing under the clue word "manias." This listing, as well as that of phobias, is derived in the main from Funk and Wagnalls Standard College Dictionary.

3. Terms for groups, males, females and the young of animals, birds, fish and other creatures are not entered separately, but appear in a chart headed "Creature Terms" under the letter C.

T.M.B.

New York, New York, September, 1975

Bernstein's
REVERSE
DICTIONARY

A

abandon, yield, give up: RELINQUISH
abandon an undertaking: SCUTTLE
abandoned, deserted, wretched, cheerless: FORLORN
abandoning of one's faith, party or principles: APOSTASY
abate, calm, quiet: SUBSIDE
abbreviation or sign representing a word such as the dollar sign: LOGOGRAM
abdominal pain resulting from muscular spasms: COLIC
abhorrence, disgust or dislike in the extreme: LOATHING
abide, continue unchanged: SUBSIST
ability, skill: PROWESS
ability to do something adroitly: KNACK
abnormal: ANOMALOUS
abnormal: TERATOID
abnormal, diverging from the natural order: PRETERNATURAL
abnormal or irregular arrangement of parts, as parts of the body: HETEROTAXIS
abominable, revolting, detestable: EXECRABLE
abominable snowman: YETI
about, approximately: CIRCA
about face: VOLTE-FACE
about to happen without delay: IMMINENT
about to occur: IMPEND
above all others in importance: PARAMOUNT
above comparison, preeminently: PAR EXCELLENCE
above the taste of the masses: CAVIAR TO THE GENERAL
abridge or make concise: CONDENSE
abridgement that is brief but comprehensive: COMPENDIUM
abrogate, repeal, revoke: RESCIND
abrupt, sharp emphasis: STACCATO

abrupt passage from one condition to another: TRANSILIENT
abruptly cause: PRECIPITATE
absence of government: ANARCHY
absence of life: ABIOSIS
absent-minded: DISTRAIT
absolute, complete: UNMITIGATED
absolute, full, complete: PLENARY
absolute, positive, final, decisive: PEREMPTORY
absolute, unreserved: IMPLICIT
absolute, without any qualifications: CATEGORICAL
absolute government by an individual: AUTOCRACY
absolute power, supreme command: IMPERIUM
absolute rule: AUTARCHY
absolve: VINDICATE
absorb, occupy completely, monopolize: ENGROSS
absorbed in one's thoughts: BROWN STUDY
absorbed in completely: RAPT
abstainer from alcoholic drinks: TEETOTALLER
abstaining from sexual intercourse, in accordance with religious vows: CELIBATE
abstract, concise summary: PRÉCIS
abstract, speculative philosophy: METAPHYSICS
abstract quality or essence of anything: DISTILLATION
abstruse, hidden: RECONDITE
abstruse, secret, unknown except by a few specially instructed individuals: ESOTERIC
absurd appearance given to something or someone: STULTIFIED
absurd, ridiculous: LUDICROUS
absurd, senseless: IRRATIONAL

absurdity of an argument or proposition demonstrated: REDUCTIO AD ABSURDUM

abundant, lavish, generous: PROFUSE

abundant, numerous: GALORE

abundant, plentiful: RIFE

abuse, handle roughly, manhandle: MAUL

abuse, vilify: REVILE

abuse by words: INVECTIVE

abuse or satirize in humorous prose or verse: LAMPOON

abusive, coarse in language: SCURRILOUS

abusive and defamatory words: OBLOQUY

abusive and loud: THERSITICAL

abusive denunciation, harangue: DIATRIBE

abusive, disgracing: OPPROBRIOUS

abusive language: VITUPERATION

accent, way of speaking a language: INTONATION

accent mark consisting of two dots over a letter (ü): DIERESIS OR UMLAUT

accent mark, hooklike, placed under a "c" (ç): CEDILLA

accent mark in form of an inverted "v" (ˆ): CIRCUMFLEX ACCENT

accent mark in Spanish and Portuguese (˜): TILDE

accent mark that runs from northeast to southwest (´): ACUTE ACCENT

accent mark that runs from northwest to southeast (`): GRAVE ACCENT

accented forcibly in music: SFORZANDO

accept as self-evident truth: POSTULATE

accept or conclude from evidence: INFER

accepted, popular, everyday speech: VULGATE

accepted practice: PRAXIS

accessory: APPURTENANCE

accidental, fortunate by chance rather than design: FORTUITOUS

accidental, random: HAPHAZARD

accidental occurrence: HAPPENSTANCE

accidentally acquired: ADVENTITIOUS

accompany factor or circumstance: CONCOMITANT

accomplice in crime: PARTICEPS CRIMINIS

accomplish, bring about: EFFECT

accomplished fact, done beyond recall: FAIT ACCOMPLI

accomplishment or realization of things worked for: FRUITION

accord, harmonious relationship: RAPPORT

accordion-like small instrument: CONCERTINA

accurate, certain: UNERRING

accurate, exact, precise: NICE

accurate reproduction: FIDELITY

accurate reproduction of a quotation indicated by this word meaning thus or so: SIC

accusation of wrongdoing made against a public official: IMPEACHMENT

accusation or the charging of a wrongdoing or fault: IMPUTATION

accusation or denunciation that is violent: INVECTIVE

accuse, charge with a crime: INDICT

accuse falsely: CALUMNIATE

accuse in return: RECRIMINATE

accuse of wrongdoing or imply guilt: INCRIMINATE

accustom oneself or someone to something: CONDITION

accustom to something difficult: INURE

accustomed or used to, habituated: WONT

acme, highest point: PINNACLE

acquainted or familiar with a subject: CONVERSANT

acquired object or entity: ACQUEST

acquit, justify: VINDICATE

acquit or free from accusation or blame: EXONERATE

acrid: PUNGENT

acrobats' canvas sheet stretched on a frame: TRAMPOLINE

across: ATHWART

acrostic form in which the final letters of successive lines form a word: TELESTICH

acrostic form in which the middle letters of successive lines form a word: MESOSTICH

act as a judge: ADJUDICATE

act as an official: OFFICIATE

acting hastily: BRASH

activate, lead, inspire, as a group: SPARKPLUG

active, lively: VIVACIOUS

actor or actress: THESPIAN

actor who feeds comedian lines: STRAIGHT MAN

actual, real: SUBSTANTIVE

acute, keen, sharp, biting: INCISIVE

acute, keen as in pleasure or pain: EXQUISITE

ad lib: EXTEMPORANEOUS

adage: APHORISM

add at the end: SUBJOIN

add or inject certain elements: INCORPO-
RATE

added syllable or group of syllables at the
end of a word: SUFFIX

adding machine of ancients: ABACUS

addition, increase, something added or
gained: INCREMENT

addition of a sound to the beginning of a
word: PROTHESIS

addition to a will: CODICIL

additions, insertions, interruptions in a
discourse, process or series: IN-
TERPOLATIONS

addressing a person or thing in a digression: APOSTROPHE

address to graduating class: BACCA-
LAUREATE

adept at many things: VERSATILE

adhesive, sticky: VISCID

adjective linked to a noun to which it normally would not apply: TRANSFERRED
EPITHET

adjunct: APPURTENANCE

adjust, temper, soften or regulate: MODU-
LATE

adjusted to a situation: RECONCILED

adjustment: ORIENTATION

adjustment to meet the demands of the environment: REALITY PRINCIPLE

adjustment to society's cultural norms:
ACCULTURATION, ENCULTURATION

administration or manner of governing:
GOVERNANCE

admirable or consummate: EXQUISITE

admittance: ACCESS

admonish or advise strongly, urge by earnest appeal: EXHORT

adorn magnificently, extol, celebrate: EM-
BLAZON

adroit, skillful: DEXTEROUS

adroit or ingenious creation or performance: TOUR DE FORCE

adultery, in law: CRIMINAL CONVERSATION

advance announcement of the coming of
someone or something: HARBINGER

advanced beyond what is usual for one's
age: PRECOCIOUS

advantage spot for observation: COIGN OF
VANTAGE

advantageous: EXPEDIENCY

adverb that is misplaced so it could modify either of two words: SQUINTING
MODIFIER

adverse, unfortunate: UNTOWARD

adversely influence or affect something:
MILITATE

advertisement or notice, usually distributed by hand: HANDBILL

advertising space measurement: AGATE
LINE

advertising that is sensational: BALLYHOO

advise of a fault: ADMONISH

advise or recommend strongly, urge by
earnest appeal: EXHORT

adviser or critic who is frank and severe:
DUTCH UNCLE

advisers, usually secret and unofficial:
CAMARILLA

advocacy or support, as of a cause: ES-
POUSAL

advocate or originator of a cause: PROPO-
NENT

aesthetic qualities associated with ancient
Greece and Rome: CLASSICISM

affectation of style or peculiarity of manner: MANNERISM

affected, artificial: FACTITIOUS

affected display of modesty: PRUDERY

affected in writing, behavior, etc.: PRE-
CIOUS

affectedly prim, elegant or dainty: MINC-
ING

affecter of attitudes to impress others: PO-
SEUR

affecting superiority, ostentatious: PRE-
TENTIOUS

affection that is foolish or excessive:
DOTAGE

affirmative expressed by negating its opposite: LITOTES

affront, insult: INDIGNITY

after-dinner: POSTPRANDIAL

after the fact: EX POST FACTO

after-the-event perception: HINDSIGHT

after death: POSTHUMOUS

aftereffect, reverberation: REPERCUSSION

aftermath: WAKE

aftermath of hay or grass in its second
growth: ROWEN

against, as in having influence or effect
against something: MILITATE

against change or progress, conservative:
REACTIONARY

age of a girl before which intercourse is
rape: AGE OF CONSENT

age or length of life beyond the ordinary:
LONGEVITY

aged, infirm, doting: SENILE

agent, deputy, substitute: VICAR
agent in financing: FACTOR
agent or adviser who is powerful but unofficial: EMINENCE GRISE
agent planted in organization to incite punishable actions: AGENT PROVOCATEUR
agent that remains unchanged while changing other components: CATALYST
agent who handles orders to buy and sell securities: BROKER
agency that sells articles to a number of periodicals: SYNDICATE
aggressive: BUMPTIOUS
aggressive, lively: FEISTY
aging and the aged, as a scientific study: GERONTOLOGY
aging, growing old: SENESCENT
agitated, worried, tense, bewildered: DISTRAUGHT
agitating violently: TURBULENT
agonizing, painful: EXCRUCIATING
agree: ACCEDE
agree: JIBE
agree exactly: COINCIDE
agreeable in manner or style, apt, well-chosen: FELICITOUS
agreeable to persuasion or change: AMENABLE
agreeableness: COMPLAISANCE
agreeing or conforming: CONGRUENT
agreement: CONCURRENCE
agreement: CONSONANCE
agreement, compact, pledge: COVENANT
agreement, treaty, contract: PACT
agreement guaranteed solely by the pledged word of the parties involved: GENTLEMAN'S AGREEMENT
agreement made by disputants pending final accord: MODUS VIVENDI
agreement of all concerned: UNANIMITY
agreement or opinion that is general: CONSENSUS
agreement that is mutual: ENTENTE
agricultural interest: AGRARIAN
aid, succor: SUBVENTION
aid or support as an auxiliary: ANCILLARY
aim, goal, purpose: INTENT
aimed straight at a target and close enough so the projectile does not fall appreciably: POINT-BLANK
aimless wandering: MEANDERING
air attack with machine-gun fire from low-flying planes: STRAFE

air column swirling around a vertical axis: WHIRLWIND
aircraft carrier: FLATTOP
aircraft enclosure, especially one housing an engine: NACELLE
aircraft on a single military mission: SORTIE
aircraft workshop or shelter: HANGAR
air-cushion vehicle: HOVERCRAFT
airhole: SPIRACLE
airplane landing that is perfect: THREE-POINT LANDING
airplane pilots' nervous disorder: AERONEUROSIS
airplane's prospective passenger who fails to claim reservation: NO-SHOW
airtight: HERMETIC
airy, light, spiritual: ETHEREAL
alarm, bell signal: TOCSIN
alarm, upset, disturb: PERTURB
Albuquerque resident: ALBUQUERQUEAN
alcoholic appetizer: APERITIF
alcoholic derelict: WINO
alcoholic liquor, given to: BIBULOUS
alcoholic liquor added in small quantity to a beverage: LACE
alcoholic strong liquor: SCHNAPPS
alcoholism, craving for alcohol: DIPSOMANIA
ale or beer and ginger ale mixed: SHANDYGAFF
alert, watchful: VIGILANT
alienated, estranged: DISAFFECTED
alignment with a margin: FLUSH
alikeness of a trait, characteristic or viewpoint: COMMON DENOMINATOR
all at one time: HOLUS-BOLUS
all life held as sacred: AHIMSA
all kinds of things accepted, as by the mind: OMNIVOROUS
all performers take part, in music: TUTTI
alleviate, extenuate: PALLIATE
alley lined with dwellings that were formerly stables: MEWS
alliance: COALITION
alliance of two or more business concerns for a venture: CONSORTIUM
all-important thing: BE-ALL AND END-ALL
allowable, permissible: TOLERABLE
allowance, salary, pension: STIPEND
allowing unusual freedom, lenient: PERMISSIVE
almighty: OMNIPOTENT
almost, nearly: WELL-NIGH
alms or charity: ELEEMOSYNARY

alone: ISOLATED
alphabetic characters of one language used to represent the letters of another: TRANSLITERATION
alphabet in small letters used in printing: LOWER CASE
alphabet matters: ABECEDARIAN
altar boy: ACOLYTE
altar boy who carries the censer: THURIFER
alter a female animal by removal of ovaries: SPAY
alter or deter the plans of someone by persuasion: DISSUADE
alteration, destruction, mutilation, especially of a legal document: SPOLIATION
alternate, change places: INTERCHANGE
altitude, instrument for measuring: ALTIMETER
altogether, entirely: IN TOTO
always prepared: SEMPER PARATUS
amaze, astound: FLABBERGAST
amazement, fear or panic that is sudden and paralyzing: CONSTERNATION
amazing, hard to believe: INCREDIBLE
amazing, wonderful: PRODIGIOUS
ambiguity, usual unintentional and because of grammatical looseness: AMPHIBOLOGY
ambiguous, insincere: LEFT-HANDED
ambiguous or oracular: DELPHIC
ambiguous talk: DOUBLE TALK
ambiguous, uncertain in origin or character, double meaning, dubious: EQUIVOCAL
ambush: WAYLAY
amends, restoration to proper condition: REPARATION
American Indian male who is married: SANNUP
among other things: INTER ALIA
amount: QUANTUM
amount by which a stock or bond may sell above its dollar value: PREMIUM
amount of stock an individual has sold even though he didn't own it and hasn't yet paid for it: SHORT POSITION
amount that must be paid by customer even though he uses his broker's credit for purchase: MARGIN
amulet or charm: TALISMAN
ammunition belt over shoulder: BANDOLIER
ammunition wagon: CAISSON
amuse, distract, entertain: DIVERT

amuse, entertain: REGALE
amuse or occupy oneself, frisk about, frolic: DISPORT
amusement: DIVERTISSEMENT
amusement, pastime: DIVERSION
anagram, or word puzzle: LOGOGRIPH
analysis of something that has happened; an after-death examination: POST-MORTEM
analysis or interpretation of a word, passage or work: EXEGESIS
analyze, break up or separate into parts: RESOLVE
ancestor dating furthest back, forefather: PRIMOGENITOR
ancestral line: PEDIGREE
ancestry, pedigree: LINEAGE
anchor for small boats: KILLICK
ancient, outmoded, old-fashioned, out of step with the times: ANTEDILUVIAN
ancient, venerable, gray- or white-haired: HOARY
ancient writing: PALEOGRAPHY
"and" symbol (&): AMPERSAND
and the following: ET SEQ.
angel of the highest rank: SERAPH
angle iron or metal bracket used to strengthen a corner or angle of a structure: GUSSET
anger, embitter: RANKLE
anger, enrage: INCENSE
anger or offense shown: BRIDLE
anger roused by injustice or baseness: INDIGNATION
angry, enraged: IRATE
angry, resentful: IN HIGH DUDGEON
angry and frowning stare: GLOWER
angry argument: ALTERCATION
angry behavior: BELLICOSITY
angry dispute, quarrel: WRANGLE
angry or irritated state: SNIT
angry or sullen look, scowl: LOWER
anguish, distress, pain, suffering: TRAVAIL
animal and plant functions and processes, as a science: PHYSIOLOGY
animal and plant structures, as a study apart from function: MORPHOLOGY
animal bereft of its horns: POLLARD
animal doctor: VETERINARIAN
animal or plant selected as representative of a new species: HOLOTYPE
animal or plant surviving from an earlier period or type: RELICT
animal preservation after death by stuffing and mounting skins: TAXIDERMY

animal worship: ZOOLATRY

animals living in a given area: FAUNA

animals that are warm-blooded and whose offspring are fed with milk from female mammary glands: MAMMALS

animate or pervade: INFORM

ankle bones, as a group: TARSUS

annihilation or destruction of an entire people or national group: GENOCIDE

annotate a text between the lines: INTERLINE

announce officially, put into effect: PROMULGATE

annoy, weary, vex: IRK

annoy or harass with taunts or questions: HECKLE

annoy or taunt by reminding of a fault: TWIT

annoying, irritating: VEXATIOUS

annoying, provoking, prodding person: GADFLY

annually recurring, said of certain Mediterranean summer winds: ETESIAN

annul: INVALIDATE

annul, as a law or a right: ABROGATE

annul, suspend: SUPERSEDE

answer sharply: RETORT

antagonist or opposing thing that threatens retribution or defeat: NEMESIS

antagonistic, hostile: INIMICAL

antagonistic, hostile, resisting: REPUGNANT

antic, caper: DIDO

antic, caper: GAMBADO

anticipatory: PREVENIENT

anti-government in any form: ANARCHIC

antiquated: ANTEDILUVIAN

anxiety: DISQUIETUDE

anxiety, agitation, nervous excitement: DITHER

anxiety about one's health, often over imagined symptoms: HYPOCHONDRIA

anxiety or concern: SOLICITUDE

anxiety or state of suspense: ON TENTERHOOKS

apartment consisting of single room with kitchenette and bathroom: EFFICIENCY APARTMENT

apartment house in which occupants own shares of stock in the building: CO-OPERATIVE

apartment house in which units are owned separately by individuals: CONDOMINIUM

apathetic: PHLEGMATIC

apathetic, lackadaisical, indifferent: LISTLESS

apathetic, unconcerned: INDIFFERENT

apathy, sluggishness, dullness: LETHARGY

apathy, stupor: TORPOR

ape-like: SIMIAN

apex, top: VERTEX

apologetic: DEPRECATORY

apologetic, meek, shy person: MILQUETOAST

apparatus that functions by itself: AUTOMATON

apparent, seeming: OSTENSIBLE

apparent to sight or understanding, evident, obvious: MANIFEST

apparently but not really correct: SPECIOUS

apparition of a person thought to be alive, seen just before or after his death: WRAITH

apparition or ghost: SPECTER

apparitions or images in a series, as in a dream: PHANTASMAGORIA

appeal earnestly, direct, command: ADJURE

appeal to prejudice, not reason: AD HOMINEM

appealing to emotions: AFFECTIVE

appear or come into view as through a mist often ominously: LOOM

appearance: SEMBLANCE

appearance, aspect: GUISE

appearance, manner: MIEN

appearance-improving: COSMETIC

appearance of truth: VERISIMILITUDE

appearance or aspect that is false in order to deceive: GUISE

appearance or look of a thing: PHYSIOGNOMY

appearance or manifestation of a deity, a showing forth: EPIPHANY

appearing in various passages in a book: PASSIM

appeasable, forgiving: PLACABLE

appease, pacify: PLACATE

appease, win good will: PROPITIATE

appease or satisfy by deceit, put off by lies or evasion: FOB

appeasement gift or bribe: SOP

append: SUBJOIN

appendix to a will: CODICIL

appetite so great as to be pathological: BULIMIA

appetizer in form of alcoholic drink: APERITIF

appetizer of toast and a spread: CANAPÉ

appetizers: HORS D'OEUVRES
appetizing, tasty: SAVORY
applauders hired for the purpose: CLAQUE
applause: PLAUDIT
applause outburst: OVATION
applicable, pertinent: RELEVANT
appoint or preempt: CO-OPT
appointment or secret meeting, as of lovers: TRYST
appointment to meet, meeting place: RENDEZVOUS
apprehension, doubt, qualm: MISGIVING
apprentice, beginner: NOVICE
approach game or prey in a stealthy manner: STALK
approachable: ACCESS
appropriate, just right: PAT
appropriate, applicable: RELEVANT
appropriate or pirate the ideas, writings, music, etc., of another: PLAGIARIZE
appropriate or seize beforehand: PREEMPT
appropriateness, fitness: EXPEDIENCY
approval: APPROBATION
approval, support, encouraging look: COUNTENANCE
approve, permit, ratify: SANCTION
approved status granted an academic institution: ACCREDITATION
approximately: CIRCA
apt, well chosen, agreeable in manner or style: FELICITOUS
Arabian hooded cloak: BURNOOSE
Arabian kerchief worn over head and shoulders: KAFFIYEH
Arabian sleeveless garment: ABA
Arabic or decimal system of counting: ALGORISM
arbitrary, overbearing: HIGHHANDED
arbor or walk with a latticework roof: PERGOLA
arch that is narrow and acutely pointed: LANCET ARCH
archeological excavation: DIG
architectural movement promoting synthesis of painting, sculpture and technology: BAUHAUS
architectural projecting block: DENTIL
architecture order of Greece characterized by fluted columns and simple capitals: DORIC
architecture order of Greece characterized by ornate, bell-shaped capitals: CORINTHIAN
architecture order of Greece characterized by scrolls on the capitals: IONIC

arctic, frigid: HYPERBOREAN
ardent, extremely fervid: PERFERVID
ardent, passionate: TORRID
ardent, violent, impetuous: VEHEMENT
ardor, intensity of emotion: FERVOR
area of authority or competency: BAILIWICK
arena for horse shows, circuses: HIPPODROME
arguable, open to question: DISPUTABLE
argue earnestly or debate: CONTEND
argue earnestly with someone about the inadvisability of some action: EXPOSTULATE
argue or contend about trifling matters: STICKLE
argue or dispute noisily: WRANGLE
argue or oppose: CONTROVERT
argue over terms or prices: HIGGLE
arguer who takes wrong side perversely: DEVIL'S ADVOCATE
argument: POLEMIC
argument in which one of the premises or the conclusion is not stated but implied: ENTHYMEME
argumentation, debate: FORENSICS
argumentative: AGONISTIC
argumentative: ERISTIC
argumentative, contentious: DISPUTATIOUS
aristocrat, member of the upper classes: PATRICIAN
arm or leg stiffness or cramp: CHARLEY HORSE
aromatic substances in a ball: POMANDER
around, about, approximately: CIRCA
arouse anger or bitterness: RANKLE
arouse interest or curiosity: INTRIGUE
arouse, startle, thrill: ELECTRIFY
arousing comment, as a piece of furniture or art: CONVERSATION PIECE
arrange or organize: COLLOCATE
arrangement according to time of occurrence: CHRONOLOGY
arrangement of parts: CONFIGURATION
arrangement of parts in abnormal or irregular fashion, as parts of the body: HETEROTAXIS
arrangement of parts that is harmonious and elegant: CONCINNITY
arrangement or plan of a book, TV show, etc.: FORMAT
arrangement or progression that is orderly or gradual: GRADATION
arrest made by citizen who sees a crime: CITIZEN'S ARREST

arrive at or reach a port: FETCH

arrogance arising from overbearing pride or passion: HUBRIS

arrogance or conceit characterizing one's ways or attitudes: OVERWEENING

arrogant: RODOMONTADE

arrogant: SUPERCILIOUS

arrogant, domineering: IMPERIOUS

arrogant, forward: PRESUMPTUOUS

arrogant assertion of beliefs: DOGMATIC

art, music or literature schools that seek to produce moods through quick glimpses of subject: IMPRESSIONISM

art and literary movement that tries to exhibit the workings of the subconscious mind: SURREALISM

art cult that rejected conventions: DADA

art for art's sake: ARS GRATIA ARTIS

art of curvilinear designs, now characterized as campy: ART NOUVEAU

art of everyday realism by U.S. Group: ASHCAN SCHOOL

art of good eating: GASTRONOMY

art or literature of a cheap, popular or sentimental quality: KITSCH

art work painted directly on a wall: MURAL

art work consisting of arrangement of flat materials pasted on a surface: COLLAGE

artery walls thickened: ATHEROSCLEROSIS

artful moves or strokes: MANEUVERS

artful strategy, cunningness, craftiness: FINESSE

article or book presenting facts on a subject: TREATISE

articulate clearly and distinctly: ENUNCIATE

artificial, affected: FACTITIOUS

artificial, counterfeit: POSTICHE

artificial part of body: PROSTHESIS

artificial manner: AFFECTATION

artificially elegant style of speech or writing: EUPHUISM

artillery or cannon, military material: ORDNANCE

artist or writer who doesn't sell his services exclusively to one employer: FREE LANCE

artistic small article: OBJET D'ART

artistically thought-of ordinary object: OBJET TROUVE

artless, candid, sincere: GUILELESS

artless, unaffected, simple, candid: NAIVE

arts movement that departs from reality to reproduce inner experience: EXPRESSIONISM

ash gray: CINEREOUS

ashamed, degraded, sneaky: HANGDOG

aside directed to a person or thing: APOSTROPHE

assistant: COADJUTOR

assistant or attendant: ACOLYTE

ask for humbly, pray earnestly for something: SUPPLICATE

ask questions, examine: INTERROGATE

aspect, phrase or side of a person or subject: FACET

aspersion: SLUR

assault from behind with intent to rob: MUG

assembling of separate parts into a whole: SYNTHESIS

assembly place: AGORA

assent: ACQUIESCENCE

assertion of something made by the negation of its opposite: LITOTES

assimilation of thoughts or facts that is gradual: OSMOSIS

assist: ABET

assistance or money furnished to advance a venture: GRUBSTAKE

assistant or servant, as of a magician or scholar: FAMULUS

associate closely with someone: FRATERNIZE

associate on close terms: HOBNOB

association, fellowship: SODALITY

association of individuals to negotiate some business: SYNDICATE

assume as a fact: POSIT

assume to be true: POSTULATE

assumed name or identity: INCOGNITO

assumptions based on evidence at hand or facts already known: EXTRAPOLATION

assumption provisionally accepted as basis for reasoning or argument: HYPOTHESIS

assure, guarantee: VOUCH

astound, confound: FLABBERGAST

astrologers' chart of position of planets and stars for fortune telling: HOROSCOPE

astringent: ACERB

at once, immediate: INSTANTER

at the home of: CHEZ

at this time: HEREAT

athlete's leap over a high horizontal bar

with the aid of a long pole: POLE VAULT

athletic, sturdy body structure: MESOMORPHIC

athletic club, gymnast association: TURNVEREIN

athletic contest in which each contestant participates in five events: PENTATHLON

athletic contest of ten field and track events in all of which each contestant participates: DECATHLON

athletically vigorous: STHENIC

atmosphere beginning at a height of about seven miles: STRATOSPHERE

atmosphere of a place or situation: AMBIENCE

atmosphere or influence that is unwholesome or noxious: MIASMA

atmospheric and weather phenomena, as a science: METEOROLOGY

atom splitting: NUCLEAR FISSION

atomic bomb: A-BOMB

atomic particle carrying a positive charge: PROTON

atomic particle carrying no charge: NEUTRON

atone for, make amends for: EXPIATE

atonement shown for wrongdoing: PENANCE

atoning: PIACULAR

atrocious, beyond decency: OUTRAGEOUS

atrocious, odious, wicked, evil: HEINOUS

atrocious, wicked: FLAGITIOUS

attach the property of a person so it can be used to pay a debt: GARNISHEE

attachment of one thing to another: APPURTENANCE

attachment to a thing or a person: FIXATION

attack, dispute or challenge the truth or validity of: IMPUGN

attack that is swift and sudden, usually in war: BLITZKRIEG

attack that is violent: ONSLAUGHT

attack with scathing criticism: FLAY

attempting: CONATION

attendant who arranges details of journey for travelers: COURIER

attendants, retainers or followers in a group: ENTOURAGE

attendants of a person of rank, escort: RETINUE

attentive: ASSIDUOUS

attentive to every detail: CIRCUMSPECT

attitudes and character of a community or individual: ETHOS

attract, cause or make likely: INVITE

attractive, pleasing: PREPOSSESSING

attractive, sweet, engaging: WINSOME

attractive in a flashy way: MERETRICIOUS

attractive photographically: PHOTOGENIC

attribute to another without just reason: ARROGATE

auction or sale that is public: VENDUE

audacity, brassiness: CHUTZPAH

audacity, boldness, impudence: EFFRONTERY

aura, halo: NIMBUS

auspices: AEGIS

auspicious, favorably disposed: PROPITIOUS

austere: ASTRINGENT

austere person: ASCETIC

authenticity lacking: APOCRYPHAL

authoritative, urgently necessary, unavoidable: IMPERATIVE

authoritative because of rank or office. EX CATHEDRA

authority or power that is absolute or supreme: IMPERIUM

authority shared: COLLEGIALITY

authorization: FIAT

authorize, empower: WARRANT

author's assumed name: NOM DE PLUME

auto driving contest: RALLY

automatic, lifeless: MECHANICAL

automatic response to a stimulus: TROPISM

automaton, mechanical man: ROBOT

automobile adjusted or re-equipped for quick starts and high speed: HOT ROD

automobile engine that works on rotary combustion: WANKEL ENGINE

automobile of standard make modified for racing: STOCK CAR

automobile with convertible design but with a rigid top: HARDTOP

auxiliary: ADMINICLE

auxiliary: ANCILLARY

avarice, greed: CUPIDITY

avenging, punitive: VINDICATORY

average, moderately good: RESPECTABLE

avert or prevent: OBVIATE

avoid, turn aside, ward off: PARRY

avoid or escape: ELUDE

avoid or outwit: CIRCUMVENT

avoidable: EVITABLE

away from the center: CENTRIFUGAL

awesome, ominous: PORTENTOUS

awesome or fearsome: FORMIDABLE

awesome or imposing: AUGUST

awaiting, until: PENDING

awkward: UNGAINLY

awkward, askew, awry: SPLAY

awkward, boorish: UNCOUTH

awkward, clumsy: GAUCHE

awkward, incompetent, clumsy: INEPT

awkward, slouching movement: LOP

awkward fellow, clown, boor: LOUT

awkward or complicated situation, predicament: PLIGHT

awkward or inexperienced person on board a ship: LANDLUBBER

awkward rustic: BUMPKIN

ax- or hatchet-shaped: DOLABRIFORM

axiomatic, terse, pithy: SENTENTIOUS

axis common to loudspeakers or transmission lines: COAXIAL

B

baby delivery by abdominal surgery: CAESAREAN SECTION

baby delivery, childbirth: PARTURITION

back country, remote area, inland region: HINTERLAND

back of horse, ox or deer, between shoulder blades: WITHERS

back of the neck: NAPE

back out of an agreement, revoke: RENEGE

backbone creatures: VERTEBRATES

backer of a cause: PROPONENT

backward looking, turning or bending: RETROVERSION

backward movement: RECOIL

backward movement, reversion: REGRESSION

backward moving, tending to recede: RECESSIVE

backward reading of a word or sentence is the same as forward reading: PALINDROME

backward reasoning, from consequence to antecedent, considered a logical fallacy: HYSTERON PROTERON

backward tending, worsening, declining: RETROGRADE

backward writing that is readable in a mirror: MIRROR WRITING

bacon or pork slice used for larding meat: LARDON

bad, evil, repulsive: VILE

bad breath: HALITOSIS

bad check: KITE

bad handwriting or spelling: CACOGRAPHY

bad in a conspicuous fashion, glaring, flagrant: EGREGIOUS

bad job: BOTCH

bad luck: AMBSACE

bad money drives out good: GRESHAM'S LAW

bad morally: UNSAVORY

badge or sign of devotion consisting of two small pieces of cloth worn about the neck by members of religious orders: SCAPULAR

bad-tempered: ATRABILIOUS

bad-tempered: CANTANKEROUS

bad-tempered, spiteful: SPLENETIC

bad-tempered outburst: TANTRUM

bag of perfumed powder: SACHET

bag used by sailors for carrying personal belongings: DITTY BAG

bag worn strapped across the shoulders used for carrying supplies: KNAPSACK

bag worn over one shoulder: HAVERSACK

baggage, supplies and equipment carried by an army: IMPEDIMENTA

bagpipe's shrill sound: SKIRL

bait, allurement, enticement: GUDGEON

balance: EQUILIBRIUM

balance, counteract or compensate for something else: OFFSET

balance or counterbalance: EQUIPONDERATE

balcony, window or porch with an excellent view, in Spanish architecture: MIRADOR

baldness: ALOPECIA

baldness, especially on top of the head: CALVITIES

balk, move restlessly sidewise or backward: JIB

balky, fretful, jittery: RESTIVE

ball game in which players hit a ball against a wall by striking it with their hands: HANDBALL

ball of small size: PELLET

ballet dancer, female: BALLERINA

ballet dancer, male: DANSEUR

ballet dancer who performs only in groups: FIGURANT

ballet dancer who ranks between the so-

loists and the corps de ballet: CORY-
PHEE
ballet dancer's whirling on the toes: PIR-
OUETTE
ballet dancing position on tiptoe: POINTE
ballet leap upward with dancer activating
legs in air: ENTRECHAT
ballet's principal female dancer: PRIMA
BALLERINA
ballet's principal male dancer: PREMIER
DANSEUR or DANSEUR NOBLE
ball's horizontal twist or spin: ENGLISH
ban or curse: ANATHEMA
banal, trite, commonplace remark: PLATI-
TUDE
band or group: COHORT
bandage, bound with a band: FASCIATE
bandage used to compress an artery to
stop the flow of blood: TOURNIQUET
banish, exile: RELEGATE
bankrupt, insufficient funds: INSOLVENT
banned, forbidden: TABOO
banner fixed to a crosspiece rather than a
pole: GONFALON
banter: CHAFF
banter, flippant talk or writing: PERSIFLAGE
banter, jesting: RAILLERY
bar, upright and forming the principal support: STANCHION
bar serving food and drink: BRASSERIE
bar used to prevent a vehicle from slipping
backward on an incline: SPRAG
barefooted, as certain religious orders:
DISCALCED
barely begun: INCHOATE
bargain, at a good bargain: A BON MARCHÉ
bargain or argue about terms: HAGGLE
baring parts of the body for sexual stimu-
lation of oneself: EXHIBITIONISM
bark or yelp: YAWP
barrel maker: COOPER
barrel stave: LAG
barren, bleak: STARK
barren, fruitless, sterile: INFECUND
barren, insipid, dry, lacking interest,
naive: JEJUNE
barren, said of cows infertile for a period:
FARROW
barren, unfruitful: STERILE
barren or weak: EFFETE
barrier made up of strong stakes: PALISADE
barrier to keep out disease: CORDON SANI-
TAIRE
base, degraded, vile: SORDID
base, dishonorable, degraded: IGNOBLE

base, weak, wretched: CAITIFF
base something on known facts or conditions: PREDICATE
baseball home run hit when there is a runner on every base: GRAND SLAM
baseball pitcher strikes out a batter: FAN
baseball pitcher who replaces another:
RELIEFER or RELIEVER
baseball barely deflected by the bat: FOUL
TIP
baseball decision by a player to try to put
out man already on base rather than
the batter: FIELDER'S CHOICE
baseball diamond space within the four
base lines: INFIELD
baseball fly hit in fielding practice by a
batsman who tosses the ball up and
strikes it as it descends: FUNGO
baseball hard hit so that it travels in an approximately horizontal trajectory:
LINE DRIVE
baseball hit on which the batter reaches
third base: TRIPLE
baseball hit that allows the batter to touch
all bases and score a run: HOME RUN
or HOMER
baseball infielder stationed between second and third bases: SHORTSTOP
baseball out made when a runner, forced
from his base by a teammate's hitting
the ball, fails to reach the next base
before the ball is caught there:
FORCE-OUT
baseball pitch by a right-hander that
curves right or by a left-hander that
curves left: SCREWBALL
baseball pitch that curves only slightly:
SLIDER
baseball pitch that curves sharply downward as it approaches home plate:
SINKER
baseball pitch that the catcher cannot
handle, thereby allowing a runner to
advance: WILD PITCH
baseball play in which a man on base
starts running with the pitch and the
batter is obligated to strike at the ball
to protect him: HIT-AND-RUN PLAY
baseball play in which a runner is caught
off base by a sudden throw: PICKOFF
baseball play in which the batter tries to
bunt the ball to allow a man on third
to score: SQUEEZE PLAY
baseball play in which three players are
put out: TRIPLE PLAY

baseball play in which two players are put out: DOUBLE PLAY

baseball player able to bat both left-handed and right-handed: SWITCH HITTER

baseball player who is used as a substitute in different positions: UTILITY PLAYER

baseball retirement of a batter with three strikes: STRIKEOUT

baseball slang for a long hit: CLOUT

baseball term for catching fly balls in practice: SHAGGING

baseball term for division of the game during which each team has a turn at bat: INNING

baseball term for fly ball or bunt that results in an out, but enables a base runner to advance: SACRIFICE

baseball term for fly ball that falls between the infield and the outfield for a base hit: TEXAS LEAGUER

baseball term for hit ball that rolls or bounces along the ground: GROUND BALL or GROUNDER

baseball term for hitting the ball lightly without swinging the bat: BUNT

baseball term for lefthanded pitcher: SOUTHPAW

baseball term for illegal pitched ball, that is wetted on one side with saliva: SPITBALL

baseball term for not swinging at a pitched ball: TAKE

baseball term for pitcher's illegal motion: BALK

baseball term for play in which a base runner trapped between two bases is put out: RUNDOWN

baseball term for obscure minor league: BUSH LEAGUE

baseball term for pen where pitchers warm up: BULLPEN

baseball term for catcher's error in failing to catch a pitch, thus allowing man on base to advance: PASSED BALL

baseball term for weakly hit ball: BLOOPER

baseless: UNFOUNDED

baseness, vileness, depravity: TURPITUDE

basic: ABECEDARIAN

basic, inherent in, fundamental: ORGANIC

basic unity in ecology, including both organisms and environment: ECOSYSTEM

basis, fundamental principle: HYPOSTASIS

basis for a discussion or conclusion: PREMISE

basket, usually large and covered: HAMPER

basket of fruit done in sculpture: CORBEIL

basketball free throw: FOUL SHOT

basketball moved by bouncing it with the hand: DRIBBLE

basketball shot made with one hand from close to the basket: LAYUP

basketball shot made by a player in the air during a jump: JUMP SHOT

bath: ABLUTION

bathing suit for women that is brief and two-piece: BIKINI

batter cake that is crisp and baked in a griddle: WAFFLE

battle formation: DEPLOYMENT

battle that is great or decisive: ARMAGEDDON

battle-ax with two sharp edges: TWIBIL

bawl, shout, exclaim loudly: VOCIFERATE

bay or stream leading into the land from a larger body of water: INLET

bay window: ORIEL

beach bathhouse: CABANA

beam going from wall to wall: CROSSBEAM

beam resting horizontally upon the walls of a building and supporting the ends of joists: SUMMER

beam-emitting device that amplifies and concentrates light waves: LASER

beams placed parallel and horizontally from wall to wall: JOISTS

bearable: TOLERABLE

beard on the chin: GOATEE

beard that is short and pointed: VANDYKE

beastlike in form: THERIOMORPHIC

beat, cudgel: FUSTIGATE

beat, overcome: DRUB

beat, thrash severely or punish: TROUNCE

beat at which the hand of the conductor is raised: UPBEAT

beat rapidly, flutter, quiver: PALPITATE

beat soundly: BELABOR

beat with the fists: PUMMEL

beating with a stick: BASTINADO

beautiful buttocks: CALLIPYGIAN

beauty: PULCHRITUDE

beauty, as a subject of study: ESTHETICS

because of this: HEREAT

become known, leak out: TRANSPIRE

become or make better: AMELIORATE

becoming sour: ACESCENT

bed, grade, layer: STRATUM

bed cover that is quilted: COMFORTER

bed of straw that lies on the floor: PALLET
bedridden the person is not: AMBULATORY
bedsore: DECUBITUS
bedspread or quilt: COUNTERPANE
bed-wetting: ENURESIS
beef cattle male: STEER
beef cut from the loin end ahead of the rump: SIRLOIN
beef marinated in vinegar before cooking: SAUERBRATEN
beef tenderloin, lean and thick, broiled: FILET MIGNON
beehive, especially one made of straw: SKEP
beehives: APIARY
beer or ale and ginger ale mixed: SHANDYGAFF
before noon: ANTEMERIDIEM
before now, previously: HERETOFORE
before the Flood: ANTEDILUVIAN
beforehand opinion: PRECONCEIVE
beg: CADGE
beg something of: SUPPLICATE
beg urgently, entreat: IMPLORE
beget, produce: PROCREATE
beggar or sponger: SCHNORRER
begging: MENDICANT
begin, commence: INAUGURATE
begin, commence, originate: INITIATE
beginner: ABECEDARIAN
beginner: FLEDGLING
beginner, apprentice: NOVICE
beginner, recent convert: NEOPHYTE
beginner, novice: TYRO
beginning, commencement: CONCEPTION
beginning, start: INCEPTION
beginning a series of lines or sentences with same word or phrase: ANAPHORA
beginning affixed to a word: PREFIX
beginning to appear, coming into existence: INCIPIENT
beginnings, earliest stages of development: INCUNABULA
behave (oneself): DEMEAN
behavior or deportment: DEMEANOR
behavior that is seemly and proper: DECOROUS
behead: DECAPITATE
behind: BUTTOCKS
behind: DERRIÈRE
behind, after, later: POSTERIOR
behold: VOILA
being, objective existence of something in the mind, actual being: ENTITY

belch: ERUCT
belief, doctrine or principle maintained as true by a person or a group: TENET
belief in a god: THEISM
belief in one god without denying the existence of others: HENOTHEISM
belief in something with too little evidence: CREDULITY
belief or opinion contrary to established doctrine: HERESY
beliefs or opinions held to be true and necessary: DOGMA
believability: CREDIBILITY
believable, apparently true but open to doubt: PLAUSIBLE
belittle: DISPARAGE
belittle, detract: DEROGATE
belittle: DEPRECIATE
belittle, put down: DISPARAGE
belittle, speak disparagingly: POOH-POOH
bell casting and ringing: CAMPANOLOGY
bell ringing variations: CHANGE RINGING
bell rung at morning, noon and night: ANGELUS
bell shaped woman's hat: CLOCHE
bell signal, alarm: TOCSIN
bell sounded slowly and at regular intervals: TOLLING
bell tolling, especially one announcing a death: KNELL
bell tower, especially one that is not part of a building: CAMPANILE
belligerent's right to use or destroy neutral's property: ANGARY
bells ringing: TINTINNABULATION
bells rung by hammers operated from a keyboard: CARILLON
belly, big and prominent: PAUNCH
belly button: NAVEL
belly button: UMBILICUS
belt buckle's tonguelike part: TANG
belt or cord put around the waist: CINCTURE
bench, upholstered and without arms: BANQUETTE
benches without roof at sporting event: BLEACHERS
bend, contort, twist: WRITHE
bend, curve in and out: SINUATE
bend, misrepresent, twist: DISTORT
bend the knee, as in worship: GENUFLECT
bendable, flexible: PLIABLE
bending, curved or bent part: FLECTION
bending easily, graceful, limber: LITHE

bending of light or heat ray as it moves from one medium to another: RE-FRACTION

bending or winding, unsteady, wavering: FLEXUOUS

beneath, below: NETHER

beneath one's dignity: INFRA DIG

beneficial: SALUTARY

beneficiary or recipient of a legacy: LEGATEE

benefit owed because of status: PERQUI-SITE

bent backward: RETROFLEX

bent like a hook: UNCINATE

berate, upbraid, scold severely: OB-JURGATE

beseeching: SUPPLIANT

beset by a difficult situation: HARDSET

beset or surround: BELEAGUER

beside the (real) point: ACCIDENTAL

bespangled with fine stars: STELLULAR

best, most distinguished: ELITE

best in given field: ARISTOCRACY

best moment, most critical time: PSY-CHOLOGICAL MOMENT

best quality, highest priced: GILT-EDGED

bestow, make known, disclose: IMPART

bet on races in which those backing winners share in the total wagered: PARIMUTUEL

betrayal: SELLOUT

betterment: MELIORATION

betterment of the world: MELIORISM

betting on a choice that has little chance of winning: LONG SHOT

betting on winners in two races: DAILY DOUBLE

betting the winnings of a previous race on a later one: PARLAY

between: INTERVENING

between acts: ENTR'ACTE

between the devil and the deep blue sea: DILEMMA

between the lines: INTERLINEAR

bevel a surface: CHAMFER

bewilder, amaze, stun: STUPEFY

bewilder, dumbfound, perplex: NONPLUS

bewilder, muddle, obscure: OBFUSCATE

bewildered: BEMUSED

bewildered, tense, worried, agitated, crazed: DISTRAUGHT

bewildered, uncertain, puzzled: PER-PLEXED

beyond the lawful powers of, forbidden: ULTRA VIRES

beyond words: INEFFABLE

bias, prejudice: PRECONCEPTION

bias or partiality preconceived: PREDILEC-TION

biased: TENDENTIOUS

biased, favoring one party, prejudiced: PARTIAL

biblical interpretation: HERMENEUTICS

bids entered simultaneously for the same stock are resolved by a flip of a coin: MATCHED AND LOST

big belly: PAUNCH

Big Board: NEW YORK STOCK EXCHANGE

big toe: HALLUX

bigoted, narrow-minded, obstinate: HIDE-BOUND

bigotry: INTOLERANCE

big, thick-skinned animals with hooves: PACHYDERMS

biggest portion (originally the whole thing): LION'S SHARE

bill for merchandise sent or services rendered: INVOICE

billiard ball caused to recoil after impact: DRAW

billiard shot in which the ball first strikes the cushion: BRICOLE

billiard shot in which the cue ball strikes two others in succession: CAROM

billiard stroke in which the cue is held perpendicularly: MASSÉ

bind one's arm to render helpless: PINION

biological classification that is a sub-division of a genus: SPECIES

biological deterioration of a strain or type, especially of man: DYSGENIC

bird cage, usually large: AVIARY

bird group terms and terms for young— see "creature terms"

bird study: ORNITHOLOGY

bird's rump or part that holds the tail feathers: UROPYGIUM

birth, buttocks first: BREECH DELIVERY

birth by abdominal surgery: CAESAREAN SECTION

birth control governing the number and spacing of offspring: PLANNED PAR-ENTHOOD

birthmark: NEVUS

biscuit baked on a griddle and served with butter: SCONE

biscuit for army and navy use that is hard and crackerlike: HARDTACK

bishop who acts as assistant or auxiliary to another bishop: SUFFRAGAN

bishopric, bishops collectively: EPIS-
COPATE

bishop's geographical area of jurisdiction:
DIOCESE

bit, scrap: SNIPPET

biting: ASTRINGENT

biting, caustic: PUNGENT

biting, sarcastic: CAUSTIC

biting, sharp, keen: INCISIVE

biting taste, manner, speech, nature:
ACRID

bitter: ACERB

bitter: ACRIMONIOUS

bitter, rancorous: VIRULENT

bitter taste, manner, speech, nature: ACRID

bitterness: ASPERITY

bizarre, fantastic: GROTESQUE

black: JET

black alloy used in cut-in decorations in
metal: NIELLO

black and blue: LIVID

black and blue mark, bruise: ECCHYMOSIS

black and white, light and shade:
CHIAROSCURO

black letter type: OLD ENGLISH

black magic, fortune telling, sorcery: NEC-
ROMANCY

blacken, disparage, defame: DENIGRATE

blackness, darkness: NIGRESCENCE

blacks in America of African descent:
AFRO-AMERICAN

blacksmith's workshop: SMITHY

bladder examination: CYSTOSCOPY

bladder inflammation: CYSTITIS

blame: CENSURE

blame, charge with fault: INCULPATE

blame, criticize, find fault with: REPRE-
HEND

blame, reprove, censure: REPROACH

blame, rebuke, disapproval: REPROOF

blame is mine: MEA CULPA

blamed person to whom mistakes of others
are attributed: SCAPEGOAT

blameless: IRREPROACHABLE

blameless, faultless: UNIMPEACHABLE

blameworthy: CULPABLE

bland, dull, tasteless, flat: INSIPID

blank, gap: LACUNA

blank, fixed, uncomprehending: GLASSY

blank check: CARTE BLANCHE

blank leaf at beginning or end of a book:
FLYLEAF

blasphemous: IMPIOUS

bleach or dry in the sun: INSOLATE

bleak, barren: STARK

bleeding condition caused by absence of a
clotting factor: HEMOPHILIA

bleeding in large quantities: HEMORRHAGE

blemish or stain: MACULATION

blend: AMALGAM

blend, combine: INTERLACE

blend and reconcile, as various philosophies: SYNCRETIZE

blend or fuse together: COALESCE

blending of two vowels generally pronounced separately: SYNERESIS

blending together as of variant readings of
a text: CONFLATION

blessing: BENEDICTION

blind alley: CUL DE SAC

blind persons, printing method for:
BRAILLE

blindly devoted: IDOLATROUS

blindness or impaired vision for blue and
yellow: TRITANOPIA

bliss, release from care and pain: NIRVANA

blister-producing: VESICANT

blind spot: SCOTOMA

block, hinder, stop, impede: OBSTRUCT

block, shut or close off: OCCLUDE

block or obstruct: STYMIE

block or stone on which a column or
statue stands: PLINTH

block that projects (architecture): DENTIL

blockhead: CLODPATE, CLODPOLL

blockhead: JACKASS

blockhead, stupid person: DOLT

blood clot in the heart or blood vessel:
THROMBOSIS

blood clotting: COAGULATION

blood infection: SEPTICEMIA

blood poisoning: TOXEMIA

blood relationship: CONSANGUINITY

bloody: SANGUINARY

bloody slaughter: CARNAGE

blossom, bloom forth, flower: EFFLORESCE

blossoming: FLORESCENCE

blossoming, late: SEROTINOUS

blotch, spot, streak: MOTTLE

blouselike garment gathered at the waist:
TUNIC

blow in puffs: WHIFFLE

blow to back of the neck in boxing: RAB-
BIT PUNCH

blue: RISQUÉ

blue appearance of skin, due to lack of oxygen in blood: CYANOSIS

blue blindness: TRITANOPIA

blundering, clumsy: MALADROIT

blunt, direct: POINT-BLANK

blunt, dull, insensible: OBTUSE

blurred piece of print, blemish or spot: MACKLE

blurring or softening colors or lines in a painting or drawing: SCUMBLE

bluster or bragging talk: GASCONADE

board with handle underneath used to hold plaster or mortar: HAWK

boards arranged for nailing together into barrels or boxes: SHOOK

boaster: GASCON

boastful, bragging: RODOMONTADE

boastful defiance: BRAVADO

boastful or bullying speech: FANFARONADE

boastfully vain: VAINGLORIOUS

boasting soldier: SWASHBUCKLER

boasting that is ostentatious: JACTITATION

boasting that is pretentious: BRAGGADOCIO

boat, flat-bottomed with battened sails, used by Chinese: JUNK

boat, narrow and light, for racing: SCULL

boat basin for pleasure craft: MARINA

boat for fishing: SMACK

boat framework that extends beyond the rail: OUTRIGGER

boat or ship term for upper edge of craft's side: GUNWALE, GUNNEL

boat race or series of boat races: REGATTA

boat, small and flat-bottomed, used along the rivers and coasts of China and Japan: SAMPAN

boat that drags a net across a fishing bank: TRAWLER

boat that services another at sea: TENDER

bodily attributes or elements: CORPORAL, CORPOREAL

bodily disorders caused by mental or emotional conditions: PSYCHOSOMATIC

bodily pleasures or place that provides them: FLESHPOT

bodily processes that continuously build up and break down protoplasm: METABOLISM

body, as distinguished from the soul: SOMATIC

body, having preoccupation with: CARNAL

body of mean summoned to assist a peace officer: POSSE

body stealer: RESURRECTIONIST

bog, marsh: MORASS

bog, swamp, backwater: SLOUGH

bog down, sink in mud: MIRE

boil down, condense: DECOCT

boil gently: SIMMER

boil partly: PARBOIL

boiling, agitated condition: CALDRON

boisterous, unruly: OBSTREPEROUS

bold, dauntless, fearless: INTREPID

bold, indecent, self-assertive: IMMODEST

bold, saucy, brazen, shameless: IMPUDENT

boldness, audacity, impudence: EFFRONTERY

boldness, daring, audacity: HARDIHOOD

bomb or grenade consisting of a bottle containing flammable liquid: MOLOTOV COCKTAIL

bomb that explodes into jagged pieces: FRAGMENTATION BOMB

bombastic: TUMID

bombastic, high-flown: INFLATED

bombastic, grandiloquent: TURGID

bombastic, pompous: GRANDILOQUENT

bombastic, ornate, florid, showy: FLAMBOYANT

bombastic, pretentious: FUSTIAN

bond, connection, link: NEXUS

bond, tie that connects: LIGAMENT

bond often lacking a specific pledge of assets: DEBENTURE

bond issue that may be redeemed by issuer before maturity: CALLABLE

bond issued by a company with a reputation for showing a profit: GILT-EDGED

bond not having owner's name registered with issuing company and payable to any holder of the bond: BEARER BOND

bond of union: VINCULUM

bond on which principal and interest are guaranteed by a company other than the issuer of the bond: GUARANTEED BOND

bond value, as it appears on the security: FACE VALUE

bone and muscle branch of surgery: ORTHOPEDICS

bone at lower end of spine: COCCYX

bone-forming process: OSSIFICATION

bones united by muscles: SYSSARCOSIS

book bound in paper rather than cloth or leather: PAPERBACK

book bound in stiff cover as distinguished from paperback: HARD-COVER BOOK

book carrying various versions of a text: VARIORUM

book containing rules of spelling, punctuation, typography, used by editors: STYLEBOOK

book cover lining, especially when it is ornamental: DOUBLURE book installment prior to publication: FAS-CICLE

book jacket matter that touts the volume: BLURB

book lover and collector: BIBLIOPHILE

book of daily prayers and offices for canonical house: BREVIARY

book or article on a single subject: MONO-GRAPH

book or list of lessons for church service: LECTIONARY

book or Bible peddler: COLPORTEUR

bookbinding leather: SKIVER

bookbinding style characterized by gilded ornamentation: GROLIER

bookbinding with leather on the spine and corners and cloth or paper on the sides: HALF BINDING

bookmaker's advantage in the betting odds he creates: VIGORISH

bookplate, from the library of: EX LIBRIS

books of an author or on a given subject listed: BIBLIOGRAPHY

books or other writings on unusual topics, often pornography: CURIOSA

books printed before 1500 A.D.: IN-CUNABULA

boor, clown, awkward fellow: LOUT

boorish: UNCOUTH

boot covering the leg to the knee in front, but cut lower in back: WELLINGTON BOOT

boot of sealskin or reindeer skin worn by Eskimos: MUKLUK

booth, newsstand, bandstand usually lightly constructed and open: KIOSK

booty, loot: PILLAGE

booty, money: PELF

booty, stolen goods, etc.: PLUNDER

border on: ABUT

border or contrasting edge: LIMBUS

bore or displease: PALL

bored, dull, or depressed state of mind: DOLDRUMS

boredom, discontent or weariness: ENNUI

boring, tedious: WEARISOME

boring, wearisome: TEDIOUS

born of the same parents as another: GERMAN

born out of wedlock: MISBEGOTTEN

born with: INHERENT

borrower's property or securities pledged to insure repayment of a loan: COL-LATERAL

borrowing stock expected to decline in order to sell it at a higher price: SHORT SALE

botany as a descriptive study: PHY-TOGRAPHY

botch a job: BUNGLE

both hands used equally well: AMBIDEX-TROUS

both sexes united in one person: AN-DROGYNOUS

bother, disturb: INCOMMODE

bother, fluster, fuss: POTHER

bother, inconvenience, trouble: DISCOM-MODE

bottle for vinegar or oil: CRUET

bottle of glass that is decorative and used for wine: DECANTER

bounce, jolt, shake up and down: JOUNCE

bound or consecrated by vow or promise: VOTARY

bound with a band, bandage: FASCIATE

boundary, restriction: PALE

boundary between the shore and the ocean: STRAND LINE

boundary line of a figure or area: PERIME-TER

bountiful, lavish, generous: MUNIFICENT

bow decoration on a ship: FIDDLEHEAD

bow decoration on a ship in the form of a carved figure: FIGUREHEAD

bow of a stringed instrument made to rebound slightly: SPICCATO

bowel stimulant, cathartic: PURGATIVE

box with feinting movements and light blows: SPAR

boxer belonging to lightest weight class, weighing 112 pounds or less: FLY-WEIGHT

boxer weighing up to 126 pounds or a wrestler up to 134 pounds: FEATH-ERWEIGHT

boxer or wrestler weighing between 127 and 135 pounds: LIGHTWEIGHT

boxer or wrestler weighing between 136 and 147 pounds: WELTERWEIGHT

boxer or wrestler weighing between 147 and 160 pounds: MIDDLEWEIGHT

boxer or wrestler weighing between 161 and 175 pounds: LIGHT HEAVY-WEIGHT

boxer or wrestler weighing over 175 pounds: HEAVYWEIGHT

boxer's deformed ear: CAULIFLOWER EAR

boxing: PUGILISM

boxing and matters pertaining to boxing: FISTIC

boxing term for a victory in a fight halted by the referee: TECHNICAL KNOCK-OUT

boxing victory based on points when there has been no knockout: DECISION

boy used in sodomy: CATAMITE

brag about: VAUNT

bragging, blustering: RODOMONTADE

bragging, boastful: THRASONICAL

bragging talk or bluster: GASCONADE

braid: PLAIT

braid that is narrow and flat, woven in a herringbone effect: SOUTACHE

brain examination that traces changes in electric potential: ELECTROENCEPH-ALOGRAM (EEG)

brain inflammation: ENCEPHALITIS

brain-lacking: ANENCEPHALOUS

brains, intellect: GRAY MATTER

brake in which friction pads press on disc that is part of wheel: DISC BRAKE

branch, offshoot: RAMIFICATION

branch or spread out, diverge: DIVARICATE

branched: RAMOSE

brand new, original condition, unused: MINT CONDITION

brave, staunch: YEOMANLY

brave, steadfast: UNFLINCHING

brave, strong, determined: STALWART

brave, warlike, disciplined: SPARTAN

bravery pretended: BRAVADO

brawl: AFFRAY

brawl, fight, conflict, uproar: FRAY

brawl marked by roughness, free-for-all: DONNYBROOK

brazen, shameless, bold, saucy: IMPUDENT

brazen audacity: CHUTZPAH

brazenly display or parade: FLAUNT

bread, usually braided, eaten by Jews on holiday: HALLAH or CHALLAH

bread made of cornmeal, eggs, milk and shortening, baked soft enough to be served with a spoon: SPOON BREAD

bread that is baked yellow then sliced and toasted: ZWIEBACK

break, as in electric service: OUTAGE

break, tear apart forcibly: REND

break apart: RUPTURE

break away, separate from: DISSOCIATE

break of a relationship: RIFT

break in continuity: INTERREGNUM

break in continuity to give an episode occurring earlier: FLASHBACK

break off from an association, or separate from an association: DISSOCIATE

break off relations with: DISAFFILIATE

break or pause in a line of verse: CAESURA

break or split, especially in layer: SPALL

break out or erupt afresh: RECRUDESCE

break up a group into small dissenting factions: BALKANIZE

break up or separate into parts, analyze: RESOLVE

breakable, brittle, fragile: FRANGIBLE

breakdown or collapse that is sudden and ruinous: DEBACLE

breakfast, late, or luncheon: DÉJEUNER

breaking of a law or a pledge: INFRACTION

breaking off in the middle of a sentence without completing the idea: APOSIO-PESIS

breaking or rushing in: IRRUPTION

breast of a woman: POITRINE

breast or chest: PECTORAL

breast removal surgery: MASTECTOMY

breast separation line in a woman: CLEAVAGE

breathe: RESPIRE

breathe noisily, as a dog following a scent: SNUFFLE

breathe or blow into or upon: INSUFFLATE

breathing difficulty caused by swelling in some parts of the body: EMPHYSEMA

breathing that is labored: DYSPNEA

breeches loose above the knees, tight below: JODHPURS

breed, multiply by natural reproduction: PROPAGATE

breed rapidly, swarm, teem: PULLULATE

breeding of special races or strains of animals and plants: STIRPICULTURE

brewing process of fermentation, as a branch of chemistry: ZYMURGY

bribe or procure one to commit perjury: SUBORN

bribe or something given as appeasement: SOP

bribery acceptable, corrupt: VENAL

brick that is sun dried: ADOBE

bride's outfit: TROUSSEAU

bridge bid that exceeds the preceding bid by more than the minimum: JUMP BID

bridge hand with no card higher than nine: YARBOROUGH

bridge victory consisting of the winning of all thirteen tricks in a round of play: GRAND SLAM

bridgelike framework for holding the rails of a traveling crane: GANTRY

brief, concise, terse: LACONIC
brief and meaningful, terse, concise: SUC-CINCT
brief general view of a work: SYNOPSIS
bright, brilliant: INCANDESCENT
bright, intense, clear: VIVID
bright, rational, clear, eásily understood: LUCID
bright idea: BRAINSTORM
brighten by rubbing: FURBISH
brilliance, radiance, splendor: RE-FULGENCE
brilliance of action or effect: ECLAT
brilliant, ostentatious oratory: PYROTECH-NICS
brilliant, speedy, dazzling: METEORIC
brilliant in a light and playful fashion: LAMBENT
brilliant or dashing performance: BRAVURA
brilliantly wise or intelligent: LUMINOUS
brim in front of a cap to shade the eyes: VISOR
brine for pickling: SOUSE
bring about, accomplish: EFFECT
bring forth, originate: SPAWN
bring on oneself: INCUR
bring something about quickly: PRECIPI-TATE
bring together: RALLY
bring up or train: NURTURE
bring up partly digested food: REGURGI-TATE
brisk, cheerful: CHIPPER
brisk, dashing, self-confident, stylish, lively: JAUNTY
briskly, lively, quickly, in music: VIVACE
bristly: SETACEOUS
bristly or spiny: ECHINATE
British Parliament member who is not a party leader: BACKBENCHER
British record of proceedings in Parliament: HANSARD
broad in tastes or understanding: CATHO-LIC
broad jump: LONG JUMP
broadcaster who coordinates reports: AN-CHOR MAN
broadheaded: BRACHYCEPHALIC
broadside or leaflet distributed free: THROWAWAY
broken, incomplete: FRAGMENTARY
broken bit of earthenware: POTSHERD
broken down: DILAPIDATED
broken down, decrepit: FLEA-BITTEN
broken-hearted: INCONSOLABLE

broken off piece: CANTLE
broken piece of pottery: SHARD
broken up into incidents, disjointed: EPI-SODIC
broker holding securities in his own name rather than in the name of his customer: STREET NAME
brokerage house that is fraudulent: BUCKET SHOP
brokers' broker: SPECIALIST
brokers on the floor of the stock exchange handling transactions for other brokers: TWO-DOLLAR BROKER
bromide, trite expression: CLICHÉ
bronze or silver gilt: VERMEIL
brook or creek: ARROYO
brothel: BORDELLO
brothers or sisters: SIBLINGS
browbeat, bully, cow: INTIMIDATE
browbeat, torment, rant, bully, bluster: HECTOR
brown paper used for bags and wrapping: KRAFT
brown or reddish brown pigment or pictures done in this pigment: SEPIA
bruise by blow or impact: CONTUSE
bruise or black-and-blue mark: ECCHY-MOSIS
Brussels resident: BRUXELLOIS
brutish, stupid, foolish, unmoved: INSEN-SATE
bubble, ripple, heave: POPPLE
bubbling over with enthusiasm or excitement: EBULLIENT
Buddhist concept of birth-death-rebirth cycle: SAMSARA
Buenos Aires native: PORTEÑO
buffet meal consisting of Scandinavian hors d'oeuvres: SMORGASBORD
buffet or sideboard, usually without legs: CREDENZA
buffoon, clown: MERRY ANDREW
bugle call in the military indicating good night or marking a military burial: TAPS
build up something with parts taken from other things: CANNIBALIZE
building construction as an art or science: TECTONICS
building of many stories: HIGH-RISE
bulging: PROTUBERANT
bulky, lumbering: PONDEROUS
bulky, of great volume: VOLUMINOUS
bulletin board for actors in a theater: CALLBOARD

bullets, missiles, rockets, etc., science of: BALLISTICS
bullfight: CORRIDA
bullfight horseman who pricks the bull's neck with a lance: PICADOR
bullfighter who kills the bull: MATADOR
bullish, like a bull: TAURINE
bully, browbeat, torment: HECTOR
bully, cow, browbeat: INTIMIDATE
bulwark, fortification: RAMPART
bump, strike against: JAR
bump or lump, protuberance: KNURL
bun or knot of hair at the back of the head, worn by women: CHIGNON
bungled action: MUFF
bungling, clumsy, or domineering: HEAVY-HANDED
bungling, inept person: SCHLEMIEL
buoyancy, elasticity: RESILIENCE
buoyant, optimistic, cheerful: SANGUINE
burden: MILLSTONE
burden, discouraging or oppressive thing: INCUBUS
burdens, drawbacks: IMPEDIMENTA
burdensome: ONEROUS
bureau of drawers, often with a mirror: CHIFFONIER
burglar's crowbar: JIMMY
burial mound: TUMULUS
burial vault: SEPULCHER
burlesque imitation of a serious literary or musical work: PARODY
burlesque or imitation that is grotesque: TRAVESTY
burlesque rigmarole: AMPHIGORY
burn quickly with great heat and light: DEFLAGRATE
burn the midnight oil in writing or studying: LUCUBRATE
burn tissue: CAUTERIZE
burn up, cremate: INCINERATE
burning, caustic: VITRIOLIC

burning fiercely: CONFLAGRANT
bursting or breaking in: IRRUPTION
bury, inter: INHUME
business that may hire nonunion workers, who are required to become union members by a specified time: UNION SHOP
businessman who assumes full control and risk of an enterprise: ENTREPRENEUR
bustle, excitement, fluster: POTHER
bustle about, rush pell-mell: HURRY-SCURRY
busybody: QUIDNUNC
butterfly or moth: LEPIDOPTERAN
buttocks: DERRIÈRE
buttocks: FUNDAMENT
buttocks: NATES
buttocks that are fat, especially in women: STEATOPYGIA
buttress joined to a wall some distance away: FLYING BUTTRESS
buy or sell order for securities good only for the day on which it is entered: DAY ORDER
buy up goods for reselling at a profit: FORESTALL
buy up with the aim of selling at a higher price: REGRATE
buyer beware: CAVEAT EMPTOR
buying and selling the same stock simultaneously in two different cities to realize a profit: ARBITRAGE
buying and selling volume of stocks relatively low: THIN MARKET
buying or selling sacred things: SIMONY
buying securities at stated intervals by the dollars' worth: MONTHLY INVESTMENT PLAN
by the very fact: IPSO FACTO
by-product, new application, incidental result: SPIN-OFF

C

cabal: CAMARILLA

cabal, intriguing group: JUNTA

cable, wire or rope used to steady or secure something: GUY

cable or rope for mooring or towing: HAWSER

cafe or restaurant that provides entertainment: CABARET

cage, usually large, for live birds: AVIARY

Cairo (Egypt) resident: CAIRENE

cajole: BLANDISH

cake, small and made of unsweetened batter: CRUMPET

cake made of butter and eggs, with fruit or nuts added: TORTE

cake made of sugar, eggs, and flour, containing no shortening and beaten very light: SPONGE CAKE

calamity: CATASTROPHE

calculating device with counters moving up and down on rods: ABACUS

calculator of risks and premiums for insurance: ACTUARY

calendar used in most of the world: GREGORIAN CALENDAR

California gold miner: ARGONAUT

calfskin or lambskin that is untanned: KIP

call, summon or draw forth: EVOKE

call in question, dispute, challenge: OPPUGN

call or whistle derisively: CATCALL

call to troops for service, review, etc.: MUSTER

call together, as a meeting: CONVOKE

call upon for aid, protection, witness: INVOKE

callow, immature, but opinionated: SOPHOMORIC

calm: DISPASSIONATE

calm, peaceful, tranquil: PLACID

calm down, quiet, abate: SUBSIDE

calm, quiet, serene: TRANQUIL

calm, serene, idyllic: HALCYON

calm, serene, unmoved: IMPASSIVE

calm, unruffled: IMPERTURBABLE

calm, untroubled, tranquil: SERENE

calmness, composure, even-temper: EQUANIMITY

Cambridge (Mass.) resident: CANTABRIGIAN

Cambridge (U.K.) resident: CANTABRIGIAN

camel with one hump: DROMEDARY

camera lens that records 180-degree field of vision: FISH-EYE LENS

camp, temporary, usually without shelter: BIVOUAC

can or cup that is small: CANNIKIN

cancel, recall, rescind, annul: REVOKE

cancer of the blood: LEUKEMIA

cancer-causing substance: CARCINOGEN

cancerous growth: CARCINOMA

candelabrum with seven branches used in the Jewish religion: MENORAH

candid, sincere, artless: GUILELESS

candidate almost unknown who wins a nomination or election: DARK HORSE

candidate list: SLATE

candidate put forward as a cover for another person: STALKING HORSE

candied or sugared, iced, frozen: GLACÉ

candlemaker: CHANDLER

candlestick that is branched: CANDELABRUM

candlestick that is branched, rotating firework: GIRANDOLE

canine tooth: CUSPID

cannibals: ANTHROPOPHAGI

cannon or artillery, military materiel: ORDNANCE

cannon with a relatively high angle of fire: HOWITZER

24

canoe that is covered except for an opening for the paddler: KAYAK

canopy or large tent, summerhouse: PAVILION

canopy over a pulpit or bed: TESTER

canopy used in religious processions: BALDACHIN

cant, lingo: JARGON

cantankerous: CROTCHETY

canvas sheet stretched on a frame and used for acrobatics: TRAMPOLINE

cap, flat and round: BERET

cap cover with long rear flap: HAVELOCK

cap of felt with a tassel, worn by Moslem men: TARBOOSH

cap that is square and stiff and worn by clergy: BIRETTA

capable of working, as a plan; able to live: VIABLE

caper, antic: DIDO

caper, antic: GAMBADO

caper, prance about: TITTUP

capital letters in type: UPPER CASE

capital that is hardly adequate used in starting a business: SHOESTRING

caprice, whim, fanciful humor: WHIMSY

capricious, willful: WAYWARD

caption or explanatory description on an illustration, chart or map: LEGEND

capture or seize: CORRAL

Caracas resident: CARAQUENO

card game called twenty-one: VINGT-ET-UN

card game series in which the series is terminated when one side has won two games: RUBBER

card game state in which a winner has made more than double his opponent: LURCH

card game that breaks a tie between players: RUBBER

card of a suit that outranks other suits during the playing of a hand: TRUMP

cards left on the table after the deal: TALON

carefree: FOOTLOOSE

carefree, light-hearted, gay: ROLLICKING

carefree, unconcerned, lighthearted: INSOUCIANT

carefree, worry-free: SANS SOUCI

carefree existence, drink and play: BEER AND SKITTLES

careful, checking every detail: CIRCUMSPECT

careful, frugal, cautious: CHARY

careful, scrupulous observance of forms: PUNCTILIOUS

careful, wise: JUDICIOUS

careful about what one says, prudent, tactful: DISCREET

careful and diligent: PAINSTAKING

carefully, cautiously: GINGERLY

carefully and delicately made: WROUGHT

careless, reckless: DEVIL-MAY-CARE

careless, reckless, weak: FECKLESS

careless, negligent: REMISS

careless or untidy person: SLOVEN

carelessly done: SLIPSHOD

caress or touch lightly as with the lips or make gentle contact, as two billiard balls: KISS

cargo cast overboard by an imperiled ship: JETSAM

carp or raise trivial objections: CAVIL

carpet of velvety texture: WILTON

carriage with hood and with high seat for horse driver: CABRIOLET

carried away by foolish love: INFATUATED

carrier of microorganisms: VECTOR

carry away wrongfully: ABDUCT

carry, haul, drag: SCHLEP

carry or move gently, float: WAFT

carry through, put into effect: IMPLEMENT

carry through or accomplish something: TRANSACT

carve, engrave, cut into: INCISE

carved design beneath the surface: INTAGLIO

carved ivory, stone, or shells: SCRIMSHAW

carving or engraving, especially on gems: GLYPTICS

case or example: INSTANCE

cash in a prize coupon, etc.: REDEEM

cash lacking: ILLIQUID

cash payment that must be made by customer when he uses his broker's credit for purchase of a security: MARGIN

cask holding half a barrel: KILDERKIN

cassock worn by Roman Catholic priest: SOUTANE

cast off, as dead skin: SLOUGH

cast off or discard a previously favored sweetheart: JILT

cast out an evil spirit by prayers or incantations: EXORCISE

cast out matter or refuse as from a volcano: EJECTA

casting or molding of footprints, etc., for

use in criminal investigation: MOU-LAGE

castle-like in structure: CASTELLATED

castrate, geld, weaken, make effeminate: EMASCULATE

castrated animal, especially a horse: GELDING

castrated man or youth: EUNUCH

castrated rooster: CAPON

casual, indiscriminate, especially sexually: PROMISCUOUS

casual, minor, secondary: INCIDENTAL

casualties sorted to fix priorities for treatment: TRIAGE

cat, particularly an old female one: GRI-MALKIN

cat family: FELINE

catch up with or get ahead of, as a ship: FOREREACH

catching: INFECTIOUS

Catholic Church list of forbidden books: INDEX EXPURGATORIUS

catlike cry, long and plaintive cry: WAUL

cat's eye: CHATOYANT

Catskill and White Mountain hotels that provide entertainment: BORSCHT CIRCUIT

cattle food: PROVENDER

cattle herder: COWBOY, COWHAND, COWPUNCHER

cattle movement to more suitable pastures: TRANSHUMANCE

caught in the act: IN FLAGRANTE DELICTO

caught in the act: RED-HANDED

cause, bring about: INDUCE

cause a result creditable or discreditable: REDOUND

cause and effect theory in philosophy, especially of human behavior: DETERMINISM

cause or make likely, attract: INVITE

cause something abruptly or unexpectedly: PRECIPITATE

cause that produces a result: FACTOR

cause to effect, prior to: A PRIORI

causes and origins as subjects of study: ETIOLOGY

caustic: ACRIMONIOUS

caustic, biting: PUNGENT

caustic, burning: VITRIOLIC

caustic, cutting, sarcastic: MORDANT

caustic, mercilessly severe, withering: SCATHING

cautious: WARY

cautious, frugal, careful: CHARY

cautious, moderate, opposed to change: CONSERVATIVE

cautious checking of every detail: CIRCUMSPECT

cautiously, carefully: GINGERLY

cautiously shrewd: CANNY

cave explorer: SPELUNKER

cave formation, cone-shaped, that is built up on the floor: STALAGMITE

cave formation, long and tapering, that hangs from the roof: STALACTITE

cave man: TROGLODYTE

cave or fall in, sink, collapse, fail: FOUNDER

caves, as a subject of study: SPELEOLOGY

cavities in the skull leading into nasal cavities: SINUSES

cease-fire, armistice: TRUCE

ceiling decorated with a painted or carved design: PLAFOND

celebrate, make merry, delight (in): REVEL

celebrity, fame: RENOWN

celestial, heavenly: SUPERNAL

celestial, sublime, superior, fiery: EMPYREAL

cellar or underground shelter used during cyclones or tornadoes: CYCLONE CELLAR

cells; study of their structure, organization and function: CYTOLOGY

cement or plaster used to surface walls: STUCCO

cemetery for paupers: POTTER'S FIELD

censor by deleting offensive passages: BOWDLERIZE

censor by removing obscene or otherwise objectionable material: EXPURGATE

censorship that is exaggerated: COMSTOCKERY

censure, blame, rebuke: REPROACH

censure, scold, reproach: UPBRAID

censure or rebuke severely: REPRIMAND

censure vehemently: INVEIGH

center in common: CONCENTRIC

center of attraction: CYNOSURE

centerless: ACENTRIC

central essential element, core: NUCLEUS

central point, hub, navel: OMPHALOS

century, era, period: SIÈCLE

century and a half: SESQUICENTENNIAL

century's end, especially the end of the 19th century; also decadence: FIN DE SIÈCLE

ceremonial procession: CORTEGE

ceremonial washing of hands: ABLUTION

ceremonies commemorating the founding of a city or university or the consecration of a church: ENCAENIA

ceremony that is pretentious or hypocritical: MUMMERY

certain: APODICTIC

certain: COCKSURE

certain, accurate: UNERRING

certain, unavoidable: INEVITABLE

certain, unquestionable: INDUBITABLE

certainly, without doubt: SANS DOUTE

certificate acknowledging debt: DEBENTURE

certificate entitling the holder to receive shares of stock, money, etc.: SCRIP

chain hanging from woman's belt to hold keys or purse: CHATELAINE

chain of colored paper, ribbon or flowers hung in loops: FESTOON

chain or closely connected series: CATENA

chain of things or events: CONCATENATION

chair of wood, with spindle back and slanting legs: WINDSOR CHAIR

chair with high back and side pieces: WING CHAIR

challenge: THROW DOWN THE GAUNTLET

challenge, dispute or attack the truth or validity of: IMPUGN

challenge the honesty or validity of: IMPEACH

chamberpot in a low chair or cabinet: COMMODE

chance occurrence: HAPPENSTANCE

change appearance of: TRANSFIGURE

change form or quality: TRANSMUTE

change in the form, character or appearance: METAMORPHOSIS

change in vowel for changed tense, etc.: ABLAUT

change into a different shape: TRANSMOGRIFY

change one substance into another: TRANSUBSTANTIATE

change opinion completely: ABOUT-FACE

change or movement that is constant: FLUX

change or vary often and in irregular manner: FLUCTUATE

change personal convictions by coercion: BRAINWASH

change places, alternate: INTERCHANGE

change plans of someone by persuasion: DISSUADE

change sides, apostatize: TERGIVERSATE

changeable: AMBIVALENT

changeable, erratic: INCONSISTENT

changeable, fickle: MUTABLE

changeable, inconstant: FICKLE

changeable, lively, clever: MERCURIAL

changeable, unstable: LABILE

changeable into different forms or shapes: PROTEAN

changeable luster: CHATOYANT

changeable person: CHAMELEON

changes in price that can be absorbed by the market in a particular security: LIQUIDITY

changes in series of plant or animal formations: SERE

changes or variations occurring irregularly, as of fortune: VICISSITUDES

changing rapidly and intricately: KALEIDOSCOPIC

channel for water, as under a road: CULVERT

chant: INTONE

chanted, nonmetrical hymn: CANTICLE

chanted formula or magic words: INCANTATION

chapel for private prayer: ORATORY

character, mark or stamp that is distinctive: IMPRESS

character and attitudes of a community or individual: ETHOS

characterization, often disparaging, of a person or thing: EPITHET

characterless: INVERTEBRATE

characterless, not distinctive: NONDESCRIPT

charcoal pencil or a sketch or drawing done in charcoal: FUSAIN

charge a public official with a crime or misdemeanor: IMPEACH

charge with a crime, accuse: INDICT

charge, fixed, that is added to bill at cabarets, hotels, clubs for entertainment or service: COVER CHARGE

charged, filled: FRAUGHT

charging of a wrongdoing or fault, accusation: IMPUTATION

charity, alms: ELEEMOSYNARY

charity case, a very poor person: PAUPER

charity to aid mankind: PHILANTHROPY

charlatan, vendor of quack medicines: MOUNTEBANK

charlatanism: SCIOLISM

charm: AMULET

charm: ENAMOR

charm as if by magic: BEWITCH

charm or amulet: TALISMAN

charm or divert: BEGUILE
charm or talisman: GRIGRI
chart containing lines representing changes in value: GRAPH
chary, stingy, economical: SPARE
chasm or fissure, as in a glacier: CREVASSE
chastise or rebuke severely: CASTIGATE
chat, talk idly: SCHMOOZE
chat or gossip: CONFABULATE
chat or informal conversation: CAUSERIE
chatter, talk senselessly: PRATE
chauvinist: JINGO
cheap, flashy dress or ornamentation: FRIPPERY
cheap, poor quality: SCHLOCK
cheap, sensational talk: CLAPTRAP
cheap, shoddy, poorly made: SLEAZY
cheap, trashy, measly: CHINTZY
cheap and showy: BRASSY
cheap and showy: TAWDRY
cheap and showy, designed merely to sell: CATCHPENNY
cheap red wine: VIN ORDINAIRE
cheat: BAMBOOZLE
cheat, dawdle, or pass time: DIDDLE
cheat, outwit: EUCHRE
cheat, swindle: ROOK
cheat, trick: HOODWINK
cheat, trick, deceive: FINAGLE
cheat a stranger: BUNCO
cheat or deceive in a petty way: COZEN
cheat or extort: GOUGE
cheat or defraud a person: MULCT
cheated or fooled easily: GULLIBLE
cheater, quibbler: PETTIFOGGER
check or restrain, as an impulse: INHIBIT
check or stop the flow of: STANCH
check stub, or stub of money order kept as record: COUNTERFOIL
checkered or plaid pattern of dark lines on a light ground: TATTERSALL
cheerful: BLITHE
cheerful: BUOYANT
cheerful, brisk: CHIPPER
cheerful, buoyant, optimistic: SANGUINE
cheerful, gay: JOCUND
cheerful, lively, urbane: DEBONAIR
cheerful, optimistic: ROSEATE
cheerful willingness: ALACRITY
cheese and crumbs crust: AU GRATIN
cheese, melted and cooked, often with beer or ale added, and served on toast or crackers: WELSH RABBIT
cheese, Italian, that is hard and is sprinkled on spaghetti or soup: PARMESAN

chess term for a draw resulting when a player can make no move without placing his king in check: STALEMATE
chest of drawers, high and often with a mirror: CHIFFONIER
chest of drawers, on short legs, about table height: LOWBOY
chest of drawers, usually in two sections, the lower on legs: HIGHBOY
chew noisily or munch: CHAMP
chewy, as spaghetti: AL DENTE
chewing food thoroughly as an aid to good health: FLETCHERISM
chicken, few months old: SPRING CHICKEN
chicken and leeks soup: COCK-A-LEEKIE
chicken pox: VARICELLA
chicken stewed in wine: COQ AU VIN
chicken stewed Italian style: CHICKEN CACCIATORE
chief commodity of a place or region: STAPLE
chief of a political party: SACHEM
chief or leader: COCK OF THE WALK
child murder: INFANTICIDE
child murder by a parent: FILICIDE
child prodigy: WUNDERKIND
child with extraordinary talent: PRODIGY
child who because of neglect spends his time in the streets: GUTTERSNIPE
childbirth, delivery: PARTURITION
childbirth pangs: TRAVAIL
childbirth ritual among primitive people in which father of newly born goes through motions as if he had given birth: COUVADE
childish, trivial, silly: PUERILE
childish talk: PRATTLE
children's diseases and hygienic care, as a study: PEDIATRICS
child's relation to parents: FILIAL
chilling: FRIGORIFIC
china or porcelain that is very thin and delicate: EGGSHELL CHINA
Chinese use of needles in medical practice: ACUPUNCTURE
chivalry: KNIGHT-ERRANTRY
chuckles of glee: CHORTLE
church architecture and decoration: ECCLESIOLOGY
church area behind the altar: RETROCHOIR
church area under jurisdiction of a bishop: DIOCESE
church rule by prelates: PRELACY
churchman of high rank: PRELATE
choice: OPTION

choice, excellence or exceptional quality: VINTAGE

choice must be made between two equally undesirable alternatives: DILEMMA

choice of what is offered or nothing: HOBSON'S CHOICE

choke to death: STRANGLE

choose, elect: OPT

choose with care: HAND PICK

chord's notes played in quick succession: ARPEGGIO

Christmas display of stable, scene of Jesus' birth: CRÈCHE

chronology as estimated by growth rings on trees: DENDROCHRONOLOGY

cigar, long and slim: PANATELA

cigar, long, slender and inexpensive: STOGIE

cigar, strong and dark: MADURO

cigar, tapering at both ends: PERFECTO

cigar, cut square at both ends: CHEROOT

circle boundary: CIRCUMFERENCE

circle or persons having an interest or interests in common: COTERIE

circle with locked arms formed by dancers in this Rumanian and Israeli folk dance: HORA

circle's circumference in relation to its diameter: PI

circling back to the original problem results after its solution raises other problems: VICIOUS CIRCLE

circular, revolving or whirling motion: GYRAL

circular graph divided into proportionate sections: PIE CHART

circulate, permeate: DIFFUSE

circumference, especially the waist: GIRTH

circumlocution, wordiness: PERIPHRASIS

cite for proof or example: ADDUCE

citizenship bestowal, freeing from slavery: ENFRANCHISEMENT

city area where vice and corruption flourish: TENDERLOIN

civic or a town resident: OPPIDAN

civil liberties advocate: LIBERTARIAN

civil magistrate or officer representing a government: SYNDIC

civilian clothes, especially those worn by one who usually wears a uniform: MUFTI

civilians arming spontaneously in times of military emergency: LEVY EN MASSE

civilities: AMENITIES

civility: COMITY

claim, require: POSTULATE

claim on property in payment of or as security for a debt: LIEN

claim without right: ARROGATE

clairvoyance, telepathy: CRYPTESTHESIA

clam: QUAHOG

clam of the littleneck variety only larger: CHERRYSTONE

clam that is the young of the quahog: LITTLENECK

clannish set: CLIQUE

clarify, enlighten, illuminate, light up: IRRADIATE

clarify, explain: INTERPRET

clarinet's lowest register: CHALUMEAU

class, sort, kind: ILK

class or group in society: CASTE

classic, venerable, time-honored: VINTAGE

classification laws and principles: TAXONOMY

clattering or rattling noise: BRATTLE

clauses in a sentence without connectives between them: PARATAXIS

claw, hoof, nail: UNGUIS

clay pottery: CERAMICS

clean, correct, flawless: IMMACULATE

clean slate: TABULA RASA

clear of blame or accusation, acquit: EXONERATE

cleanse or wipe off: DETERGE

cleansing agent: ABLUENT

clear, bright, intense: VIVID

clear, comprehensible: INTELLIGIBLE

clear, definite, straightforward, outspoken: EXPLICIT

clear, easily understood, rational, bright, shining: LUCID

clear, lucid, understandable: PERSPICUOUS

clear, rounded, full voice: OROTUND

clear, transparent, lucid, pure: LIMPID

clear, understandable: PELLUCID

clear, understandable in one way only: UNEQUIVOCAL

clear and resounding: CLARION

clear of accusation: VINDICATE

clear the throat audibly: HAWK

clearing area in a fog bank: FOGDOG or SEADOG

clearing in the woods: GLADE

clergyman's salary paid out of church revenues: PREBEND

clerical cap that is square and stiff: BIRETTA

clerical garb that is loose and white and has wide sleeves: SURPLICE

clerical or professional worker: WHITE COLLAR
clever, skillful, inventive: INGENIOUS
clever man, thinker: SOPHIST
clever remark: BON MOT
cliché: BROMIDE
clicking pieces for keeping time to music, especially Spanish: CASTANETS
cliff at the rim of a plateau: SCARP
cliff on the side of a hill: SCAR
cliff projecting into the water: HEADLAND
cliff that extends a distance: PALISADES
cliff's edge, dangerous situation: PRECIPICE
climax: APOGEE
climax in coitus: ORGASM
climb, as a tree, by clasping it with the arms and legs: SWARM
clinging, retentive: TENACIOUS
clinging closely: OSCULANT
clique: CAMARILLA
clique or group: FACTION
close association, confidential friendship: INTIMACY
close but not touching: CONTIGUOUS
close off, block or shut up: OCCLUDE
close one's eyes to something as if it had not happened: CONDONE
close one's eyes to wrongdoing: CONNIVE
close quarters, close contact: HAND-TO-HAND
close together, jammed: CHOCKABLOCK
closed or secret session: IN CAMERA
closed session to consider confidential business: EXECUTIVE SESSION
closed to others' opinions or beliefs: INTOLERANT
closed to outside influence, incapable of being passed through: IMPERVIOUS
closemouthed, reserved: TACITURN
closeness: PROPINQUITY
clot formation causing dead tissue: INFARCTION
cloth containing an intricate design that usually includes loops ending in curlicues: PAISLEY
cloth laid on the lap of a bishop officiating at a mass or ordination: GREMIAL
cloth of yellowish brown: KHAKI
clothe richly: CAPARISON
clothed negligently or partly: DISHABILLE
cloud formation, dense, usually white, with domed top and horizontal base, seen in fair weather: CUMULUS

cloud of rounded mass appearing before a thunderstorm: THUNDERHEAD
cloud streamers, or wisps of precipitation: VIRGA
cloud study, as a branch of meteorology: NEPHOLOGY
clouds, long and fibrous, supposed to foretell a storm: MARE'S TAIL
clouds in a fine, whitish veil, giving a hazy appearance: CIRROSTRATUS
clouds in a mass of fleecy globular cloudlets: CIRROCUMULUS
clouds in large globular masses, disposed in waves, groups or bands: STRATOCUMULUS
clouds in a white wispy tufts or bands across the sky: CIRRUS
cloudy: TURBID
cloudy, foggy, obscure, indefinite: NUBILOUS
cloudy or overcast: LOWERY
clown, buffoon: MERRY ANDREW
cloying, oversweet or rich: LUSCIOUS
clumsily done: BOTCHED
clumsy, awkward, heavy in appearance or movement: LUMBERING
clumsy, awkward, incompetent: INEPT
clumsy, blundering: MALADROIT
clumsy, boorish, awkward: GAUCHE
clumsy, bungling, or domineering: HEAVY-HANDED
clumsy, labored: PONDEROUS
clumsy, lacking skill: INAPT
clumsy, stupid person: CLODHOPPER
clumsy in handling things: BUTTERFINGERS
clumsy job: BUNGLE
clumsy rustic: BUMPKIN
clump along pompously: GALUMPH
clump or tuft, as of grass or hair: TUSSOCK
coal mining by stripping off soil rather than sinking a shaft: STRIP MINING
coarse, abusive in language: SCURRILOUS
coarse, loud, rough in sound: RAUCOUS
coarse, unrefined, natural: EARTHY
coarse food: ROUGHAGE
coarsely or vulgarly joking: RIBALD
coat lapel: REVERS
coat of which the sleeves are in one piece up to the collar: RAGLAN
coat or covering, as of a seed: TEGMEN
coats of arms, genealogies, etc.: HERALDRY
coax or flatter to persuade: WHEEDLE
coax with flattery: CAJOLE

cock less than a year old: COCKEREL

coddle: COCKER

coddle or pamper: COSHER

code deciphering: CRYPTANALYSIS

coded writing: CRYPTOGRAPHY

codfish that is young: SCROD

coercion, compulsion: DURESS

coercive measures taken to force a country to comply with demands: SANCTIONS

coffee, black: CAFE NOIR

coffee, small cup of: DEMITASSE

coffee or coffee-flavored: MOCHA

coffee with milk: CAFE AU LAIT

coffin of stone: SARCOPHAGUS

coffin-supporting framework: CATA-FALQUE

coherence lacking: DISJOINTED

coiled: TORTILE

coiled spirally: HELICOID

coin a word: MINT

coin or medal space for date, place of coining, etc.: EXERGUE

coined money: SPECIE

coins, medals, etc., as a study: NUMIS-MATICS

cold in the head: CORYZA

cold sore: HERPES LABIALIS

coil up intricately: CONVOLUTE

coincidence: CONJUNCTION

collapse, fail, sink: FOUNDER

collapse inward violently: IMPLODE

collar or cord used in executions: GAR-ROTE

colleague or fellow member: CONFRERE

collect, gather or store as in a granary: GARNER

collect, incorporate, make part of a whole: EMBODY

collected excerpts from literary works: ANALECTS

collection during a religious ceremony: OFFERTORY

collection of choice extracts for instruction in a language: CHRESTOMATHY

collection of poems, stories, etc.: AN-THOLOGY

collection of things, mass, heap: CONGERIES

collection of works and roles of a perform-ance or company: REPERTORY

collection or cluster that is heterogeneous: CONGLOMERATE

collective farm in Soviet Union: KOLKHOZ

collective farm or settlement in Israel: KIBBUTZ

collector or connoisseur of works of art: VIRTUOSO

college enrollment: MATRICULATION

color blindness: ACHROMATOPSIA

color blindness: DALTONISM

color blindness to one of the three primary colors: DICHROMATIC

color or tint uniform throughout: ISOCHROOUS

color slightly: TINGE

color study: CHROMATICS

colored differently in different parts: PAR-TICOLORED

coloring matter: PIGMENT

colorless, pale: PALLID

colors changing in different lights: VER-SICOLOR

colors of the rainbow in shifting hues and patterns: IRIDESCENCE

column in form of a female figure: CARYATID

columns that are regularly spaced: COL-ONNADE

collusion in a lawsuit to get share of mat-ter sued for: CHAMPERTY

combative: PUGNACIOUS

combination of circumstances or events: CONJUNCTURE

combination of two or more substances: AMALGAM

combine, blend and reconcile, as various philosophies: SYNCRETIZE

combustible substance that will ignite with a spark: TINDER

come forth into the open, emerge: DE-BOUCH

come between, especially as a barrier: IN-TERPOSE

come into office or dignity: ACCEDE

come into view or appear as through a mist often ominously: LOOM

comedian who is the star: TOP BANANA

comedy that is broad or exaggerated: FARCE

comedy that is loud and crude: SLAPSTICK

comfort in grief: SOLACE

comic antics: HARLEQUINADE

coming from without, unrelated to the matter at hand: EXTRANEOUS

coming in continually as of people or things: INFLUX

coming into a country not one's own: IM-MIGRANT

coming into existence, beginning to ap-pear: INCIPIENT

coming together, or a crowd: CONCOURSE
command, order, forbid: ENJOIN
command level: ECHELON
commandeer a plane in transit: HIJACK
commence, begin: INAUGURATE
commence, originate, begin: INITIATE
commencement headgear with a flat, square top: MORTARBOARD
commendation: PLAUDIT
commendatory: LAUDATORY
comment that is not binding, a remark made in passing: OBITER DICTUM
comment-arousing object: CONVERSATION PIECE
commentary, explanatory note: GLOSS
commerce, communication, exchange: INTERCOURSE
commissions and other costs of distribution included in the price paid by the purchaser of securities: LOAD
commit or do something, as a crime or hoax: PERPETRATE
committee consisting of all members of a legislative body: COMMITTEE OF THE WHOLE
committee formed for specific purpose: AD HOC COMMITTEE
common, vulgar: PLEBEIAN
common, widely practiced: PREVALENT
common people, masses: HOI POLLOI
common people, pertaining to: DEMOTIC
common people's language: VULGAR
common rather than literary language: VERNACULAR
common run, ordinary people: RUCK
common sense: MOTHER WIT
common stock earnings as affected by bond interest and preferred stock dividends: LEVERAGE
common to the masses: VULGAR
commonplace: TOLERABLE
commonplace, banal, trite remark: PLATITUDE
commonplace, basic: BREAD-AND-BUTTER
commonplace, dull: STODGY
commonplace, ordinary, simple: EXOTERIC
commonplace, trite idea or expression: CLICHÉ
commonplace, trite statement: PLATITUDE
commonplace, uninspired, unimaginative: PROSAIC
commotion: TURBULENCE
commotion, fluster, bustle: POTHER
communication, exchange, commerce: INTERCOURSE

communication of minds in other than normal sensory means: TELEPATHY
communication system for immediate, direct exchange in an emergency: HOT LINE
communication system that is secret and usually person to person: GRAPEVINE
Communist emblem: HAMMER AND SICKLE
compact, agreement, pledge: COVENANT
companionship: SODALITY
company that uses its capital to invest in other companies: INVESTMENT TRUST
compare critically, as writings or facts: COLLATE
comparison implied in a figure of speech: METAPHOR
compatible, congenial: SIMPATICO
compel or force to go: HALE
compelling, fascinating: IRRESISTIBLE
compensate, make up, offset: COUNTERVAIL
compensate, pay back: REIMBURSE
compensate, pay for: REMUNERATE
compensate, repay in kind: REQUITE
compensate, right a wrong: REDRESS
compensate for or counteract something else: OFFSET
compensation for injury to the feelings: SOLATIUM
compensation for loss or damage, exemption from penalties or liabilities: INDEMNITY
compete: VIE
competent legally to take care of one's own affairs: SUI JURIS
competition or rivalry: CONTENTION
competitive: EMULOUS
complacent, self-satisfied: SMUG
complain: CARP
complain, find fault: CRAB
complain, fret: REPINE
complaining, whining: QUERULOUS
complaint, grievance: PLAINT
complaint receiver in government, consumer organizations, etc.: OMBUDSMAN
complement or mate to another: COUNTERPART
complete, absolute: UNMITIGATED
complete, absolute, full: PLENARY
complete, entire: INTEGRAL
complete confidence: CERTITUDE
completely organized and active: FULL-FLEDGED
completeness: INTEGRITY

complex, subtle, highly intellectual: METAPHYSICAL

compliant, manageable: TRACTABLE

complicate, confuse, entangle: EMBRANGLE

complicate, disconcert, hamper: EMBARRASS

complicated, involved, puzzling: INTRICATE

complicated or confused state of affairs: IMBROGLIO

complicated or refined in design: SOPHISTICATED

complicated situation, predicament: PLIGHT

complication, intertwining, entanglement: INVOLUTION

comply, either in fact or only apparently: TEMPORIZE

comport (oneself): DEMEAN

compose or write out: REDACT

composure, coolness: SANG-FROID

composure, even-temper, calmness: EQUANIMITY

composure, serenity, self-assurance: POISE

comprehension or awareness independent of the senses: ESP (EXTRASENSORY PERCEPTION)

compressed: ANGUSTATE

compulsive, excessive preoccupation with a thought or feeling: OBSESSION

compulsory service: CONSCRIPTION

computer design and apparatus: HARDWARE

computer information delivered in printed form: PRINTOUT

computer information that is fed into the apparatus: INPUT

computers and human nervous system under study: CYBERNETICS

conceal, pretend, dissemble: DISSIMULATE

conceal, disguise, feign, make a false show of: DISSEMBLE

concealed: ABSTRUSE

concealed, secret or sheltered: COVERT

concealing language: AESOPIAN LANGUAGE

concealment by a public official of an offense or crime, or wrongdoing by such an official: MISPRISION

concealment of one's real activities or designs: COVER-UP

conceit, egotism: EGO

conceit or arrogance characterizing a person's ways of attitudes: OVERWEENING

conceited, arrogant: BUMPTIOUS

conceited, boastful: VAINGLORIOUS

concentration of psychic energy upon a person, idea, fantasy: CATHEXIS

concerned: SOLICITOUS

concerning, in the matter of: IN RE

conciliate, win over: PROPITIATE

conciliate opposing sides: MEDIATE

concise: TERSE

concise, terse, brief: LACONIC

concise, terse, meaningful: SUCCINCT

concise summary or abstract: PRECIS

conclude or accept from evidence: INFER

conclude or suppose from incomplete evidence: CONJECTURE

conclusion in a sentence that emerges from the PROTASIS, or condition: APODOSIS

concretize, make real: REIFY

concurrent: SIMULTANEOUS

condemn: CENSURE

condemn, prohibit, outlaw: PROSCRIBE

condemn or denounce: DECRY

condense: ABBREVIATE

condense: ABRIDGE

condense, boil down: DECOCT

condescend: DEIGN

condescend to, grant or permit: VOUCHSAFE

condition existing at a particular time: STATUS QUO

condition or stipulation: PROVISO

condition set forth in a clause that leads to APODOSIS, or conclusion: PROTASIS

conditional transaction authorized for when, as and if a security is issued: WHEN ISSUED

cone or pyramid with top sliced off: FRUSTUM

conference: POWWOW

conference of opposing sides, talk: PARLEY

conference or conversation that is formally arranged: COLLOQUY

confidence lacking, timidity, shyness: DIFFIDENCE

confidential friendship, close association: INTIMACY

confidential or private, as a conversation: TÊTE-À-TÊTE

confine, imprison: INCARCERATE

confine, surround, enclose within walls, imprison: IMMURE

confine or detain, as during war: INTERN

confined without means of communication: INCOMMUNICADO

confining or checking item, as a rope: TETHER

confinement that is forced, imprisonment: DURANCE

conflicting, mismated, discordant: INCOMPATIBLE

conflicting tendencies: AMBITENDENCY

conforming, done in accordance with: PURSUANT

conforming or agreeing: CONGRUENT

conformity forced ruthlessly: PROCRUSTEAN

confuse, defeat the plans of, frustrate: DISCOMFIT

confuse, divert: DISTRACT

confuse, mix up: DISORIENT

confuse, muddle: EMBROIL

confuse, obscure, bewilder: OBFUSCATE

confuse, upset, frustrate: DISCONCERT

confuse or mix up, as ideas or things: CONFOUND

confused: ADDLED, ADDLE-BRAINED, ADDLEHEADED, ADDLEPATED

confused, disjointed: INCOHERENT

confused, disorderly situation, from military slang acronym "situation normal, all fouled [not sic] up": SNAFU

confused, random: INDISCRIMINATE

confused, vague: HAZY

confused and hurried: HELTER-SKELTER

confused condition, mess: MARE'S NEST

confused mixture, medley: FARRAGO

confused or complicated state of affairs: IMBROGLIO

confused or meaningless talk: GALIMATIAS

confused state: TURBIDITY

confusion, hodgepodge: KATZENJAMMER

confusion that is noisy: BEDLAM

congenial, compatible: SIMPATICO

congratulate: FELICITATE

congratulation on a witty retort or a successful point made: TOUCHÉ

conjunctions omitted: ASYNDETON

connect like links of a chain: CATENATE

connect with a crime or fault: IMPLICATE

connection, bond, link: NEXUS

connive or conspire: COLLUDE

connoisseur: MAVEN, MAVIN

connoisseur, collector of works of art: VIRTUOSO

conscious of oneself as being observed by others, ill at ease: SELF-CONSCIOUS

conscious perception: APPERCEPTION

consciously or deliberately done: WITTINGLY

consciousness: SENTIENCE

consecrate, make holy: HALLOW

consecrated or bound by vow or promise: VOTARY

consent: ACCEDE

consent given passively: SUFFERANCE

consent quietly: ACQUIESCE

consequence: AFTERMATH

consequence: SEQUELA

consequence or result that is normal: COROLLARY

conservative, almost reactionary workers: HARD HATS

conservative, reactionary: RIGHTIST

conservative in beliefs, especially in politics: TORY

conservative or old-fashioned person: FOGY

conservative person: MOSSBACK

consider as real: HYPOSTATIZE

consider carefully, think about, reflect: PONDER

consign to an obscure place or inferior position: RELEGATE

consistency brought about, as in ideas: RECONCILED

consolation in grief: SOLACE

conspicuous, striking, standing out: SALIENT

conspicuous public position: LIMELIGHT

conspiracy, plot, secret and underhanded activity: INTRIGUE

conspire, connive: COLLUDE

conspire, scheme: MACHINATE

constant: INVARIABLE

constant movement or change: FLUX

constantly cause irritation, rankle: FESTER

constipated: COSTIVE

construction material of plaster and fiber that is temporary: STAFF

contact at a single point or along a line: TANGENT

contagious disease that breaks out suddenly and affects many individuals at the same time: EPIDEMIC

contain or include: COMPRISE

container: RECEPTACLE

container, usually metal, for tea, spices: CANISTER

container of miscellaneous things: CATCHALL

container's weight deducted to find weight of contents: TARE

contemplation of the navel: OMPHALO-SKEPSIS

contemporary: COEVAL

contemptible, trivial, petty: PALTRY

contemptible, vile: DESPICABLE

contemptuous sound: BRONX CHEER

contend or argue about trifling matters: STICKLE

contentious, argumentative: DISPUTATIOUS

contentment or smugness: COMPLACENCY

contest in which each player engages every other player: ROUND ROBIN

contest won without much opposition: WALKAWAY

continue unchanged, abide: SUBSIST

continuing, lasting a long time: CHRONIC

continuing, undecided: PENDING

continuing throughout the year or lasting a long time: PERENNIAL

continuing without interruption: INCESSANT

continuity interrupted to give an episode occurring earlier: FLASHBACK

continuous, pitiless: RELENTLESS

continuum of four dimensions—three of space plus time: SPACE-TIME

contraceptive intrauterine device: LOOP

contraceptive medication for women: PILL (THE PILL)

contraceptive or anti-infection sheath for the penis: CONDOM

contraceptive pessary: DIAPHRAGM

contract obligating a person to work for another for a period: INDENTURE

contracted: ABBREVIATED

contradict, deny, oppose: GAINSAY

contradict, repudiate, deny: DISAFFIRM

contradiction, inconsistency: DISCREPANCY

contradictory-appearing statement that is really true: PARADOX

contradictory terms combined in one phrase: OXYMORON

contradictory thoughts or attitudes: AMBIVALENCE

contrary, nonconforming: PERVERSE

contrary to: ATHWART

contrast: ANTITHESIS

contrast by reverse parallelism in phraseology: CHIASMUS

contrition: PENITENCE

control and communication as they apply to the operation of complex machines and functions of human organisms: CYBERNETICS

control artfully: MANIPULATE

controlled course of living: REGIMEN

conventional, proper: ORTHODOX

conventional person uninformed about culture or aesthetics: PHILISTINE

conversational: COLLOQUIAL

conversation about unimportant things: SMALL TALK

conversation or conference that is formally arranged: COLLOQUY

conversation that is informal, chat: CAUSERIE

conversational wit: REPARTEE

convert, transform: RESOLVE

convert by intensive indoctrination: BRAINWASH

convert into a different shape: TRANSMOGRIFY

convert or try to convert a person to one's religion: PROSELYTE

convert the energy of instinctual drives into socially acceptable manifestations: SUBLIMATE

convincing: COGENT

convincing, influential: POTENT

convulsive: SPASMODIC

convulsive seizure, as in pregnancy or childbirth: ECLAMPSIA

cook gently: CODDLE

cookery, or the kitchen: CULINARY

cooking, its style and quality: CUISINE

cooking pot that is airtight and prepares food quickly under pressure: PRESSURE COOKER

cool, casually indifferent: NONCHALANT

coolness, composure: SANG-FROID

coop or pen for small animals: HUTCH

cooperative, working together: SYNERGETIC

cooperate secretly: COLLUDE

coordinator of a broadcasting team: ANCHOR MAN

copy, duplicate made by the originator: REPLICA

copy in form, as a legislative bill: ENGROSS

copy or reproduction that is exact: FACSIMILE

copying device made up of four rods in parallelogram shape: PANTOGRAPH copying process employing electrostatic attraction: XEROGRAPHY

copyright or patent has run out: PUBLIC DOMAIN

cord or belt worn around the waist: CINCTURE

cord or metal collar used in executions: GARROTE

cordlike decoration used on clothes: PIPING

corduroy ridge: WALE

core, central or essential element: NUCLEUS

core group: CADRE

cornmeal dough ball fried in deep fat: HUSH PUPPY

cornstalks: STOVER

corporation embracing companies in unrelated industries: CONGLOMERATE

corporation that holds securities of another corporation that it normally controls: HOLDING COMPANY

corporation's total amount of securities issued: CAPITALIZATION

corporeal, physical: SOMATIC

corpulent, very fat: OBESE

correct or change a literary work, especially after scholarly study: EMEND

correctable or reformable: CORRIGIBLE

correctness of judgment, uprightness: RECTITUDE

corrode or corrupt: CANKER

corrosive, caustic: ESCHAROTIC

corrupt: ADULTERATE

corrupt: PERVERT

corrupt, invalidate, debase: VITIATE

corrupt, morally degraded: SCROFULOUS

corrupt, pervert: DEPRAVE

corrupt, rotten: PUTRID

corrupt, seduce, deprave: DEBAUCH

corrupt, sinful: PECCANT

corrupt, subject to bribery: VENAL

corrupt, undermine the morale: SUBVERT

costs of transaction included in the price paid by a purchaser of securities: LOAD

costs or continuous operating expenses of a business: OVERHEAD

cottage cheese: SMEARCASE

cottage or duplex apartment: MAISONETTE

couch or sofa, upholstered and without back or arm rests: DIVAN

couch without arms or back: OTTOMAN

couchlike chair with elongated seat to support legs: CHAISE LONGUE

cough drop: TROCHE

cough up (phlegm): HAWK

couldn't care less: APATHETIC

counterbalance: EQUIPONDERATE

countercharge: RECRIMINATION

counterfeit, artificial: POSTICHE

counterfeit, illegitimate: SPURIOUS

counterpart: OBVERSE

counting time in reverse: COUNTDOWN

countries that are underdeveloped and belong to neither the communist nor the capitalist bloc: THIRD WORLD

country home, Russian: DACHA

country person who is awkward: BUMPKIN

courage, initiative, shrewd common sense: GUMPTION

courage, pluck, spirit: METTLE

courage inspired by alcohol: DUTCH COURAGE

courageous, valiant: METTLESOME

course for advanced study: SEMINAR

court clerk who is chief: PROTHONOTARY

court command that a thing be done: MANDAMUS

court engaged in arbitrary or illegal procedures: STAR CHAMBER

court has it under consideration: SUB JUDICE

court official's cry to obtain silence: OYEZ

court order to appear and testify: SUBPOENA

court that is unauthorized and irregular: KANGAROO COURT

court writ ordering production of documents or other evidence: SUBPOENA DUCES TECUM

courteous, gallant, generous: CHIVALROUS

courtesy: COMITY

courtly or gallant man: CAVALIER

court-martial in the field for an offense committed during operations: DRUMHEAD COURT-MARTIAL

cover or suffuse with a liquid or color: PERFUSE

coverall worn by paratroops, mechanics, etc., or a woman's similar lounging garment: JUMP SUIT

covered with matted woolly hair: TOMENTOSE

covered with matted woolly masses: FLOCCULENT

covering or outer coating, especially a natural covering: INTEGUMENT

cow, not fertile: FARROW

cow, young and not yet having produced a
calf: HEIFER
coward: POLTROON
coward or sneak: DASTARD
cowardly: CRAVEN
cowardly, unfaithful: RECREANT
cowardly, weak: PUSILLANIMOUS
cowardly or timid: CHICKEN-HEARTED or
CHICKEN-LIVERED
cowboy's leather trousers: CHAPS
co-worker: COADJUTOR
coy, shy, modest, reserved: DEMURE
crablike: CANCROID
crack, cleft, chink: CREVICE
crack, small space: INTERSTICE
cracked or fissured, chinky: RIMOSE
crackle or rattle: CREPITATE
cracklings: GREAVES
cracks that intersect, as in glazed pottery:
CRAZE
craft, cunning: SLEIGHT
craftiness, cunning: WILE
craftsman: ARTIFICER

crafty, foxlike, sly: VULPINE
crafty, insincere: DISINGENUOUS
cramp or muscle pain: MYALGIA
cramped, uncomfortably small: INCOM-
MODIOUS
cranky, stubborn: PERVERSE
crashing noisily, as waves: PLANGENT
crave, yearn, desire: HANKER
craven, mean-spirited person: POLTROON
craving: APPETENCE
crawl face downward, lie prostrate:
GROVEL
craze for irrational interest in one thing:
MONOMANIA
craze, obsession: MANIA
crazed: DISTRAUGHT
crazy: CRACKBRAINED
crazy: HAYWIRE
crazy, absurd: COCKAMAMIE
creating ill will or dislike: INVIDIOUS
creation that turns on its creator: FRANK-
ENSTEIN'S MONSTER
creative, original: PROMETHEAN

CREATURE TERMS

Creature	Group	Male	Female	Young
antelope	herd	buck	doe	kid
ass	herd, drove, pace	jack	jenny	colt, foal
badger	cete	boar	sow	
bear	sloth			cub
beaver				kitten
bee	swarm, hive	drone	queen	
boar	sounder			squeaker, calf
buffalo	herd	bull	cow	
camel	herd, flock	bull	cow	foal, calf, colt
cat	kindle (young), clowder, cluster	tom	she-cat, queen (fancy breed)	kitten
cattle	herd, drove	bull	cow	calf, heifer (female)
chicken	brood, flock	rooster, cock	hen	chicken, pullet (f) cockerel (m)
cod			codling, sprag	
crane	herd			
crow	murder			
deer	herd	buck, stag	doe	fawn

Creature	Group	Male	Female	Young
dog	pack, kennel	hound	bitch	puppy, whelp
duck	team (in flight) paddling (in water)	drake	duck	duckling
eagle	convocation			eaglet
eel	swarm			elver
elephant	herd	bull	cow	calf
elk	gang	bull	cow	calf
ferret	business	dog	bitch	
finch	charm			
fish (general)	shoal, school, run			fry
frog	army			
fox	earth, skulk	vix	vixen	cub
giraffe	herd			
goat	flock, herd, tribe	billy	nanny (colloq)	kid
goose	flock, skein (on the wing), gaggle (on water)	gander	goose	gosling
grouse	covey (family), pack (larger group)			
gull	colony			
hare	drove, trace	buck	doe	leveret
hawk	flight			eyas
heron	siege			
herring	army, glean, shoal			
hippopotamus				calf
horse	herd, stable	stallion	mare	colt, foal
hummingbird	charm			
jay	band			
kangaroo	troop			joey
lark	exaltation			
leopard	leap	leopard	leopardess	
lion	pride, flock, troop	lion	lioness	cub
lobster			hen	chicken lobster
mackerel	shoal			spike, blinker, tinker
monkey	troop, tribe			
moose		bull	cow	calf
mouse	nest			
mule	barren, rake			
nightingale	watch			
owl	store			owlet
otter		dog	bitch	
ox	herd, drove			
parrot	flock			
partridge	covey			squeaker
peafowl	muster	peacock	peahen	
pheasant	nye (young), brood			
pigeon	flight, flock			squab, squealer, squeaker

Creature	Group	Male	Female	Young
pig	herd	boar	sow	pig, farrow, shote
polecat		hob	jill	
porpoise	school			
quail	bevy			
raven	unkindness			
rhinoceros	crash			
seal	crash, herd, pod			cub
sheep	flock	ram	ewe	lamb
sparrow	host			
squirrel	dray			
starling	chattering			
stork	mustering			
swallow	flight			
swan	herd, wedge	cob	pen	cygnet
swine	sounder	boar	sow	
tiger		tiger	tigress	cub
toad	knot			
trout	hover			
turkey	flock	tom	hen	poult
turtle	bale			
whale	herd, school, gam, pod	bull	cow	calf
wolf	herd, rout, pack	dog wolf	bitch	whelp, cub
wren	herd			
zebra	herd			foal, colt

credit amount that may legally be advanced by brokers to customers for purchase of securities: REGULATION T

credit for an achievement: KUDOS

credits in film or TV show that move vertically on screen: CRAWL

credulous, unaffected, simple, candid, artless: NAIVE

creek or stream: KILL

cremate, burn up: INCINERATE

crescent or crescent-shaped: MENISCUS

cricket, to deflect a ball by a slight turn of the bat: DRAW

cricket over, or period, in which no runs are scored: MAIDEN OVER

crime, criminals and prisons as a study: PENOLOGY

crime, proof of a: CORPUS DELICTI

crime or concealment of an offense by a public official: MISPRISION

crime such as murder, rape, arson or burglary: FELONY

crime study: CRIMINOLOGY

criminal, evildoer: MALEFACTOR

cringe fondly, toady: FAWN

crisis or conflict between two opposing political groups: CONFRONTATION

crisis or critical situation: CONJUNCTURE

criterion or standard for testing the qualities of something: TOUCHSTONE

critic or adviser who is frank and severe: DUTCH UNCLE

critical: CAPTIOUS

critical, demanding immediate action, urgent: EXIGENT

critical, harsh remark: BRICKDAT

critical to an excessive degree, hard to please: HYPERCRITICAL

critical year or period: CLIMACTERIC

criticism: ANIMADVERSION

criticism or difficulties from both sides: GANTLET

criticism that is bitter or malicious: DIATRIBE

criticism that is petty: QUIBBLE

criticism that is severe: STRICTURE

criticize, as if by perforation: RIDDLE

criticize, find fault with, rebuke, blame: REPREHEND

criticize angrily, caustically: VITRIOLIC

criticize sharply: SCARIFY

cross bearer: CRUCIFER

cross from one side to another: TRANS-VERSE

cross in form of an x, intersect: DECUSSATE

cross shaped: CRUCIATE

cross shaped: CRUCIFORM

cross threads in cloth: WEFT

cross with circle behind crossbeam: CELTIC CROSS

cross woman, old-fashioned in dress: FRUMP

crossbreed: INTERBREED

cross-country race along a course containing obstacles: STEEPLECHASE

cross-country runner: HARRIER

cross-country skiing run: LANGLAUF

crossed the equator by ship: SHELLBACK

cross-eyed condition: STRABISMUS

cross-fertilization: XENOGAMY

crouch or shrink in servility: CRINGE

crowbar used by burglars: JIMMY

crowd: RUCK

crowd, or a coming together: CONCOURSE

crowd, or a flocking together: CONFLUENCE

crowd or push roughly, shake up, elbow, shove: JOSTLE

crowded, densely populated: IMPACTED

crowded dwelling: WARREN

crown or headband: DIADEM

crownlike, jeweled headdress worn by women: TIARA

crucially important, essential: PIVOTAL

crude: INDELICATE

crude, lacking polish: INURBANE

crude, unrefined, rough: UNCOUTH

cruel, stubborn: TRUCULENT

cruel, vicious, inhuman: FELL

cruel exercise of power: TYRANNY

cruel or hideous being: OGRE

cruel or wantonly pitiless person: HELLKITE

crumbly or pulverizable: FRIABLE

crusade or fanatic campaign: JIHAD

crush, subdue utterly, silence: SQUELCH

crushable or crumbly: FRIABLE

cry, wail, whimper: PULE

cry loudly, scream, bawl: SQUALL

cry or whine with low, broken sounds: WHIMPER

cry that is long and plaintive, like a cat's: WAUL

cuddle: SNUGGLE

cuddle, snuggle for comfort: NESTLE

culminating point: SOLSTICE

culminating or highest point: ZENITH

cultivate deliberately the confidence or favor of others: INGRATIATE

cultivation capability, of land: ARABLE

cultural change in one society being affected by culture of another: ACCULTURATION

cunning, craft: SLEIGHT

cunning, craft, deceit: GUILE

cunning, craftiness: WILE

cunning, ingenious, intricate: DAEDAL

cunning, treacherous, wily: INSIDIOUS

cunningness, artful strategy, craftiness: FINESSE

cup for drinking, large, often with a cover: TANKARD

cup holder of filigreed metal, for a hot coffee cup: ZARF

cup or glass filled to the brim: BUMPER

cup or glass for measuring liquor: JIGGER

curative, healing: THERAPEUTIC

curb about a hatchway or skylight to keep out water: COAMING

cure-all, remedy for all ailments: PANACEA

curious to an offensive degree: INQUISITORIAL

curling, to play the stone gently: DRAW

curse, call down a calamity: IMPRECATE

curse, denounce violently: EXECRATE

curse against someone, slander, calumny: MALEDICTION

curse or ban: ANATHEMA

cursing: BLASPHEMY

curtain at rear of stage: BACKDROP

curtain in a doorway: PORTIÈRE

curve, especially inward: INCURVATE

curve in and out, bend: SINUATE

curve pattern that circles around a central point or in either direction around an axis: SPIRAL

curved or bent part, bending: FLECTION

curved wall or screen usually containing pictures: CYCLORAMA

curving inward: CONCAVE

curving outward: CONVEX

custard or other easily digested dish: FLUMMERY

custodian, superintendent, in charge of a museum or similar institution: CURATOR

customary practice, habit: WONT

custom-made (British): BESPOKE

customs or folkways of a social group: MORES

cut, scratch: SCOTCH

cut across, divide: INTERSECT

cut expenses: RETRENCH

cut into, carve, engrave: INCISE

cut off by ecclesiastical authority: EX-COMMUNICATE

cut or mark the edge of border with notches: INDENT

cut or notch carved out by a saw or ax: KERF

cut or part into two sections: DICHOT-OMIZE

cut or split into long thin pieces: SLIVER

cut or trim the branches as from a tree: LOP

cut out, excise: EXSCIND

cut the top or end from: TRUNCATE

cut up or stir the surface, as of topsoil: SCARIFY

cutlet, especially veal: SCHNITZEL

cutoff of operation or service by accident: OUTAGE

cutting, intersecting: SECANT

cutting, splitting: SCISSION

cutting off: ABSCISSION

cutting teeth, teething: DENTITION

cyclone in the western Pacific: TYPHOON

cynical, sneering, scornful: SARDONIC

D

dabbler with a superficial interest in an art or science: DILETTANTE

dagger mark, double, in printing (‡): DIESIS

dagger or sword with wavy-edged blade: KRIS

daily: DIURNAL

daily expense allowance: PER DIEM

daily occurrence: QUOTIDIAN

daily prayers said by Catholic clergy: BREVIARY

dainty, elegant or affectedly prim: MINCING

dainty, oversensitive: FASTIDIOUS

dam placed in a stream to divert the water, as in irrigation: WEIR

damage as if by perforation: RIDDLE

damage or destruction done deliberately to obstruct a cause: SABOTAGE

damage to a person's reputation done through a false or malicious written statement or graphic representation: LIBEL

damages awarded in excess of actual loss: EXEMPLARY DAMAGES

damaging or destruction of property willfully: VANDALISM

damnation, hell: PERDITION

damp, moist: HUMID

dance in which couples form sets in squares: SQUARE DANCE

dance in which the performer's shoes sharply accentuate the rhythm with the toes and heels: TAP DANCE

dance like a slow polka: SCHOTTISCHE

dance movement in which a couple swing round with hands joined: POUSETTE

dance of Rumanians and Israelis in which dancers lock arms in a circle: HORA

dance of Slavs in which a man performs the prisiadka, a step in which from a squatting position each leg is kicked out alternately: KAZATSKY

dancer: TERPSICHOREAN

dancing art: CHOREOGRAPHY

dancing mania, characteristic of a nervous disorder: TARANTISM

dancing muse: TERPSICHORE

dandified man or one who dresses over-fastidiously: FOP

dandruff: FURFUR

dandruff or similar scales shed by the skin: SCURF

dandy, fop, man who dresses flashily: DUDE

danger: JEOPARDY

danger on both sides: BETWEEN SCYLLA AND CHARYBDIS

danger sign, warning, especially in zoology: SEMATIC

danger that is imminent: SWORD OF DAMOCLES

dangerous speed: BREAKNECK

dangerous to society: PESTILENT

daring, audacity, impudence, boldness: HARDIHOOD

dark: APHOTIC

dark, gloomy: CIMMERIAN

dark, gloomy: TENEBROUS

dark, gloomy, infernal: STYGIAN

dark, obscure, misty: MURKY

dark complexioned, dusky: SWARTHY

dark and threatening, as the weather: LOWERING

dark appearance or dark pigmentation: MELANOID

dark shape or profile with a light background: SILHOUETTE

darkened or tinged with brown, as a part of an insect's wing: INFUSCATE

dash, enthusiasm, vivacity: ÉLAN

dash, spirited style: PANACHE

dash, vigor: VERVE
dashing, gay, smart: RAKISH
dashing, large, vigorous, swift: SPANKING
dashing, self-confident, stylish, lively, brisk: JAUNTY
date on which a loan or bond comes due: MATURITY
daughter's sexual attachment to her father: ELECTRA COMPLEX
dauntless, fearless, bold: INTREPID
dawdle, waste time: DILLYDALLY
dawdle, waste time: PIDDLE
dawdle, pass time, cheat: DIDDLE
dawn: COCKCROW
day blindness: HEMERALOPIA
day by day account of events: CHRONOLOGY
day or month added to the calendar: INTERCALARY
day when night and day are of equal length, marking start of spring or autumn: EQUINOX
daydreaming: musing: REVERIE
daydreaming tendency: AUTISM
days and nights are equal at these times, March 21 and September 21: VERNAL EQUINOX AND AUTUMNAL EQUINOX
daytime rather than nighttime: DIURNAL
dazzling, brilliant, swift: METEORIC
dazzling, shining with brilliance, vividly bright: RESPLENDENT
dead, extinct: DEFUNCT
dead; say nothing but good about them: DE MORTUIS NIL NISI BONUM
dead at birth: STILLBORN
dead or rotten flesh: CARRION
dead person: DECEDENT
deaden, paralyze with fear: PETRIFY
deadlocked situation: STALEMATE
deadly, fatal: LETHAL
deadly, injurious malicious: PERNICIOUS
deadly to both sides of a group: INTERNECINE
deaf mute alphabet: DACTYLOLOGY
dealer or trader: MONGER
dealing with people or situations delicately and without giving offense: TACT
death: DEMISE
death, resurrection, immortality, as a subject of study: ESCHATOLOGY
death anniversary observed by Jews: YAHRZEIT
death blow or mortal blow: COUP DE GRACE

death investigation: INQUEST
death omen: KNELL
death only apparent not real: ANABIOTIC
death that is painless and peaceful: EUTHANASIA
deathly looking: CADAVEROUS
debase: ADULTERATE
debase, corrupt, invalidate: VITIATE
debase oneself as from fear or servility: GROVEL
debatable or so hypothetical as to be without significance: MOOT
debate or argue earnestly: CONTEND
debate, argumentation: FORENSICS
debate that is formal: DISPUTATION
debauched, immoral: DISSOLUTE
debt-acknowledging certificate: DEBENTURE
debt acknowledgment that is non-negotiable and usually exchangeable for goods or services: DUE BILL
debt or liability extinguished gradually, as by installment payments: AMORTIZED
decay, rot: PUTREFY
decay or decline as in art or morals: DECADENCE
decayed: CARIOUS
decayed, neglected, shabby: DILAPIDATED
deceit, cunning, craft: GUILE
deceit, dishonest dealing: INDIRECTION
deceitful: MENDACIOUS
deceitful, treacherous: DOUBLE-DEALING
deceitfulness, trickery, double-dealing: DUPLICITY
deceitfulness, trickery, rascality: KNAVERY
deceive: BEGUILE
deceive, cheat, trick: FINAGLE
deceive, mislead: EQUIVOCATE
deceive or cheat in a petty way: COZEN
deceiver: IMPOSTOR
deception, trickery: HOCUS-POCUS
deception or pretended blow meant to distract: FEINT
deceptive, pretended, sham: FEIGNED
deceptive explanation designed to cover up a defect or a fault: GLOSS
deceptively appearing to be true or correct: SPECIOUS
decided previously by judicial authority: RES JUDICATA
deciding statement: CLINCHER
deciding vote: CASTING VOTE
decimal system of counting: ALGORISM
decision maker in a dispute: ARBITER

decisive, final, absolute, positive: PEREMPTORY

declare relevant and operative, as a law: INVOKE

declare solemnly: ASSEVERATE

decline or decay as in art or morals: DECADENCE

declining, worsening, going backward: RETROGRADE

declining market: BEAR MARKET

decoding: CRYPTANALYSIS

decorate, dress up: TITIVATE

decorate, ornament: EMBELLISH

decorate an initial page or word of a manuscript with designs or bright colors: ILLUMINATE

decorate lavishly as with jewels: INCRUST, ENCRUST

decorate or dress up with showy ornaments: PRANK

decorate or enrich with engraved or inlaid work: ENCHASE

decorated with material embedded flush with the surface: INLAID

decorative horizontal strip, as along the top of a wall: FRIEZE

decorative plan of a room: DECOR

decree: RESCRIPT

decree, command or prohibition: EDICT

decree, establish: ORDAIN

decree, law: STATUTE

decree that is official and arbitrary: UKASE

dedicate or sign a book for presentation: INSCRIBE

dedicatory words or lines at the end of a poem: ENVOY

deduce by logical methods: RATIOCINATE

deduction, conjecture: INFERENCE

deduction, discount: REBATE

deduction, inference: ILLATION

deductive reasoning: SYNTHESIS

deductive reasoning formula: SYLLOGISM

deep in intellect or feeling: PROFOUND

deep involvement: IMMERSION

deep red or purplish red: CARMINE

deep-rooted, firmly established: INGRAINED

deep-sea chamber: BATHYSPHERE

deeply established habits: SECOND NATURE

deer meat: VENISON

deer's tail: FLAG

defamation that is spoken: SLANDER

defame, dishonor: SMIRCH

defame, disparage, blacken: DENIGRATE

defame, disparage, despise: VILIPEND

defame, revile: VILIFY

defame, say malicious things: TRADUCE

defame, traduce: MALIGN

defamatory and abusive words: OBLOQUY

defeat, nullify, prevail over: OVERRIDE

defeat but with great losses: CADMEAN VICTORY, PYRRHIC VICTORY

defeat by cleverness: OUTWIT

defeat by skillful maneuver: CHECKMATE

defeat the plans or purposes of, frustrate, vanquish: DISCOMFIT

defeat suffered abruptly: REBUFF

defeat utterly: DRUB

defeated officeholder with some time to remain in office: LAME DUCK

defect existing at birth: CONGENITAL DEFECT

defendable, maintainable: TENABLE

defense or justification: APOLOGIA

defense system that is a form of jujitsu: JUDO

defenseless, cannot be defended, as an attitude: UNTENABLE

defensive tactic: PARRY

defer, put off, postpone: WAIVE

defiance of established doctrine: HERESY

defiant in an aggressive way: TRUCULENT

deficiency: INSUFFICIENCY

defile, besmirch, soil: SULLY

defile, dirty: POLLUTE

definite, clear, straightforward, outspoken: EXPLICIT

definitive, judicial, established by decree: DECRETORY

deflect, turn aside, distract, amuse, entertain: DIVERT

deformation of the earth's crust, forming mountains, continents: DIASTROPHISM

defraud or cheat a person: MULCT

defy, scoff, mock, jeer: FLOUT

degrade: DEMEAN

degraded, base, dishonorable: IGNOBLE

degraded, morally debased: SCROFULOUS

degraded, sneaky, skulking: HANGDOG

degree of personal excellence: CALIBER

degree or range of occurrence: INCIDENCE

degree or strength of some feeling, quality, action: INTENSITY

deification: APOTHEOSIS

deign to grant or permit: VOUCHSAFE

dejected: CHAPFALLEN

dejected: DISPIRITED

dejected: INCONSOLABLE

dejected, depressed: CRESTFALLEN

dejected, gloomy, saddened: DISCONSOLATE

dejection of spirits, hopelessness: DESPONDENCY

dejection or despair: SLOUGH OF DESPOND

delay, hinder, put obstacles in the way of: IMPEDE

delay, hinder, slow: RETARD

delay, postponement, interval of relief or rest: RESPITE

delay, temporary: ABEYANCE

delay authorized in some specific activity: MORATORIUM

delayed reaction to a joke or unusual situation: DOUBLE TAKE

delaying: DILATORY

delete obscene or otherwise objectionable material: EXPURGATE

deletion, erasure: EXPUNCTION

deliberate decision: VOLITION

deliberately or consciously done: WITTINGLY

delicate, flimsy substance: GOSSAMER

delicately and carefully made: WROUGHT

delicious, sometimes sweet in excess, cloying: LUSCIOUS

delight, give unusual pleasure, entertain: REGALE

delight (in), celebrate, make merry: REVEL

delightful, entrancing: RAVISHING

deliver up or surrender an accused individual to another state or country: EXTRADITE

delusions of persecution or grandeur: PARANOIA

demand for a customer to put money or securities with his broker: MARGIN CALL

demand or summons: REQUISITION

demand rigorously, require as a matter of justice: EXACT

demanding constant hard work: EXACTING

demanding insistently: IMPORTUNATE

demolish, level to the ground: RAZE

demon that takes possession of a living person: DYBBUK

demon-possessed: DEMONIAC

demonstrable: APODICTIC

demonstrate convincingly, show clearly: EVINCE

denounce, condemn: DECRY

denounce violently, curse: EXECRATE

dense, incomprehensible: IMPENETRABLE

dentistry branch that is devoted to gums and bones supporting the teeth: PERIODONTICS

dentistry that strives to prevent and correct tooth irregularities: ORTHODONTICS

denunciation: REPROBATION

denunciation, loud and violent: FULMINATION

denunciation or accusation that is violent: INVECTIVE

denunciation or threat, especially from a divine source: COMMINATION

denunciatory speech: TIRADE

deny, repudiate: DISAFFIRM

deny, oppose, contradict: GAINSAY

deny oneself something: ABSTAIN

deny or renounce one's own rights, etc.: ABNEGATION

depart suddenly: ABSCOND

dependable, firm: STAUNCH

dependency: APPANAGE

dependent on luck: ALEATORY

deportment, or manner in which one bears oneself: DEMEANOR

deposit eggs or roe: SPAWN

deprave, corrupt, seduce: DEBAUCH

depravity, baseness, vileness: TURPITUDE

depreciatory or derogatory: PEJORATIVE

depressed, bored, or dull state of mind: DOLDRUMS

depressed, dejected: CRESTFALLEN

depressed, downhearted: DISPIRITED

depressed, gloomy, dusky: SOMBER

depressed mood: FUNK

depressing, unhappy: DOWNBEAT

deprive as a punishment: AMERCE

deprive as of rights or possessions, strip as of clothes: DIVEST

deprive of, strip, rob: DESPOIL

deprive of rights or privileges, as of a citizen's right to vote: DISFRANCHISE

deputy, agent, substitute: VICAR

deranged mentality: ABERRATION

deride, sneer, laugh coarsely, jeer: FLEER

derisive or mocking speech or manner: JEER

derisive sound: BRONX CHEER

derivations and development of words, as a study: ETYMOLOGY

derogatory or depreciatory: PEJORATIVE

descendant, offspring: SCION

descent of an individual traced from a certain ancestor: GENEALOGY

describe, portray, paint, or draw: LIMN

description of a person, as of a criminal for identification: SIGNALMENT

desecrate, pollute: PROFANE

desert, change sides: TERGIVERSATE

deserted, wretched, abandoned, cheerless: FORLORN

deserter, traitor: RENEGADE

desertion of faith or principles: APOSTASY

deserved or suitable, as a punishment: CONDIGN

design cut on a gem: GLYPTOGRAPH

design in nature, as studied in cosmology: TELEOLOGY

design in relief, as in metal: REPOUSSÉ

design or shape that doesn't adhere to any rigid pattern: FREE-FORM

desire: APPETENCE

desire, crave, yearn: HANKER

desire, feel the need for or the lack of: DESIDERATE

desire or lust for something belonging to another: COVET

desolate or saddened through loss: BEREAVED

despair or dejection: SLOUGH OF DESPOND

despise, defame, disparage: VILIPEND

despise, scorn: CONTEMN

despotic subordinate governor: SATRAP

despotism: ABSOLUTISM

destroy completely, wipe out: OBLITERATE

destroy or kill a large proportion of: DECIMATE

destroy or weaken the affection of: DISAFFECT

destroy utterly, pull up by the roots, uproot, erase: ERADICATE

destroy wholly, root out: EXTIRPATE

destroyer of images, or of venerated objects or ideas: ICONOCLAST

destruction, mutilation or alteration, especially of a legal document: SPOLIATION

destruction, ruin: HAVOC

destruction of great scope, especially by fire: HOLOCAUST

destruction or extermination of an entire people or national group: GENOCIDE

destructive force that is slow and irresistible: JUGGERNAUT

detached, isolated: INSULAR

detached, unbiased: OBJECTIVE

detail, declare, state: EXPOUND

detailed examination or discussion: CANVASS

detain or confine, as during war: INTERN

detective (humorous use): HAWKSHAW

deter or alter the plans of someone by persuasion: DISSUADE

detergent: ABLUENT

deteriorated, rickety: RAMSHACKLE

deterioration, biologically, of a strain or type, especially of man: DYSGENIC

determined, brave, strong: STALWART

determined, resolved, unflinching: RESOLUTE

detest: ABHOR

detestable, revolting, abominable: EXECRABLE

detestation: ABHORRENCE

detract, take away from: DEROGATE

detraction: DISPARAGEMENT

develop, sit on and hatch eggs: INCUBATE

develop or work out gradually: EVOLVE

develop to the utmost, make the most of: OPTIMIZE

developed or advanced more rapidly than is usual: PRECOCIOUS

deviating from normal rule: ANOMALOUS

deviating from the right way: ABERRANCE

deviating from what is generally accepted: PERVERSE

deviation: ABERRATION

deviation from the main current: EDDY

deviation from the normal: PERVERSION

devil, in Moslem countries: SHAITAN

devilish: CLOVEN-HOOFED

devious: AMBAGIOUS

devious: TORTUOUS

devise, think out carefully: EXCOGITATE

devise or make up: CONCOCT

devitalize, sap the strength of, weaken: ENERVATE

devoted: ASSIDUOUS

devoted blindly: IDOLATROUS

devotee: AFICIONADO

devotee of a particular pursuit, enthusiast: VOTARY

dexterity or skill in manipulation: SLEIGHT

dexterous: ADROIT

diagonal: CATER-CORNERED

diagonal or oblique line: BIAS

diagram showing a sequence of operations for a program or process: FLOW CHART

diagram, synopsis or summary, as of a process: SCHEMA

diagrams, charts, drawings, etc., used as explanatory matter: GRAPHICS dialect, especially one that is crude: PATOIS

dialect of a region that has become the language of a larger area: KOINE

dialect or jargon mixed with English: PIDGIN ENGLISH

dialogue: INTERLOCUTION

diameter-measuring instrument: CALIPERS

diametrically opposed: ANTIPODAL

dictatorial, imperious: PEREMPTORY

dictionary compiling: LEXICOGRAPHY

die without having made a will: INTESTATE

differ in opinion: DIVERGE

difference: DISSIMILITUDE

difference, as of opinion: DIVERGENCE

difference of opinion, discord, quarrel: DISSENSION

differences in outlook between individuals: PERSONAL EQUATION

different: DIVERSE

different, dissimilar, distinct: DISPARATE

different directions, move in: DIVERGE

differing: DISSIDENT

differing, not all alike: HETEROGENEOUS

differing in names that show a relationship: HETERONYMOUS

difficult, stubborn, unruly: INTRACTABLE

difficult and interminable: SISYPHEAN

difficult or puzzling, as a problem: STICKLER

difficult position: QUAGMIRE

difficult situation: MORASS

difficult to accomplish: HERCULEAN

difficult to deal with: SCABROUS

difficult to understand: ABSTRUSE

difficulties or criticism from both sides: GANTLET

diffuse or scatter, as if by sowing: DISSEMINATE

diffusion of a fluid through a membrane: OSMOSIS

dig out the facts: PLUMB

dig up a corpse or some buried thing: EXHUME

digest or summary: CONSPECTUS

digestion that is good: EUPEPSIA

dignified, well-bred air: DISTINGUÉ

digress, wander or stray from the subject: DIVAGATE

digression: APOSTROPHE

digressive, rambling: EXCURSIVE

digs, study of: ARCHEOLOGY

diligent, constant, working steadily: SEDULOUS

diligent and careful: PAINSTAKING

dim, obscure, pertaining to twilight: CREPUSCULAR

diminish: ABATE

diminish or lessen: DWINDLE

dimming of lights: BROWNOUT

dimple or small depression: FOSSETTE

dinner menu with each item having a separate price: A LA CARTE

dinner menu with a complete meal at a set price: TABLE D'HÔTE

dinner precooked and frozen in an aluminum-foil tray: TV DINNER

dining hall in a college or monastery: REFECTORY

dip into liquid for pickling: SOUSE

dip lightly or suddenly into water, as a bird does: DAP

diphtheria test: SCHICK TEST

diplomatic, prudent, wise: POLITIC

diplomatic etiquette: PROTOCOL

direct, blunt: POINT-BLANK

direct, plain: FLAT-FOOTED

direct into set channels: CANALIZE

direct opposite: ANTITHESIS

directed firmly, unwavering, steadfast: INTENT

direct relationship, freedom from intervention: IMMEDIACY

direction or sense of direction lost or mixed up: DISORIENTATION

dirge, funeral hymn: EPICEDIUM

dirge, funeral song: THRENODY

dirty, defile: POLLUTE

dirty, foul, appearing neglected: SQUALID

dirty, squalid: SORDID

disable: INCAPACITATE

disadvantage: DRAWBACK

disadvantage imposed on contestants of superior ability in a contest or race: HANDICAP

disagree: DISSENT

disagreeable, offensive: UNSAVORY

disagreeable, ugly, unpleasant in appearance: ILL-FAVORED

disagreement: DISSIDENCE

disagreement, quarreling: AT LOGGERHEADS

disappear by degrees, vanish gradually: EVANESCE

disappointment over one's own acts: CHAGRIN

disapproval: ANIMADVERSION

disapprove, plead against: DEPRECATE

disarrayed or partly dressed: DISHABILLE

disaster that brings violent change: CATACLYSM

disavow a former belief: RECANT

disbelief or denial of purpose in existence or in customary institutions: NIHILISM

disbelieving, doubting: INCREDULOUS

discard or cast off a previously favored sweetheart: JILT

discard something that hampers: JETTISON

discerning, perceptive, keen: PERSPICACIOUS

discernment, wisdom: SAGACITY

discharge of repressed emotions: CATHARSIS

discharge suddenly and quickly, exclaim: EJACULATE

disciplinarian of extreme militaristic severity: MARTINET

disciplinary action that is swift: CRACKDOWN

disclose, bring to light, reveal: EXHUME

disclose, make known, bestow: IMPART

disclose, reveal, give vent to: UNBOSOM

disclose, reveal, tell: DIVULGE

disclosure in a trial or hearing that a defendant is compelled to make: DISCOVERY

disconcert, impede, complicate: EMBARRASS

disconcerted by some occurrence: ABASHED

disconnect: UNCOUPLE

disconnected, lacking in coherence: DISJOINTED

disconnected, separate: DISCRETE

discontent or illness, a chronic feeling of either: DYSPHORIA

discord, quarrel, difference of opinion: DISSENSION

discord, harsh disagreement: DISSONANCE

discordant: ABSONANT

discordant, harsh sound: JANGLE

discordant, conflicting, mismated: INCOMPATIBLE

discordant sound: CACOPHANY

discourage: DISHEARTEN

discourteous or rude manner: INCIVILITY

discover with the eye, discern, observe: DESCRY

discovery and investigation as a way of learning: HEURISTICS

discriminate or distinguish: SECERN

discriminating taste in food and drink: GOURMET

discussion or series of remarks: DESCANT

discussion that is informal and rambling: CRACKER-BARREL

disdainful, arrogant: SUPERCILIOUS

disease breaking out suddenly and affecting many individuals at the same time: EPIDEMIC

disease correction by manipulation of parts of the body: OSTEOPATHY

disease moving from one part of the body to another: METASTASIS

disease of the intestine usually caused by eating undercooked pork: TRICHINOSIS

disease-preventing treatment: PROPHYLAXIS

disease treatment effected by producing incompatible conditions: ALLOPATHY

diseases and their nature, as a branch of medicine: PATHOLOGY

diseases classified and described: NOSOGRAPHY

disembowel or remove vital part of: EVISCERATE

disentangle, free from entanglement: EXTRICATE

disgrace, infamy: OBLOQUY

disgrace attached to a person or group: STIGMA

disgraceful: INGLORIOUS

disgraceful, shocking, notorious: FLAGRANT

disgracing, abusive: OPPROBRIOUS

disguise, feign, conceal, make a false show of: DISSEMBLE

disguise or shelter: COVERTURE

disguise to avoid recognition: INCOGNITO

disguise to blend with environment: CAMOUFLAGE

disgust or dislike in the extreme, abhorrence: LOATHING

disgusting, offensive, hateful, repugnant: ODIOUS

disgusting, offensive, stinking, noxious: NOISOME

dish, deep and covered, for serving soup: TUREEN

dish made light by adding beaten egg whites: SOUFFLÉ

dish of chopped meat, eggs, onions, anchovies: SALMAGUNDI

disharmony in a relationship: RIFT

disheveled, untidy: UNKEMPT

dishonesty, deceitfulness, trickery: KNAVERY

dishonesty, lack of integrity: IMPROBITY

dishonor, defame: SMIRCH

dishonorable: IGNOMINIOUS

dishonorable, degraded, base: IGNOBLE

disinterested, free from bias, fair: IMPARTIAL

disjoint, dislocate: LUXATE

disjointed, broken up into separate incidents: EPISODIC

disjointed, confused: INCOHERENT

dislike of debate, argument, or reasoning: MISOLOGY

dislike or disgust in the extreme, abhorrence: LOATHING

dislocate, throw out of joint: LUXATE

dismayed: AGHAST

dismiss in disgrace: CASHIER

dismissal or leavetaking: CONGÉ

disobedient: INSUBORDINATE

disobedient, insolently so: CONTUMACIOUS

disobedient, stubborn, rebellious: RECALCITRANT

disorder, confusion: HUGGER-MUGGER

disorder, destruction or carnage, scene of: SHAMBLES

disorder and inertness as an irreversible tendency of a system: ENTROPY

disorder resulting from lack of leader or plan: ANARCHY

disordered, jumbled, topsy-turvy: HIGGLEDY-PIGGLEDY

disorderly, boisterous, rude: RAMBUNCTIOUS

disorderly, loud: RAUCOUS

disorderly, wild haste: PELL-MELL

disown, reject, refuse to accept: REPUDIATE

disparage, defame, blacken: DENIGRATE

disparage, treat with contempt: VILIPEND

disparaging term used to describe something inoffensive: DYSPHEMISM

dispel, waste, squander: DISSIPATE

display ostentatiously: FLOURISH

display or parade brazenly or gaudily: FLAUNT

displease or bore: PALL

dispose of, make unnecessary: OBVIATE

dispose of a matter quickly: DISPATCH

dispose of by fraud or trickery: FOB

dispose of swiftly: MAKE SHORT SHRIFT OF

dispose quickly of a matter: DISPATCH OR WITH DISPATCH

disposition, tendency, leaning: PROCLIVITY

dispossession that is unlawful: DISSEIZIN

disproportionate, inadequate: INCOMMENSURATE

disprove, demonstrate an error: REFUTE

dispute: ALTERCATION

dispute, challenge, attack the truth or validity of: IMPUGN

dispute, challenge, call in question: OPPUGN

disregard, forgetfulness: OBLIVION

disregard, neglect: SLIGHT

disregard for the rules or for fact to achieve artistic effect: POETIC LICENSE

disreputable, ill-tempered, perverse woman, hussy: JADE

disreputable, tawdry, vulgar: RAFFISH

disrespect toward one to whom deference is due: LESE MAJESTY

disrespectful, insulting: INSOLENT

dissension, disagreement, lack of harmony: DISCORD

dissenter: RECUSANT

dissimilar, distinct, different: DISPARATE

dissimilar, unrelated, unlike: HETEROGENEOUS

dissolute, lustful: WANTON

distance around: CIRCUMFERENCE

distance light travels in a vacuum in one year: LIGHT-YEAR

distance measured by determination of angles: TELEMETRY

distance of an eighth of a mile: FURLONG

distance of 3,280.8 feet: KILOMETER

distant, unknown region: ULTIMA THULE

distended, swollen: TURGID

distinct, different, dissimilar: DISPARATE

distinct, separate, disconnected from others: DISCRETE

distinctive mark: CACHET

distinguish or discriminate: SECERN

distinguished: PRESTIGIOUS

distinguished, dignified, well-bred: DISTINGUÉ

distinguished, renowned: ILLUSTRIOUS

distinguishing characteristic, facial contour or feature: LINEAMENT

distort, misapply: PERVERT

distort, pervert: WREST

distorted vision or view: ASTIGMATISM

distortion of shape: ANAMORPHISM

distract, amuse, entertain: DIVERT

distract, turn aside, deflect: DIVERT

distress, cause of: BANE

distress, pain, suffering, anguish: TRAVAIL

distress or disturb the mind or feelings painfully: HARROW

distribute or divide in proportion: PRORATE

district of a city in which a minority lives: GHETTO

distrust or hatred of mankind: MISANTHROPY

distrustful: ASKANCE

disturb, alarm, upset: PERTURB

disturb, bother: INCOMMODE

disturb, trouble, inconvenience: DISCOMMODE

disturb or ruffle: DISTEMPER

disturb the mind or feelings painfully, distress: HARROW

disturb the smoothness of: RUFFLE

disturbance, civil disorder: DISTEMPER

disturbance of the peace: AFFRAY

ditch or moat artificially created: FOSSE

dive in which one does a back flip and plunges into the water head first and facing the board: HALF GAINER

dive down suddenly, as a whale when harpooned: SOUND

diverge, spread apart or branch out at a wide angle: DIVARICATE

divergency, inconsistency: DISCREPANCY

diverse, varied to a great degree: MULTIFARIOUS

diversify or vary by adding something different: INTERLARD

diversity of sources used: ECLECTIC

divert, confuse: DISTRACT

diverted by thought, preoccupied: BEMUSED

divide, separate, part: DISSEVER

divide or shape a voting area to advance the interests of one political party: GERRYMANDER

divide by cutting or passing across: INTERSECT

divide into opposing groups or views: POLARIZE

divide into two sections: DICHOTOMIZE

divide or distribute in proportion: PRORATE

divide or spread out into divisions: RAMIFY

divided in half: DIMIDIATE

dividend, either regular or scheduled, that has been omitted: PASSED DIVIDEND

dividend on stock, paid in securities instead of cash: STOCK DIVIDEND

divination by means of figures formed when particles of earth are thrown down at random: GEOMANCY

divination by use of a divining rod: RHABDOMANCY

divinatory, mystical or magical arts: OCCULT

divine or supernatural intervention in human affairs: THEURGY

division: SCISSION

division of a church or other organization into factions: SCHISM

dizziness: VERTIGO

dizzy, whirling, spinning: VERTIGINOUS

do or commit something, as a crime or hoax: PERPETRATE

do away with, as a law or a right: ABROGATE

do penance, be humbled: GO TO CANOSSA

doctor serving apprenticeship in a hospital: INTERN

doctor who treats animals: VETERINARIAN

doctor's auxiliary or assistant: PARAMEDIC

doctrine, belief or principle maintained as true by a person or a group: TENET

doctrine that all life is sacred: AHIMSA

doctrine that holds reality has existence independent of the mind: OBJECTIVISM

doctrines held to be true and necessary: DOGMA

document accrediting an envoy to a foreign power: LETTER OF CREDENCE

document wholly in the handwriting of the person whose signature it bears: HOLOGRAPH

dodge, avoid: SIDESTEP

dodge or device to avoid unpleasantness: SUBTERFUGE

dogmatic, arrogant, haughty, pompous: PONTIFICAL

dogmatic or unproved assertion: IPSE DIXIT

doll made of wood representing spirit ancestors of Pueblo Indians: KACHINA

dollar per share of stock: POINT

domain: DEMESNE

domain of authority: BAILIWICK

dome, or roof that is rounded: CUPOLA

dominant, prevalent: REGNANT

dominate thoughts, engross: PREOCCUPY

domination of one state over another or leadership: HEGEMONY

domineering, arrogant: IMPERIOUS

domineering, overwhelming: OVERBEARING

done beyond recall, accomplished fact: FAIT ACCOMPLI

done or said for effect or as a formality: GESTURE

done with great effort: LABORED

doomed to failure: FORLORN HOPE

door, entrance: PORTAL

door divided horizontally so that either half can be opened separately: DUTCH DOOR

door or window part, above the opening and supporting structure above it: LINTEL

doorkeeper of a building: CONCIERGE

doorway curtain that replaces a door: PORTIERE

doorway or window drapery that covers only top half of opening: LAMBREQUIN

doorway side post: JAMB

dormant: LATENT

dots of many colors used as a method of painting: POINTILLISM

dots or hyphens in a horizontal row serving to guide the eye across a page: LEADER

dots or shadings used in photoengraving: BENDAY

dots over the second of two adjacent vowels to indicate it is pronounced separately (ö): DIERESIS

dots used to indicate the omission of words: SUSPENSION POINTS

dotted pattern woven into fabric: SHARKSKIN

double, two or paired: BINARY

double dagger symbol used in printing (‡): DIESIS

double dealer: AMBIDEXTER

double dealing, trickery: DUPLICITY

double image, blot: MACKLE

double meaning: AMBIGUOUS

double meaning, ambiguous, uncertain in origin or character, dubious: EQUIVOCAL

double meaning attributable to grammatical looseness: AMPHIBOLOGY

double or become doubled: GEMINATE

double or twofold: DUPLE

double pulse beat with each heartbeat: DICROTIC

double tablet, picture or carving, often depicting a religious subject: DIPTYCH

double vision: DIPLOPIA

doubling of a syllable or sound in a word: REDUPLICATION

doubling the stakes in gambling, to recover previous losses: MARTINGALE

doughnut in elongated, twisted shape: CRULLER

doubt, qualm, apprehension: MISGIVING

doubter: SKEPTIC

doubtful: DUBIOUS

doubtful state: DUBIETY

doubtfulness: INCERTITUDE

doubting, disbelieving: INCREDULOUS

doubting, resisting, ignoring attitude: NEGATIVISM

dowdy, sometimes ill-tempered woman: FRUMP

down in spirits, dejected: DISPIRITED

down in the dumps, down in the mouth: DOLDRUMS

down in the mouth: CHAPFALLEN

down to earth, practical rather than speculative: PRAGMATIC

downcast: DISPIRITED

downhearted, depressed: DISPIRITED

downy, covered with soft fine hair: LANUGINOUS

dowry, woman's marriage portion: DOT

drab, frumpish, not smartly dressed: DOWDY

draft: CONSCRIPTION

drag in the mud, lag, follow slowly: DRABBLE

drag or haul: SCHLEP

drapery or board across the top of a window: VALANCE

draw, paint, engrave with dots instead of lines: STIPPLE

draw a line around: CIRCUMSCRIBE

draw back, as claws: RETRACT

draw forth, call, or summon: EVOKE

draw forth, evoke, bring to light: ELICIT

draw or scribble aimlessly: DOODLE

draw or a tie, as in a game: STANDOFF

drawback, burden: IMPEDIMENTA

drawing a conclusion, based on reasoning from general to particular: DEDUCTION

drawing to create the illusion of depth and distance while keeping the proper proportions: FORESHORTEN

drawing together, reconciliation: RAPPROCHEMENT

drawn-out speech or writing: LONGWINDED

dread, abnormal and persistent, of a particular thing: PHOBIA (and see listing under that word)

dreaded or hated object or person: BÊTE NOIRE

dream interpreter: ONEIROCRITIC

dreamer or visionary: FANTAST

dreamlike, visionary: HYPNAGOGIC

dreamy repose caused by smoking narcotics: KEF

dregs of wine or liquor: LEES

dregs or lees, refuse grain from breweries and distilleries: DRAFF

drench or stain, especially with blood: IMBRUE

dress fussily: PRIMP

dress hanging straight from the shoulders: CHEMISE

dress showily, primp: PREEN

dress up or decorate: TITIVATE

dressed negligently or partially: DISHABILLE

dressing in garments of the opposite sex, a compulsion to do so: TRANSVESTITISM

dressing room for a woman: BOUDOIR

dressmaker, male: COUTURIER

dribbling of saliva: SLAVER

drink: IMBIBE

drink, given to: BIBULOUS

drink and play, carefree existence: BEER AND SKITTLES

drink greedily or to excess: GUZZLE

drink heartily: QUAFF

drink of mild nature to wash down hard liquor: CHASER

drink or eat greedily, gorge: INGURGITATE

drink sparingly: ABSTEMIOUS

drink that is drugged: MICKEY FINN

drinkable: POTABLE

drinking bowl or its contents: JORUM

drinking cup or goblet: MAZER

drive a sharp stake through: IMPALE

drive away, dispel: DISSIPATE

drive off, dispel, scatter: DISPERSE

drive away or remove, as by scattering: DISPEL

drive back, ward off: REPEL

drive or force to action, urge on: IMPEL

drive out of hiding: FERRET

drivel, incoherent talk: MAUNDER

driving force: IMPETUS

driving too closely behind another vehicle: TAILGATING

droop, hang loosely: LOLL

droop, weaken: FLAG

droop gradually, pine, weaken: LANGUISH

droop or hang down loosely: LOP

drop heavily and clumsily, flop: FLUMP

drop of liquid, in pharmacy: GUTTA

drop or plunge straight down: PLUMMET

dropping of sounds or letters from the middle of a word: SYNCOPE

dropping a sound at the end of a word: APOCOPE

dropping the initial letter or sound in a word: APHERESIS

dropping to earth of particles after a nuclear explosion: FALLOUT

drowning as a form of execution: NOYADE

drowsy: SOMNOLENT

drudge, one who hires himself out to do routine or tedious work: HACK

drug salesman: DETAIL MAN

drug that is incapable of doing harm or good: ADIAPHOROUS

drug that overcomes effects of sedatives: ANALEPTIC

drug withdrawal: COLD TURKEY

drugs as a science: PHARMACOLOGY

drum: TAMBOUR

drum, small and double-headed, with a wire string across the bottom: SNARE DRUM

drum in the form of a hollow hemisphere with a parchment top: KETTLEDRUM

drum or tap monotonously: THRUM

drum or trumpet signal for a parley: CHAMADE

drumbeat with two sticks striking almost simultaneously: FLAM

drumhead with jingles in its rim: TAMBOURINE

drumlike: TYMPANIC

drumming continuously: TATTOO

drunk: BESOTTED

drunk: INEBRIATED

drunkard: TOPER

drunken, gluttonous: CRAPULENT

drunken revelry: BACCHANAL

drunk-making: INTOXICANT

dry: BRUT

dry, lacking interest, naive, barren, insipid: JEJUNE

dry or roast by exposing to heat: TORREFY

dry up, make thirsty: PARCH

dry up or out: EXSICCATE

drying: SICCATIVE

dryness: XERIC

dualism in theology, belief in two co-equal gods: DITHEISM

dubious use of ploys to gain an advantage: GAMESMANSHIP

dueling sword with sharp point and no cutting edge: EPEE

dull: LACKLUSTER

dull, commonplace: STODGY

dull, depressed or bored state of mind: DOLDRUMS

dull, heavy, lethargic: LOGY

dull, inactive, sluggish: TORPID

dull, insensible, not acute: OBTUSE

dull, lifeless, insipid, flat: VAPID

dull, light-resistant: OPAQUE

dull, mediocre, prosaic: PEDESTRIAN

dull, monotonous: HUMDRUM

dull, ordinary, uninspired: PROSAIC

dull, tasteless, flat, bland, vapid: INSIPID

dull, trite: BANAL

dull, zestless: PERFUNCTORY

dull or become stupid: HEBETATE

dulled from overindulgence, worn-out, exhausted, sated: JADED

dullness, apathy, sluggishness: LETHARGY

dullness, stagnation, weakness, fatigue, dreaminess, spiritlessness: LANGUOR

dullness, yawning: OSCITANCY

dupe or tool: CAT'S-PAW

dumbfound, perplex, bewilder: NONPLUS

duplicate: DITTO

duplicate of a work made by the originator, close copy: REPLICA

duplication of a word for rhetorical effect: GEMINATION

durable, binding: INDISSOLUBLE

durable, permanent: PERDURABLE

durable products such as automobiles, refrigerators, furniture: HARD GOODS

dusky, dark complexioned: SWARTHY

dusky, gloomy, depressed: SOMBER

dusty, powdery: PULVERULENT

dwarf, midget: HOMUNCULUS

dwell or stay temporarily: SOJOURN

dwelling: ABODE

dwelling, house, home, abode: DOMICILE

dwelling that is wretched and small, shed: HOVEL

dying work, as of a writer or composer: SWAN SONG

E

eager curiosity or excitement: AGOG
eager for food in quantity: VORACIOUS
ear deformed by blows: CAULIFLOWER EAR
ear diseases, as a study: OTOLOGY
ear reception: AURAL
earache: OTALGIA
earliest stages of development, beginnings: INCUNABULA
earlike projections for holding something, as a pot or kettle: LUGS
early edition of a newspaper: BULLDOG EDITION
early in the morning: MATUTINAL
early morning: COCKCROW
earnest, warm, glowing: FERVENT
earnestly appeal: ADJURE
earnings of common stock as affected by bond interest and preferred stock dividends: LEVERAGE
ears ringing: TINNITUS
earth inhabitant: TELLURIAN
earth study of materials, their structure and characteristics: GEOGNOSY
earthenware, glazed, usually blue and white: DELFT
earthenware piece in broken condition: POTSHERD
earthly: TERRESTRIAL
earthquake: TEMBLOR
earthquake measuring scale: RICHTER SCALE
earthquake phenomena, as a science: SEISMOLOGY
earth's physical structure, as a science: GEOLOGY
earth's structure and the forces that change it, as a scientific study: TECTONICS
earth's surface above sea level treated as a science: HYPSOGRAPHY

easily: HANDILY
easily achieved, ready or quick in performance, skillful: FACILE
easing, as of discord, between nations: DETENTE
easterly wind in Mediterranean regions: LEVANTER
eastern hemisphere: ORIENT
easy mark: GULL
easy to approach: AFFABLE
eat, especially with someone: BREAK BREAD
eat greedily: ENGORGE
eat ravenously: GUTTLE
eat or drink greedily, gorge: INGURGITATE
eat sparingly: ABSTEMIOUS
eat voraciously or gluttonously: GOURMANDISE
eater and drinker with discriminating taste: GOURMET
eater of much food: TRENCHERMAN
eater to excess: GOURMAND
eating as an art: GASTRONOMY
eating at the same table: COMMENSAL
eating implements: CUTLERY
eating or wearing away of a substance: CORROSION
eating to excess: GLUTTONOUS
eating many foods: POLYPHAGIA
eats all kinds of food both animal and vegetable: OMNIVOROUS
ebb, flowing back: REFLUX
ebbing, flowing back: REFLUENT
eccentric or queer: CRANKY
eccentric, irregular, nonconforming: ERRATIC
ecclesiastical council: SYNOD
ecclesiastical cutting of one off from fellowship of a church: EXCOMMUNICATION

ecclesiastical property transferred to laymen: IMPROPRIATED

echo, response: REPLICATION

echoic as pertaining to words: ONOMATOPOEIC or ONOMATOPOETIC

echoing loudly: REBOANT

ecology, basic unit including both organisms and environment: ECOSYSTEM

ecology—nonavailable water of the soil: ECHARD

ecology—plant adjustment to a new habitat: ECESIS

ecology—soil rather than climate as an affective factor: EDAPHIC

ecology—zone wherein two different species contend for dominance: ECOTONE

ecology of plant and animal communities: SYNECOLOGY

economic self-sufficiency: AUTARKY

economic union of Belgium, Netherlands and Luxembourg: BENELUX

economic union of Western Europe: COMMON MARKET

economical, chary, stingy: SPARE

economy or thrift in managing: HUSBANDRY

economy spur of governmental expenditures financed by borrowing: DEFICIT FINANCING

ecstasy of a religious nature: THEOPATHY

edge of fabric so woven as not to ravel: SELVAGE

edge of paper that resembles the ragged edge of handmade paper: DECKLE EDGE

edge or outer part: PERIPHERY

edge that slopes: BEVEL

edging, selvage, strip, as of cloth: LIST

edging decorated with a series of indentations: ENGRAILED

edging of small loops of ribbon or thread: PICOT

edible: ESCULENT

edit: REDACT

edit prudishly: BOWDLERIZE

editing of a text by reference to varying manuscripts: RECENSION

editor of manuscripts in newspaper or publishing house: COPY EDITOR

educated people or individuals collectively: INTELLIGENTSIA

eel fishing by putting bait into the eels' hiding places: SNIGGLING

eel-shaped: ANGUILLIFORM

eerie, strange, weird, unnatural: UNCANNY

efface, destroy completely: OBLITERATE

effect, result: RAMIFICATION

effect that balances another effect: COUNTERPOSE

effective: POTENT

effective, moving, working: OPERATIVE

effective at a specified past time: RETROACTIVE

effeminate: EMASCULATED

effeminate, sexless: EPICENE

efficacy, potency: VIRTUE

efficient quickness: DISPATCH

eggs baked with crumbs in a buttered dish: SHIRRED EGGS

eggs cooked and served on toast spread with anchovy paste: SCOTCH WOODCOCK

eggs laid at one time: CLUTCH

egg white: ALBUMEN

egg-white glaze: GLAIR

egg yolk: VITELLUS

eight tones above or below a given one: OCTAVE

eight-year period: OCTENNIAL

elaborate, speak or write more fully: EXPATIATE

elasticity, buoyancy: RESILIENCE

elate or excite to a degree of frenzy: INTOXICATE

elated: COCK-A-HOOP

elderly woman of dignified bearing and wealth: DOWAGER

eldest or senior member of a group: DOYEN

elect, choose: OPT

election held between regular ones: BY-ELECTION

election that finally decides: RUN-OFF

electioneer on a political trip: STUMP

electric strength, unit that measures: AMPERE

electromotive force measured in volts: VOLTAGE

electronic devices without moving parts or heated elements: SOLID STATE

electronic solid-state device that controls flow of current without use of a vacuum: TRANSISTOR

element that causes a thing to be what it is: FACTOR

elemental, original, primitive: PRIMORDIAL

elementary: ABECEDARIAN

elementary: RUDIMENTARY

elementary instruction: PROPAEDEUTIC

elephant in a state of sexual frenzy: MUST
elephant keeper and driver, in India: MAHOUT
elevator for conveying food from floor to floor: DUMBWAITER
eleven-sided figure: HENDECAGON
elf or sprite: PIXIE
elite group within an organization: CADRE
elk, large North American deer: WAPITI
emaciate, become thin: MACERATE
emaciated: TABETIC
emaciated, haggard, hollow-eyed, gloomy, desolate: GAUNT
emaciation: MARASMUS
emanate, exude: EFFUSE
emanation: EFFLUX
emanation, especially foul-smelling exhalation from decaying matter: EFFLUVIUM
emancipate, liberate, free: MANUMIT
emasculate: CASTRATE
embarrassed: ABASHED
embarrassing occurrence: CONTRETEMPS
embarrassment at what one has done himself: CHAGRIN
embed a material such as gold or ivory into a surface so as to form a decorative pattern: INLAY
embellish, as ornamental lines or figures: FLOURISH
embellish a speech or writing with quotations, etc.: LARD
embellishment: GARNITURE
embezzle, steal funds, especially public funds: PECULATE
embezzle or misappropriate: DEFALCATE
embitter: ACERBATE
embitter: ENVENOM
embitter, stir enduring ire: RANKLE
embodiment of an attribute or a quality in a person: PERSONIFICATION
embroidery at the ankle of a sock or stocking: CLOCK
embroidery that is rich: ORPHREY
emerge, come forth into the open: DEBOUCH
emergency or temporary as applied to a ship's rigging: JURY-RIGGED
emergency program that has top priority: CRASH PROGRAM
emotion, subjective aspect of: AFFECT
emotional in appeal: AFFECTIVE
emotional for effect, theatrical: HISTRIONIC
emotional intensity, ardor: FERVOR

emotional or mental block: INHIBITION
emotional or sentimental, tearfully so: MAUDLIN
emotional shock, injury: TRAUMA
emotionless: APATHETIC
employer who is excessively demanding: SLAVE DRIVER
employer's barring employes from work until they accept his terms: LOCKOUT
employes tend to rise to their level of incompetence: PETER PRINCIPLE
employment of more workers than needed: FEATHERBEDDING
empower, authorize: WARRANT
emptiness: VACUITY
empty compliment or flattery: FLUMMERY
empty tomb: CENOTAPH
enact, establish, decree: ORDAIN
enamel-and-metal work: CLOISONNÉ
enamel- or lacquer-ornamented metalware: TOLE
enchantress who changed men into swine: CIRCE
enclose within walls, imprison, confine, surround: IMMURE
encourage: ABET
encourage: HEARTEN
encouragement, exhortation: HORTATORY
encroach, infringe: IMPINGE
end a parliamentary session: PROROGUE
end, cease: SURCEASE
end, termination: EXPIRY
end of the world: CRACK OF DOOM
end-of-the-world battle between good and evil: ARMAGEDDON
end or withdraw by plan: PHASE OUT
end unexpectedly: ABORT
ending of debate in parliamentary procedure: CLOSURE, CLOTURE
ending of one or more syllables affixed to a word: SUFFIX
ending section of a book or a play that adds commentary or explanation: EPILOGUE
endless: INTERMINABLE
endless and difficult: SISYPHEAN
endowment: APPANAGE
endowment or gift, as of a church: PATRIMONY
ends touching: ABUTTING
endurance, vigor, strength: STAMINA
endurance test: MARATHON
endurance test, painful experience: ORDEAL
energetic, in music: VIGOROSO

energy, enthusiasm: VERVE

energy and matter, as a science: PHYSICS

energy or force held as the basis for phenomena of the universe: DYNAMISM

enfeebled, worn out by age or use: DECREPIT

engine mounted on the rear of a small boat: OUTBOARD MOTOR

English dessert consisting of spongecake soaked in wine and topped with jam, custard and whipped cream: TRIFLE

engrave, cut into, carve: INCISE

engraver of precious stones: LAPIDARY

engross, dominate thoughts: PREOCCUPY

engross, involve deeply: IMMERSE

engrossed intensely: RAPT

engulf, overpower, submerge: WHELM

enigmatic, mysterious: INSCRUTABLE

enigmatic, prophetic: ORACULAR

enjoyment: DELECTATION

enjoyment of possessions: FRUITION

enlarge: AGGRANDIZE

enlarge a hole: REAM

enlarge excessively, increase unduly, puff up: INFLATE

enlargement: AMPLIFICATION OR AMPLIATION

enlarging, growing, waxing: INCRESCENT

enlighten, benefit, uplift: EDIFY

enlighten, illuminate, light up, make clear: IRRADIATE

enmity, malice: RANCOR

enormous, hideous: MONSTROUS

enormous, unwieldy, ponderous: ELEPHANTINE

enormous, vast: PRODIGIOUS

enrage, anger: INCENSE

enraged, angry: IRATE

enroll or register in a college or university as a candidate for a degree: MATRICULATE

entangle, complicate, confuse: EMBRANGLE

entangle, intertwine, involve: IMPLICATE

entanglement, complication, intertwining: INVOLUTION

enter office or dignity: ACCEDE

enter without leave or invitation: INTRUDE

entertain, amuse, distract: DIVERT

entertain, delight, give unusual pleasure: REGALE

enthusiasm, dash, vivacity: ÉLAN

enthusiasm, energy: VERVE

enthusiasm, zest: GUSTO

enthusiast: AFICIONADO

enthusiastic, fervent: ZEALOUS

enthusiastic or excited, bubbling: EBULLIENT

entice by flattery or guile, draw, cajole: INVEIGLE

entire range of anything: GAMUT

entirely: TOUT À FAIT

entirely, altogether: IN TOTO

entrance, going in: INGRESS

entrance hall, lobby: FOYER

entrance or gate: PORTAL

entreating earnestly and humbly: SUPPLIANT

entreaty or appeal for assistance: INVOCATION

entreaty or prayer in behalf of others: INTERCESSION

entry: ACCESS

envelope markings used instead of stamps: INDICIA

environment, setting: MILIEU

environment in relation to organisms: ECOLOGY

environmental distinctiveness: AMBIENCE

epidemic among animals: EPIZOOTIC

episode that is minor: INCIDENT

epithet or title substituted for proper name: ANTONOMASIA

equal before the law, or in ability or social position: PEER

equal in size: COMMENSURATE

equal intervals of time: ISOCHRONAL

equal number of parts: ISOMEROUS

equal or equivalent: TANTAMOUNT

equal political power in a government: ISOCRACY

equality, social and political: EGALITARIAN

equality in dimensions or measurements: ISOMETRIC

equality in rank, power, condition, etc.: PARITY

equality of racial and ethnic groups: INTEGRATION

equilibrium of an organism: HOMEOSTASIS

equipment, gear, personal effects: PARAPHERNALIA

equivalent or equal: TANTAMOUNT

equivocate, be evasive: TERGIVERSATE

equivocate, lie: PREVARICATE

era, period, century: SIÈCLE

eradicate, dislocate, uproot: DERACINATE

erase, delete: EXPUNGE

erase, destroy utterly, pull up by the roots, uproot, erase: ERADICATE erase, rub out, cancel, obliterate: EFFACE

erection of the penis as a persistent pathological condition: PRIAPISM

ermine in its brown summer coat: STOAT

erratic, unexpected: WAYWARD

erring, wicked: PERVERSE

erroneous name: MISNOMER

erroneous placement of something in time: ANACHRONISM

erroneous or misleading: FALLACIOUS

error in reading or speaking lines: FLUFF

error in speaking that is thought to disclose a person's true thinking: FREUDIAN SLIP

errorless, faultless, flawless: IMPECCABLE

errors in a list: ERRATA

escape from the law by secret departure: ABSCOND

escape or avoid: ELUDE

escort, attendants of a person of rank: RETINUE

essence of a legal complaint or accusation: GRAVAMEN

essence of something: QUIDDITY

essence of something in concentrated form: QUINTESSENCE

essence or abstract quality of anything: DISTILLATION

essential, indispensable: SINE QUA NON

essential, whole: INTEGRAL

essential, inherent: INTRINSIC

essential element: INHERENT

essential qualities of anything: DISTILLATION

essential source of life, actions, energy: ANIMA

essential theme or part, gist: PITH

established firmly, deep-rooted: INGRAINED

established firmly by long continance: INVETERATE

established rule or principle: CANON

esteem, high regard: REPUTE

estimate based on a guess: GUESSTIMATE

estimate from evidence at hand, project on the basis of facts already known: EXTRAPOLATE

estranged, alienated: DISAFFECTED

eternity or period of time that is incalculable: EON

ethical consequences of all one's acts (Buddhism and Hinduism): KARMA

ethics or science of moral obligation: DEONTOLOGY

etiquette in diplomacy: PROTOCOL

Eucharist as given just before death: VIATICUM

eulogy or praise formally delivered: ENCOMIUM

European Economic Community: COMMON MARKET

evangelist preacher: REVIVALIST

evasion of main point by stressing a trivial point: QUIBBLE

evasion of painful emotions or unacceptable impulses by adjusting behavior or mental attitude: DEFENSE MECHANISM

evasive action to gain time: TEMPORIZATION

even on the same line or with a margin: FLUSH

even beat as in music or speech: CADENCE

evening prayers or services: VESPERS

evening star: HESPERUS

evergreen: INDECIDUOUS

every two weeks: BIWEEKLY

everyday speech, popular, accepted: VULGATE

everything included: OVERALL

everywhere at once: UBIQUITOUS

everywhere present simultaneously: OMNIPRESENCE

evidence that a defendant is compelled to disclose in a trial or hearing: DISCOVERY

evidence that if unrefuted establishes the fact alleged: PRIMA FACIE EVIDENCE

evident, manifest, obvious: PATENT

evident, obvious, plainly apparent: MANIFEST

evident, open, unconcealed: OVERT

evil, repulsive, flagrantly bad: VILE

evil, vile: NEFARIOUS

evil, wicked, odious, atrocious: HEINOUS

evil eye protection: AMULET

evil notoriety: INFAMY

evil person: SHAITAN

evildoer, criminal: MALEFACTOR

evildoer, villain: MISCREANT

evoke, draw forth, bring to light: ELICIT

evolution of any animal or plant group: PHYLOGENY

exact, accurate: PRECISE

exact, honest: SCRUPULOUS

exact, precise, accurate: NICE

exact, scrupulous observance of forms: PUNCTILIOUS

exact copy or reproduction: FACSIMILE

exact words of the original: LITERAL

exaggerate a narrative with fictitious details: EMBROIDER

exaggerated sense of buoyancy and vigor: EUPHORIA

exaggeration or overstatement intended for effect and not to be taken seriously: HYPERBOLE

exalting human to divine status: APOTHEOSIS

examination of something that has already happened: POST-MORTEM

examination of tissue removed from a living organism: BIOPSY

examination or discussion that is detailed: CANVASS

examine carefully: SCRUTINIZE

examine or analyze minutely, sift: WINNOW

example or case: INSTANCE

examine by feeling or touching: PALPATE

examine or read thoroughly, scrutinize: PERUSE

examine or scrutinize carefully: TRAVERSE

example of excellence: PARAGON

example or model: PARADIGM

excavation for archeological purposes: DIG

excavations, study of, as history: ARCHEOLOGY

exceed, excel: OUTSTRIP

exceed a limit: TRANSCEND

excel: TRANSCEND

excel, beat, surpass: TRUMP

excel, exceed: OUTSTRIP

excellence exemplified: PARAGON

excellence or exceptional quality, choice: VINTAGE

excellent or fine: COPESETIC

exercises to promote grace and health: CALISTHENICS

excerpts or selections from literary works: ANALECTS

excess, abundance beyond need: SUPERFLUITY

excess in eating or drinking: SURFEIT

excess word or phrase: PLEONASM

excessive: INORDINATE

excessive, unrestrained: WANTON

excessive or insincere: FULSOME

excessive beyond usual limits: EXORBITANT

excessive or extreme: INTEMPERATE

excessively: UNDULY

exchange, as ideas: INTERCHANGE

exchange by two countries of concessions: RECIPROCITY

exchange of something for something else: QUID PRO QUO

excite, enliven, stimulate: QUICKEN

excite, exhilarate, intoxicate: INEBRIATE

excite, rouse to action, stimulate: GALVANIZE

excite, stimulate, raise the spirits of: ELATE

excite, stimulate, sharpen: WHET

excite or elate to a degree of frenzy: INTOXICATE

excited, confused, hasty: HECTIC

excited to a feverish pitch: FRENETIC

excitement that is great and intense: WHITE HEAT

exciting or producing similar reactions in others: INFECTIOUS

exclaim, discharge suddenly and quickly: EJACULATE

exclaim loudly, shout, bawl: VOCIFERATE

exclamation, often profane: EXPLETIVE

exclamation, usually one word: INTERJECTION

exclude, make impossible, shut out: PRECLUDE

exclude, shut out: OSTRACIZE

exclude from sacraments and solemn services, as in the Roman Catholic Church: INTERDICT

exclusive control of a product or service: MONOPOLY

exclusive set: CLIQUE

excrement: FECES

excrete waste matter: DEFECATE

excusable, pardonable, as a fault: VENIAL

excuse or exempt, as from a regulation: DISPENSE

excuse or reason for being: RAISON D'ÊTRE

excuse or try to excuse from blame: EXTENUATE

excuse that clears from censure, criticism or suspicion: EXCULPATION

excuse that is not quite honest: SALVO

execute or attack with a cord or metal collar, which is tightened: GARROTE

exemption as from a rule or law: DISPENSATION

exemption from local law granted to members of the diplomatic corps: DIPLOMATIC IMMUNITY

exemption from obligation or penalty, resistance to harmful influence or disease: IMMUNITY

exemption from penalties or liabilities, compensation for loss or damage: INDEMNITY

exemption or freedom from punishment, harm or unpleasant consequences: IMPUNITY

exhausted, helpless, lying flat: PROSTRATE

exhibit in which modeled figures are set in a naturalistic foreground, which blends into a painted background: DIORAMA

exhibition or parade that is spectacular: PAGEANT

exhilarate, excite: INEBRIATE

exhortation, encouragement: HORTATORY

existing, surviving: EXTANT

exit, or going out: EGRESS

exiled person: EXPATRIATE

expand, grow, increase step by step: ESCALATE

expand, stretch out, swell: DISTEND

expand, widen, swell: DILATE

expand a business by increasing the variety of its products: DIVERSIFY

expanding with age: ACCRESCENCE

expectorated matter: SPUTUM

expedient and wise: POLITIC

expedition or journey: SAFARI

expenditures limited or regulated, as by law: SUMPTUARY

expense account: SWINDLE SHEET

expenses or continuous costs of operating a business: OVERHEAD

expense allowance for each day: PER DIEM

experience alone as the source of knowledge: EMPIRICISM

experiment subject: GUINEA PIG

expert: ADROIT

expert: MAVEN, MAVIN

expert in matters of art and taste: CONNOISSEUR

expert on recorded music: DISCOPHILE

expertness, manual skill: HANDINESS

explain, make clear: INTERPRET

explain actions or thoughts on rational grounds, which may not be the real motives: RATIONALIZE

explain away: GLOZE

explain away: RESOLVE

explain or interpret: EXPLICATE

explainer or promoter: EXPONENT

explanation that is detailed: EXPLICATION

explanation of a word, passage or work: EXEGESIS

explanatory description or caption on a chart, map or illustration: LEGEND

explanatory note, commentary: GLOSS

explicit, most accurate and complete: DEFINITIVE

explode suddenly and with violence: DETONATE

exploration of enemy positions: RECONNAISSANCE

explosive effect: BRISANCE

explosive force of a thousand tons of TNT: KILOTON

explosive sounds, or throwing off small particles as by frying meat: SPLUTTER

explosive that is trinitrotoluene: TNT

expose actual or alleged corruption: MUCKRAKE

expose to the sun as for bleaching: INSOLATE

exposure to risk to achieve some end: BRINKMANSHIP

express by gestures: GESTICULATE

expurgate: BOWDLERIZE

extemporize: AD LIB

extend, spread out: SPLAY

extended to great subtleness: FINE-DRAWN

extension: AMPLIFICATION or AMPLIATION

extent, scope, range: PURVIEW

extenuate, alleviate: PALLIATE

extermination or destruction of an entire people or national group: GENOCIDE

extinct or dead: DEFUNCT

extinguish or satisfy thirst: QUENCH

extirpate, uproot, dislocate, eradicate: DERACINATE

extort: EXACT

extort or swindle to get goods or money: FLAY

extra day in leap year: BISEXTILE

extra something given beyond obligation: LAGNIAPPE

extra vowel inserted into word: ANAPTYXIS

extract or passage, especially from the Bible: PERICOPE

extraneous, superfluous: SUPEREROGATORY

extraordinary happening: PHENOMENON

extrasensory perception of distant objects: TELESTHESIA

extravagance as in entertaining or in style of living: LUCULLAN extravagance to impress: CONSPICUOUS CONSUMPTION

extravagant, pompous: HIGHFALUTIN

extravagant, wasteful, lavish: PRODIGAL

extravagant ornamentation: BAROQUE

extravagantly praise: ADULATE

extreme or excessive: INTEMPERATE

extrinsic: ADVENTITIOUS

exude, emanate: EFFUSE

exult over another's bad luck: GLOAT

eye, make eyes at suggestively: OGLE

eye disease marked by pressure within the eyeball: GLAUCOMA

eye disorder in which both eyes cannot be focused simultaneously on the same spot: STRABISMUS

eye examination to determine response to light and shadow: SKIASCOPY

eye examiner: OPTOMETRIST

eye for an eye, a tooth for a tooth: RETALIATION

eye in which the iris is light-colored: WALLEYE

eye or sight: OCULAR

eye sees an object double: DIPLOPIA

eyebrows bushy and prominent: BEETLE-BROWED

eyeglass dealer: OPTICIAN

eyeglasses that grip the bridge of the nose: PINCE-NEZ

eyeglasses with handle into which they may be folded: LORGNETTE

eyeglasses with three-part lenses: TRIFOCALS

eyeglasses with two-part lenses: BIFOCALS

eyelet of metal: GROMMET

eyes, as a medical study: OPHTHALMOLOGY

eyes dark and velvety: SLOE-EYED

eyes see what appear to be specks or threads: MUSCAE VOLITANTES

F

fable or tale with a moral: APOLOGUE

fabric edge so woven as not to ravel: SELVAGE

fabric gathered in parallel rows: SHIRRING

fabric piece, usually triangular, inserted in a garment for roomier fit: GUSSET

fabric sample: SWATCH

fabric surface of velvet, plush or corduroy: PILE

fabric with a soft pile: VELOUR

fabric with fibers that make the surface fuzzy: NAPPED

fabric woven with a dotted pattern: SHARKSKIN

fabrication, fiction: FIGMENT

face or facial expression: VISAGE

face that is pale and sallow: WHEYFACE

face to face: VIS-À-VIS

face upward, lying on the back: SUPINE

face-down lying position: PRONE

face-to-face meeting: CONFRONTATION

facial contour or feature, distinguishing characteristic: LINEAMENT

facial expression indicative of pain or annoyance: GRIMACE

facial features regarded as clues to character: PHYSIOGNOMY

facile, too glib: PAT

facilitate, quicken, speed up: EXPEDITE

facing toward one: OBVERSE

factual condition as distinguished from legal condition: DE FACTO

fail, sink, collapse: FOUNDER

fail disastrously: COME A CROPPER

fail to carry out a mission: ABORT

fail to keep a promise: RENEGE

failure in duty, willful omission or neglect: DERELICTION

failure or neglect to meet an obligation: DEFAULT

failure that is complete or humiliating: FIASCO

failure to realize one's intentions: MISCARRIAGE

faint, hidden, unclear: OBSCURE

fair, disinterested: IMPARTIAL

fair, impartial: UNBIASED

fair, impartial, reasonable: EQUITABLE

fairness, impartiality, justness: EQUITY

fairy, elf, goblin: SPRITE

faithful devotion to obligations: FIDELITY

faithful follower: MYRMIDON

faithful forever: SEMPER FIDELIS

faithfulness, obligation owed, loyalty: FEALTY

falconry term for the short strap on each leg of a hawk, used for attaching a leash: JESS

fall or cave in, sink, collapse, fail: FOUNDER

fall straight down, plunge: PLUMMET

fall that is heavy: CROPPER

fall upon, strike against: IMPINGE

falling behind, slow; a straggler: LAGGARD

falling objects always roll to the most inaccessible spot: BERNSTEIN'S FIRST LAW

falling off or shedding as petals, leaves, fruit: DECIDUOUS

false, artificially invented, not real: FICTITIOUS

false, fraudulently invented: TRUMPED-UP

false, not genuine: SPURIOUS

false, ridiculous or self-contradictory statement: PARADOX

false appearance, pretense: GUISE

false conception or deceptive appearance: ILLUSION

false charges: ASPERSIONS

false front: FACADE

false pathos: BATHOS
false sentimentality: MAWKISHNESS
false step, mistake, error especially in etiquette: FAUX PAS
false story circulated for political purposes: ROORBACK
false story or rumor: CANARD
falsehood: FABRICATION
falsehood, deception, humbug, sham: FLAM
false or malicious written statement or graphic representation that damages a person's reputation: LIBEL
falsetto and normal chest tones alternated in song: YODEL
falsify or misrepresent: BELIE
fame, celebrity: RENOWN
familiar phrase or person that represents a type: BYWORD
family name: COGNOMEN
family name: PATRONYMIC
family or branch of a family: STIRPS
family or kindred, collectively: COUSINRY
family tree, descent of an individual from a certain ancestor: GENEALOGY
famous: RENOWNED
famous, distinguished: ILLUSTRIOUS
fan: AFICIONADO
fanatic, partisan to excess: ZEALOT
fanatical, raging: RABID
fanatical enthusiast, one possessed by evil spirits: ENERGUMEN
fanciful humor, caprice: WHIMSY
fanciful idea or notion that emerges suddenly: WHIM
fanciful thought or expression: CONCEIT
fancy trappings, finery: REGALIA
fanfare, as of trumpets: FLOURISH
fan-shaped structure: FLABELLUM
fantastic: CHIMERICAL
farewell: ADIEU
farewell: VALE
farewell drink: STIRRUP CUP
farewell speech: VALEDICTORY
farm on which vegetables are grown for market: TRUCK FARM
farm operated cooperatively: COLLECTIVE
farming: HUSBANDRY
farming or rural affairs: GEORGIC
farseeing: PRESCIENT
farsightedness as an abnormal condition of the eye: HYPERMETROPIA
farsightedness that accompanies aging: PRESBYOPIA
farthest possible point: ULTIMA THULE

fascinate, beguile: INTRIGUE
fascinating, enchanting: IRRESISTIBLE
fashionable: DE RIGUEUR
fashionable, wealthy people: JET SET
fast time in music: ALLEGRO
fasten firmly: RIVET
fasten or tie together: COLLIGATE
faster than the speed of sound: SUPERSONIC
fastidious, overly exacting: FINICKY
fasting or other ascetic practices to keep from sinning: MORTIFICATION
fat: ADIPOSE
fat, very stout: OBESE
fat and red-faced: BLOWZY
fat and short person: SQUAB
fat of hogs in melted form: LARD
fat or fleshy: CORPULENT
fatal, deadly,: LETHAL
fate: KISMET
fatigue, spiritlessness, dreaminess, dullness, stagnation: LANGUOR
father of newly born child in primitive tribes going through motions as if he had given birth, such as going to bed: COUVADE
fatherly: PATERNAL
fatlike substance: LIPOID
fats of beef or mutton, used in making soap and candles: TALLOW
fats that limit cholesterol level: POLYUNSATURATED
fatten: BATTEN
fatty buttocks, especially in women: STEATOPYGIA
fatty substance linked to atherosclerosis: CHOLESTEROL
faucet or valve used to drain off water or air: PETCOCK
fault in character that is minor: FOIBLE
fault or trivial sin: PECCADILLO
faultfinder: MOMUS
faultfinding: CAPTIOUS
faultfinding: CENSORIOUS
faultfinding: QUERULOUS
faultfinding, berating: VITUPERATION
faultless, blameless: UNIMPEACHABLE
faultless, flawless, errorless: IMPECCABLE
faulty or illogical reasoning: PARALOGISM
favorable, mild, gentle: BENIGN
favorably disposed, auspicious gracious: PROPITIOUS
favoring one party, prejudiced, biased: PARTIAL

favoritism shown to relative in jobs: NEP-OTISM

fawn upon someone: ADULATE

fawn, cower: CRINGE

fawning, servile, overly obedient: OB-SEQUIOUS

fawning, servile person: TOADY

fear, abnormal and persistent, of a particular thing: PHOBIA (and see listing under that word)

fear, amazement or panic that is sudden and paralyzing: CONSTERNATION

fear-inspiring, formidable: REDOUBTABLE

fear of losing sexual power: APHANISIS

fearful, timid: TIMOROUS

fearful anxiety: TREPIDATION

fearful feeling that something is about to happen: PRESENTIMENT

fearful or timid, trembling: TREMULOUS

fearless, bold, dauntless: INTREPID

fearsome or awesome: FORMIDABLE

feast, picnic or pleasure trip: JUNKET

feather beginning to pierce the skin: PIN-FEATHER

feathers on the neck of a rooster or pigeon or hairs on the neck of a dog: HACKLES

feces, waste matter from bowels: EXCRE-MENT

federal funds appropriated to help an official with his constituents: PORK BARREL

federally regulated amount of credit that a bank may extend to a customer for the purchase of stock: REGULATION U

fee paid to obtain the services of an attorney or a consultant: RETAINER

feebleminded: ANILE

feebleminded person: AMENT

feed, support, rear, train: NURTURE

feed or fodder for cattle: STOVER

feed or supply to excess: SURFEIT

feeding on other animals, exploiting others: PREDATORY

feeding on vegetables, plant-eating: HER-BIVOROUS

feeding through a stomach tube: GAVAGE

feel about with the hands, grope, sprawl, flounder: GRABBLE

feel of a place or situation: AMBIENCE

feel or examine by touching: PALPATE

feeling sharing or emotion sharing with another: EMPATHY

feign, conceal, disguise, make a false show of: DISSEMBLE

fellow member or colleague: CONFRERE

fellowship: CAMARADERIE

fellowship, association: SODALITY

female and male sexual organs in one individual: HERMAPHRODITES

female demon: SUCCUBUS

female external genitals: PUDENDUM

female figure forming a column or pillar: CARYATID

female line of kinship: ENATE

female line or maternal branch of family: DISTAFF SIDE

female opera singer of note, prima donna: DIVA

female professional singer: CANTATRICE

female singer in the principal position: PRIMA DONNA

femininity, womanhood: MULIEBRITY

fence of rails crossed at ends so that the fence zigzags: WORM FENCE

fence made up of strong stakes: APLISADE

fence or wall placed in a ditch so as not to interfere with the view: HA-HA

fermentation, as in brewing: ZYMOLYSIS

ferocious, stubborn, defiant: TRUCULENT

fertile: PROLIFIC

fertile, fruitful: FERACIOUS

fertile, fruitful, prolific: FECUND

fertilize, saturate, permeate: IMPREG-NATE

fervid to an extreme, ardent: PERFERVID

fester, form pus: SUPPURATE

fetus killed: FETICIDE

fetus that is malformed, monstrosity: TERATISM

fetus's lodging place within the mother before birth: PLACENTA

feud, usually a blood feud, involving families: VENDETTA

fever: PYREXIA

feverish: FEBRILE

feverishly excited: FRENETIC

feverless: AFEBRILE

few words his mark: LACONIC

fewer words than the original: ABRIDG-MENT

fewness, small quantity: PAUCITY

fickle: INCONSTANT

fickle: SKITTISH

fickle, changeable: MUTABLE

fickle, frivolous, shallow: FLIGHTY

fickle, unstable, fleeting, transient: VOLA-TILE

fickle person, variable thing: WEATHER-COCK

fickleness, lightness, gaiety that is inappropriate, frivolity: LEVITY

fiction, fabrication: FIGMENT

fictitious: MYTHICAL

fictitious name, pen name: PSEUDONYM

fidgety, unruly, restless: RESTIVE

field near a stable where horses are exercised: PADDOCK

fiendish: DEMONIAC

fierce, harsh: FELL

fierce, malicious, unruly: VICIOUS

fierce, wild, unsociable: FAROUCHE

fifth of a gallon, especially of liquor: FIFTH

fight, brawl or dispute that is noisy: FRACAS

fight, conflict, uproar, brawl: FRAY

fight among people that is confused and noisy: MELEE

fighter in an independent raiding band: GUERRILLA

fighting in public: AFFRAY

fighting over words, verbal contention: LOGOMACHY

fighting with an imaginary foe: SCIAMACHY

figure of speech, figurative language: TROPE

figure of speech endowing inanimate things with human qualities: PERSONIFICATION

figure of speech implying a comparison: METAPHOR

figure of speech or construction in which a word modifying two or more words acquires different meanings: SYLLEPSIS

figure of speech in which a word modifying two others relates correctly to one of them: ZEUGMA

figure of speech in which an assertion is made by the negation of its opposite: LITOTES

figure of speech in which an attribute or an associated term is substituted for the name of the thing itself: METONYMY

figure of speech in which contradictory ideas are combined: OXYMORON

figure of speech in which normal order of things or events is reversed: HYSTERON PROTERON

figure of speech in which two nouns joined by "and" are used instead of noun and modifier: HENDIADYS

figure of speech that describes an event as happening before it could have happened: PROLEPSIS

figure of speech that makes a comparison by use of "as" or "like": SIMILE

filled, laden: FRAUGHT

film director or maker with personal style: AUTEUR

film documentary close to reality: CINÉMA VÉRITÉ

film of part of a television series used for trial purposes: PILOT FILM

film of tiny size for reproducing texts, pictures, etc.: MICROFILM, MICROFICHE

filtering action: LEACH

filth or indecency in art or literature: COPROLOGY

filthy or foul sediment: FECULENCE

final contestant of a team: ANCHORMAN

final deciding election: RUN-OFF

final lines of a poem, usually a dedication: ENVOY

final unraveling or solution in a plot: DENOUEMENT

finalism, final causes as studied in cosmology: TELEOLOGY

financial: FISCAL

fine change or gradation in meaning: NUANCE

fine or excellent: COPESETIC

fine point of behavior or etiquette: PUNCTILIO

fine point or subtlety: NICETY

finery, fancy trappings: REGALIA

finger: DIGIT

finger beside the little finger: RING FINGER

finger snap or quick tap with the nail of a finger that has been snapped: FILLIP

fingerless: ADACTYLOUS

fingerprint: DACTYLOGRAM

fingerprint ridge: WHORL

fingertip infection that is painful: WHITLOW

finicky, fussy: NIGGLING

finish used to coat fabrics, paper or other surfaces: SIZE

fire-breathing monster, part goat, lion and serpent: CHIMERA

firecracker that burns with a spitting sound before exploding: SQUIB

firefighter who parachutes into or near a forest fire: SMOKE JUMPER

fireflies' fire: LUCIFERIN

firelike: IGNEOUS

fireplace or furnace floor: HEARTH

fireplace support for wood: ANDIRON
fireproof: INCOMBUSTIBLE
fireworks: PYROTECHNICS
fireworks that rotate, branched candlestick: GIRANDOLE
firm, dependable: STAUNCH
firm, durable: INDISSOLUBLE
firm, hard, obdurate: FLINTY
firm, solid, forthright: FOURSQUARE
firm, unshakable: IMPREGNABLE
firm foundation of anything: HARDPAN
firm in chewing, as spaghetti: AL DENTE
firmly established by long continuance:
INVETERATE
firmly faithful, unwavering: STEADFAST
first, original, principal: PRIMAL
first in rank: PREMIER
first mention or suggestion: BROACH
first principle or fundamental: RUDIMENT
fish, as a branch of zoology: ICHTHYOL-
OGY
fish basket used by anglers: CREEL
fish cured by splitting and drying in the
air, without salting: STOCKFISH
fish eggs, especially in masses: SPAWN
fish group terms—see "creature terms"
fish or hunt illegally: POACH
fish resembling a sardine: SPRAT
fishing by dragging a hook and line near
the surface: TROLLING
fissure or chasm, as in a glacier: CRE-
VASSE
fissured or cracked, chinky: RIMOSE
fit of bad temper: TANTRUM
fit together, unify, bring together into a
whole: INTEGRATE
fitness or agreement: CONGRUITY
fitting, as to proportion: COMMENSURATE
five-line stanza: CINQUAIN
five-year period: LUSTRUM
fix in place: IMMOBILIZE
fix the eyes or attention of: RIVET
fix upon a sharp stake: IMPALE
fixed, blank, uncomprehending: GLASSY
fixed, unchangeable: INFLEXIBLE
fixed amount, as of work to be done in a
specified time: STINT
fixed idea: IDÉE FIXE
fixed in one place: STABILE
fixed price for a whole meal: PRIX FIXE
flabby, intellectually or morally: INVER-
TEBRATE
flag fixed to a crosspiece rather than a
pole: GONFALON

flagrant, glaring, conspicuously bad:
EGREGIOUS
flaming, flaring: IGNESCENT
flaming, said of food served flaming with
ignited brandy or other liquor:
FLAMBÉ
flaring, flaming up: IGNESCENT
flash like lightning: FULGURATE
flashy, cheap dress or ornamentation:
FRIPPERY
flat, bland, dull, tasteless,: INSIPID
flat, broad piece: SLAB
flat, dull, lifeless, insipid: VAPID
flat, knifelike instrument for spreading, as
plaster or cake icing: SPATULA
flat and open country: CHAMPAIGN
flatter or coax to persuade: WHEEDLE
flatter or wheedle: BLANDISH
flatter servilely: ADULATE
flatterer who is servile, parasite: SYCO-
PHANT
flattery contrived as a means of persuasion: SNOW JOB
flattery or empty compliment: FLUMMERY
flatulence remedy: CARMINATIVE
flavor, taste: SAPOR
flavor-enhancing chemical: MONOSODIUM
GLUTAMATE
flavor or odor imbued in a substance:
TINCTURE
flawless, errorless, faultless: IMPECCABLE
flawless, warranting no criticism: UNEX-
CEPTIONABLE
fleet of large merchant ships: ARGOSY
fleeting, transient, fickle, unstable: VOLA-
TILE
fleeting, transitory: EVANESCENT
fleeting, quickly passing: FUGACIOUS
flesh-eating mammals: CARNIVORES
fleshly: CARNAL
fleshy or fat: CORPULENT
fleshy part below the lower jaw: JOWL
flexible, bendable: PLIABLE
flexible, easily changed: SUPPLE
flexible, pliable: MALLEABLE
flickering, radiating softly: LAMBENT
flighty, haughty: HOITY-TOITY
flighty, giddy, foolish: HAREBRAINED
flimsily built: JERRYBUILT
flimsy, delicate, thin: TENUOUS
flimsy, delicate substance: GOSSAMER
flippant, light style of writing or talk:
PERSIFLAGE
flippantly humorous, jesting: FACETIOUS

flirt or act in a trifling manner: COQUET

float, carry or move gently: WAFT

floating cylinder or boat to support a temporary bridge: PONTOON

floating objects on a body of water: FLOTSAM

floating or swimming: NATANT

floating wreckage: FLOTSAM

flocking together, a crowd: CONFLUENCE

flood, pertaining to, especially the flood at the time of Noah: DILUVIAL

flood of the tide in an estuary: EAGRE

flood or overwhelm with abundance or excess: INUNDATE

floodlight used in making motion pictures: KLIEG LIGHT

floors of inlaid woodwork: PARQUETRY

florid, overelaborate: ROCOCO

florid, showy, bombastic, ornate: FLAMBOYANT

florid, showy, excessively ornamented: ORNATE

flounder, splash: SLOSH

flourish at the end of a signature: PARAPH

flourish or mark after a signature: RUBRIC

flow of water beneath and opposite to the surface current: UNDERTOW

flower, bloom forth, blossom: EFFLORESCE

flower and ornamental plant culture: FLORICULTURE

flowering, flourishing: INFLORESCENCE

flowerless: ANANTHOUS

flowers, in a bunch: BOUQUET

flowery, excessively ornate: FLORID

flowery, metaphorical: FIGURATIVE

flowery speech or writing: EUPHUISM

flowing and sweet sounding: MELLIFLUOUS

flowing back, ebb: REFLUX

flowing back, ebbing: REFLUENT

flowing in: INFLUENT

flowing or a discharge: FLUX

flowing out: EFFLUENCE

flowing together: CONFLUENCE

fluctuate, swing back and forth: OSCILLATE

flushed, ruddy: FLORID

fluster, excitement, bustle: POTHER

flute with eleven finger holes and a plug, or fipple, near the mouthpiece: RECORDER

fluted or crimped ornamentation, as along the edge of fabric: GOFFER

flutter, beat rapidly: PALPITATE

flying, able to fly: VOLANT

flying men's nervous disorder: AERONEUROSIS

foam, scum, froth: SPUME

fodder, food suitable for horses and cattle: FORAGE

fodder or feed for cattle: STOVER

fog containing ice particles: POGONIP

fog or mist: BRUME

foggy, misty, indefinite: NUBILOUS

foil, frustrate, obstruct: THWART

fold of cloth doubled back and pressed flat: PLEAT

folded backward, also to reply, to reproduce itself or oneself: REPLICATE

folded fanlike: PLICATED

foliage that has fallen in a forest: DUFF

folk singers' meeting for a public performance: HOOTENANNY

folkways or customs of a social group: MORES

follies or vices attacked by ridicule or wit: SATIRE

follow closely upon something: SUPERVENE

follower or favorite who behaves servilely: MINION

followers, retainers or attendants in a group: ENTOURAGE

followers or companions in a group: COHORT

following, as an effect or conclusion: CONSEQUENTIAL

following in time: SUBSEQUENT

fond of one's wife to excess or submissive to her: UXORIOUS

fond of others' company: GREGARIOUS

food: ALIMENT

food: NUTRIMENT

food, cheap and popular among Southern blacks: SOUL FOOD

food, especially choice food: VIAND

food, means of support, livelihood: SUSTENANCE

food expert: EPICURE

food for body or mind: ALIMENT

food prepared by highly skilled chefs: HAUT CUISINE

food reheated: RECHAUFFÉ

food suitable for horses or cattle, fodder: FORAGE

food that is coarse: ROUGHAGE

fooled or cheated easily: GULLIBLE

foolhardiness, heedlessness: TEMERITY

foolish, flighty, giddy: HAREBRAINED

foolish, idiotic, stupid: FATUOUS

foolish, stupid, brutish, unmoved: INSEN-SATE

foolish, talkative person: BLATHERSKITE

foolish appearance given to something or someone: STULTIFIED

foolish love, unreasoning passion: INFATUATION

foolish or excessive affection: DOTAGE

foolish or senseless talk: DRIVEL

foolishly wasteful, involved procedure: RIGMAROLE

foot and toenail treatment: PEDICURE

foot race 26 miles long: MARATHON

foot section above the arch between the ankle and the toes: INSTEP

foot that is flat and turned out: SPLAYFOOT

foot treatment: PODIATRY

football area between goal line and end line where a touchdown may be scored: END ZONE

football defensive player stationed just behind the linemen: LINEBACKER

football field corner at goal line: COFFIN CORNER

football illegality consisting of blocking from behind an opponent who is not carrying the ball: CLIPPING

football kick in which ball is dropped, then kicked, as it bounces up from ground: DROP KICK

football kicked after being dropped from the hands but before touching the ground: PUNT

football line parallel to the goal line along which teams take positions at start of play: LINE OF SCRIMMAGE

football lineman between the guard and the end: TACKLE

football maneuver in which one back hands the ball to another: HANDOFF

football mass play after the ball has been snapped by the center: SCRIMMAGE

football offensive formation with the quarterback behind the center and the fullback behind him flanked by the halfbacks: T FORMATION

football official supervising at the sidelines: LINESMAN

football pass that moves parallel to the passer's goal line rather than forward: LATERAL PASS

football place kick that starts play at the beginning of each half or following a touchdown: KICKOFF

football play in which a player grounds the ball behind his own goal line after it has been moved there by an opponent: TOUCHBACK

football play in which the ball is thrown toward the opponent's goal: FORWARD PASS

football player, one of a pair who with the quarterback and fullback make up the backfield: HALFBACK

football player stationed behind the quarterback: FULLBACK

football player who calls the signals: QUARTERBACK

football players behind the linemen: BACKFIELD

football players providing protection for the ball carrier: INTERFERENCE

football score of six points made by touching the ball down behind the opponent's goal line: TOUCHDOWN

football scoring of one or two extra points after a touchdown: CONVERSION

football term for a member of the backfield stationed far out before the ball is put in motion: SLEEPER

football term for a player's touching the ball to the ground behind his own goal line at the cost of two points: SAFETY

football term for being ahead of the ball before it is snapped by the center: OFFSIDE

football term for charging the opposing quarterback by rushing through the line: RED-DOG

football term for putting the ball in play: SNAP

footprint or other trace of a wild animal: SPOOR

footstool, usually upholstered: HASSOCK

for example, or, by way of example: E.G. (EXEMPLI GRATIA)

forbid a person to have or do something: INTERDICT

forbidden: VERBOTEN

forbidden, banned: TABOO

forbidden, beyond the lawful powers of: ULTRA VIRES

force, use of: DURESS

force of destruction that is slow and irresistible: JUGGERNAUT force one's thoughts or self upon others: INTRUDE

force oneself, or one's opinion, on someone else: OBTRUDE

force or compel to go: HALE

force or drive to action, urge on: IMPEL

force or pack down by repeated pressure: TAMP

force or spirit from within that guides: NUMEN

force that balances another force: COUNTERPOISE

force that is overpowering or coercive: FORCE MAJEURE

force that sets a body in motion: IMPETUS

force unjustly: EXACT

forced feeding: GAVAGE

forced labor, particularly for repairing roads: CORVÉE

forces at work in any field: DYNAMICS

forcible separation: AVULSION

foreboding: PREMONITION

foreboding: PRESENTIMENT

forever: AD INFINITUM

forefather, earliest ancestor: PRIMOGENITOR

forefather or source: PROGENITOR

forefinger: INDEX FINGER

forehead just above the nose and between the eyebrows: GLABELLA

foreknowledge: PRESCIENCE

forerunner, preliminary: PRECURSOR

foreshadow: ADUMBRATE

foreshadow, warn: PORTEND

foresight, prudent economy: PROVIDENCE

foreskin: PREPUCE

forests of a certain region and their characteristics: SILVA

foretell: VATICINATE

foretell, indicate beforehand: PROGNOSTICATE

foreteller of events: SOOTHSAYER

foretelling by omens: AUGURY

foretelling the future, prophecy: DIVINATION

forethought: CALCULATION

forgetfulness, disregard: OBLIVION

forgetfulness, oblivion: LETHE

forgivable, as sins: REMISSIBLE

forgiveness: ABSOLUTION

forgiving, appeasable: PLACABLE

forgo, relinquish, give up: WAIVE

fork with three broad tines, one sharp: RUNCIBLE SPOON

forked, branching: FURCATE

forked twig or branch popularly thought to be effective in finding underground water: DIVINING ROD

form, shape, outline: FIGURATION

form a point of view beforehand: PRECONCEIVE

form lacking or indefinite: AMORPHOUS

form only: PRO FORMA

formal in an artificial way, pompous: STILTED

formation in ranks or steps as with troops, fleets or airplanes: ECHELON

formed into a rounded mass: GLOMERATE

formed or fashioned: WROUGHT

former: QUONDAM

formidable, fear-inspiring: REDOUBTABLE

formless: INCHOATE

forsaking one's faith, party or principles: APOSTASY

forte, one's occupation for which he is particularly suited: MÉTIER

forthright, firm, solid: FOURSQUARE

fortification, bulwark: RAMPART

fortified place: BASTION

fortnightly: BIWEEKLY

fortune telling, sorcery, black magic: NECROMANCY

fortune telling from the lines of the palm: PALMISTRY

fortuneteller, sorceress: SIBYL

forward, overconfident, arrogant: PRESUMPTUOUS

fossil study or examination of prehistoric forms of life: PALEONTOLOGY

foul or filthy sediment: FECULENCE

foul-smelling: MEPHITIC

foundation of stones thrown together: RIPRAP

foundation or basic facilities of a community: INFRASTRUCTURE

four, group of four: TETRAD

four-dimensional continuum—three of space plus time: SPACE-TIME

four-year period: QUADRENNIUM

foxlike, sly, crafty: VULPINE

fracas, rough-and-tumble clash: SCRIMMAGE

fragment, as of pottery: SHARD

fragments or particles separated from rock masses by erosion or glaciers: DETRITUS

fragments or selections from literary works: ANALECTS

fragrant, suggestive of something: REDO-
LENT
fragrant odor: ODOROUS
frame of mind: DISPOSITION
frame of mind: POSTURE
framework like a bridge for holding the
rails of a traveling crane: GANTRY
framework or structure: FABRIC
frank, innocent, simple, naive, straightforward: INGENUOUS
fraudulent or tricky action: JOCKEYING
fraudulently invented, false: TRUMPED-UP
freakish, strange: OUTLANDISH
freckle: LENTIGO
free, emancipate, liberate: MANUMIT
free and easy, offhand: CAVALIER
free from blame, prove innocent: EXCUL-
PATE
free from bondage or restraint: EMAN-
CIPATE
free from fever: AFEBRILE
free from slavery, admit to citizenship:
ENFRANCHISE
free of charge: GRATIS
free will denied or minimized in regard to
human behavior: DETERMINISM
freedom from restrictions: LATITUDE
freedom or exemption from punishment,
harm or unpleasant consequences:
IMPUNITY
free-for-all, brawl marked by roughness:
DONNYBROOK
freight train's rear car: CABOOSE
French for good day: BON JOUR
French for good evening: BON SOIR
French working girl, especially one with
free and easy manners: GRISETTE
frenzied, raging: MADDING
frequent visitor to a place: HABITUÉ
frequently occurring: PREVALENT
fresh, springlike, youthful: VERNAL
fret, complain: REPINE
fretful, jittery, balky: RESTIVE
fried rapidly with little fat: SAUTÉ
friend who is exceedingly close to one:
ALTER EGO
friendly: AFFABLE
friendly: AMICABLE
friendly and solicitous toward guests:
HOSPITABLE
friendship or loyalty weakened or destroyed: DISAFFECTION
frighten with threats: INTIMIDATE
frightened, panicky mood: FUNK

frightened easily: SKITTISH
frightful: HORRENDOUS
frigid, arctic: HYPERBOREAN
fringed: LACINIATE
frisk about, frolic: DISPORT
frisk about or prance: CAVORT
frivolity, fickleness, lightness, gaiety that
is inappropriate: LEVITY
frivolous, impulsive, irresponsible:
FLIGHTY
frivolous, restless, superficial: YEASTY
frolic, skip or leap about: GAMBOL
frolic or amuse oneself, frisk about: DIS-
PORT
frolic with hilarity: SKYLARK
front or primary side of something, such
as a coin: OBVERSE
froth, foam, scum: SPUME
frozen, icy: GELID
frugal, careful, cautious: CHARY
frugal, chary, stingy: SPARE
fruit-bearing: FRUITION
fruit-eating: FRUGIVOROUS
fruitful: PROCREANT
fruitful, fertile: FERACIOUS
fruitful, fertile, prolific: FECUND
fruitful, inventive, productive: PREGNANT
fruitless, unsuccessful: INEFFECTUAL
fruits stewed in syrup: COMPOTE
frustrate, confuse, defeat the plans of:
DISCOMFIT
frustrate, obstruct, foil: THWART
frying pan, of iron and with a long handle:
SPIDER
fulfillment: FRUITION
full, absolute, complete: PLENARY
full, overflowing: TEEMING
full, rounded voice: OROTUND
full, sated, amply supplied: REPLETE
full attendance, as in a legislative body:
PLENUM
full length: IN EXTENSO
full moon after the harvest moon:
HUNTER'S MOON
full of meaning: PREGNANT
full power conferred: PLENIPOTENTIARY
fuller statement, addition for fuller explanation: EPEXEGESIS
fullness of a container lacking by this
amount: ULLAGE
full-sounding, loud: SONOROUS
fumble, bungle, misplay: FOOZLE
fumbler who drops things: BUTTERFINGERS
fun, quip, playfulness: JEST

fun that is noisy and rough: HORSEPLAY
fund invested so that its gradual accumulations will pay a debt: SINKING FUND
fundamental, basic, inherent in: ORGANIC
fundamental principle, basis: HYPOSTASIS
funeral hymn, dirge: EPICEDIUM
funeral hymn, lament: DIRGE
funeral pile: PYRE
funeral rites: OBSEQUIES
funeral song, dirge: THRENODY
funnier than average: UPROARIOUS
fur, or other covering of a mammal: PELLAGE
fur hat worn by hussars, etc.: BUSBY
furious, enraged: LIVID
furiously angry, maddened: HORN-MAD
furnace floor or fireplace: HEARTH
furnace or oven for baking or drying bricks, pottery, cement: KILN

furnish, supply: PURVEY
furtive: CLANDESTINE
furtively move about: SKULK
fuse or blend together: COALESCE
fuss, commotion in a relatively simple situation: TSIMMES
fuss over something trivial: FOOFARAW
fussy, old-fashioned person: FUDDY-DUDDY
fussy, overprecise, finicky: NIGGLING
fussy, precise, overly fastidious, exacting: FINICKY
futile, unsuccessful: UNAVAILING
futile endeavor: WILD-GOOSE CHASE
future event referred to as if it had already happened: PROLEPSIS
future generations: POSTERITY
fuzzy or hairy, in botany: COMATE

G

gad about, walk about idly or aimlessly:
TRAIPSE
gadget or device, the name of which is
forgotten: DINGUS
gaiety: JOLLITY
gaiety or merriment that is exuberant and
noisy: HILARITY
gaiety that is inappropriate, frivolity, fickleness, lightness: LEVITY
gallant, courteous, generous: CHIVALROUS
gallant or courtly man: CAVALIER
gallery or portico that is arcaded and built
into the side of a building: LOGGIA
gallows: GIBBET
gambling or luck as a cause or reason:
ALEATORY
gambling system in which one doubles the
stakes to recover previous losses:
MARTINGALE
game in which one team fails to score:
SHUTOUT
game of ball, popular in Latin America,
played with a curved basket fastened
to the arm: JAI ALAI
gangrenous: SPHACELATE
gap, blank: LACUNA
gap, opening, break or interruption of
continuity: HIATUS
gap in a mountain through which a torrent
passes: FLUME
gape, stare stupidly: GAWK
gaping or expanse of open mouth: RICTUS
garden cultivation: HORTICULTURE
garden for quiet pleasure: PLEASANCE
garment, one piece and tight-fitting, worn
by acrobats and dancers: LEOTARD
garment like a skirt worn by both sexes in
the Malay Archipelago: SARONG
garment of one piece often worn over regular clothes: COVERALL
garment with no sleeves, worn by Arabs:
ABA

garment worn by an official or a clergyman: VESTMENT
garments that dry quickly after washing
and need no ironing: DRIP-DRY
garments that need no ironing after washing: WASH-AND-WEAR
gas in the intestine: FLATUS
gash, cut: INCISION
gasoline that vaporizes at a relatively low
temperature: HIGH-TEST
gate controlling flow of water into canal
lock: HEAD GATE
gate that revolves to admit passengers
after deposit of fare: TURNSTILE
gateway or porch, covered, at the entrance
of a building: PORTE-COCHÈRE
gather or store, as in a granary; accumulate: GARNER
gather sheets of manuscript into a unified
whole: COLLATE
gathered into a mass: AGGLOMERATE
gathering of people, animals or things:
CLUTCH
gauge or pattern used to copy something
accurately, as in woodworking:
TEMPLATE
gaunt, pale, ghastly: CADAVEROUS
gaunt, wild or worn look, as from fatigue,
hunger or anxiety: HAGGARD
gay, carfree, light-hearted: ROLLICKING
gay, cheerful: JOCUND
gay, puckish, strange: FEY
gay, smart, dashing: RAKISH
gear, equipment, personal effects: PARA-
PHERNALIA
geld, weaken, castrate, make effeminate:
EMASCULATE
gem cutting, engraving or polishing: LAP-
IDARY
gem measurement: CARAT
gem that is cut in oblong shape:
BAGUETTE

gems, as a study: GEMOLOGY
genealogies, armorial bearings, etc.: HERALDRY
general epidemic, widespread, universal: PANDEMIC
general idea, vague concept: NOTION
general pardon: AMNESTY
general store: EMPORIUM
general to particular, as in reasoning: DEDUCTION
generalization to particular instances: A PRIORI
generous: BOUNTEOUS
gemerous, bountiful, lavish: MUNIFICENT
generous, high-minded, great of soul: MAGNANIMOUS
generous in giving or spending: LAVISH
gentle, mild, favorable: BENIGN
gentle, reproof: ADMONITION
geometry that deals with three-dimensional figures: SOLID GEOMETRY
germ killer: GERMICIDE
German for "so long": AUF WIEDERSEHEN
German prisoner-of-war camp: STALAG
German song: LIED
gestures without words: PANTOMIME
get by begging: CADGE
get rid of, shed: SLOUGH
get something from a person by violence or threats: EXTORT
getting even with someone: REPRISAL
ghastly, sepulchral: CHARNEL
ghost: REVENANT
ghost believed to cause sounds: POLTERGEIST
ghost or apparition: SPECTER
ghostly double of someone not yet dead: DOPPELGANGER
ghostly or weird: EERIE
gibberish: GALIMATIAS
gibberish, speech that is confused or meaningless: JARGON
gibe or witty remark: QUIP
giddy, flighty: HOITY-TOITY
giddy, flighty, foolish: HAREBRAINED
gift given at start of new year or new venture: HANDSEL
gift of money, tip: GRATUITY
gift that is small and comes from one who can barely afford it: WIDOW'S MITE
gift to a beggar: HANDOUT
gifts bestowed liberally: LARGESS
gigantic, strong, having power to great proportions: HERCULEAN

gigantic unidentified water beast: LEVIATHAN
gilt of bronze or silver: VERMEIL
gin or vodka mixed with bouillon as a cocktail: BULLSHOT
gin or vodka mixed with dry vermouth as a cocktail: MARTINI
gin or vodka mixed with water and sweetened lime juice: GIMLET
girl (Spanish): MUCHACHA
girls in a group: BEVY
gist, essential theme or part: PITH
give and take: BANDY
give back: RETROCEDE
give cause for just complaint: AGGRIEVE
give grudgingly: STINT
give off or send forth as light or heat: EMIT
give out, distribute: DISPENSE
give to another in a will: BEQUEATH
give up: ABDICATE
give up, abandon, yield: RELINQUISH
give up, relinquish, forgo: WAIVE
give up conditionally: CAPITULATE
give up or turn over something to someone: CONSIGN
give up rights, etc.: ABNEGATE
give up something: CEDE
give up something as a penalty: FORFEIT
give vent to, reveal, disclose: UNBOSOM
given without requirement of payment or return: GRATUITOUS
giver of benefits or favors: BENEFACTOR
giving or spending generously: LAVISH
giving up or resigning an office: DEMISSION
glaciers, as a scientific study: GLACIOLOGY
glance at, read quickly: SCAN
glance over or read hastily: SKIM
glandular secretion that is internal: ENDOCRINE
Glasgow resident: GLASWEGIAN
glass, broken or refuse, which is gathered for remelting: CULLET
glass or cup filled to the brim: BUMPER
glass or cup for measuring liquor: JIGGER
glass showcase, as for art objects: VITRINE
glass that is colored and used in mosaics: SMALTO
glasses with three lenses: TRIFOCALS
glasses with two lenses: BIFOCALS
glassware with embedded ornaments of colored glass: MURRHINE GLASS
glassy: VITREOUS
glaze made of raw egg white: GLAIR

gleeful chuckles: CHORTLE

glib, talkative, speaking fluently: VOLUBLE

glib and swift talk: PATTER

glide or skim over water: SKITTER

glide or slide, as a snake: SLITHER

gliding, sinuous motion: UNDULATION

glitter: SPANGLE

glitter, flash, sparkle: SCINTILLATE

globular: CONGLOBATE

gloomy, dark: CIMMERIAN

gloomy, dark: TENEBROUS

gloomy, dejected: DISCONSOLATE

gloomy, depressed, murky: SOMBER

gloomy, desolate, haggard: GAUNT

gloomy, grave, morose: SATURNINE

gloomy, ill-humored, sullen: MOROSE

gloomy, infernal, dark: STYGIAN

gloomy, melancholy: SEPULCHRAL

gloomy, peevish: DYSPEPTIC

gloomy, saddened, dejected: DISCONSOLATE

gloomy, stern, morose, ill-tempered: DOUR

Gloria Patri, Gloria in excelsis Deo: DOXOLOGY

glorification: APOTHEOSIS

glorify, idealize: TRANSFIGURE

glory of the world thus passes away: SIC TRANSIT GLORIA MUNDI

gloss producing machine, used on paper or fabric: CALENDER

glove part uniting back and front parts of adjacent fingers: FOURCHETTE

glowing: LUMINOUS

glowing or luminous with heat: INCANDESCENT

glum, resentfully morose: SULLEN

glut, offer more than enough: SATIATE

gluttonous or drunken: CRAPULENT

go about, roam in search of diversion: GALLIVANT

go in peace: VADE IN PACE

go without sleep, keep vigil: WATCH

goad, incite, foment, provoke, spur on to some drastic action: INSTIGATE

goat or sheep newly born: YEANLING

goatlike, lustful: HIRCINE

go-between: INTERMEDIARY

go-between: INTERNUNCIO

goblet or large drinking cup: MAZER

God as the uncaused creator of all things: FIRST CAUSE

God conceived as having human characteristics: THEANTHROPISM

God evidenced in every feature of the universe: PANTHEISM

God's existence denied: ATHEISM

God's existence questioned: AGNOSTICISM

going before, preceding: PREVENIENT

going in, entrance: INGRESS

going or traveling from place to place: ITINERANT

going out, or exit: EGRESS

gold-colored alloys used in cheap jewelry and ornaments: ORMOLU

Golden Fleece searchers with Jason: ARGONAUTS

golf course obstacle or trap: HAZARD

golf play in which the ball goes into the hole on the drive from the tee: HOLE IN ONE

golf shot, short and lofted, made in approaching the green: CHIP SHOT

golf situation in which an opponent's ball lies on the green in a direct line between a player's ball and the hole: STYMIE

golf stroke on the green to move the ball into or near the hole: PUTT

golf term for one stroke over par on a hole: BOGEY

golf term for one stroke under par on a hole: BIRDIE

golf term for two strokes under par on a hole: EAGLE

golf term indicating ball on the green on a line perpendicular to line of approach: HOLE-HIGH

golfer's shouted warning that the ball is about to be hit: FORE

good breeding: SAVOIR-VIVRE

good deed (Hebrew): MITZVAH

good living: CAKES AND ALE

good luck piece: AMULET

good nature: BONHOMIE

good or benevolent spirit: EUDEMON

good things of life: AMENITIES

goodbye: ADIEU

goodbye (Spanish): HASTA LA VISTA or HASTA LUEGO or HASTA MAÑANA

good-natured, polite remark: PLEASANTRY

goodness, moral excellence: VIRTUE

goods accumulated as a reserve: STOCKPILE

goods paid for by dealer only after they've been sold: ON CONSIGNMENT

goods sold in a miscellany collection to a retailer: JOB LOT goods that may not be imported or exported: CONTRABAND

goof or social blunder: FAUX PAS

goose flesh: HORRIPILATION

gospel-spreading through preaching and revival meetings: EVANGELISM

gossip: BRUIT

gossip carelessly: BANDY

gossip or chat: CONFABULATE

gourmet, sensualist: EPICURE

gout: PODAGRA

government administration by inflexible officials: BUREAUCRACY

government by a few: OLIGARCHY

government by holy men: HAGIARCHY or HAGIOCRACY

government by men only: PATRIARCHY

government by priests or members of the clergy: HIEROCRACY

government by the military: STRATOCRACY

government by the old: GERONTOCRACY

government by the rich: PLUTOCRACY

government by women or a woman: GYNARCHY

government council, local or national, in the Soviet Union: SOVIET

government expenditures financed by borrowing in order to increase productivity and consumption: DEFICIT FINANCING

government in which people as a whole control production and distribution of goods: COLLECTIVISM

government or authority shared jointly by two men: DUUMVIRATE

governmental organization of a state or society: POLITY

government publication on a relatively less important subject: WHITE PAPER

government seizure, usually sudden and often accompanied by violence: COUP D'ETAT

government with absolute power: AUTARCHY

government-must-go theory: ANARCHISM

government's unlimited authority: ABSOLUTISM

gown, loose and flowing, gathered from the neckline: MUUMUU

graceful, slender young woman: SYLPH

graceful, smooth, expressive: FLUENT

graceful in bending, bending easily, limber: LITHE

graceful structure or movement: EURYTHMIC

gracious: BENIGNANT

gracious gesture: BEAU GESTE

gradation or subtle change in meaning: NUANCE

grade, layer, bed: STRATUM

gradual reduction and extinction of debt or liability, as by installment payments: AMORTIZATION

graduation address: BACCALAUREATE

graduation speech of farewell: VALEDICTORY

grain that has been or is to be ground, meal: GRIST

grammatical change of construction within a sentence: ANACOLUTHON

grammatical or syntactical violation: SOLECISM

grammatical system consisting of a set of rules for producing sentences: GENERATIVE GRAMMAR

grammatical term for possessive case: GENITIVE

grammatical theory that holds that all sentences are kernel sentences or transformations of them in accordance with transformational rules: TRANSFORMATIONAL GRAMMAR

grammatically analyze a sentence by giving form, function and syntactical relationship of its words: PARSE

grand, stately, impressive: IMPOSING

grand jury report on an offense based on its own knowledge and with no indictment: PRESENTMENT

grand or imposing: GRANDIOSE

grandiloquent: TURGID

grant with condescension: VOUCHSAFE

grape cultivation for wine: VINICULTURE

grape growing: VITICULTURE

grape refuse after pressing, from which brandy is distilled: MARC

graph in form of a circle divided into proportionate sections: PIE CHART

graphic symbol representing an object or idea: IDEOGRAPH

grasping, greedy: RAPACIOUS

grasping, holding: PREHENSION

grass in second growth after regular cutting, usually tall and rank: FOG

grass or hay in its second growth; aftermath: ROWEN

grass-covered land, turf: SWARD

grass-eating: GRAMINIVOROUS

grassland or open country of South Africa: VELDT

gratify or yield to one's desires: INDULGE

grating, shrill: STRIDENT

gratuity, something extra given: LAGNIAPPE

grave, gloomy, morose: SATURNINE

grave robber: GHOUL

grave robber, of bodies: RESURRECTIONIST

graveyard shift in newspaper work: LOBSTER SHIFT

gravy in natural form included: AU JUS

gray or graying hair: GRIZZLED

gray- or white-haired, ancient, venerable: HOARY

grayish, often with a mottled appearance: GRISEOUS

grease or oil something: LUBRICATE

greasy, slippery feeling: UNCTUOUS

great of soul, generous, high-minded: MAGNANIMOUS

great style: BRAVURA

great work, masterpiece: MAGNUM OPUS

greed, avarice: CUPIDITY

greedy: COVETOUS

greedy: INSATIABLE

greedy, grasping: RAPACIOUS

greedy, insatiable, immoderate: VORACIOUS

greedy, rapacious person: HARPY

Greek architecture characterized by elaborateness: CORINTHIAN

Greek architecture characterized by ornamental scrolls on capitals: IONIC

Greek architecture characterized by simplicity and plain capitals on columns: DORIC

Greek monster with head and trunk of man, body and legs of horse: CENTAUR

green, grassy: VERDANT

green coating on bronze or copper: PATINA

green crops for animal fodder: SOILAGE

green pigment in plant cells involved in photosynthesis: CHLOROPHYLL

greenish: VIRESCENT

greenish-yellow: LUTEOUS

greeting: SALUTATION

greeting in the Orient consisting of a low bow with the right palm at the forehead: SALAAM

grief or sorrow, to cause: AGGRIEVE

grief or weeping that is false: CROCODILE TEARS

grievance: GRAVAMEN

grievance, complaint: PLAINT

grieve or sympathize with someone: CONDOLE

grim, severe, strict: STARK

grin, laugh: RISUS

grind or scrape harshly, cut, pierce: GRIDE

grinding of teeth, especially during sleep: BRUXISM

gritty like sand: SABULOUS

groggy: PUNCH-DRUNK

grooved, striped: STRIATED

grooved timber, in which wings of a stage set slide: COULISSE

grooved with long, rounded channels: FLUTED

ground, as of a region or territory: TERRAIN

ground plan of a building or other structure: ICHNOGRAPHY

ground that is solid and unbroken: HARDPAN

group arranged by rank: HIERARCHY

group of girls: BEVY

group of persons sharing same interest or interests: COTERIE

group of two or more business concerns for a venture: CONSORTIUM

group or clique: FACTION

group spirit: ESPRIT DE CORPS

group with common interests living together: COMMUNE

grow, increase, expand step by step: ESCALATE

growing, waxing, enlarging: INCRESCENT

growing along the ground, lying down: DECUMBENT

growing old, aging: SENESCENT

growing or coming together: CONCRETION

growing plants in solutions rather than in soil: HYDROPONICS

growing white: ALBESCENT

growing with age: ACCRESCENCE

growth arrested: ATROPHY

growth on a field, as of corn: STAND

growth rings on trees as means of determining approximate dates of past events: DENDROCHRONOLOGY

growth that is gradual: ACCRESCENCE

gruesome, horrible, ghastly: MACABRE

gruff or irritable person, usually elderly: CURMUDGEON

grumble, complain: GROUSE

guarantee: WARRANTY

guarantee, assure: VOUCH

guarantee, promise: STIPULATE

guard, watchman, keeper: WARDER

guard against, hinder or prevent in advance: FORESTALL

guard line, as of men or ships enclosing an area: CORDON

guardian, trustee: FIDUCIARY

guarding and watching carefully: WARY

guess: CONJECTURE

guess correctly, surmise: DIVINE

guessing game, based on pantomimed actions: CHARADES

guide or interpreter for travelers in the Near East: DRAGOMAN

guide who explains to tourists: CICERONE

guidebook: BAEDEKER

guidebook, manual: HANDBOOK

guidebook for travelers: ITINERARY

guiding or animating spirit from within: NUMEN

guiding principle or example; star used as guide in navigation: LODESTAR

guilt feeling: COMPUNCTION

guilt feeling, self-reproach: REMORSE

guilt or wrongdoing implied: INCRIMINATION

Gulf State inhabitant, Spanish American or West Indian of European descent: CREOLE

gullibility: CREDULITY

gully that is deep and dry: ARROYO

gum inflammation: GINGIVITIS

gunfire that sweeps across the length of a trench or a troop of men: ENFILADE

gush forth, squirt: SPURT

gush or spurt of liquid from a narrow orifice: JET

gushing, overdemonstrative: EFFUSIVE

gut reaction, deeply felt: VISCERAL

gutter or channel of a street: KENNEL

gymnast association, athletic club: TURNVEREIN

gymnastics to promote grace and health: CALISTHENICS

gypsy: TZIGANE

H

habit, customary practice: WONT
habits deeply established: SECOND NATURE
habitual or hardened in a particular character or opinion: INVETERATE
habitual or usual way of reacting: DISPOSITION
habituated, accustomed or used to: WONT
habitue or inhabitant: DENIZEN
hack, mangle, cut unskillfully: HAGGLE
hack writers: GRUBSTREET
hades: ACHERON
hag: CRONE
hag, hateful old woman: HARRIDAN
hag who is ugly and malicious: BELDAM
haggard, hollow-eyed, gloomy, desolate, emaciated: GAUNT
hair covering that is matted and woolly: TOMENTOSE
hair covering that is soft like velvet: VELUTINOUS
hair growing to a point on the forehead: WIDOW'S PEAK
hair of a woman: TRESSES
hair remover: DEPILATORY
hair sticking up: COWLICK
hair that is woolly or crispy: ULOTRICHOUS
hairdo in which the hair is bound by a ribbon in back and hangs loosely below it: PONYTAIL
hairdresser (male): COIFFEUR
hairs in the nostrils: VIBRISSA
hairy: HIRSUTE
hairy or fuzzy, in botany: COMATE
half, portion, share: MOIETY
half-breed, mixed origin: HYBRID
half-man, half-horse monster of Greek mythology: CENTAUR
half turn made by horse with rider: CARACOLE
Halifax resident: HALIGONIAN

hallucination-causing or mind-intensifying: PSYCHEDELIC
halo: AUREOLE
halo: GLORIOLE
halo, aura: NIMBUS
halved: DIMIDIATE
ham, spicy and thin: PROSCIUTTO
ham that is smoked or cured: GAMMON
hammered or stamped, as the figure or design on a coin: INCUSE
hand down, transmit, grant in will: BEQUEATH
hand measure, with the thumb and little finger extended: SPAN
hand over or give up something to someone: CONSIGN
handbag, small, used by women: RETICULE
handbook or manual: ENCHIRIDION
handcuff, fetter, shackle: MANACLE
handle, especially of a knife, sickle, sword: HAFT
handle or move skillfully: MANIPULATE
handrail supported by balusters: BALUSTRADE
hands on hips: AKIMBO
handsome man: ADONIS
handwriting art: CHIROGRAPHY
handwriting or spelling that is bad: CACOGRAPHY
handwriting or type that resembles it: SCRIPT
handwritten by the signer: HOLOGRAPH
hang around, waste time, loiter: DAWDLE
hang down or droop loosely: LOP
hang loosely, droop: LOLL
hanger-on: CAMP FOLLOWER
hanging in a loose position: PENSILE
hanging in a swinging position: PENDULOUS

hanging on in spite of difficulties: TENA-
CIOUS
haphazard: RANDOM
happen, take place: SUPERVENE
happen or come into being as a final outcome: EVENTUATE
happening at the same rate: SYNCHRONOUS
happening or event: INCIDENT
happiness, relaxation, well-being: EU-
PHORIA
happiness or well-being as found in the
life of moderation: EUDEMONIA
happy and healthy: EUPEPTIC
happy condition: SEVENTH HEAVEN
happy, optimistic: UPBEAT
harangue, abusive denunciation: DIATRIBE
harangue that is lengthy: SCREED
harass or annoy with taunts or questions:
HECKLE
harass with persistency: IMPORTUNE
harass, worry: CHEVY
hard, cruel, obdurate: FLINTY
hard legendary mineral: ADAMANT
hard or impossible to explain, as of something causing wonder: UNCANNY
hard shelled: TESTACEOUS
hard, stony: PETROUS
hard to believe, amazing: INCREDIBLE
hard to express: JE NE SAIS QUOI
hard to grasp: ELUSIVE
hard to handle because of size, strength or
difficulty: FORMIDABLE
hard to please: FASTIDIOUS
hard to please, excessively critical: HY-
PERCRITICAL
hard to understand: ABSTRUSE
harden, become rigid: OSSIFY
harden, deaden, paralyze with fear: PET-
RIFY
hardened, unfeeling: INDURATE
hardhearted, stubborn, pitiless: OBDURATE
hardness: CALLOSITY
harm the reputation of: DISCREDIT
harmful, injurious: NOCUOUS
harmful, unwholesome: NOXIOUS
harmful, mischievous: MALEFICENT
harmful, noxious: VIRULENT
harmful with intent, spiteful: MALICIOUS
harmless: INNOCUOUS
harmless: INNOXIOUS
harmless substance given to comfort a patient or as a test control: PLACEBO
harmonious or pleasing in sound, smooth:
EUPHONIOUS
harmonious relationship, accord: RAPPORT

harmony, in sympathy: EN RAPPORT
harmony and elegance in arrangement of
parts: CONCINNITY
harmony restored: RECONCILED
harpsichord or small piano: SPINET
harsh: ACERB
harsh, caustic, withering: SCATHING
harsh, discordant sound: JANGLE
harsh, fierce: FELL
harsh, high sound: STRIDENT
harsh, merciless: INCLEMENT
harsh, pitiless: RELENTLESS
harsh, stern: ASTRINGENT
harsh cry or sound like a donkey's:
BRAY
harsh sound: CACOPHANY
harshness: ASPERITY
haste, turmoil, excitement: HECTIC
hasten, hurry: HIE
hastening the tempo, in music: STRIN-
GENDO
hasty, rash, impulsive: IMPETUOUS
hasty or impulsive actions or speech:
HALF-COCKED
hat, round and close-fitting: TOQUE
hat with brim turned up to form three
sides: TRICORN
hat with broad brim turned up at the sides:
SHOVEL HAT
hatchet- or ax-shaped: DOLABRIFORM
hate, deep enmity: RANCOR
hated or dreaded object or person: BÊTE
NOIRE
hateful, repugnant, loathsome, disgusting,
offensive: ODIOUS
hatred: ANIMUS
hatred of men: MISANDRY
haughty, arrogant: CAVALIER
haughty, arrogant, pompous, dogmatic:
PONTIFICAL
haughty person: BRAHMIN
haughty person who sets great store by
social status, wealth, etc.: SNOB
haul, drag, carry: SCHLEP
haunt, place to which one often returns:
PURLIEU
Hawaiian feast with entertainment: LUAU
Hawaiian salutation: ALOHA
hay fever: POLLENOSIS
hay or grain raked into a long ridge or
pile: WINDROW
haystack with the top fashioned to protect
interior from rain: RICK
hazy, misty, vague, unclear: NEBULOUS
head cold: CORYZA

head enlargement caused by excess of fluid in cranium: HYDROCEPHALUS

head of a human joined to animal body: ANDROCEPHALOUS

head of the line: VAN

head that is broad: BRACHYCEPHALIC

head to foot: CAP-A-PIE

headache on one side as in migraine: HEMICRANIA

headband or crown: DIADEM

headdress, crownlike and jeweled, worn by women: TIARA

headdress of Moslems consisting of wound cloth: TURBAN

headland, high land extending into the sea: PROMONTORY

headless: ACEPHALOUS

healing: SANATIVE

healing, curative: THERAPEUTIC

health-conscious person unduly anxious about illness: VALETUDINARIAN

health or spirits: FETTLE

health resort: SANITARIUM

health that is sound and vigorous, robust: HALE

healthful: SALUBRIOUS

healthy and happy: EUPEPTIC

heap, mass or collection of things: CONGERIES

heard by someone but not positively known to be true: HEARSAY

hearing diminution that accompanies aging: PRESBYCUSIS

heart attack: CORONARY THROMBOSIS

heart attack factor, according to experimental evidence: CHOLESTEROL

heart examination that traces changes in electric potential: ELECTROCARDIOGRAM (EKG)

heart rhythm disturbance: EXTRASYSTOLE

heart-shaped: CORDIFORM

heartbeat abnormality, with double pulse beat: DICROTIC

heartbeats that are weak and irregular: FIBRILLATION

heartburn: PYROSIS

heart's regular contraction: SYSTOLE

heat and cold sensitivity: THERMESTHESIA

heat causing or producing: PYROGENIC

heat energy employed after nuclear fusion: THERMONUCLEAR

heat measurement: CALORIMETRY

heat or light ray bent in passage from one medium to another: REFRACTION

heat or warmth producing, like a mustard plaster: CALEFACIENT

heat producing: CALORIFIC

heat-producing medical treatment: DIATHERMY

heat that is oppressive or overpowering: SWELTERING

heavenly, celestial: SUPERNAL

heavens, sky: FIRMAMENT

heavy, clumsy, awkward in appearance or movement: LUMBERING

heavy shoe: BROGAN

hedge or wall set low in a ditch so as not to obstruct the view: HA-HA

heedless, inattentive: UNAWARE

heedlessness, foolhardiness: TEMERITY

heel-stamping Spanish dance, flamencolike: ZAPATEADO

height, instrument for measuring: ALTIMETER

height of power, exuberance: HEYDAY

held notes, prolonged tempo, in music: SOSTENUTO

held or sustained, in music: TENUTO

helicopter landing place: HELIPORT

hell: INFERNO

hell: NETHER WORLD

helmet worn as protection against the sun: TOPEE

help: ABET

help: ADMINICLE

helpful person or rescuer: SAMARITAN

helping to make possible: CONDUCIVE

helpless, ineffective: IMPOTENT

helplessness, ineffectiveness: IMPOTENCE

hen that has been spayed: POULARD

hence: ERGO

herald or announcement of the coming of something or someone: HARBINGER

heraldic blue banner with three fleurs-de-lis of gold: ORIFLAMME

heraldic vertical band through the middle of the shield: PALE

heraldic white or silver: ARGENT

heraldry device placed above the shield in a coat of arms: CREST

heraldry position of a beast reared on its hind legs: RAMPANT

heraldry term for animal walking with a forepaw raised: PASSANT

heraldry term for a square table set diagonally, displaying arms of a deceased person: HATCHMENT

heraldry term for design with many small figures: SEMÉ

heraldry term for division of the quarter usually on the dexter side: CANTON

heraldry term for left: SINISTER

heraldry term for sitting with the forelimbs upright: SEJANT

heraldry term for two coats of arms placed side by side on an escutcheon: IMPALE

heraldry term for vertical bands of alternating colors: PALY

here and there in a book: PASSIM

heredity study to improve quality of humans: EUGENICS

hermaphroditic: ANDROGYNOUS

hermit: ANCHORITE

hero as a rogue in fiction: PICARESQUE

hesitancy or uneasiness regarding a question of moral right: SCRUPLE

hesitate, take exception, object: DEMUR

hesitate in speaking: HAW or HEM AND HAW

hesitating: IRRESOLUTE

hidden: ABSTRUSE

hidden, profound: RECONDITE

hidden, unclear, faint: OBSCURE

hidden goods or articles: CACHE

hidden or secret: ARCANE

hidden or unknown difficulty: JOKER

hidden tendency: UNDERCURRENT

hide or obscure: CAMOUFLAGE

hideous, enormous: MONSTROUS

hideous or cruel being: OGRE

hiding of one's real activities or designs: COVER-UP

hiding place for goods or articles: CACHE

hieroglyphics key: ROSETTA STONE

high, harsh sound: STRIDENT

high and mighty: HAUGHTY

high birth or rank: AUGUST

high fashion: HAUT COUTURE

high level land: PLATEAU

high on a hill or mountain, said of a house or stronghold: AERIE

high or culminating point: SOLSTICE

high priest, prelate: HIERARCH

high regard, esteem: REPUTE

high society: HAUT MONDE

high spirits or elated: COCK-A-HOOP

high voice above natural register: FALSETTO

higher price on a stock transaction than the preceding transaction price: UP TICK, PLUS-TICK

highest bid to buy and lowest offer to sell a given stock at a given time: QUOTATION

highest grade, usually said of diamonds and pearls: FIRST WATER

highest honors attending graduation: SUMMA CUM LAUDE

highest in kind, quality, or degree: SUPERLATIVE

highest in rank: PARAMOUNT

highest or culminating point: ZENITH

highest point: APOGEE

highest point: PINNACLE

highest point, topmost stone: CAPSTONE

highest point of anything, zenith: MERIDIAN

highest priced or best quality: GILT-EDGED

high-minded, great of soul, generous: MAGNANIMOUS

high-pressure peddling by phone of stocks of dubious value: BOILER ROOM

high-wire acrobat: AERIALIST

high-wire walker: FUNAMBULIST

highway interchange with overpass and curved ramps: CLOVERLEAF

hill or small round mound: KNOLL

hilly, moundy: TUMULOSE

hinder, block or guard against in advance: FORESTALL

hinder, impede, crowd with useless additions: ENCUMBER

hinder, interfere with the movements of, impede: HAMPER

hinder, put obstacles in the way of, retard: IMPEDE

hinder, slow, delay: RETARD

hinder or obstruct: CRIMP

hindrance, impediment: TRAMMEL

Hindu ascetic philosophy that involves deep meditation: YOGA

Hindu mythology triad of Brahma, Vishnu and Siva: TRIMURTI

Hindu system of exercises practiced in the Yoga discipline: YOGA

Hindu women's garment consisting of a long piece of fabric artfully wound about the body: SARI

hint, imply: INTIMATE

hint, notion, slight suggestion, vague idea: INKLING

hint, sly intimation: INSINUATION

hint, suggestion, insinuation, usually derogatory: INNUENDO

hint at, signify: IMPLY

hired applauders: CLAQUE

hissing sound: SIBILANT
history study based on excavations: AR-CHEOLOGY
hit and rebound: CAROM
hit repeatedly: PELT
hit repeatedly with the fists: PUMMEL
hit sweepingly along the side: SIDESWIPE
hives, nettle rash: URTICARIA
hoarding riches: AVARICE
hoax: SPOOF
hobos' section of a city: SKID ROW
hockey enclosure to seat players removed as a penalty: PENALTY BOX
hockey foul of touching opponent's body with stick held in both hands: CROSS-CHECK
hockey term for illegal entry of opponent's zone ahead of the puck: OFF-SIDE
hockey term for moving the puck with light taps of the stick: DRIBBLE
hockey term for starting play by dropping the puck between the sticks of two opposing players: FACE OFF
hocus-pocus, sleight of hand, trickery: LEGERDEMAIN
hodgepodge, confusion: KATZENJAMMER
hodgepodge, hash: GALLIMAUFRY
hodgepodge, medley: MÉLANGE
hoggish, piggish, swinish: PORCINE
hold back from something: ABSTAIN
hold forth, discuss: DESCANT
hold someone by binding the arms: PINION
holding, as of land or a term of office: TENURE
holding of an office: INCUMBENCY
holding together: COHERENT
hole drilled through the ocean floor: MO-HOLE
hole in a paved road: POTHOLE
holiday spent in activity similar to one's regular work: BUSMAN'S HOLIDAY
holiness or righteousness pretended: SANCTIMONIOUS
hollow in a wall, as for a bust, statue or the like: NICHE
holy men forming the government: HAGIARCHY or HAGIOCRACY
holy oil: CHRISM
holy water basin: STOUP
homage, respect, reverence: OBEISANCE
home: ABODE
home, house or dwelling: DOMICILE
homeless, roaming: NOMADIC
homeless, wandering youngster: GAMIN

homeless person forced by a war, to live in a foreign country: DISPLACED PERSON
homeless wanderer: WAIF
homeless rover, vagabond: VAGRANT
homesickness that is severe: NOSTALGIA
homosexual male: URANIST, URNING
homosexual female: LESBIAN
homosexuality, especially among males: URANISM
honest, conscientious: SCRUPULOUS
honest, morally proper: UPRIGHT
honest, straightforward dealing: PLAIN-DEALING
honest, upright: INCORRUPT
honesty: VERACITY
honesty, probity: INTEGRITY
honeylike, semifluid, sticky: VISCOUS
honor with festivities: FETE
honorable, respectable; in good usage: REPUTABLE
honored for excellence in one's achievements: LAUREATE
honors awarded according to property owned, as a form of government: TIMÓCRACY
honors included, as at graduation: CUM LAUDE
hood and mask worn at masquerades: DOMINO
hooded: COWLED
hooded cloak: BURNOOSE
hoof, nail, claw: UNGUIS
hook at the end of the pole for landing large fish: GAFF
hooked or curved: AQUILINE
hooklike: UNCIFORM
hoot, wail, howl: ULULATE
hope with little or no expectation of getting what is desired: FORLORN HOPE
hopeless, incapable of being reformed: INCORRIGIBLE
hopeless plight: CHANCERY
hopelessness, dejection of spirits: DE-SPONDENCY
hormone of male sex: ANDROSTERONE
horn overflowing with fruit, vegetables, grain: CORNUCOPIA
horn that is low-pitched, especially one used on ships to signal alarms: KLAXON
horn-bereft animal: POLLARD
hornlike or horny: CORNEOUS
horrible fancy: CHIMERA
horrified: AGHAST

horse breed notable for its trotters and pacers: STANDARDBRED

horse command word meaning to turn left: HAW

horse of light tan with ivory-colored mane and tail: PALOMINO

horse of medium size used for ordinary driving or riding: HACKNEY

horse race in which any entry is subject to purchase at a previously set price: CLAIMING RACE

horse race in which the competitors are selected far in advance: FUTURITY

horse race with only one starter: WALK-OVER

horse racing information sheet: DOPE SHEET

horse racing term for designated weight carried by a horse in a handicap race: IMPOST

horse that has been castrated: GELDING

horse that is male and uncastrated: STALLION

horse that races well on a muddy track: MUDDER

horse whose coloring is permeated whth gray or white: ROAN

horse-drawn two-wheeled vehicle for one person: SULKY

horselike mythical animal with one horn: UNICORN

horse's lifting of a forefoot and the opposite hind foot without moving forward or backward: PIAFFER

horses or horsemanship: EQUESTRIAN

horses or oxen in a matched pair: SPAN

horses used for heavy work: PERCHERONS

horse-training term for a gait in which a horse moves partly sidewise: VOLT

hospital department in which outpatients are treated: POLICLINIC

hospital or ship for the treatment of contagious diseases: LAZARETTO

hostile, antagonistic: INIMICAL

hostile, inharmonious, incongruous: DISSONANT

hostile, resisting, antagonistic: REPUGNANT

hostile behavior: BELLICOSITY

hostile feeling: ANIMUS

hot, scorched: TORRID

hot days of July and August: DOG DAYS

hotel designed to accommodate motorists: MOTEL

hotel system in which the price includes room, service and meals: AMERICAN PLAN

hotel system of charging for room and service without meals: EUROPEAN PLAN

hourly: HORAL

house with a view: BELVEDERE

house with each floor half a story above or below the adjacent one: SPLIT-LEVEL

household: MÉNAGE

household gods: LARES AND PENATES

howl, hoot, wail: ULULATE

hubbub, turmoil: HURLY-BURLY

huge: TITANIC

huge or powerful thing or creature: LEVIATHAN

human attributes ascribed to inanimate things: PATHETIC FALLACY

human attributes ascribed to inanimate things in figurative speech: PERSONIFICATION

human embodiment: INCARNATION

human emotions or passions attributed to gods or objects: ANTHROPOPATHY

human form or characteristics ascribed to something not human: ANTHROPOMORPHISM

human improvement through control of environment: EUTHENICS

human improvement through control of factors that affect heredity: EUGENICS

human knowledge as a subject of study, cognition: EPISTEMOLOGY

human shaped: ANDROID

humanly made object or art: ARTIFACT

humble and earnest entreating: SUPPLIANT

humiliate: ABASE

humorous: WAGGISH

humpback, curvature of the spine: KYPHOSIS

hundredfold: CENTUPLE

hunger that is continuous: BULIMIA

hungry, greedy: ESURIENT

hungry in a wild or greedy way: RAVENOUS

hunt or fish illegally: POACH

hunted creature: QUARRY

hurl from a height: PRECIPITATE

hurried and confused: HELTER-SKELTER

hurry: POSTHASTE

hurry, hasten: HIE

hurry off, run: SCAMPER

hurtful: DELETERIOUS

hurtful to the feelings in a sharp way: POIGNANT

hurtle through air: CATAPULT

husband of a reigning female sovereign: PRINCE CONSORT

husband of an unfaithful wife: CUCKOLD

husband or wife: CONSORT

husband who murders his wife: UXORICIDE

husbandly excessive fondness for or submissiveness to wife: UXORIOUS

husk, shell or pod: SHUCK

hussy: JADE

hybrid offspring of a stallion and a female ass: HINNY

hymn for the dead: REQUIEM

hymn or verse in praise of God: DOXOLOGY

hyprocrisy: PHARISAISM

hypocrisy: SANCTIMONY

hypocrite: AMBIDEXTER

hypocrite: TARTUFFE

hypocrite: WHITED SEPULCHER

hypocrite who is fawning and scheming: URIAH HEEP

hypocritical, insincere: PECKSNIFFIAN

hypocritical, pretentious or ostentatious ceremony: MUMMERY

hypocritical behavior: DISSEMBLANCE

hypocritical pious expressions: CANT

hypothetical, academic, debatable: MOOT

hysterical outburst or rage: CONNIPTION

I

I am at fault: MEA CULPA
I came, I saw, I conquered: VENI, VIDI, VICI
ice game, in which heavy stones are slid toward a goal: CURLING
iced or chilled beverages as a dessert: FRAPPÉ
icy, frozen: GELID
increase power, rank or wealth: AGGRANDIZE
increasing the number of shares of a company by dividing the outstanding shares: SPLIT
idea conference: BRAINSTORMING
idealize, glorify: TRANSFIGURE
identification card: ID CARD
identifying oneself with other persons or objects: INTROJECTION
idiocy: AMENTIA
idiom, language, speaking style: PARLANCE
idiot: AMENT
idiotic, inane, stupid: FATUOUS
idle, dormant: FALLOW
idle, lazy: OTIOSE
idle, unoccupied: VACUOUS
idle chatter; also a discussion: PALAVER
idle talk: PRATE
idle tramp who is subject to arrest: VAGRANT
idler, do-nothing: FAINEANT
idyllic, serene, calm: HALCYON
if anything can go wrong, it will: MURPHY'S LAW
if you please; please: S'IL VOUS PLAÎT
ignorant: BENIGHTED
ignoring the complexity of problems, oversimplifying them: SIMPLISTIC
ignorance: NESCIENCE
ignorance pretended to expose errors of opponent's argument: SOCRATIC IRONY
ill will, spitefulness: RANCOR
ill temper, spitefulness, peevishness: SPLEEN
ill-assorted, incongruous: DISSOCIABLE
ill-disposed, wishing evil toward others: MALEVOLENT
illegal bargain made in a lawsuit to get share of matter sued for: CHAMPERTY
illegal commerce in goods that may not be exported or imported: CONTRABAND
illegal influencing of a judge or jury: EMBRACERY
illegitimate, counterfeit: SPURIOUS
ill-humored, cross, gloomy: SULKY
ill-humored, sullen, gloomy: MOROSE
illiterate, uneducated: UNLETTERED
illiterate who is unable to learn to read: FUNCTIONAL ILLITERATE
ill-natured or rude person: CHURL
illness, disorder: DISTEMPER
illness or discontent, a chronic feeling of either: DYSPHORIA
illness or disorder of mind or body: DISTEMPER
illness that is slight: INDISPOSITION
illogical or faulty reasoning: PARALOGISM
ill-starred: STAR-CROSSED
ill-tempered or peevish: BILIOUS
illusion of reality, in art or decoration: TROMPE L'OEIL
illusion that a new experience has happened before: DÉJÀ VU
illustrate a book already in print with illustrations from another book: GRANGERIZE
illustrative: EXEMPLARY
illustrious, shining: SPLENDENT
image: EIDOLON

image in the mind, specter: PHANTASM

image, likeness, picture, usually an object of veneration: ICON

image, likeness, representation, usually crudely done of a disliked person: EFFIGY

images in works of art studied to determine thematic significance of the subject: ICONOGRAPHY

imaginable, possible, secular: EARTHLY

imaginary, assumed, supposed: HYPOTHETICAL

imaginary, flimsy: INSUBSTANTIAL

imaginary, unrealistic: VISIONARY

imaginary grotesque monster: CHIMERA

imaginary or visionary semblance: SIMULACRUM

imaginative resources: INGENUITY

imagined symptoms as part of anxiety about one's health: HYPOCHONDRIA

imitate, look or act like someone or something: SIMULATE

imitate in attempt to equal or surpass: EMULATE

imitation, especially in literature and art: MIMESIS

imitation by a word of some sound: ECHOIC

imitation of a literary or musical work, meant humorously: PARODY

imitation marble: SCAGLIOLA

imitation or burlesque that is farcical: TRAVESTY

imitation or reproduction of the original: ECTYPE

immature: CALLOW

immature, callow but opinionated: SOPHOMORIC

immature, inexperienced: UNFLEDGED

immediate: INSTANTANEOUS

immediately: TOUT DE SUITE

immediately, at once: INSTANTER

immediately following this: HEREUPON

immoral, debauched: DISSOLUTE

immoral man, roué: RAKE

immortality: ATHANASIA

immovable: ADAMANT

immune, resistant: INSUSCEPTIBLE

immune to injury, unconquerable: INVULNERABLE

immunity to disease, as a study: IMMUNOLOGY

immunize by an injection: INOCULATE

impair, spoil: VITIATE

impair secretly, weaken by degrees: UNDERMINE

impart gradually: INSTILL

impartial, fair: UNBIASED

impartial, fair, reasonable: EQUITABLE

impartial, unbiased: DISINTERESTED

impartial, objective: DISPASSIONATE

impartiality, justness, fairness: EQUITY

impassioned: FERVID

impassive, unfeeling: STOLID

impassive, unaffected by pain or pleasure: STOICAL

impede, block, hinder, stop: OBSTRUCT

impede, disconcert, complicate: EMBARRASS

impede, hinder, obstruct, crowd with useless additions: ENCUMBER

impede, restrain, interfere with the movements of: HAMPER

impediment, hindrance: TRAMMEL

impending, threatening: IMMINENT

imperious, dictatorial: PEREMPTORY

impetuous: BRASH

impetuous, ardent, violent: VEHEMENT

impetus of a body in motion: MOMENTUM

implant ideas or opinions: INSEMINATE

implicate: INVOLVE

implication of a word, an expression or a text: CONNOTATION

implied, not directly stated: TACIT

imply, hint: INTIMATE

imply or give the appearance of fact, often falsely: PURPORT

important: CONSEQUENTIAL

important, essential: PIVOTAL

important, highly regarded: PRESTIGIOUS

important, outstanding feature: HIGHLIGHT

important person: HIGH MUCK-A-MUCK

important person in a group: KINGPIN

impose, introduce or insert fraudulently: FOIST

imposing, awesome: AUGUST

imposing, pretentiously grand: GRANDIOSE

impossible to extricate oneself from, impossible to disentangle or undo: INEXTRICABLE

impress on the mind, instill: INCULCATE

impressive, grand, stately: IMPOSING

imprison: INCARCERATE

imprison, confine, surround enclose within walls: IMMURE

imprisonment, forced confinement: DURANCE

improbable person or event introduced to untangle a story plot: DEUS EX MACHINA

improper: UNSEEMLY

improper, unseemly: UNTOWARD

improve: AMELIORATE

improvements to property: CAPITAL EXPENDITURE

improvise: AD LIB

improvised: EXTEMPORANEOUS

improvised musical passage: CADENZA

improvised to fill a need temporarily: STOPGAP

imprudent: IMPOLITIC

imprudent, unwise: INDISCREET

impudence: CHUTZPAH

impudence, boldness, audacity: EFFRONTERY

impudent young woman: BAGGAGE

impudently or ostentatiously display: FLAUNT

impulse that is creative: AFFLATUS

impulsive, hasty, rash: IMPETUOUS

impulsive or hasty action or speech: HALF-COCKED

impulsive without forethought: SPONTANEOUS

impure, to make: ADULTERATE

in name alone, not in fact: NOMINAL

in on a secret: PRIVY

in opposition to: ATHWART

in place of: LIEU

in the matter of, concerning: IN RE

in the morning, early: MATUTINAL

in wine there is truth: IN VINO VERITAS

inability to understand or use objects: APRAXIA

inactive, indolent, listless: SUPINE

inactive, settled, seated a great part of the time: SEDENTARY

inactive sluggish, dull: TORPID

inactive, still, placid: QUIESCENT

inactive for a period, especially winter: HIBERNATING

inadequate, disproportionate: INCOMMENSURATE

inadequate, not quite enough: SCANT

inadvertent or random action, accidental homicide: CHANCE-MEDLEY

inane or idle thing: VACUITY

inanimate objects possess souls, as a belief: ANIMISM

inappropriate, at odds with, unsuitable: INCONGRUOUS

inappropriate, out of place: MALAPROPOS

inattentive, heedless: UNAWARE

inborn: INHERENT

inborn: INNATE

incantation used to conjure an evil spirit: INVOCATION

incarnation of a quality or idea: AVATAR

incapable of being passed through: IMPERVIOUS

incapable of being transferred or removed: INALIENABLE

incautious, thriftless, rash: IMPROVIDENT

incense ingredient: TACAMAHAC

incentive, motivating force: IMPETUS

incentive, stimulus: FILLIP

incident or controversy attracting wide attention: CAUSE CÉLÈBRE

incidental result, by-product, new application: SPIN-OFF

incised carving: INTAGLIO

incite, foment, provoke, spur on, goad to some drastic action: INSTIGATE

incite, instigate, stir up: FOMENT

inclination, tendency, bent: PROPENSITY

inclination or slope of countryside: VERSANT

inclination or tendency: BENT

incline downward, be of greater weights: PREPONDERATE

incline linking different levels: RAMP

include or embrace: COMPRISE

include or take in as a part of the whole: INCORPORATE

incoherent, rapid talk: GIBBERISH

incoherent talk: GABBLE

income in dollars of individuals adjusted to take account of inflation: REAL INCOME

incompetence tends to be the level achieved by the promotion of employes: PETER PRINCIPLE

incompetent, clumsy, awkward: INEPT

incomplete, broken: FRAGMENTARY

incomprehensible, dense: IMPENETRABLE

incongruity, lack of harmony: DISSONANCE

incongruous, ill-assorted: DISSOCIABLE

inconsistency, contradiction: DISCREPANCY

inconsistent or opposed, antagonistic: REPUGNANT

inconstant, changeable: FICKLE

inconvenience, bother, trouble: DISCOMMODE

incorporate, collect, make part of a whole: EMBODY

incorrect though popular idea of the origin of a word: FOLK ETYMOLOGY

increase, addition, something added or gained: INCREMENT

increase, grow, expand step by step: ESCALATE

increase unduly, puff up, enlarge excessively: INFLATE

increasing, enlarging, growing: INCRESCENT

incriminate: INCULPATE

incriminating position: RED-HANDED

indecency or pornography in art or literature: COPROLOGY

indecent: UNSEEMLY

indecent, bold, self-assertive: IMMODEST

indecent, risqué: SCABROUS

indecisive: VACILLATING

indefinable something: JE NE SAIS QUOI

indefinite, misty, foggy: NUBILOUS

indefinite or vague: INTANGIBLE

indention of all lines of a paragraph except the first, as in the format of this entry: HANGING INDENTION

independent: AUTONOMOUS

independent, needing no help: SELF-SUFFICIENT

independent, particularly in politics: MUGWUMP

independent and supreme authority: SOVEREIGN

independent in resources: SUBSTANTIVE

independent of an original or main body or group: SPLINTER

independent of outside control: AUTONOMOUS

index to words in a particular book: CONCORDANCE

Indiana resident: INDIANIAN, HOOSIER

indicate, point out, signify: DENOTE

indifference, dullness, stagnation, weakness, fatigue, spiritlessness: LANGUOR

indifference to pleasure or pain: STOICAL

indifferent: APATHETIC

indifferent, apathetic: PHLEGMATIC

indifferent, apathetic, lackadaisical: LISTLESS

indifferent, uncaring: POCOCURANTE

indifferent in a casual way, cool: NONCHALANT

indigenous: ABORIGINAL

indigenous, native: ENCHORIAL

indignity: AFFRONT

indirect, not obvious: SUBTLE

indirect, slanted: OBLIQUE

indirect and unexpected stroke: BRICOLE

indirect mention: ALLUSION

indirect method of proceeding: AMBAGE

indirect or roundabout: CIRCUITOUS

indirect words used to say something: PERIPHRASTIC

indiscretions of youth: WILD OATS

indiscriminate, especially sexually: PROMISCUOUS

indispensable, without which not (nothing): SINE QUA NON

indispensable, essential, whole: INTEGRAL

indispensable, required: REQUISITE

indisputable: APODICTIC

indisputable, unquestionable: INCONTESTABLE

individuals or items chosen in the expectation they will be representative of a whole group: RANDOM SAMPLE

indoctrination that is coercive: BRAINWASHING

indolent, irresponsible individual: LOTUS-EATER

indolent, listless, inactive: SUPINE

induce or bribe one to commit perjury: SUBORN

indulgence that is excessive: DISSIPATION

industrial worker: BLUE COLLAR

indwelling: IMMANENCE

inebriate: INTOXICATE

ineffective, lazy, useless: FAINEANT

ineffectual, useless: OTIOSE

ineffectual person: WEAK SISTER

inequality, unlikeness: DISPARITY

inertness and disorder as an irreversible tendency of a system: ENTROPY

inevitable, unavoidable: INELUCTABLE

inevitability: FATALISM

inexperienced: CALLOW

inexperienced: VERDANT

infallible authority, wise person: ORACLE

infamy, disgrace: OBLOQUY

infantile concept of a parent or loved one persisting in the adult: IMAGO

infer from incomplete evidence: CONJECTURE

inference or deduction: ILLATION

inference resulting from concealment or misrepresentation of facts: SUBREPTION

inferior, paltry, pitiable: SORRY

inferior in any way: SUBORDINATE

inferior in rank: SUBALTERN

inferior quality: SHODDY

inferior substitute: ERSATZ
inferior to an appalling degree: EXECRABLE
infernal, dark, gloomy: STYGIAN
infinitive in which an adverb intervenes between the ''to'' and the verb: SPLIT INFINITIVE
inflamed, sore: IRRITATED
inflated, bombastic, as a style of speech: TURGID
inflated, overloaded: PLETHORIC
inflated, pompous: TUMID
inflated, pretentious: OVERBLOWN
inflation designed by government to bring back a former price structure: REFLATION
inflection of words: ACCIDENCE
inflexible, rigid: HARD-SHELL
inflict or enforce in an arbitrary fashion: IMPOSE
inform: APPRISE
informal noisy gathering: CLAMBAKE
informal word or phrase: COLLOQUIALISM
informed, acquainted with facts: AU FAIT
informed on current things: AU COURANT
informer for the police: STOOL PIGEON
ingenious, cunning, skillful: DAEDAL
ingenious, refined: SUBTLE
inhabitant or habitue: DENIZEN
inharmonious, incongruous, hostile: DISSONANT
inharmonious: DISSONANCE
inherent: INNATE
inherent, essential: INTRINSIC
inhuman, cruel, vicious: FELL
initial, beginning: INCEPTIVE
initial letter or sound dropped in the development of a word: APHERESIS
initial letter or sound the same in a series of words: ALLITERATION
initial letters of a series of words combined to form a word: ACRONYM
initial letters of lines forming a word: ACROSTIC
initiate someone by subjecting him to pranks and humiliating horseplay: HAZE
inject or add certain elements: INCORPORATE
injection under the skin: HYPODERMIC
injured or victimized by one's plans to injure another: HOIST BY ONE'S OWN PETARD
injured feeling, resentment: UMBRAGE
injurious: DELETERIOUS

injurious, deadly, malicious: PERNICIOUS
injurious, harmful: NOCUOUS
injurious, unwholesome: NOXIOUS
injury, damage: LESION
injury, harmful action, ill service: DISSERVICE
injury or emotional shock that is severe: TRAUMA
ink blot test used to analyze personality: RORSCHACH TEST
inland region, remote area, back country: HINTERLAND
inlet of sea between steep cliffs: FIORD
inlet of the sea or mouth of a river where tide and current meet: ESTUARY
inmost parts as in a house of worship: PENETRALIA
inn or hostelry: CARAVANSARY
innards, internal organs such as stomach, heart, lungs: VISCERA
inner force that animates or guides: NUMEN
innkeeper: BONIFACE
innocence, peace and simplicity portrayed as associated with rural life: PASTORAL
innocence-proving: EXCULPATORY
innocent young woman: INGÉNUE
innumerable, vast indefinite number: MYRIAD
insanity: ALIENATION
insatiable, immoderate, greedy: VORACIOUS
inscribe or adorn with names or symbols: BLAZON
inscription on a tomb or monument: EPIGRAPH
inscriptions, scribblings or drawings on walls: GRAFFITI
insect study: ENTOMOLOGY
insensible, blunt, dull: OBTUSE
insert, as an additional day in the calendar: INTERCALATE
insert, throw in between other things, introduce abruptly: INTERJECT
insert an organ within the body: IMPLANT
insert unacknowledged addition in order to falsify a text: INTERPOLATE
insertion, as in a wooden joint, to hide a bad fitting or to replace a broken piece: DUTCHMAN
insertion of a sound or letter into a word: EPENTHESIS
insertion of a word between the parts of a compound word: TMESIS

insertion of one thing into another: IN-TROMISSION

insertion sign in typewritten or printed matter (˄): CARET

inside exclusive group: CLIQUE

inside of a curved surface: CONCAVITY

inside talk of a special group: CANT

insider, one in the know: COGNOSCENTE

insignia that is V shaped: CHEVRON

insignificant, trifling, tiny: MINUTE

insignificant, unimportant, trifling: PETTY

insignificant amount: IOTA

insignificant or trifling size or amount: NEGLIGIBLE

insincere, ambiguous: LEFT-HANDED

insincere, crafty: DISINGENUOUS

insincere, hypocritical: PECKSNIFFIAN

insincere or excessive: FULSOME

insincere religious or moralistic talk: CANT

insincere sympathy: BATHOS

insinuation, hint, suggestion, usually derogatory: INNUENDO

insipid, dry, lacking interest, naive, barren: JEJUNE

insipid, flat, dull, lifeless: VAPID

insolent: BRASSY

insolence, rudeness: IMPERTINENCE

insolent or rebellious: CONTUMACIOUS

insolent treatment: AFFRONT

inspection of one or a few typical things out of many, to insure quality: SPOT CHECK

inspire, activate, lead, as a group: SPARK-PLUG

inspire with ideas: IMBUE

install, as an official: INAUGURATE

install or place in office formally: INVEST

installment ceremony: INVESTITURE

instantly: IN A TRICE

instigate, incite, stir up: FOMENT

instigate an evil act: SUBORN

instill, impress on the mind: INCULCATE

institute legal proceedings: PROSECUTE

instruct in doctrines, principles or systems of belief: INDOCTRINATE

instructional, boringly pedagogical: DIDACTIC

instrument similar to the xylophone: MARIMBA

instrument that is long and tubular with a curving stem: BASSOON

instrument to measure diameter of thickness: CALIPERS

insubstantial, nonmaterial, spiritual: IN-CORPOREAL

insult, affront: INDIGNITY

insult openly: AFFRONT

insulting: ABUSIVE

insulting, disrespectful: INSOLENT

insulting rudeness in speech: CONTUMELY

insurance risk and premium calculator: ACTUARY

insurrection: INSURGENCE

intact: INVIOLATE

intangible: IMPALPABLE

integrity, honesty: PROBITY

integrity lack, dishonesty: IMPROBITY

intellect, brains: GRAY MATTER

intellectual activity: NOETIC

intellectual quickness, keenness: ACUMEN

intellectual perception of something unknowable through the senses: NOUMENON

intemperance: DISSIPATION

intensify: AGGRANDIZE

intensify or elevate: HEIGHTEN

inter, bury: INHUME

interbreeding of races: MISCEGENATION

interest not compounded but computed on the original principal alone: SIMPLE INTEREST

interesting and agreeable: SAPID

intermediate point between two extremes, sometimes an average: MEAN

interminable and difficult: SISYPHEAN

internal organs, innards, such as stomach, heart, lungs: VISCERA

internal rhyme, in which a word within a line of verse rhymes with the final word of the line: LEONINE RHYME

internal-examining machine: FLUORO-SCOPE

International Criminal Police Organization: INTERPOL

interpret or explain: EXPLICATE

interpretation, especially of the Bible: HERMENEUTICS

interpretation of a word, passage or work: EXEGESIS

interpretation of words, spiritual and mystical: ANAGOGE

interpretation or performance of a text, role, etc.: RENDITION

interpreter or guide for travelers in the Near East: DRAGOMAN

interrupted, broken: DISCONTINUOUS

interruption, as of electric service: OUTAGE

interruption or break in continuity: IN-TERREGNUM

interruptions, insertions, additions in a discourse, process or series: INTERPOLATIONS

intersect, cross in form of an x: DECUSSATE

intersecting, cutting: SECANT

intertwining, entanglement, complication: INVOLUTION

interval between events or activities, recess: INTERMISSION

intervene in behalf of another or to mediate: INTERCEDE

interweave: PLEACH

intestinal: ENTERIC

intestinal disease usually caused by eating undercooked pork: TRICHINOSIS

intestinal inflammation: COLITIS

intestinal waves of contraction that push the contents outward: PERISTALSIS

intimate friend: ALTER EGO

intimate relation: A DEUX

intimately: CHEEK BY JOWL

intricate: INVOLVED

intricate, skillful, cunning, ingenious: DAEDAL

intriguers, cabal: JUNTA

intriguing secret group: CABAL

introduce, impose, insert fraudulently: FOIST

introduce abruptly, throw in between other things: INTERJECT

introduce additions, comments, interruptions into a discourse or process: INTERPOLATE

introduce ideas or opinions into the mind of: INOCULATE

introduce or bring in something new: INNOVATE

introduce some new element into: INJECT

introduce subtly and gradually: INSINUATE

introduction, as to a field of study: ISAGOGE

introduction or preface: PREAMBLE

introduction to a book or thesis: PREFACE

introduction to an art or science: PROPAEDEUTIC

introductory remark, foreword: PROLEGOMENON

introductory statement, preface: PROEM

intrude, meddle in the affairs of others: INTERLOPE

intrude gradually, make inroads, trespass, advance beyond proper limit: ENCROACH

intrude oneself or one's opinion on someone else: OBTRUDE

intuitive, emotional: VISCERAL

intuitive knowledge, direct awareness: IMMEDIACY

invalid: VALETUDINARIAN

invalidate, debase, corrupt: VITIATE

invasion, raid: INCURSION

invasion that is sudden: IRRUPTION

invent, produce, perform without previous thought or preparation: IMPROVISE

invent a word: MINT

invent details to compensate for loss of memory: CONFABULATE

invent or make up as a story or a lie: FABRICATE

invented, false, not real: FICTITIOUS

inventive, clever, skillful: INGENIOUS

inventive, fruitful, productive: PREGNANT

inversion of the structure of the second of two parallel clauses: CHIASMUS

inverted order of words: ANASTROPHE

inverted "v" placed under a line to indicate insertion: CARET

investigate or search for information: DELVE

investigation, officially done, of the beliefs and activities of individuals: INQUISITION

investigation and discovery as a way of learning: HEURISTICS

invigorate, cheer up, pep up, stimulate: EXHILARATE

inviolable, as an oath: STYGIAN

inviting attack, vulnerable: PREGNABLE

involve, entangle, intertwine: IMPLICATE

involve in trouble: EMBROIL

involve necessarily or naturally: IMPLY

iota: TITTLE

involved, complicated, puzzling: INTRICATE

involved, foolishly wasteful procedure: RIGMAROLE

invulnerable, unfeeling: IMPASSIBLE

inward violent collapse: IMPLOSION

iridescence: OPALESCENCE

iridescence, especially on pottery: REFLET

iridescent: VERSICOLOR

iridescent, pearl-like: NACREOUS

iridescent, resembling a peacock's tail: PAVONINE

Irish pronunciation: BROGUE

iron for pressing clothes that is pointed at both ends: SADIRON

irony: ANTIPHRASIS

irregular: ANOMALOUS
irregular, eccentric, nonconforming: ERRATIC
irregular, occasional: SPORADIC
irregularity: ABNORMALITY
irrelevance: IMPERTINENCE
irrelevant: INAPPOSITE
irrelevant remark: NON SEQUITUR
irreligious, unbelieving: HEATHEN
irresistibly attractive: BEWITCHING
irresponsible, reckless, wild: HARUM-SCARUM
irreverent: IMPIOUS
irreverent remarks about God or sacred things: BLASPHEMY
irritability or excitability in any part of the body to an abnormal degree: ERETHISM
irritable, quick-tempered: IRASCIBLE
irritable, unruly, cranky, rebellious: FRACTIOUS
irritable or gruff person, usually elderly: CURMUDGEON
irritableness, peevishness: PETULANCE
irritate: ACERBATE
irritate, embitter: RANKLE
irritate or upset: RUFFLE
irritated or angry state: SNIT
irritating, annoying: VEXATIOUS
is it not so? (German): NICHT WAHR?

islamic prophet or messiah expected before the end of the world: MAHDI
island or reef especially one of coral, low and beside a coast: KEY
islands, chain of: ARCHIPELAGO
Isle of Man native: MANXMAN
isn't it so?: N'EST-CE PAS?
isolate: INSULATE
isolate a thought: PRESCIND
isolated, detached: INSULAR
isolated, private room: SANCTUM
isolated, separated: SPORADIC
Israeli and Rumanian folk dance in which dancers lock arms in a circle: HORA
Israeli collective farm or settlement: KIBBUTZ
Israeli Constituent Assembly: KNESSET
Israeli native: SABRA
Italian dessert containing layers of different ice creams: SPUMONI
Italian frothy dessert made of eggs, sugar, and wine: ZABAGLIONE
Italian small eating place: TRATTORIA
itemized list of securities held by a person or an institution: PORTFOLIO
items too small or too numerous to be separately specified: SUNDRIES
ivory, bone, or shells ornamented by cutting or carving: SCRIMSHAW

J

jabbering: BLITHERING
jacket that binds the arms to the body to restrain a violent person: STRAIT-JACKET
jammed, close together: CHOCK-A-BLOCK
Japanese American of the third generation: SANSEI
Japanese art of paperfolding: ORIGAMI
Japanese broad sash with a bow in the back: OBI
Japanese classical drama: NO
Japanese dish of thinly sliced meat and vegetables usually cooked rapidly at the table: SUKIYAKI
Japanese play on popular or comic themes: KABUKI
Japanese ritual suicide by disembowelment: HARA-KIRI
Japanese stringed musical instrument: KOTO
Japanese suicidal air attack: KAMIKAZE
Japanese syllabic writing: KANA
Japanese translucent paper screen used as a partition or door: SHOJI
Japanese verse form: HAIKU or HOKKU
Japanese wrestling system that uses size and strength of an opponent against him: JUJITSU
jar, in which moisture is retained, for storing cigars and tobacco: HUMIDOR
jar or pot, broad-mouthed and of earthenware: OLLA
jargon: ARGOT
jargon or vocabulary of a profession or class: LINGO
jaundice: ICTERUS
jaunty, gay, dashing: RAKISH
jaw, pertaining to: GNATHIC
jazz that is loud and improvised: BARREL-HOUSE
jeer, defy, scoff, mock: FLOUT

jeer, deride, sneer, laugh coarsely: FLEER
jeer or reproach sarcastically: TAUNT
jeer, taunt: GIBE
jelly making substance: PECTIN
jerky, unsteady movement: JIGGLE
jesting, flippantly humorous: FACETIOUS
jesting, playful: JOCOSE
jesting, teasing talk: RAILLERY
Jesus' saying not found in Bible: AGRAPHA
jewelers' or watchmakers' magnifying glass: LOUPE
jewelers' weights system: TROY
jewels set so closely as to hide metal: PAVÉ
Jewish boy's coming-of-age ceremony at 13: BAR MITZVAH
Jewish civil and religious law and commentaries thereon: TALMUD
Jewish dietary standards observed: KOSHER
Jewish girl's coming-of-age ceremony: BAS (or BAT or BATH) MITZVAH
Jewish greeting: SHALOM
Jewish law and literature, also the Pentateuch: TORAH
Jewish leather cases containing Scriptural passages that are placed on the forehead and left arm during morning prayers: PHYLACTERIES
Jewish marriage broker: SCHATCHEN
Jewish mourning prayer: KADDISH
Jewish New Year: ROSH HASHANA
Jewish observance of mourning period: SIT SHIVA
Jewish Passover feast commemorating the exodus from Egypt: SEDER
Jewish school or college: YESHIVA
Jewish scroll in a small tube that is affixed to a doorpost: MEZUZA
Jewish seven-day period of mourning: SHIVA

Jews' dispersion: DIASPORA

Jews of Spanish or Portuguese descent: SEPHARDIM

jittery, balky, fretful: RESTIVE

joined together: CONJUNCTIVE

joint formed in carpentry: MITER

joint government or authority shared by two men: DUUMVIRATE

jointed: ARTICULATED

joke, mischief: WAGGERY

joke, mock: JAPE

joker: WAG

joker, wag: FARCEUR

jolt, bounce, shake up and down: JOUNCE

jolting of the neck or base of the brain, as in an automobile crash: WHIPLASH

jot: TITTLE

journey, usually short and for pleasure: JAUNT

journey made for safety or as an escape: HEGIRA

journey or expedition: SAFARI

journey or laborious trip: TREK

joy of living: JOIE DE VIVRE

joy to the utmost, ecstasy: RAPTURE

joyful, triumphant: JUBILANT

joyful, vigorous, vital, spirited: EXUBERANT

jubilant, triumphant, joyful: EXULTANT

judge: ADJUDICATE

judge: ARBITER

judge's private room in court: CAMERA

judgment lacking: INJUDICIOUS

judicial, definitive, established by decree: DECRETORY

judicial order requiring one to take, or refrain from, certain action: INJUNCTION

jug, narrow-necked and often enclosed in wickerwork: DEMIJOHN

jug or mug in form of an old man wearing a three-cornered hat: TOBY

jug or pitcher with wide mouth: EWER

juice of grapes or other fruit that is unfermented: MUST

juicy: SUCCULENT

July and August hot sultry days: DOG DAYS

jumbled, topsy-turvy, disordered: HIGGLEDY-PIGGLEDY

jumbled heap: AGGLOMERATE

jumpy, shy: SKITTISH

jurors summoned to fill vacancies: TALES

jury of twelve selected after each party strikes a given number of names from a panel: STRUCK JURY

just right, appropriate: PAT

justice, prudence, temperance and fortitude: CARDINAL VIRTUES

justice that is ideal with the good rewarded and the evil punished: POETIC JUSTICE

justify: VINDICATE

justify, sufficient grounds for: WARRANT

juvenile, trivial, silly: PUERILE

juxtaposition of words, one to explain the other: APPOSITION

K

keen, acute as in pleasure or pain: EXQUISITE

keen, cutting, acute, sharp: INCISIVE

keen, discerning, perceptive: PERSPICACIOUS

keen, discriminating: SUBTLE

keen, incisive: TRENCHANT

keenly desirous, as for food: SHARP-SET

keenness of mind: ACUMEN

keep back, suppress: STIFLE

keep vigil, go without sleep: WATCH

keeper, guard, watchman: WARDER

kept man: GIGOLO

kerchief worn by Arabs over head and shoulders: KAFFIYEH

kerchief worn on head: BABUSHKA

kettledrums: TIMPANI

key to hieroglyphics: ROSETTA STONE

kidnap: ABDUCT

kidney bean and other edible beans: HARICOT

kidney disease: NEPHRITIS

kidney removal by surgery: NEPHRECTOMY

kill by choking: STRANGLE

kill or destroy a large portion of: DECIMATE

killing action: QUIETUS

killing of a human being by another: HOMICIDE

killing of a king: REGICIDE

killing of a legislative bill by a chief executive: VETO

killing of one's brother or one's countrymen: FRATRICIDE

kind disposition: BENIGN

kind, sort, class: ILK

kind or type, as in art of literature: GENRE

kindly disposed, auspicious: PROPITIOUS

King Arthur's legendary court site: CAMELOT

king-killing: REGICIDE

king's deputy who rules a country, colony, etc.: VICEROY

kinship, nearness: PROPINQUITY

kissing: OSCULATION

kitchen utensil with small holes through which potatoes and other foods are pressed: RICER

knack: INSTINCT

knapsack: RUCKSACK

knee inflammation: HOUSEMAID'S KNEE

knee tendon: HAMSTRING

kneel on one knee, as in worship: GENUFLECT

knickknacks: BRIC-A-BRAC

knife with blade at right angles to the handle: FROE

knife with blade folded in that springs open when a button is pressed: SWITCH-BLADE KNIFE

knife-sharpening stone: WHETSTONE

knife that is swordlike: SNICKERSNEE

knife with a handle at each end: DRAWKNIFE

knitted fabric, machine made: TRICOT

knitted to follow the contour of the leg or body: FULL FASHIONED

knitting stitch that gives a ribbed appearance: PURL

knob, knot, or swelling: NODE

knobby: TOROSE

knock about or cuff: BUFFET

knock-kneed: VALGUS

knot or bun of hair worn by women at the back of the head: CHIGNON

knot that forms a loop having no free ends: HARNESS HITCH

known or able to be known, characterized by awareness: PRESENTATIVE

knowing all things, all-knowing: OMNISCIENT

knowing or perceiving: COGNITION

knowing something before it occurs: PRE-
SCIENCE
knowledge, skill: EXPERTISE
knowledge derived from sense perception:
PERCEPT
knowledge of something without conscious attention or reasoning: INTU-
ITION

knowledge of the right thing to say or do:
SAVOIR-FAIRE
knowledge or cognition as a subject of
study: EPISTEMOLOGY
knowledge or familiarity of a subject:
CONVERSANT
knowledge that is superficial: SCIOLISM
knowledgeable: GNOSTIC

L

"l" pronounced like "r" or "w," or "r" pronounced like "w": LALLATION

label someone as infamous: BRAND

labored, clumsy: PONDEROUS

laborer on river vessels or on the waterfront: ROUSTABOUT

labor, toil: TRAVAIL

lace in which patterns are held together by connecting threads rather than by a net ground: GUIPURE

lack, scarcity, famine: DEARTH

lack of energy: ANERGY

lack of power or ability, impotence: IMPUISSANCE

lackadaisical: LANGUID

lackadaisical, indifferent, apathetic: LISTLESS

lacking animation, weak, listless: LANGUID

lacking any easing: UNMITIGATED

lacking common measure or standard of comparison: INCOMMENSURABLE

lacking fulfillment, unsuccessful: MANQUÉ

lacking particular character, not distinctive: NONDESCRIPT

lacking understanding: PURBLIND

ladder hung over the side of a ship: ACCOMMODATION LADDER

lady's maid: ABIGAIL

lag, follow slowly, drag in the mud: DRABBLE

lamb chunks broiled on a skewer: SHASHLIK

lamb or other meat chunks skewered and broiled with tomatoes, onions, peppers: SHISH KEBAB

lambskin or calfskin that is untanned: KIP

lament, woeful tale, complaint: JEREMIAD

lamentation or mourning in verse or song: ELEGY

lamentation or wailing for the deceased: KEEN

lamp with light directed upward by a bowl reflector: TORCHIER

land, usually a narrow piece, extending into a body of water and connecting two larger land masses: ISTHMUS

land between hills, especially along a river: INTERVALE

land cultivation based on scientific principles: AGRONOMY

land extending in a narrow point from the shore into the water: SPIT

land extending into the sea, the high point of it: PROMONTORY

land or soil capable of being cultivated: ARABLE

land or water vehicle or creature: AMPHIBIAN

land projecting into water: PENINSULA

land strip plowed or cleared to prevent spread of fire: FIREBREAK

land tenure or distribution: AGRARIAN

landing of a plane using only electronic signals: INSTRUMENT LANDING

landing of a spacecraft on water: SPLASHDOWN

landlord who lets slum dwellings run down: SLUMLORD

language, as a science or a study: LINGUISTICS

language, idiom, speaking style: PARLANCE

language, usually hybrid, that is used as a common speech by people having different tongues: LINGUA FRANCA

language invented for international use: ESPERANTO

language lacking sincere meaning or intention: RHETORIC

language or grammatical forms that are customary: USAGE

language mixture: POLYGLOT

language native to an area, common rather than literary language: VERNACULAR

language study that assumes a formal system of signs and examines their nature and arrangement: STRUCTURAL LINGUISTICS

language that conceals: AESOPIAN LANGUAGE

language that is deliberately ambiguous and deceptive (Orwell coinage): NEWSPEAK

language, informal and substandard, that consists of coined words and new meanings of existing words: SLANG

language theory that stresses tagmemes, the smallest meaningful grammatical forms: TAGMEMICS

language's smallest meaningful unit: MORPHEME

lapel of a coat: REVERS

large, as capital letters: MAJUSCULE

large groups involved: MACROSCOPIC

large system regarded as a unity: MACROCOSM

lasso, lariat: RIATA

last, often inferior, remnant: RUMP

last part or remnant, usually of no further use: FAG END

last stage of any journey or project: HOMESTRETCH

last syllable of a word: ULTIMA

lasting a short time, transitory, fleeting: EPHEMERAL

lasting condition, sometimes specifically for life: PERPETUITY

lasting or continuing a long time: CHRONIC

lasting through the year: PERENNIAL

late blossoming: SEROTINOUS

latest fashion or word: DERNIER CRI

Latin American term for a foreigner, especially an American or Englishman: GRINGO

latitude, additional space for freedom of action: LEEWAY

laugh at with contempt: DERIDE

laugh immoderately or noisily: CACHINNATE

laughable or having the power to laugh: RISIBLE

laughing: RIANT

laughter in a loud boisterous burst: GUFFAW

laughter that is uproarious and irrepressible: HOMERIC LAUGHTER

launch at high speed: CATAPULT

lavish, copious, generous: PROFUSE

lavish, bountiful: MUNIFICENT

lavish, overflowing: EXUBERANT

law derived from custom, usage or court opinions: COMMON LAW

lavish, wasteful, extravagant: PRODIGAL

law, especially of a municipal body: ORDINANCE

law and its administration, as a science: JURISPRUDENCE

law based on usage rather than legislation: UNWRITTEN LAW

law of locality not applied to foreign diplomats: DIPLOMATIC IMMUNITY

laws to protect investors against securities frauds: BLUE SKY LAWS

law that limits the time during which a particular legal action may be brought: STATUTE OF LIMITATIONS

law violation less serious than a felony: MISDEMEANOR

lawbreaker whose violations are habitual: SCOFFLAW

lawful: LICIT

lawful act performed in an unlawful way: MISFEASANCE

lawless confusion: ANARCHY

lawmaker, particularly a wise one: SOLON

lawsuit: LITIGATION

lawyer, not highly competent, who deals with small cases: PETTIFOGGER

lawyer expelled from the profession: DISBARRED

lawyer who is unethical or deceitful: SHYSTER

layer, bed, grade: STRATUM

lazy: SHIFTLESS

lazy: SLOTHFUL

lazy, idle: INDOLENT

lazy, useless, futile: OTIOSE

lazy person: SLUGGARD

lazy person, idler: FAINÉANT

lead, inspire, activate, as a group: SPARKPLUG

lead astray: DELUDE

lead-colored: LIVID

leader of a group that follows sheeplike: BELLWETHER

leader of singing in church: PRECENTOR

leader or chief: COCK OF THE WALK

leader or one who sets an example: FUGLEMAN

leader who appeals to prejudices and passions: DEMAGOGUE

leaderless: ACEPHALOUS

leaders of new movements: AVANT GARDE

leadership or domination of one state over another: HEGEMONY

leadership person lacking real power: FIGUREHEAD

leadership quality that captures imagination and inspires loyalty: CHARISMA

leading character in a drama or a cause: PROTAGONIST

leading to: CONDUCIVE

leafy: FOLIATE

leak out, become known: TRANSPIRE

lean, thin: SPARE

lean body structure: ECTOMORPHIC

leaning, lying down, reclining: RECUMBENT

leaning, usually toward something objectionable: PROCLIVITY

leaning, weighing or resting upon something: INCUMBENT

leaning or bent, liking, tendency: INCLINATION

leap year's extra day, Feb. 29: BISSEXTILE

learn the facts, fathom: PLUMB

learned, scholarly: ERUDITE

learned person: PUNDIT

learned person, scholar: SAVANT

learned response: CONDITIONED REFLEX

learner: ABECEDARIAN

learning, branch of: DISCIPLINE

learning or teaching through discovery and investigation: HEURISTICS

least amount possible: AMBSACE

leather produced by some process not using tanning liquor: TAW

leather used for bookbinding: SKIVER

leatherlike: CORIACEOUS

leave one country to settle in another: EMIGRATE

leaves own country to live elsewhere: EMIGRANT

leavetaking or dismissal: CONGÉ

leaving one's faith, party or principles: APOSTASY

lecherous, lewd, obscene: SALACIOUS

lecherous man: SATYR

lecherous or malicious look: LEER

lecture, sermonize: PRELECT

lecture briefly setting forth details: BRIEFING

lecture with diagrams made on blackboard: CHALK TALK

lecturer, tutor, teacher without faculty rank: DOCENT

left- and right-handed: AMBIDEXTROUS

left side as opposed to right side or dexter, especially in heraldry: SINISTER

left side of a vessel as one faces forward: PORT

left-hand page of a book: VERSO

left-handed: SINISTRAL

leftover: REMNANT

leftover part, remainder: RESIDUE

leg or arm stiffness or cramp: CHARLEY HORSE

legs kicked out alternately from a squatting position in this Slavic folk dance by a male: KAZATSKY

legal arrangement by which diplomatic corps members are exempt from local law: DIPLOMATIC IMMUNITY

legal questions to which medical knowledge is applied: MEDICAL JURISPRUDENCE

legal right to use and profit from the property of another: USUFRUCT

legally based; by law: DE JURE

legislative body's calling to account of an administrative official: INTERPELLATION

legislative receptacle, figuratively, for bills to be taken up at a future time: HOPPER

legs far apart: ASTRIDE

leisurely gait: AMBLE

lender who charges illegal rates of interest: LOAN SHARK

lengthened toward the poles: PROLATE

lenient: INDULGENT

lenient, tolerating unusual freedom: PERMISSIVE

lens used in movies or TV that adjusts rapidly for close-up or distance shots while holding focus: ZOOM LENS

less severe, more moderate, milder: MITIGATED

less than one would expect: NOMINAL

lessen: ABATE

lessen: ABRIDGE

lessen in quality or value, make worse: IMPAIR

lessen or diminish: DWINDLE

lessen the guilt or odiousness of an offense: EXTENUATE

lessening of productivity in proportion to increase in expenditure: DIMINISHING RETURNS lessening of speed: RETARDATION

let go, give up: RELINQUISH

let it stand, as a direction used in proof-reading: STET

lethargy: HEBETUDE

letter, long and formal: EPISTLE

letter delivered from same postoffice at which it was posted: DROP LETTER

letter or sound inserted into a word: EPENTHESIS

letter that each member of a group signs: ROUND ROBIN

letters in early Greek and Latin manuscripts resembling rounded modern capitals: UNCIAL

letting business act without regulation: LAISSEZ FAIRE

level land with few or no trees: SAVANNA

level of command: ECHELON

level to the ground, demolish: RAZE

lewd, grossly ribald: ITHYPHALLIC

lewd, lustful: LECHEROUS

lewd, sexually aroused: RANDY

lewd, obscene, lecherous: SALACIOUS

lewd, sexually abandoned: LICENTIOUS

lewd or dissipated person: DEBAUCHEE

lewd or lascivious: LUBRICOUS

lewd or wanton: CYPRIAN

liability or debt gradually extinguished, as by installment payments: AMORTIZED

liability to conviction and punishment: JEOPARDY

liable or possible: CONTINGENT

liable to err, be misled or deceived: FALLIBLE

liable to injury, attack, or criticism: VULNERABLE

liberal or radical political figure: LEFTIST

liberal or unorthodox in attitudes or beliefs: LATITUDINARIAN

liberate, free, emancipate: MANUMIT

lie: FABRICATION

lie: PREVARICATE

lie, equivocate: PALTER

lie, humbug, sham: FLAM

lie or lean in a relaxed manner: LOLL

lie that is trivial and told to be polite or spare someone's feelings: WHITE LIE

life and matter viewed as inseparable: HYLOZOISM

life insurance policy in which the payment is double the face value in case of accidental death: DOUBLE INDEMNITY

life is generated from living organisms only: BIOGENESIS

life is like that: C'EST LA VIE

lifeless, automatic: MECHANICAL

lifeless state: ABIOSIS

life-manifesting: VITAL

life-size drawing or illustration: MACROGRAPH

lift up your hearts: SURSUM CORDA

lifting to test weight or gauge: HEFT

light, according to wavelengths: SPECTRUM

light, airy, spiritual: ETHEREAL

light and frothy dish fixed in that condition by adding beaten egg whites: SOUFFLÉ

light and shade, black and white: CHIAROSCURO

light beam passes over a surface for television or other production: SCAN

light emitted by a substance after exposure to some form of energy: PHOSPHORESENCE

light meal: COLLATION

light or heat ray bent in passage from one medium to another: REFRACTION

light thrown by a candle on one square foot of surface one foot away: FOOTCANDLE

light wind: CAT'S-PAW

light-admitting but not transparent: TRANSLUCENT

lighthearted: BUOYANT

lighthearted, carefree, unconcerned: INSOUCIANT

lighthearted, gay, carefree: ROLLICKING

lighthouse: PHAROS

lightness, gaiety that is inappropriate, frivolity, fickleness: LEVITY

lightning without thunder, in fitful play usually near horizon on hot evenings: HEAT LIGHTNING

light-producing or light-conveying: LUMINIFEROUS

light-resistant, dull: OPAQUE

light up, make clear, enlighten, illuminate: IRRADIATE

light-wave or sound-wave change that seems to accompany change in distance between source and observer: DOPPLER EFFECT

like it or not: WILLY-NILLY

likeness, image, representation, usually crudely done of a disliked person: EFFIGY

likeness in sound: ASSONANCE

likening one thing to something else in a

figure of speech using "like" or "as": SIMILE

liking, tendency, trend, leaning or bent: INCLINATION

liking for something: PENCHANT

limber, bending easily and gracefully: LITHE

limit freedom: TRAMMEL

limit or range, as of power or action: TETHER

limited as by human or natural conditions: FINITE

limited, narrow, provincial: PAROCHIAL

limitless: AD INFINITUM

limitless or vast: INFINITE

limits: AMBIT

line, as of men or ships, enclosing an area: CORDON

line over a vowel indicating long sound: MACRON

line that slants, used in printing or writing: VIRGULE

linear markings: STRIATION

lined: LINEATE

linen for a household: NAPERY

lines that make up a page, an article, an ad, etc.: LINAGE

linger or walk aimlessly: LOITER

lingo, cant: JARGON

linguistical study of the structure of words: MORPHOLOGY

link, connection, bond,: NEXUS

linked things or events: CONCATENATION

lion-like: LEONINE

lip deformity consisting of a cleft, usually on the upper lip: HARELIP

liplike: LABIATE

liqueurs served in layers: POUSSE-CAFÉ

liquid measure of about 63 gallons: HOGSHEAD

liquid medicine: POTION

liquid poured ceremonially, as in honor of a deity: LIBATION

liquor mixed with water, soda, ginger ale, etc. and served in a tall glass: HIGH-BALL

liquor quantity, a fifth of a gallon: FIFTH

list, with definitions, of technical, obscure or foreign words of a work or field: GLOSSARY

list of acknowledgments in film or TV show: CREDITS

list of acknowledgments in film or TV show that moves vertically on screen: CRAWL

list of articles on hand with description and quantity of each: INVENTORY

list of candidates: SLATE

list of goods being shipped: WAYBILL

list of merchandise sent or services rendered; including price to purchaser: INVOICE

list of names: ROSTER

list of securities held by a person or an institution: PORTFOLIO

list of supplications, with a fixed response after each: LITANY

listen: HARK

listen in at a college class: AUDIT

listless: LACKADAISICAL

listless, inactive, indolent: SUPINE

listless, lacking animation, weak: LANGUID

listless discontent or weariness, boredom: ENNUI

literal translation of word or construction from one language to another: LOAN TRANSLATION

literary club: ATHENEUM

literary composition in a mixture of languages: MACARONIC

literary effort that is labored and pedantic: LUCUBRATION

literary study or scholarship: PHILOLOGY

literary work that is short, depicting something subtly: VIGNETTE

literature: BELLES-LETTRES

literature or art of a cheap, popular or sentimental quality: KITSCH

lithe, pliant, supple, agile: LISSOME

little universe: MICROCOSM

live in distressing conditions: LANGUISH

live or reside in, occupy as a home: INHABIT

live passively, monotonously, dully: VEGETATE

live together: COHABIT

live well at another's expense: BATTEN

lively, active, spirited: VIVACIOUS

lively, aggressive: FEISTY

lively, brisk, dashing, self-confident: JAUNTY

lively, changeable, volatile: MERCURIAL

lively, cheerful, urbane: DEBONAIR

lively, energetic: VIBRANT

lively, quickly, briskly, in music: VIVACE

lively, racy: PIQUANT

lively, saucy: PERT

lively in one's behavior: TITTUP

lively or playful movement in music:
SCHERZO
lively person: GRIG
lively spirits, vivacity, gaiety, sparkle:
EFFERVESCENCE
livelihood, food, means of support: SUS-
TENANCE
liveliness: ALACRITY
liveliness: BRIO
living together of dissimilar organisms,
usually in a mutually advantageous
partnership: SYMBIOSIS
liver inflammation: HEPATITIS
Liverpool resident: LIVERPUDLIAN
load a missile can lift and carry to a target:
THROW-WEIGHT
loafer, spendthrift: WASTREL
loafer or idler who lives off others: DRONE
loan or prepayment of money from public
funds: IMPREST
loan that may be terminated at any time:
CALL LOAN
loathesome, hateful, repugnant, disgusting: ODIOUS
loathing: ABHORRENCE
lobby, entrance hall: FOYER
lobster liver, considered a delicacy: TOM-
ALLEY
local road: VICINAL ROAD
lockjaw: TRISMUS
lodging for soldiers in a private home:
BILLET
lodging place that is part-time or temporary: PIED-À-TERRE
lofty, impressive, noble, as in quality or
style: SONOROUS
logic formula in which two premises are
laid down and a conclusion is drawn
from them: SYLLOGISM
logic, reasoning from general to particular: DEDUCTION
logical argument in examining ideas or
opinions: DIALECTIC
logical rather than intuitive: DIANOETIC
loincloth or waistcloth of printed calico
worn by Samoan natives: LAVA-LAVA
loiter or waste time: DAWDLE
London press: FLEET STREET
Londoner of East End: COCKNEY
long and polysyllabic, as of words: SES-
QUIPEDALIAN
long and wordy, tedious: PROLIX
long jump, as formerly known: BROAD-
JUMP

long life: LONGEVITY
long live: VIVE
longing for something distant in time or
place: NOSTALGIA
long-drawn-out explanation or narrative:
MEGILLAH
longheaded: DOLICHOCEPHALIC
long-sleeved robe, sashed, worn in Mediterranean countries: CAFTAN
long-winded: DIFFUSE
long-windedness: CIRCUMLOCUTION
look, countenance, face: VISAGE
look at closely, scrutinize: SCAN
look like or act like someone or something: SIMULATE
look or appearance lacking reality: SEM-
BLANCE
look that implies malice, lechery or sly-
ness: LEER
loose, not rigid: LAX
loose, weak: SLACK
loose morals: WANTON
lopsided, unsymmetrical: SKEWED
Los Angeles resident: LOS ANGELENO, LOS
ANGELEAN, ANGELINO
lose heart, withdraw in fear: QUAIL
losing contender or one expected to lose:
UNDERDOG
loss from sale of assets: CAPITAL LOSS
loss of an unaccented vowel at the beginning of a word: APHESIS
loss of income anticipated from eventual
reduction in supply of natural resources: DEPLETION
loss of memory: AMNESIA
loss of muscular coordination: ATAXIA
loss of power of speech: APHASIA
loss of sight without organic defect:
AMAUROSIS
lottery, often based on a horse race, in
which all the wagers may be won by
one or a few bettors: SWEEPSTAKES
loud, full-sounding: SONOROUS
loud, rough in sound: RAUCOUS
loud and abusive: THERSITICAL
loud and noisy: UPROARIOUS
loud to an extreme: STENTORIAN
loudness measure: DECIBEL
loud-voiced person: STENTOR
Louisiana descendant of the Acadian
French: CAJUN
louse infestation: PEDICULOSIS
love affair that is secret or illicit: IN-
TRIGUE

love feast: AGAPE

love insincerely (applied to a man): PHI-LANDER

love letter: BILLET-DOUX

love of mankind: ALTRUISM

love of women: PHILOGYNY

love potion: PHILTER

lover or gallant of a married woman: CI-CISBEO

lover or illicit sexual companion: PAR-AMOUR

lovers, secret meeting of: ASSIGNATION

low neckline in a dress: DECOLLETAGE

lowdown, rumor, gossip: SCUTTLEBUTT

lower: NETHER

lower in dignity or reputation: DEMEAN

lower middle class: PETITE BOURGEOISIE

lower oneself to do something: CONDE-SCEND

lower price on a stock transaction than on the preceding transaction: DOWN TICK, MINUS-TICK

lower someone in prestige or estimation: ABASE

lowering of esteem: DISPARAGEMENT

lowest point: NADIR

lowest point in an orbit: PERIGEE

low-priced stocks, selling at less than $1 a share: PENNY STOCKS

loyal: STAUNCH

loyal adherent: MYRMIDON

loyalty, obligation owed, faithfulness: FEALTY

loyalty or friendship weakened or destroyed: DISAFFECTION

lozenge, medicated as for a sore throat: TROCHE

lucid, clear, understandable: PERSPICUOUS

lucid, pure, clear, transparent: LIMPID

lucky discoveries made accidentally: SERENDIPITY

lucky stroke, good luck: FLUKE

ludicrous or ridiculous situation: FARCE

lukewarm: TEPID

lumbering, bulky: PONDEROUS

luminous or glowing with heat: INCAN-DESCENT

lump or bump, protuberance: KNURL

lunatic or maniac: DEMONIAC

lurch or twist from side to side: CAREEN

lust for or desire something belonging to someone else: COVET

lust or sexual desire: CONCUPISCENCE

lustful: LASCIVIOUS

lustful: LIBIDINOUS

lustful, dissolute: WANTON

lustful, lewd: LECHEROUS

lustful, amorous: RANDY

luxurious, sensual: VOLUPTUOUS

luxury-loving person: VOLUPTUARY

lying: MENDACIOUS

lying abnormally: MYTHOMANIA

lying down, growing along the ground: DECUMBENT

lying down, reclining, leaning: RECUM-BENT

lying down or reclining: COUCHANT

lying face down: PRONE

lying flat, helpless, exhausted: PROSTRATE

lying on the back, face upward: SUPINE

lying under oath: PERJURY

M

machine for giving gloss to paper or fabric: CALENDER

"madam-I'm-Adam" type of sentence: PALINDROME

maddened, furiously angry: HORN-MAD

made to order: BESPOKE

Madrid resident: MADRILENIAN, MADRILEÑO

magic: CONJURATION

magic: THEURGY

magic tricks: PRESTIDIGITATION

magic tricks: SLEIGHT OF HAND

magic word: ABRACADABRA

magic words or formula: INCANTATION

magical, mystical or divinatory arts: OCCULT

magical, occult, relating to alchemy: HERMETIC

magician: THAUMATURGE

magician or sorcerer: CONJURER

magnifying glass used by jewelers or watchmakers: LOUPE

maid to a lady, lady's maid: ABIGAIL

maiden name of a married woman: NÉE

mail sent without charge as by congressmen: FRANKED MAIL

main clause of a sentence at the beginning: LOOSE SENTENCE

main clause of the sentence at the end: PERIODIC SENTENCE

main course of a meal: ENTREE

main dish or chief item in a collection: PIÈCE DE RÉSISTANCE

main idea or substance of an argument, discussion, question: GIST

Main resident: MAINER

maintainable, defendable: TENABLE

majestic: AUGUST

make amends for, atone for: EXPIATE

make eyes at suggestively, stare at: OGLE

make faces: GRIMACE

make known, disclose, bestow: IMPART

make merry, delight (in), celebrate: REVEL

make noteworthy or call attention to: SIGNALIZE

make or become better: AMELIORATE

make outwardly real: EXTERNALIZE

make over, renovate: REVAMP

make poor or fruitless: IMPOVERISH

make specific: CONCRETIZE

make up, compensate: COUNTERVAIL

make up or devise: CONCOCT

make up or invent as a story or lie: FABRICATE

making sense: COHERENT

makeup of a book, newspaper, etc.: FORMAT

male adoption of female clothing and mannerisms: EONISM

male and female sexual organs in one individual: HERMAPHRODITE

male ballet dancer: DANSEUR

male ballet dancer who is the principal performer: PREMIER DANSEUR

male counterpart of a ballerina: DANSEUR NOBLE

male figure used as a supporting pillar: TELAMON

male figure with pointed ears, horns and goat's legs, in Greek mythology: SATYR

male flirt: PHILANDERER

male genitals subjected to oral contact: FELLATIO

male government: PATRIARCHY

male homosexual: URANIST, URNING

male line relationship: AGNATION

male of beef cattle: STEER

male sex hormone: ANDROSTERONE, TESTOSTERONE

male singer in the principal position: PRIM'ORO

male sterilization by surgery: VASECTOMY

malevolent: ILL-DISPOSED

malformation: ABNORMALITY

malice, hate: RANCOR

malice, spite: VENOM

malicious, cutting: SNIDE

malicious, fierce, unruly: VICIOUS

malicious, unprovoked, unjust: WANTON

malicious, wicked: PERNICIOUS

malicious, wishing evil toward others: MALEVOLENT

malicious or lecherous look: LEER

malicious or mean behavior: DOGGERY

malignant, as a disease: VIRULENT

malnutrition: CACHEXIA

mammals bringing forth living young: VIVIPAROUS

man about town: BOULEVARDIER

man as center: ANTHROPOCENTRIC

man hatred: MISANDRY

man in relation to environment: ANTHROPONOMY

man of great beauty: ADONIS

man supported by a woman to whom he is not married: GIGOLO

man to whom a woman is engaged: FIANCÉ

man who dresses flashily: DUDE

manage shrewdly: MANIPULATE

manage to live: SUBSIST

manageable, compliant: TRACTABLE

management or superintendance: INTENDANCE

manager, sponsor or organizer of performers for entertainment: IMPRESARIO

manager of another's affairs: PROCURATOR

Manchester native: MANCUNIAN

maneuver, especially in diplomacy: DÉMARCHE

maneuver, trick, device for obtaining advantage: STRATAGEM

maneuver by craftiness: FINAGLE

maneuver for an advantage: JOCKEY

maneuver or stratagem to outwit someone: PLOY

maneuvering, methods or management to gain an end: TACTICS

maneuvering with ploys to gain an advantage: GAMESMANSHIP

mangle, cut unskillfully, hack: HAGGLE

mangle, tear raggedly: LACERATE

manhandle, abuse, handle roughly: MAUL

mania: CACOETHES

maniac or lunatic: DEMONIAC

manias.

(In the following listing read the words "obsession with" ahead of each entry.)

alcoholic liquor: DIPSOMANIA

animals: ZOOMANIA

ballet: BALLETOMANIA

bees: APIMANIA

birds: ORNITHOMANIA

books: BIBLOMANIA

cats: AILUROMANIA

children: PEDOMANIA

crowds: OCHLOMANIA

dancing: CHOREOMANIA

dogs: CYNOMANIA

eating: SITOMANIA

fire: PYROMANIA

fish: ICHTHYOMANIA

flowers: ANTHOMANIA

gaiety: CHEROMANIA

grandiose things: MEGALOMANIA

horses: HIPPOMANIA

ideas: IDEOMANIA

insects: ENTOMOMANIA

money: CHREMATOMANIA

nakedness: GYMNOMANIA

one subject or thing: MONOMANIA

pleasure: HEDONOMANIA

reptiles: OPHIDIOMANIA

roaming: DROMOMANIA

solitude: AUTOMANIA

speech: LALOMANIA

stealing: KLEPTOMANIA

stillness: EREMIOMANIA

travel: HODOMANIA

wealth: PLUTOMANIA

women: GYNEMANIA

manic-depressive condition that is mild: CYCLOTHYMIA

manifest, demonstrate convincingly, show clearly: EVINCE

manifest, evident, obvious: PATENT

manifestation or appearance of a deity, a showing forth: EPIPHANY

manipulation of parts of the body to correct diseases: OSTEOPATHY

mankind hater: MISANTHROPE

manlike: ANDROID

manlike apes and man: HOMINOIDS

manly vigor: VIRILITY

manner: MIEN

manner in which one bears oneself, deportment: DEMEANOR

manner of operating: MODUS OPERANDI

manner of speech: LOCUTION

mannerism, personal peculiarity: QUIRK

mannerism, quirk, habit peculiar to an individual: IDIOSYNCRASY

man's nature regarded as consisting of decisive actions rather than inner dispositions: EXISTENTIALISM

manual guidebook: HANDBOOK

manual or handbook: ENCHIRIDION

manual skill, expertness: HANDINESS

manual training system: SLOYD

manual worker: BLUE COLLAR

manuscript copier: AMANUENSIS

manuscript of a play, film, or television show: SCRIPT

manuscript sheets gathered into a unified whole: COLLATED

man-woman relationship without sexual activity: PLATONIC

many and varied forms: MANIFOLD

many-sided: VERSATILE

map making: CARTOGRAPHY

map of the earth with parallel longitude lines intersected by parallel latitude lines: MERCATOR PROJECTION

map or survey used for taxation basis: CADASTER

mapping of regions or districts: CHOROGRAPHY

mapping or charting of area in detail: TOPOGRAPHY

marble used for shooting: TAW

marginal note of explanation: SCHOLIUM

marginal, not essential: PERIPHERAL

marine animal and plant organisms that drift or float: PLANKTON

mark or mark as infamous: BRAND

mark, stamp or character that is distinctive: IMPRESS

mark between parts of a compound word: HYPHEN

mark like a hook under letter ç: CEDILLA

mark of authenticity: CACHET

mark of identification: EARMARK

mark of infamy or disgrace: STIGMA

mark or proof of genuineness or high quality: HALLMARK

mark out boundaries or limits, separate: DEMARCATE

mark out limits: CIRCUMSCRIBE

marked with lines, striped: LINEATE

marker or memorial of heaped-up stones: CAIRN

market, outdoor, for dealing in second-hand goods: FLEA MARKET

market on the decline: BEAR MARKET

market on the rise: BULL MARKET

marketable: VENDIBLE

marketplace: AGORA

markings of a spotted animal or plant: MACULATION

markings on an envelope used in place of stamps: INDICIA

marriage a man is forced into because of sexual relations with the woman: SHOTGUN WEDDING

marriage after the death or divorce of first spouse: DIGAMY

marriage between unequals in which titles and estates are not passed on to the inferior partner: MORGANATIC

marriage broker, Jewish: SCHATCHEN

marriage for the second time: DEUTEROGAMY

marriage in trial form: COMPANIONATE MARRIAGE

marriage relationship: CONJUGAL

marriage with one of lower position: MÉSALLIANCE

marriage within the group or tribe, inbreeding: ENDOGAMY

marriageable because of physical maturity: NUBILE

married male American Indian: SANNUP

married man: BENEDICT

married state: CONNUBIAL

married woman: FEME COVERT

married woman's acknowledged lover or gallant: CICISBEO

married woman's legal status: COVERTURE

marrying while still married: BIGAMY

marsh, bog: MORASS

marshy body of water: BAYOU

marshy ground, bog: QUAGMIRE

marshy low ground: SWALE

martini served with pickled onion: GIBSON

marvelous, wonderful: PRODIGIOUS

marvelous or wonderful to tell: MIRABILE DICTU

masculine, strong, sturdy: VIRILE

masculine woman: AMAZON

masculinity: VIRILITY

masculinity, aggressive virility: MACHISMO

mask for the eyes, worn at masquerades: DOMINO

masochism or sadism: ALGOLAGNIA

mass, heap or collection of things: CONGERIES

mass of things indiscriminately thrown together: AGGLOMERATE

Massachusetts resident: MASSACHUSETT- SAN, BAY STATER

massacre, especially directed against Jews: POGROM

massacre or slaughter: CARNAGE

masses: DEMOS

masses, common people: HOI POLLOI

masses, pertaining to: DEMOTIC

mast or boom on a sailboat: SPAR

master of technique: VIRTUOSO

masterpiece, great work: MAGNUM OPUS

masterstroke, sudden telling blow, brilliant stratagem: COUP

masturbation or interruption of coitus: ONANISM

matchless: INIMITABLE

matchless, unequaled: NONPAREIL

mate or complement to another: COUNTERPART

material, real, having definite shape: TANGIBLE

materialize, concretize: REIFY

maternal or female line of a family: DISTAFF SIDE

mathematical sequence in which the ratio between each two numbers is the same: GEOMETRIC PROGRESSION

mathematical term indicating parts into which the whole is to be divided: DENOMINATOR

mathematics is incapable of expressing it in rational numbers: SURD

matter and energy, as a science: PHYSICS

mattress of straw: PALLIASSE

mature: FULL-FLEDGED

maxim: APOTHEGM

maxim: AXIOM

maxim, rule, moral guide: PRECEPT

maxim, wise saying: GNOME

maze, an intricate structure: LABYRINTH

meal: REPAST

meal, particularly dinner: PRANDIAL

meal at which guests serve themselves: BUFFET

meal served in a restaurant complete at a fixed price: TABLE D'HÔTE

meal that is light: REFECTION

meal that is light and informal: COLLATION

meals and room included in hotel rate: AMERICAN PLAN

mean: PETTY

mean or malicious behavior: DOGGERY

mean or stingy practice: CHEESE-PARING

meaning, purport, general course: TENOR

meaning of language forms: SEMANTIC

meaning that is exact as stated: LITERAL

meaning that is suggested, significance: PURPORT

meaningless, merely sociable, as applied to talk: PHATIC

meaningless, worthless: NUGATORY

meaningless performance: CHARADE

meaningless speech: BALDERDASH

meaningless talk: ABRACADABRA

meanings of language forms, as a subject of study: SEMANTICS

means of support, livelihood, food: SUSTENANCE

meantime, time between periods or events: INTERIM

measure, especially by the hand, with thumb and little finger extended: SPAN

measure of length for yarn: SPINDLE

measure that is practical rather than scientifically accurate: RULE OF THUMB

measure the depth of water with, or plumb: PLUMB

measured from side to side: BREADTH

measurement of advertising space: AGATE LINE

measurement of distance by determination of angles: TELEMETRY

meat and vegetable stew and its broth: POT-AU-FEU

meat broiled on a skewer: BROCHETTE

meat chunks marinated: KEBAB

meat pie topped with mashed potatoes: SHEPHERD'S PIE

meat portion, that is small: COLLOP

mechanical man, automaton: ROBOT

mechanical way of doing something or doing it solely by memory: ROTE

meddle, intrude in the affairs of others: INTERLOPE

meddler in the affairs of others: KIBITZER

mediating factor between opposite things: TERTIUM QUID

medical auxiliary or assistant: PARAMEDIC

medical graduate serving in and living at a hospital for clinical training: INTERN

medical knowledge applied to questions of law: FORENSIC MEDICINE medical oath setting forth a code of ethics: HIPPOCRATIC OATH

medical profession symbol, wand or staff of Mercury: CADUCEUS

medical technique employing needles inserted into body: ACUPUNCTURE

medical term for the branch of medicine dealing with functions and diseases of women: GYNECOLOGY

medical-appearing substance given to comfort a patient or as a test control: PLACEBO

medicinal liquid injected into the colon as a purgative: ENEMA

medicine obtainable without prescription: OFFICINAL

medicine of one's own invention, quack medicine, cure-all: NOSTRUM

medicine that causes vomiting: EMETIC

medicine that eases irritation: ABIRRITANT

medicine that increases flow of urine: DIURETIC

medicines described and listed in a book: PHARMACOPOEIA

medieval chemistry: ALCHEMY

mediocre: INDIFFERENT

mediocre, prosaic, dull: PEDESTRIAN

meditate or ponder: RUMINATE

medium, moderate, in music: MEZZO

medley: SALMAGUNDI

medley, confused mixture: FARRAGO

medley, mixture: POTPOURRI

meek, apologetic, shy person:MILQUETOAST

meeting at the same point, simultaneous: CONCURRENT

meeting or secret appointment, as of lovers: TRYST

meeting place, meeting or appointment to meet: RENDEZVOUS

meeting to confer on a particular subject: SYMPOSIUM

melancholy: ATRABILIOUS

melancholy, gloomy: SEPULCHRAL

melancholy, pessimism, romantic world-weariness: WELTSCHMERZ

Melbourne resident: MELBURNIAN

melodic: ARIOSE

melodious, soothing, pleasant: DULCET

melodious or musical: CANOROUS

melody added to another melody: COUNTERPOINT

melting: LIQUESCENT

members or items chosen out of a group in the expectation they will be representative of the whole group: RANDOM SAMPLE

membership on a stock exchange: SEAT

memorable or prominent object in the landscape: LANDMARK

memorandum to remind one of something in the future: TICKLER

memory: RETENTION

memory aid: MNEMONIC

memory alone as a way of doing something, mechanical action: ROTE

memory blocks, speech errors or faulty actions: PARAPRAXIS

memory involving clear visualization of objects previously seen: EIDETIC IMAGERY

memory loss: AMNESIA

memory loss concerning muscular movements: APRAXIA

menacing, threatening: MINACIOUS, MINATORY

men's clothes and matters pertaining thereto: SARTORIAL

men's furnishings: HABERDASHERY

menstruation cessation: MENOPAUSE

mental age times 100 divided by chronological age: INTELLIGENCE QUOTIENT (IQ)

mental confusion: AMENTIA

mental derangement: ALIENATION

mental disorder marked by separation of thought from emotions: SCHIZOPHRENIA

mental disorders treated by study of the unconscious: PSYCHOANALYSIS

mental lapse: ABERRATION

mental or emotional block: INHIBITION

mental position, frame of mind: POSTURE

mental powers impaired: DEMENTIA

mental quickness, keenness: ACUMEN

mental telepathy: CRYPTESTHESIA

mental torpor, pathological: ACEDIA

mentally deficient person: AMENT

mentally retarded person: IMBECILE

mentally unsound: NON COMPOS MENTIS

mention of something by saying it will not be mentioned: APOPHASIS

mention or suggest for the first time: BROACH

menu with each item having a separate price: A LA CARTE

mercenary, subject to bribery: VENAL

merciless: RUTHLESS

merciless, unrelenting: IMPLACABLE

mercy killing: EUTHANASIA

merge gradually one into another: IN-TERGRADE

merging into one of two vowels generally pronounced separately: SYNERESIS

merited or deserved, as a punishment: CONDIGN

merriment or spirited gaiety: MIRTH

merry-go-round: WHIRLIGIG

mess, confused condition: MARE'S NEST

messenger, especially one on urgent or diplomatic business: COURIER

messiah or prohet in Islam: MAHDI

metal condition, as regards hardness and elasticity: TEMPER

metal disk or spangle: PAILLETTE

metal-and-enamel work: CLOISONNÉ

metals and alloys, as a science: METAL-LURGY

metalware with enameled or lacquered design: TOLE

metaphorical, flowery: FIGURATIVE

meter mixed within a poem: LOGAOEDIC

Mexican dish of hot-seasoned meat and corn, wrapped in corn husks: TA-MALES

Mexican farm laborer who enters United States illegally: WETBACK

Mexican flat, round cake: TORTILLA

Mexican strong, alcoholic liquor: TE-QUILA

Michigan resident: MICHIGANITE, MICHI-GANDER

microscopic, small to the point of being incalculable: INFINITESIMAL

middle class: BOURGEOIS

middle number in a series of statistics: MEDIAN

middle way: VIA MEDIA

middleman handling transactions between company issuing new securities and the public: INVESTMENT BANKER

midget, dwarf: HOMUNCULUS

midway in the action rather than at the start: IN MEDIAS RES

mighty, powerful: PUISSANT

mild, gentle, favorable: BENIGN

mild or bland word substituted for one that might give offense or pain: EUPHE-MISM

milder, less severe, more moderate: MITI-GATED

mildly given reproof: ADMONITION

milieu: AMBIENCE

military aircraft on a single mission: SOR-TIE

military class in command of the government: STRATOCRACY

military court: COURT-MARTIAL

military detachment designated to do a particular job: DETAIL

military equipment and supplies: MA-TERIEL

military equipment of the heavy variety: HARDWARE

military headgear with visor and a flat top: KEPI

military materiel, cannon: ORDNANCE

military persecution: DRAGONNADE

military position taken on enemy side of a river, defile, etc.: BRIDGEHEAD

military science that deals with procurement, maintenance, movement, disposition of all supplies and personnel: LOGISTICS

milk included: AU LAIT

milklike: LACTESCENT

milk fermented by a bacterium: YOGURT

milk from mare or camel, fermented: KUMISS

milk's thin part that separates from solids, as in making cheese: WHEY

milky: LACTEAL

milky liquid: EMULSION

million tons of TNT as the measurement of an explosive: MEGATON

mimic, play the part of: IMPERSONATE

mind controlling matter: PSYCHOKINESIS

mineral springs treatment of disease: BALNEOLOGY

mingle in a friendly fashion with people of an enemy or conquered country: FRATERNIZE

minor, secondary, casual: INCIDENTAL

minor league of no note: BUSH LEAGUE

minority incursion into a neighborhood used to frighten homeowners into selling: BLOCKBUSTING

miracles, as a study: THAUMATOLOGY

mirage, especially as observed in the Strait of Messina: FATA MORGANA

mirror between two windows: PIER GLASS

mirror for signaling by flashes of light: HELIOGRAPH

mirror hung on horizontal pivots in a frame: CHEVAL GLASS

misapply, distort: PERVERT

misappropriate or embezzle: DEFALCATE

miscarry: ABORT
miscarry, said of animals: SLINK
miscellany: POTPOURRI
mischief, joke: WAGGERY
mischief-maker: HELLION
mischievous, harmful: MALEFICENT
misconduct of an official: MISPRISION
miser: SKINFLINT
miserable person: WRETCH
miserliness: PARSIMONY
miserly: AVARICIOUS
miserly, hard man: SCROOGE
misery, suffering: TRIBULATION
misfortune: AMBSACE
misgiving, fear: QUALM
mishaps in actions, speech, or memory:
    PARAPRAXIS
mislead: BAMBOOZLE
mislead: DELUDE
mislead or deceive: EQUIVOCATE
misleading talk: HUMBUG
mismated, conflicting, discordant: IN-
    COMPATIBLE
misrepresent: BELIE
misrepresent, twist, bend: DISTORT
missile with two or more warheads aimed
    at separate targets: MIRV
missile's forward separable section de-
    signed to stand intense heat: NOSE
    CONE
missile's nose containing the explosive:
    WARHEAD
misstroke or misplay: FOOZLE
mist or fog: BRUME
mistake, error, false step: FAUX PAS
mistress of any fashionable household:
    CHATELAINE
misty, unclear, dark: MURKY
misuse of words: CATACHRESIS
miswriting of words or phrases generally
    caused by cerebral injury: PARA-
    GRAPHIA
mix up, confuse: DISORIENT
mix up ingredients for a drink or a dish:
    CONCOCT
mixed fruits or vegetables used as dessert
    or salad: MACEDOINE
mixed metaphor: CATACHRESIS
mixed meter in a poem: LOGAOEDIC
mixed origin, half-breed: HYBRID
mixed-up: ADDLED,   ADDLE-BRAINED,
    ADDLEHEADED, ADDLEPATED
mixture, medley: POTPOURRI
mixture in a society of ethnic, racial, re-

ligious, or cultural groups: PLURAL-
    ISM
mixture in an artistic composition of fea-
    tures from various sources: PASTICHE
mixture of a confused mass of elements:
    MEDLEY
mixture of languages in one literary com-
    position: MACARONIC
mob rule: OCHLOCRACY
mobile-home area: TRAILER PARK
mock, jeer, defy, scoff: FLOUT
mock, joke: JAPE
model, pattern, typical example: EX-
    EMPLAR
model of an apparatus or structure:
    MOCKUP
model of the human body used to show
    off clothes: MANNEQUIN
model or perfect standard: PROTOTYPE
moderate, cautious, opposed to change:
    CONSERVATIVE
moderate, restrained: TEMPERATE
moderate tempo in music: ANDANTE
moderately good, average: RESPECT-
    ABLE
moderation produced by addition of an-
    other element: TEMPER
modest, shy, coy, reserved: DEMURE
modesty: PUDENCY
modification of the causes of a result by
    the result itself: FEEDBACK
moist, damp: HUMID
moisten and rub the body with oil: EM-
    BROCATE
moisture absorbing: DELIQUESCENT
moisture measurement (in the air): HY-
    GROMETRY
mold in which something is cast or
    shaped: MATRIX
moldable: PLASTIC
molding around the walls, close to the
    ceiling: CORNICE
molding or casting of footprints, etc., for
    use in criminal investigation: MOU-
    LAGE
monetary matters: PECUNIARY
money, booty: PELF
money bet or invested by supposedly
    knowing people: SMART MONEY
money carried by a woman on a date to let
    her get home alone if need be: MAD
    MONEY
money changing: AGIOTAGE
money given to one who helped a person

or company obtain a job or contract: KICKBACK

money in circulation lessened, resulting in a decline in prices: DEFLATION

money or assistance furnished to advance a venture: GRUBSTAKE

money paid to a person to prevent his disclosing something: HUSH MONEY

money pooled for any specific purpose: KITTY

money used for corrupt political purposes: SLUSH FUND

money-making: LUCRATIVE

mongolism: DOWN'S SYNDROME

monkey or ape: SIMIAN

monk's haircut, with the crown of the head shaved: TONSURE

monochromatic: HOMOCHROMATIC

monologue: SOLILOQUY

monstrosity, in biology: TERATISM

monstrous act, wickedness: ENORMITY

monthly: MENSAL

monument to a dead person containing no body: CENOTAPH

moo like a cow: LOW

moon's surface, as a subject of scientific study: SELENOGRAPHY

mooring rope or cable: HAWSER

moral corruption: DRY ROT

moral decline or decay: DECADENCE

moral guide, maxim, rule: PRECEPT

moral sense of right and wrong lacking: AMORPHOUS

moralizing, pedantic; DIDACTIC

moralizing, trite: SENTENTIOUS

morally bad: UNSAVORY

morally debased, degraded: SCROFULOUS

morally degraded: DEGENERATE

morally neutral: ADIAPHOROUS

morally unrestrained, unchaste: LIBERTINE

more than one wife or husband at once: POLYGAMY

more than the regular number: SUPERNUMERARY

morning call by bugle or drum signaling the time to rise: REVEILLE

morning song: MATIN

morose, gloomy, grave: SATURNINE

mortal blow or death blow: COUP DE GRACE

mortar that is thin and used to fill crevices between bricks or tiles: GROUT

mosaic pattern: TESSELLATED

mosaic piece, as of stone or glass: TESSERA

mosaic woodwork style, popular in Renaissance Italy: INTARSIA

Moscow resident: MOSCOVITE

Moses books in Bible: TORAH, PENTATEUCH

Moslem law as observed by the orthodox: SUNNA

Moslem prince or commander, especially in Arabia: EMIR

Moslem scholars: ULEMA

Moslem term for devil: SHAITAN

Moslem title of respect for one who has memorized the Koran: HAFIZ

Moslem's sacred book: KORAN

Moslems who slew during Crusades: ASSASSINS

moth or butterfly: LEPIDOPTERAN

mother as the head of the family: MATRIARCHY

mother-of-pearl shellfish: ABALONE

mother worship that is psychologically harmful: MOMISM

mother's side of the family, in kinship: ENATE

motion picture art and production: CINEMATOGRAPHY

motion picture or recording term for an uninterrupted run of a camera or recording apparatus: TAKE

motion study without reference to particular forces or bodies: KINEMATICS

motionless: STOCK-STILL

motionless, not moving: IMMOBILE

motionless with horror or awe: TRANSFIXED

motivating force, incentive: IMPETUS

motivation or reward offered for an action: INDUCEMENT

motor mounted on the rear of a small boat: OUTBOARD MOTOR

mottled, especially in white and black: PIEBALD

motto or quotation prefixed to a book: EPIGRAPH

mound, manmade, often of great size and very old: TUMULUS

mound or small round hill: KNOLL

moundy, hilly: TUMULOSE

mountain base or foot of a mountain: PIEDMONT

mountain mass of separate peaks: MASSIF

mountain nymph: OREAD

mountain range or chain: SIERRA
mountaineering term for descent of a cliff, using a rope: RAPPEL
mountains, as a study: OROGRAPHY
mournful, sad, painful: DOLOROUS
mournful, sad in a ludicrous manner: LUGUBRIOUS
mournful, sorrowful: PLAINTIVE
mournful, wretched: WOEBEGONE
mourning or lamentation in verse or song: ELEGY
mouth, opening: ORIFICE
mouth and its diseases, as a branch of medicine: STOMATOLOGY
mouth gaping, expanse of open mouth: RICTUS
move, especially in diplomacy: DÉMARCHE
move across: TRAVERSE
move ahead slowly but steadily: FORGE
move backward, withdraw: RECEDE
move designed to gain an advantage: GAMBIT
move dreamily or idly: MAUNDER
move heavily and clumsily: FLUMP
move or roll tumultuously: WELTER
move rapidly, scour, search: SKIRR
move sideways: SIDLE
move swiftly and with force: HURTLE
move the camera so as to photograph an entire scene, in movies or television: PAN
move unsteadily or irregularly at sea: YAW
move with exaggerated tosses of the body: FLOUNCE
move with rumbling noise, move clumsily: LUMBER
movement of inanimate objects without apparent external cause: TELEKINESIS
movement or change that is constant: FLUX
movements or strokes that are artful: MANEUVERS
movement or structure that is gracefully proportioned: EURYTHMIC
movie: FLICK
movie change in sound track from original language to another: DUBBING
movie device to translate dialogue from one language to another by superimposing lines on the screen: SUBTITLE
movie making: CINEMATOGRAPHY
movie showing in advance of regular showings: SNEAK PREVIEW

moving abruptly from one condition to another: TRANSILIENT
moving imperceptibly but harmfully: INSIDIOUS
moving in an emotional way, touching: POIGNANT
moving out in a different direction: DIVERGENT
moving rapidly: SPANKING
much, very much, in music: MOLTO
mud or silt deposited by flowing water: SULLAGE
muddle, bewilder, obscure: OBFUSCATE
muddle or confuse: EMBROIL
muddled, confused: TURBID
mug or jug in form of an old man wearing a three-cornered hat: TOBY
multilingual: POLYGLOT
multiply by natural reproduction, breed: PROPAGATE
mumps: PAROTITIS
munch or chew noisily: CHAMP
municipal government by elected commission: COMMISSION PLAN
mural painting using pigments mixed with waterglass: STEREOCHROMY
murder of husband by wife or wife by husband: MARITICIDE
murderous: HOMICIDAL
murmuring softly, rustling, whispering: SUSURRANT
murmuring sound, as of the wind: SOUGH
muscle and bone branch of surgery: ORTHOPEDICS
muscle pain or cramp: MYALGIA
muscle sense: KINESTHESIA
muscle spasm that pulls the head to one side: TORTICOLLIS
muscle that surrounds an opening or tube in the body and can open or close it: SPHINCTER
muscles, as a scientific study: MYOLOGY
muscular coordination loss: ATAXIA
muscular development that is light: ASTHENIC
muscular rigidity and irresponsiveness to stimuli: CATALEPSY
muscular rigidity, stupor, occasional mental agitation: CATATONIA
muscular spasm: CLONUS
muscular strengh: BRAWN
museum or library overseer: CURATOR
music at performer's pleasure: A CAPRICCIO

music by a small group, as a string quartet: CHAMBER MUSIC

music direction calling for slowness: LENTO

music direction to perform very loudly: FORTISSIMO

music lacking tonality because of disregard of key: ATONALITY

music played between stanzas of a hymn or acts of a play: INTERLUDE

music style that is smooth and flowing: LEGATO

music swelling in loudness: CRESCENDO

music tempo that is moderate: ANDANTE

music tempo that is slow: LARGO

music with fast time: ALLEGRO

musical, dramatic or ballet offering given between acts of play or opera: INTERMEZZO

musical bass instrument, large, of brass and having three to five valves: TUBA

musical brass wind instrument with coiled tube and flaring bell: FRENCH HORN

musical brass wind instrument with long, doubled-up tube: TROMBONE

musical composition for a story that is sung but not acted: CANTATA

musical composition for several male voices, having no accompaniment: GLEE

musical composition for solo instruments and orchestra: CONCERTO

musical composition in which a theme is repeated contrapuntally: FUGUE

musical composition on a religious subject for voices and orchestra: ORATORIO

musical composition suggestive of improvisation: RHAPSODY

musical composition that is playful and lively: HUMORESQUE

musical direction meaning more: PIU

musical double-reed woodwind instrument: OBOE

musical flourish: CADENZA

musical instrument in the flute category: PICCOLO

musical instrument like a piano in which strings are plucked: HARPSICHORD

musical instrument that has wooden bars of graduated length that are struck with wooden hammers: XYLOPHONE

musical instrument with double reed and low pitch: ENGLISH HORN

musical instrument with metal bars that produce bell-like tones when struck: GLOCKENSPIEL

musical instrument with metal strings that is played with two small hammers: DULCIMER

musical notation for some stringed instruments that indicates rhythm and fingering: TABULATURE

musical note that ornaments or embellishes a more important note: GRACE NOTE

musical notes that are short and detached: STACCATO

musical or melodious: CANOROUS

musical passage ending a composition: CODA

musical passage or movement that is stately: MAESTOSO

musical piece consisting of parts of different songs: MEDLEY

musical play in a light vein: OPERETTA

musical section once considered essential to a proper performance but now often optional: OBLIGATO

musical sliding effect: GLISSANDO

musical solo composition or an exercise designed to perfect some technique: ETUDE

musical style of West Indies: CALYPSO

musical term for gradual slackening of tempo: RITARDANDO

musical term for medium, moderate: MEZZO

musical term for quick: PRESTO

musical term for slowing down gradually: RALLENTANDO

musical term for slightly, somewhat: POCO

musical term for very fast: PRESTISSIMO

musical term for very soft: PIANISSIMO

musical trembling effect caused by rapid, tiny variations in pitch: VIBRATO

musical use of syllables, as do, re, mi, etc.: SOLMIZATION

musician of eminence or a master in any art: MAESTRO

musing, daydreaming: REVERIE

muslin of a thin weave: TARLATAN

mustard plaster: POULTICE

musty, moldy, old-fashioned: FUSTY

mutilate a book by cutting out the illustrations: GRANGERIZE

mutilation, destruction or alteration, especially of a legal document: SPOLIATION

mutual: RECIPROCAL, BILATERAL
mysterious: ARCANE
mysterious: CABALISTIC
mysterious, defying understanding: IN-SCRUTABLE
mystery story: WHODUNIT
mystic or secret system: CABALA
mystical: ANAGOGIC
mystical poem or song: RUNE

mystical status attributed to a person, an institution, an activity, etc.: MYS-TIQUE
mystifying, secret, hidden, puzzling: CRYPTIC
myths explained on the premise that they are based on actual events: EUHE-MERISM

N

nag at: BADGER
nagging, petty: NIGGLING
nail, claw, hoof: UNGUIS
nail that is slender and small with a small head: BRAD
naive, insipid, dry, lacking interest, barren: JEJUNE
naive, straightforward, frank, innocent, simple: INGENUOUS
name: APPELLATION
name derived from a place, place name: TOPONYM
name of broker rather than customer used in securities holdings: STREET NAME
name of individual used for a class: ANTONOMASIA
name of one person taken by another: ALLONYM
name of person from which name of a state or institution is derived: EPONYM
name of plant or creature in common rather than scientific language: VERNACULAR
name of writer at head of article: BYLINE
name only, nominal: TITULAR
name plate, signature, trademark, etc., on a single type plate: LOGOTYPE
name replaced by title or epithet: ANTONOMASIA
nameless, anonymous: INNOMINATE
namely: VIZ
namely, to wit: SCILICET
names, terminology: NOMENCLATURE
names, as a study: ONOMASTICS
naming a parent after his or her child: TEKNONYMY
naming a thing by substituting one of its attributes or a term it suggests: METONYMY

nape: SCRUFF
nape, back of the neck: NUCHA
narcotic made from Indian hemp: HASHISH
narrow, close or small margin or space: HAIRBREADTH
narrow, limited, provincial: PAROCHIAL
narrow, unsophisticated: PROVINCIAL
narrow elevated walking space: CATWALK
narrow or limited in outlook, provincial: INSULAR
narrowed: ANGUSTATE
narrow-minded: PETTY
narrow-minded, bigoted, obstinate: HIDEBOUND
nasal tone: SNUFFLE
nation's total production of goods and services: GROSS NATIONAL PRODUCT (G.N.P.)
native, indigenous: ENCHORIAL
native language of a place: VERNACULAR
native person, animal or thing: INDIGENE
native to a given area, peculiar to a given country or people: ENDEMIC
native to a region: INDIGENOUS
native to or in a place: ABORIGINAL
natural, coarse, unrefined: EARTHY
natural, existing from birth: INBORN
natural accompaniment, attribute or endowment: APPANAGE
natural attraction: AFFINITY
natural resources diminishing in supply therefore reducing income from them: DEPLETION
natural response to stimulus: INSTINCT
natural roughness or lack of polish: AGRESTIC
natural virtues: CARDINAL VIRTUES
nauseated: QUEASY, SICKENED
nauseated or shocked easily, prudish: SQUEAMISH

navel: UMBILICUS
navel contemplation: OMPHALOSKEPSIS
near, neighboring, adjoining: VICINAL
nearly, almost: WELL-NIGH
nearness: CONTIGUITY
nearness: PROXIMITY
nearness, kinship: PROPINQUITY
nearsighted, obtuse: MYOPIC
necessarily: PERFORCE
necessary means: WHEREWITHAL
neck ailment caused by muscle contraction: TORTICOLLIS
neck or base of the brain jolted, as in an automobile crash: WHIPLASH
necklace worn high around the throat: CHOKER
neckline cut low in a dress: DECOLLETAGE
necktie, wide and soft, knotted loosely: WINDSOR TIE
necktie or scarf: CRAVAT
neck's back part: SCRUFF
need for, lack of, or desire for: DESIDERATE
needle-pricking body tissues to diagnose or remedy ills: ACUPUNCTURE
needful or right to be: BEHOOVE
negative of a statement's opposite used to express an affirmative: LITOTES
neglect, disregard: SLIGHT
neglect, overlook, disregard: PRETERMIT
neglect or failure to meet an obligation: DEFAULT
neglect or willful omission, failure in duty: DERELICTION
neglected, abandoned, unused condition: DESUETUDE
neglected, decayed, in disrepair: DILAPIDATED
negligent, careless: REMISS
negotiations between organized workers and their employers: COLLECTIVE BARGAINING
neighboring, near: VICINAL
nerve inflammation: NEURITIS
nervous excitement, anxiety, agitation: DITHER
nervous or restless movements: FIDGET
nervous system and its disorders, as a study: NEUROLOGY
nervously excited, overstrained: OVERWROUGHT
nest in high place of a predatory bird: AERIE
network: RETICULATION

network, complicated interconnection of parts: PLEXUS
network or system to catch a criminal: DRAGNET
neurotic condition caused by feelings of inferiority: INFERIORITY COMPLEX
nevertheless: NOTWITHSTANDING
new birth, revival: RENASCENCE
new convert, beginner, novice: NEOPHYTE
new life, restoration, reconstitution: REGENERATION
new movement leaders: AVANT GARDE
new word or new meaning for existing word: NEOLOGISM
New York Stock Exchange: BIG BOARD
newcomer to an organization, cult, fraternity: INITIATE
newly born: YEANLING
newly conceived, just developing: NASCENT
newly introduced element: INNOVATION
newly married man: BENEDICT
newly rich or influential, upstart: PARVENU
news correspondent who works part time for a paper elsewhere: STRINGER
newspaper or magazine listing of editors, staff and owners: MASTHEAD
newspaper section in European papers usually at the bottom of the page, where fiction is printed: FEUILLETON
newspaper with sheets half the standard size, and usually emphasizing pictures: TABLOID
newspaper work shift beginning during the late night hours: LOBSTER SHIFT
newspaper's early edition: BULLDOG EDITION
newsstand, bandstand, booth, usually lightly constructed and open: KIOSK
next: PROXIMATE
next to nothing: AMBSACE
next to the last: PENULTIMATE
niches for cinerary urns or as vaults for the dead: COLUMBARIUM
nickname: SOBRIQUET
night and day of equal length, marking start of spring or autumn: EQUINOX
night club with recorded music for dancing: DISCOTHÈQUE
night or moon blindness: NYCTALOPIA
night vigil over a body before burial: WAKE
nightmare: INCUBUS

nine inches long: SPAN
nine-day prayer recitation: NOVENA
ninefold: NONUPLE
90 to 100 years old: NONAGENARIAN
nipple's dark circular background: ARE-OLA
no fraud or trickery: ABOVEBOARD
no ifs, ands, or buts: CATEGORICAL
no let-up: CONTINUOUS
nobility's obligations (French): NOBLESSE OBLIGE
noble, lofty or impressive, as in quality or style: SONOROUS
no-contest plea in criminal case without admission of guilt: NOLO CONTENDERE
nodding of the head: NUTATION
noise measure: DECIBEL
noise that is clattering: BRATTLE
noise that is shrill, creaking or grating: STRIDOR
noisily crashing, as waves: PLANGENT
noisy: CLAMOROUS
noisy: VOCIFEROUS
noisy and loud: UPROARIOUS
noisy commotion of a crowd: TUMULT
noisy confusion: BEDLAM
noisy disturbance: FRACAS
noisy gaiety, boisterous merriment: HILARITY
noisy ghost: POLTERGEIST
nominal, in name only: TITULAR
nonconforming, contrary: PERVERSE
nonconformist: MAVERICK
nonconformist: RECUSANT
nonconformity: DISSENT
nonessential attribute: ACCIDENTAL
noninterference, especially by government in business: LAISSEZ FAIRE
nonmaterial, spiritual, insubstantial: INCORPOREAL
nonsense: ABRACADABRA
nonsense: AMPHIGORY
nonsense: BALDERDASH
nonsense, meaningless chatter: SKIMBLE-SCAMBLE
nonsense, worthless, rubbish: TRUMPERY
nonviolent opposition: PASSIVE RESISTANCE
noodles, broad and flat, served with butter or a sauce: FETTUCCINE
normal consequence: COROLLARY
North African city's crowded section: CASBAH

nose, humorous name for a large nose: PROBOSCIS
nose and its diseases, as a branch of medicine: RHINOLOGY
nosebleed: EPISTAXIS
not concrete: ABSTRACT
not inherent: ADVENTITIOUS
not moving, motionless: IMMOBILE
"not to mention . . . :" APOPHASIS
notch or cut carved out by a saw or ax: KERF
notched at the edge: SERRATED
notched or indented, as a battlement on a fortress: CRENELATED
notched pattern on edge of fabric: PINKED
notches along an edge or border, space from a margin: INDENTION
notes in music lengthened or shortened arbitrarily: RUBATO
notes in music that are short and detached: STACCATO
notes of chord played in quick succession: ARPEGGIO
notify: APPRISE
notion or fancy that emerges suddenly: WHIM
notoriety that is evil: INFAMY
notoriously bad: ARRANT
notoriously bad, odious, vile reputation: INFAMOUS
nouns linked by conjunction that express same thought as noun with modifier: HENDIADYS
nourish, rear, train: NURTURE
nourishment: ALIMENT
novel that includes actual persons under fictitious names: ROMAN À CLEF
novel that is brief and often contains a moral: NOVELLA
novice: ABECEDARIAN
novice, beginner: NEOPHYTE
novice, beginner: TYRO
noxious, harmful: VIRULENT
noxious, unwholesome atmosphere, influence, effect, etc.: MIASMA
nuclear bomb: A-BOMB
nucleus or core of a group: CADRE
nudge or touch with a slight jar, shake lightly, stimulate: JOG
null and void: DIRIMENT
null and void: INVALID
numb: TORPID
number in arithmetic from which the subtrahend is to be subtracted: MINUEND

number of members necessary for an assembly to transact business: QUORUM

number sequence in which the ratio between each two terms is the same: GEOMETRIC PROGRESSION

number symbols from 0 to 9: DIGITS

number that is divisible by two or more numbers: COMMON MULTIPLE

number the pages of a book: FOLIATE, PAGINATE

number to be subtracted from another: SUBTRAHEND

number-using computer: DIGITAL COMPUTER

numberless: MYRIAD

numerous, great numbers: MULTITUDINOUS

nun's headdress covering head, cheeks, and neck: WIMPLE

nuptial poem or song: EPITHALAMIUM

nurse who rears a child without suckling it: DRY NURSE

nutrition and its processes: TROPHIC

nutrition that is defective or perverted: DYSTROPHY

nymph dwelling in or presiding over woods and trees: DRYAD

nymph fabled to live and die in the tree which she inhabited: HAMADRYAD

O

oath plus written statement: AFFIDAVIT
oath taken by a prospective witness or juror: VOIR DIRE
oath taker: JURANT
obedience or servility that is excessive: OBSEQUIOUS
obedient: DUTEOUS
object made by man: ARTIFACT
object of attention: CYNOSURE
object to, hesitate, take exception to: DEMUR
object serving as a boundary mark or guide to travelers: LANDMARK
object regarded as having magical powers: FETISH
objection that is trivial: QUIDDITY
objectionable, offensive: OBNOXIOUS
objective, impartial, unbiased: DISPASSIONATE
objective, unbiased: DISINTERESTED
objectivity: DISINTEREST
obligation or penalty established by authority: IMPOSITION
obligation owed, faithfulness, loyalty: FEALTY
obligatory: INCUMBENT
obligatory: IRREMISSIBLE
obligatory, required: MANDATORY
obligingness: COMPLAISANCE
oblique direction taken: SKEW
oblique earth deposited by water: ALLUVIUM
oblique or diagonal line: BIAS
oblivion, forgetfulness: LETHE
oblivion-producing potion: NEPENTHE
oblong-shaped cut gem: BAGUETTE
obscene: SCATOLOGICAL
obscene, lecherous, lewd: SALACIOUS
obscene, vulgar: FESCENNINE
obscene talk or conduct: BAWDRY
obscure: AMBIGUOUS

obscure: INCOMPREHENSIBLE
obscure, dim, pertaining to twilight: CREPUSCULAR
obscure, muddle, bewilder,: OBFUSCATE
obscure, overshadow, surpass: ECLIPSE
obscure, unclear, misty, dark: MURKY
obscure or ambiguous saying, riddle, puzzle: ENIGMA
obscure poem or song: RUNE
obsequious, servile: SUBSERVIENT
observation and analysis of one's own thoughts and feelings: INTROSPECTION
observation area built on the roof of a house: WIDOW'S WALK
observation spot or point: COIGN OF VANTAGE
observe, discern, discover with the eye: DESCRY
obsession: IDÉE FIXE
obsession, craze: MANIA. For a listing of such conditions see "manias"
obsolete, outdated, discarded: SUPERANNUATED
obstacle: IMPEDIMENT
obstinacy: PERTINACITY
obstinate, narrow-minded, bigoted: HIDEBOUND
obstinate, sinful: UNREGENERATE
obstinate, shrewd, practical: HARDHEADED
obstinate, unmanageable: REFRACTORY
obstinately resistant: DIE-HARD
obstruct, block: STYMIE
obstruct, frustrate, foil: THWART
obstruct, hinder: CRIMP
obstruction of action through time-killing tactics: FILIBUSTER
obtain by entreaty: IMPETRATE
obtrude or force oneself or one's will on another without right: IMPOSE

119

obtrusive, forward, pushy: OFFICIOUS

obtuse, nearsighted: MYOPIC

obvious, manifest, evident: PATENT

occasional: SPORADIC

occult: CABALA

occupation, avocation, interest: PURSUIT

occupation, career: VOCATION

occupation for which one is suited and well equipped: MÉTIER

occupy, amuse oneself: DISPORT

occupy completely, monopolize, absorb: ENGROSS

occurring or existing at the same time: SIMULTANEOUS

occurring together: CONCOMITANT

ocean grave of the drowned: DAVY JONES'S LOCKER

ocean wave, destructive, caused by underwater earthquake: TSUNAMI

oceanic: PELAGIC

oceanic: THALASSIC

odd, freakish: WHIMSICAL

odd, unconventional: OUTRÉ

odd, wild idea: VAGARY

odious, notoriously bad, vile reputation: INFAMOUS

odor from decaying matter: EFFLUVIUM

off-color, suggestive: RISQUÉ

offense against sovereign authority, treason: LESE MAJESTY

offense given or taken: UMBRAGE

offense not so serious as a felony, in law: MISDEMEANOR

offensive, disagreeable: UNSAVORY

offensive, disgusting, stinking, noxious: NOISOME

offensive, objectionable: OBNOXIOUS

offensive because of excessiveness or insincerity: FULSOME

offer: PROFFER

offer, as money: TENDER

offhand: CASUAL

offhand, free and easy: CAVALIER

offhand, spur of the moment: IMPROMPTU

office or position that pays, but involves few or no duties: SINECURE

offices filled through political power: PATRONAGE

official approval as of a literary work: IMPRIMATUR

official arbitrary decree: UKASE

official defeated in an election but filling out an unexpired term: LAME DUCK

official who is pompous or pretentious: PANJANDRUM

official who is tyrannical: SATRAP

officials, etc., arranged by rank: HIERARCHY

offset: COUNTERBALANCE

offset, make up, compensate: COUNTERVAIL

offshoot, branch: RAMIFICATION

offspring: PROGENY

offspring, descendant: SCION

offspring of a stallion and a female ass: HINNY

offspring of parents of different racial stock: HALF-BREED

offstage waiting room for performers: GREEN ROOM

oil consecrated for use in church: CHRISM

oil or grease something: LUBRICATE

oil well from which oil spouts: GUSHER

oily: OLEAGINOUS

oily, greasy: PINGUID

oily-tongued, suave to an excess: UNCTUOUS

old, infirm, doting: SENILE

old age, senility: DOTAGE

old age, as a branch of medicine: GERIATRICS

old age weakness: CADUCITY

old-fashioned: ANTEDILUVIAN

old fashioned: DÉMODÉ

old-fashioned: PASSÉ

old-fashioned, fussy person: FUDDYDUDDY

old-fashioned, musty, moldy: FUSTY

old-fashioned, out of step with the times, ancient, outmoded: ANTEDILUVIAN

old-fashioned or ultra-conservative person: FOGY

old maid: SPINSTER

old men forming a governing body: GERONTOCRACY

old salt, veteran sailor: SHELLBACK

Old Testament interpretation largely mystical: ANAGOGE

old-woman-like: ANILE

omelet prepared with ham, onion, and green pepper: WESTERN OMELET

omen, portent: AUGURY

omen, warning, portent: PRESAGE

omen of death: KNELL

ominous, awesome: PORTENTOUS

omission of conjunctions: ASYNDETON

omission of understood word or words: ELLIPSIS

omission of words from a sentence but leaving the meaning intact: ELISION

omit a vowel or syllable in pronunciation:
ELIDE
omitting, passing over: PRETERITION
omnipresent: UBIQUITOUS
on the agenda for consideration: ON THE
TAPIS
on the alert, wide-awake: ON THE QUI
VIVE
on the up-and-up: ABOVEBOARD
on your mark, get set, go: ASYNDETON
one behind the other, as on a bicycle built
for two: TANDEM
one-colored: MONOCHROME
one dollar per share of stock: POINT
one-eyed: POLYPHEMUS
one following another: SERIATIM
one hundred years: CENTENARY, CENTEN-
NIAL
one husband at a time: MONANDROUS
one leg on each side of something:
ASTRIDE
one-man rule with absolute power: AU-
TOCRACY
one of a kind, unique: SUI GENERIS
one side only: UNILATERAL
one-sided: EX PARTE
one-sided in heaviness or size: LOPSIDED
onomatopoeia: ECHOISM
ooze or trickle forth: EXUDE
open: ABOVEBOARD
open, unconcealed, evident: OVERT
open out, develop: EVOLVE
open paved area adjoining a home: PATIO
open to injury, attack, or criticism: VUL-
NERABLE
open to question, arguable: DISPUTABLE
open to the sky, unroofed: HYPETHRAL
open-handed in giving: MUNIFICENT
opening, break or interruption of continuity, gap: HIATUS
opening, mouth: ORIFICE
opening cut in an interior wall of a church
to allow those in a side aisle to see
the main altar: HAGIOSCOPE
opening move in chess: GAMBIT
opening or slit in the upper part of a dress
or skirt: PLACKET
opening oration at a commencement: SA-
LUTATORY
opening performance: PREMIERE
open-minded: PERVIOUS
opera in which music is subordinated to
words: SINGSPIEL
opera singer of note: DIVA
opera's verbal text: LIBRETTO

operetta form in Spain: ZARZUELA
opinion adopted beforehand: PRECONCEP-
TION
opinion or agreement that is general:
CONSENSUS
opinion or belief contrary to established
doctrine: HERESY
opinionated, but immature: SOPHOMORIC
opponent who takes wrong side perversely: DEVIL'S ADVOCATE
oppose, argue: CONTROVERT
oppose, contradict, deny: GAINSAY
oppose, thwart: TRAVERSE
oppose or protest by pleading: REMON-
STRATE
opposed or inconsistent: REPUGNANT
opposed to change or progress, conservative: REACTIONARY
opposed to usual beliefs: HETERODOX
opponent, pursuer, or antagonist who is
unusually tenacious: NEMESIS
opposite: POLAR
opposite or reversed in order or effect:
INVERSE
opposite sides: ANTIPODAL
opposite word: ANTONYM
opposite meaning to words said sarcastically or humorously or with opposite
result to what is expected: IRONY
opposite terms combined in one phrase:
OXYMORON
opposition expressed: ADVERSATIVE
opposition that is nonviolent: PASSIVE RE-
SISTANCE
opposition to human education: OB-
SCURANTISM
oppressive thing, burden: INCUBUS
optical device in which pictures on both
sides of a card or disk appear to
blend when the card is twirled:
THAUMATROPE
optimistic, buoyant, cheerful: SANGUINE
optimistic, happy: UPBEAT
optimistic about rising prices, as in the
stock market: BULLISH
oracular or ambiguous: DELPHIC
oral, not written, referring especially to
wills: NUNCUPATIVE
oral, spoken: VIVA VOCE
oral defamatory statement: SLANDER
oral teaching: CATECHESIS
oration opening a commencement: SALU-
TATORY
oratory that is bombastic and artificial:
DECLAMATION

orbital point farthest from the earth: APOGEE

orbital point of a celestial body or satellite that is nearest to the earth: PERIGEE

orbital point that is nearest the sun: PERIHELION

orbiting man-made body: SATELLITE

orchestra seats in a theater: PARQUET

order, command, forbid: ENJOIN

order, decree, enact: ORDAIN

order or send back: REMAND

order requiring certain action: MANDAMUS

order requiring one to take, or refrain from, a certain action: INJUNCTION

order that is positive and authoritative: FIAT

order to buy or sell at the most advantageous price: MARKET ORDER

order to buy or sell securities that is good only for the day on which it was entered: DAY ORDER

ordinary, commonplace: MUNDANE

ordinary, simple, commonplace: EXOTERIC

ordinary, uninspired, commonplace: PROSAIC

ordinary or hackneyed: BANAL

ordinary people, common run: RUCK

organ that uses reeds and resembles a harmonium: MELODEON

organic equilibrium: HOMEOSTASIS

organic whole has a reality other and greater than the sum of its parts, according to this theory: HOLISM

organisms derived asexually from a common ancestor: CLONE

organisms in relation to their environment: ECOLOGY

organizer, manager or sponsor of performers for entertainment: IMPRESARIO

organ-like instrument with steam whistles: CALLIOPE

orgy: BACCHANAL

origin: PROVENANCE

original, creative: PROMETHEAN

original, first, principal: PRIMAL

original, primitive, elemental: PRIMORDIAL

original condition, unused, brand new: MINT CONDITION

original pattern: ARCHETYPE

originate, begin, commence: INITIATE

originate, bring forth: SPAWN

ornament, decorate: EMBELLISH

ornament or mark used in typography: DINGBAT

ornament or trinket either gaudy or trifling: FALLAL

ornament resembling a twisted cable or cord: TORSADE

ornament that hangs: PENDANT

ornament the edge with a series of indentations: ENGRAIL

ornament with raised figures worked on a surface as decoration: EMBOSS

ornamental openwork usually composed of interlaced parts: FRETWORK

ornamental stand with shelves: ÉTAGÈRE

ornamentation done with tools, as on leather: TOOLING

ornamentation or style that is extravagant: BAROQUE

ornamentation with wavy lines or patterns, or with inlaying or etching, as on iron or steel: DAMASCENE

ornamented excessively: ORNATE

ornamental relief work in metal: TOREUTICS

ornamented tastelessly, showy and cheap: TAWDRY

ornate, excessively flowery: FLORID

ornate, florid, showy, bombastic: FLAMBOYANT

ornate writing: PURPLE PROSE

ornateness to excess: FROUFROU

ostentatious, affecting superiority: PRETENTIOUS

ostracize: BLACKBALL

ostracize, banish from society: SEND TO COVENTRY

O the times! O the customs!: O TEMPORA! O MORES!

out and out: ARRANT

out of action: HORS DE COMBAT

out of business: DEFUNCT

out of control: RAMPANT

out of date, not current: OBSOLETE

out of place, inappropriate: MALAPROPOS

out of proportion, not in accordance: INCOMMENSURABLE

out-of-the-blue element introduced to untangle a story plot: DEUS EX MACHINA

outbreak of violence: RAMPAGE

outburst of passion or emotion: ACCESS

outburst that is sudden and turbulent: PAROXYSM

outcast, one socially rejected: PARIAH

outcome in a plot: DENOUEMENT

outcome that is possible: EVENTUALITY

outcry, clamor, shouting: HUE AND CRY

outdated, obsolete, discarded: SUPER-
ANNUATED
outdoor celebration, especially a dinner or
bazaar: FETE
outdoor party: FETE CHAMPETRE
outer coating or covering, especially a natural covering: INTEGUMENT
outflow: EFFLUENT
outgoing person: EXTROVERT
outgrowth that is unnatural such as a wart:
EXCRESCENCE
outlaw, condemn, prohibit: PROSCRIBE
outline: PROSPECTUS
outline, form, shape: FIGURATION
outline, trace out, describe: DELINEATE
outline of the main points of a course of
study: SYLLABUS
outline or structure of something: CON-
FORMATION
outline sketchily: ADUMBRATE
outlying areas: PURLIEU
outmoded, old-fashioned, ancient, out of
step with the times: ANTEDILUVIAN
outmost limit: JUMPING-OFF PLACE
outpatient department of hospital: POLI-
CLINIC
outpouring, as of words: SPATE
outrageous, notorious, shocking, disgraceful: FLAGRANT
outside, not central: PERIPHERAL
outside the jurisdiction of a state or country: EXTRATERRITORIAL
outside the nature of something: EXTRIN-
SIC
outspoken, definite, clear, straightforward:
EXPLICIT
outstanding: PREEMINENT
outstanding, important feature: HIGHLIGHT
outwardly real, or made outwardly real:
EXTERNALIZED
outwit, avoid: CIRCUMVENT
outwit, cheat: EUCHRE
ovary removal from a female animal:
SPAY
oven or furnace for baking or drying
bricks, pottery, cement: KILN

overabundance: PLETHORA
overbearing, arbitrary: HIGHHANDED
overcome, beat: DRUB
overdemonstrative: EFFUSIVE
overdo, as an argument: BELABOR
overelaborate, florid: ROCOCO
overflowing: INUNDANT
overflowing, full: TEEMING
overflowing, lavish: EXUBERANT
overflow or rise of a stream occurring suddenly: FRESHET
overlapping edges as in tiles or shingles:
IMBRICATE
overloaded, inflated: PLETHORIC
overlook, disregard: PRETERMIT
overlook something as if it had not happened: CONDONE
overly polite: CEREMONIOUS
overnice, squeamish: FASTIDIOUS
overprecise, finicky: NIGGLING
overrefined in behavior, writing, etc.:
PRECIOUS
overrun, occur in large numbers so as to
be annoying or dangerous: INFEST
overshadow, obscure, surpass: ECLIPSE
overshadowing: ADUMBRAL
oversight: INADVERTENCE
oversimplifying problems: SIMPLISTIC
overspread, as with color: SUFFUSE
overstatement or exaggeration intended for
the effect and not to be taken seriously: HYPERBOLE
overstrained, nervously excited: OVER-
WROUGHT
overthrow of a government, usually sudden and often accompanied by violence: COUP D'ÉTAT
overthrow or undermine: SUBVERT
overwhelming, domineering: OVER-
BEARING
overwhelm, swallow up: ENGULF
owned by a proprietor, protected as by
patent or copyright: PROPRIETARY
ownership of securities: LONG
Oxford resident: OXONIAN
oxygen in liquid form: LOX

P

pacesetter, leader: FUGLEMAN

pacify, soothe: SALVE

pacify, appease, quiet down: MOLLIFY

pack animal, beast of burden: SUMPTER

pack or force down by repeated pressure: TAMP

packed or wedged firmly, thickly populated: IMPACTED

packing material composed of thin wood shavings: EXCELSIOR

page at start of a book: FRONTISPIECE

page in a book or magazine that is larger than page size and can be unfolded: GATEFOLD

page number in a book: FOLIO

page on the left-hand side of a book: VERSO

pages of a magazine or newspaper that face each other and include related material: DOUBLE TRUCK OR SPREAD

pain, suffering, anguish, distress: TRAVAIL

pain combating: ANALGESIC

pain free: ANALGESIA

pain inflicted on others as a source of pleasure for the inflicter: SADISM

pain relieving: ANODYNE

painful, agonizing: EXCRUCIATING

painful, sad, mournful: DOLOROUS

painful experience, endurance test: ORDEAL

painful inflammation near shoulder: BURSITIS

pains that are violent: THROES

painstaking, overly precise about details: METICULOUS

paint, engrave or draw with dots instead of lines: STIPPLE

painting, using shades of gray only, often in imitation of bas-relief: GRISAILLE

painting in water colors on wet plaster: FRESCO

painting in which pigment is applied thickly to a surface: IMPASTO

painting medium made from a mixture of water and other substances such as egg yolks or glue: TEMPERA

painting method of using varicolored dots: POINTILLISM

painting using opaque colors mixed with water and gum: GOUACHE

pair of matched horses or oxen: SPAN

pair of objects considered as a single unit: DUAD

paired, double or two: BINARY

pairs or separated into pairs: DICHOTOMIZED

pale, colorless: PALLID

pale, ghastly, gaunt: CADAVEROUS

pale, sallow face: WHEYFACE

pale and thin: PEAKED

palm of the hand: THENAR

palm of the hand, sole of the foot: VOLAR

palm off: FOB

palmistry: CHIROMANCY

paltry, pitiable, inferior: SORRY

paltry, trivial: PICAYUNE

pamper: CODDLE

pamper or coddle: COSHER

pamper or pet: COSSET

pampered, overindulged: SPOON-FED

panacea: CATHOLICON

pancakes, thin and rolled in hot orange sauce: CRÊPES SUZETTE

pancakes, thin, with filling: CRÊPES

panel of prospective jurors: VENIRE

paneled lower part of an inner wall: WAINSCOT

panic, amazement or fear that is sudden and paralyzing: CONSTERNATION

pantomime, especially in which Harlequin and clown play leading parts: HARLEQUINADE pantomime in shadows thrown on a screen or wall: GALANTY SHOW

papal envoy who carries insignia to new cardinals: ABLEGATE

papal letter addressed to the bishops of the world: ENCYCLICAL

paper at front and back of book, one half of which is pasted to the binding: END PAPER

paper chewed into a wet wad for throwing: SPITBALL

paper cover slipped around a book: DUST JACKET

paper fastener of thin wire: STAPLE

paper in units of 480 to 516 sheets: REAM

paper mark of translucent lines or designs: WATERMARK

paper money in small amounts: SCRIP

paper of high grade with smooth surface: WIRE-WOVE

paper scrap: SCRIP

paper size, 23 by 31 inches: IMPERIAL

paper that does not carry the marks of the wire gauze on which it was laid: WOVE PAPER

paper that measures 13 by 16 inches: FOOLS-CAP

paper used by lawyers and usually measuring about 8½ x 13 inches: LEGAL CAP

paper watermarked with fine parallel lines: LAID PAPER

parade: CAVALCADE

parade of persons or animals fastened together: COFFLE

parade or display brazenly or gaudily: FLAUNT

parade or exhibition that is spectacular: PAGEANT

paradise: ELYSIAN FIELDS

paragon, unequaled: NONPAREIL

parallel lines slanting on each side of a spine: HERRINGBONE

parallelogram with oblique angles and its opposite sides equal: RHOMBOID

paralysis of one side of the body: HEMIPLEGIA

paralysis of the lower part of the body: PARAPLEGIA

paralyze with fear, harden, deaden: PETRIFY

parched, arid: TORRID

parchment or tablet in which earlier writing has been erased to make room for a new one: PALIMPSEST

pardon by a government given in general: AMNESTY

pardonable, as sins: REMISSIBLE

pardonable, excusable, as a fault: VENIAL

parent killing: PARRICIDE

parentage or line of descent: FILIATION

parents in common with another: GERMAN

parents of adopted child: ADOPTIVE PARENTS

parley so as to gain time: TEMPORIZE

part, divide, separate: DISSEVER

part of a debt or of a serial story: INSTALLMENT

part used to stand for the whole: SYNECDOCHE

partiality or bias held in advance: PREDILECTION

particle, negatively charged, that forms part of an atom: ELECTRON

particle or speck: MOTE

particular application, not general: AD HOC

particularize: INDIVIDUATE

partisan to excess, fanatic: ZEALOT

partnership of dissimilar organisms: SYMBIOSIS

partnership or company distinguished from a corporation: FIRM

part-time, amusement: DIVERSION

part-time or temporary lodging place: PIED-À-TERRE

party given in the evening: SOIREE

pass assuring the bearer protection on a journey, as in time of war: SAFE-CONDUCT

pass away, slip by (said of time): ELAPSE

pass imperceptibly from one shade or degree to another: GRADATE

pass through, survive, as a crisis: WEATHER

pass through tissue: TRANSPIRE

passage of ornate writing: PURPLE PROSE

passage or extract, especially from the Bible: PERICOPE

passageway, as between house and garage: BREEZEWAY

passing abruptly from one condition to another: TRANSILIENT

passing lightly from one subject to another, wandering from the point: DISCURSIVE

passing out of use, becoming obsolete: OBSOLESCENT

passion or love that is foolish or unreasoning: INFATUATION

passionate, ardent: TORRID

passive consent: ACQUIESCENCE
passive consent: SUFFERANCE
Passover book containing story of the Exodus: HAGGADAH
passport endorsement granting entry into or passage through a country: VISA
password, rallying cry: WATCHWORD
password, test word: SHIBBOLETH
pasta in the form of dumplings: GNOCCHI
pastoral or rustic: BUCOLIC
pastry shell, fried, in which food may be served: TIMBALE
pastry shell to be filled with meat or fish: VOL-AU-VENT
pastry store: PATISSERIE
path: ACCESS
path of an object moving through space: TRAJECTORY
path that is winding or circuitous: AMBAGE
patient treated at a hospital but not staying there: OUTPATIENT
patriot of an aggressive and boastful nature: JINGO
patriotism that is overzealous: CHAUVINISM
patronizing: CONDESCENDING
pattern, model example: PARADIGM
pattern, model, typical example: EXEMPLAR
pattern or gauge used to copy something accurately, as in woodworking: TEMPLATE
pause or interruption of continuity, gap, opening: HIATUS
pause temporarily or stop at intervals: INTERMIT
pay back, compensate: REIMBURSE
pay for, compensate: REMUNERATE
pay larger than normal given to a dismissed employe: SEVERANCE PAY
pay or fee for a service: EMOLUMENT
pay out: DISBURSE
pay to a clergyman from church revenues: PREBEND
paying back money originally invested: SELF-LIQUIDATING
payment, from earnings of a corporation, to be made to shareholders: DIVIDEND
payment beyond regular salary or profit: PERQUISITE
payment by each of his own meal ticket, party fee, etc.: DUTCH TREAT
payment for release of seized person or property: RANSOM

payment extorted to prevent disclosure: BLACKMAIL
payment immediately on delivery: SPOT CASH
payment in addition to salary, such as pension, insurance, etc.: FRINGE BENEFIT
peace be with you: PAX VOBISCUM
peace of mind: ATARAXIA
peace pipe: CALUMET
peaceable, showing good will: AMICABLE
peaceful, placid: PACIFIC
peaceful, tranquil, calm: PLACID
peaceful in purpose: IRENIC
pearl-like, iridescent: NACREOUS
pear-shaped: PYRIFORM
peculiar to a given country or people, native to a given area: ENDEMIC
peculiarity in behavior or speech, affectation of tyle: MANNERISM
pedantic: DIDACTIC
pedantic, dogmatic teacher: PEDAGOGUE
pedantic, moralizing: DIDACTIC
pedantic, smug, overexacting person: PRIG
pedantic literary effort: LUCUBRATION
peddle, cry goods in the street: HAWK
peddler of Bibles and other books: COLPORTEUR
peddler of food, liquor, etc. to an army: SUTLER
pedestal on which a statue or column stands: PLINTH
pedestal part between base and cornice: DADO
pedestrian who disregards traffic rules: JAYWALKER
pedigree record of thoroughbred stock: STUD BOOK
peep show, street show: RAREE SHOW
peeping Tom: VOYEUR
peevish: PETTISH
peevish, gloomy: DYSPEPTIC
peevish, ill-tempered: BILIOUS
peevishness, ill temper, spitefulness: SPLEEN
peevishness, irritableness: PETULANCE
pelt, shower, spatter: PEPPER
pen name: NOM DE PLUME
penalty in which something is given up or taken away: FORFEIT
penalty or obligation established by authority: IMPOSITION
pencil lead: GRAPHITE
penetrable, open-minded: PERVIOUS

penetrate, spread through completely: PERMEATE

penis erection as a persistent pathological condition: PRIAPISM

penis in rigid, enlarged condition: ERECTION

penis-like: PHALLIC

penis-like representation: PHALLUS

penmanship art: CHIROGRAPHY

penmanship that is beautiful: CALLIGRAPHY

penniless, poor: IMPECUNIOUS

pension, allowance, salary: STIPEND

Pentateuch, also Jewish law and literature: TORAH

people collectively, especially those outside a specific profession or occupation: LAITY

people forced by circumstances to listen: CAPTIVE AUDIENCE

people's protector or champion: TRIBUNE

pep up, cheer up, stimulate, invigorate: EXHILARATE

perceive, recognize as different: DISCERN

perceived below the threshold of consciousness: SUBLIMINAL

percentage of total that must be paid by customer when he uses his broker's credit to buy a security: MARGIN

perception after the event: HINDSIGHT

perception independent of senses: EXTRASENSORY PERCEPTION (ESP)

perception of distant objects by other than normal sensory means: TELESTHESIA

perception of one's own consciousness: APPERCEPTION

perception or knowing of a fact: COGNIZANCE

perception that has no external stimulus: HALLUCINATION

perceptive, keen, discerning: PERSPICACIOUS

perfect example: ARCHETYPE

perfection: NE PLUS ULTRA

perform, invent or produce without previous thought or preparation: IMPROVISE

perform a ceremony: SOLEMNIZE

perform the functions of an office: OFFICIATE

performance added in response to audience demand: ENCORE

performance or interpretation of a text, role, etc.: RENDITION

performer having a very small part, as in a play: WALK-ON

performer's special talent or piece of business: SHTICK

performing services for a fixed payment: STIPENDIARY

performing to win applause or approval: GRANDSTAND PLAY

perfumed powder in a bag: SACHET

peril that is imminent: SWORD OF DAMOCLES

period, century, era: SIÈCLE

period of happiness, comfort or wealth: MILLENNIUM

period of time that is incalculable, eternity: EON

period that divides some longer or periodic process: INTERLUDE

periodical of a company for its employes: HOUSE ORGAN

perjure oneself: FORSWEAR

permanent: INDELIBLE

permanent, durable: PERDURABLE

permeable through pores: POROUS

permeate, circulate: DIFFUSE

permeate, fertilize: IMPREGNATE

permeation gradually of thoughts or facts: OSMOSIS

permission given or implied by failure to prohibit: SUFFERANCE

permit, ratify, approve: SANCTION

permit with condescension: VOUCHSAFE

perplex, dumbfound, bewilder: NONPLUS

perplexing situation: QUANDARY

persecution complex: PARANOIA

persecution imposed by the military: DRAGONNADE

persevering: ASSIDUOUS

persevering, stubborn: INDOMITABLE

persistent: ASSIDUOUS

persistent, stubborn: PERTINACIOUS

persistent, tough, stubborn: TENACIOUS

persistent striving: PERSEVERANCE

persistently demand: IMPORTUNE

person, animal or plant that lives off another: PARASITE

person acting as if mechanically: AUTOMATON

person from whom a family descends: STIRPS

person from whom a nation, city, or epoch is said to derive its name: EPONYM

person moved out of a destroyed or threatened area: EVACUEE

person or thing uncommonly large or fine: SPANKER

person thought of as a perfect example: PERSONIFICATION

person with specialized knowledge, expert: COGNOSCENTE

person who buys and sells for another, on commission: BROKER

person who drops things: BUTTERFINGERS

person who enjoys good living: BON VIVANT

person who is a cultured or aristocratic snob: BRAHMIN

person who utters unheeded prophecies of disaster: CASSANDRA

personal excellence: CALIBER

personal feelings or one's mind as the source of judgment, as opposed to objective: SUBJECTIVE

personal need as motivation: BREAD-AND-BUTTER

personal property: CHATTEL

personality test made through interpretation of standard ink blots: RORSCHACH TEST

personification: PROSOPOPEIA

personified: INCARNATE

personnel reduction through retirement, etc.: ATTRITION

persons to whom secrets are confided: CONFIDANT

perspiration that is copious: DIAPHORESIS

persuadable, tractable: PLIANT

persuade one to act or speak: INDUCE

persuade or try to persuade by flattery: WHEEDLE

persuasive, insincere flattery: SNOW JOB

persuasively forceful: COGENT

pertinent, appropriate: RELEVANT

pertinent, related to what is being discussed, relevant: GERMANE

pervade, saturate, wet thoroughly: IMBUE

pervade or animate: INFORM

pester, press a debtor for payment: DUN

pessimism, melancholy, romantic world-weariness: WELTSCHMERZ

pessimistic about stock prices: BEARISH

pet name or endearing diminutive: HYPOCORISM

pet phrase: BYWORD

petitioner: POSTULANT

petty, cheap, sleazy: CHINTZY

petty, contemptible, trivial: PALTRY

petty, nagging: NIGGLING

petty, trivial: INSIGNIFICANT

petty, trivial, mean: PICAYUNE

petulant, self-important: HOITY-TOITY

phallus that is large, as in certain primitive art: ITHYPHALLIC

phantom: EIDOLON

phase, side or aspect of a person or subject: FACET

phobias

    (In the following listing read the words "irrational fear of" ahead of each entry.)

air or drafts: AEROPHOBIA

aloneness: AUTOPHOBIA

animals: ZOOPHOBIA

being touched: HAPTEPHOBIA

blood: HEMOPHOBIA

burial alive: TAPHEPHOBIA

cats: AILUROPHOBIA

children: PEDOPHOBIA

cold: PSYCHROPHOBIA

contamination: MYSOPHOBIA

crowds: DEMOPHOBIA, OCHLOPHOBIA

dead bodies: NECROPHOBIA

death: THANATOPHOBIA, NECROPHOBIA

depths: BATHOPHOBIA

dogs: CYNOPHOBIA

eating: PHAGOPHOBIA

England, the English: ANGLOPHOBIA

fire: PYROPHOBIA

foreigners, strangers: XENOPHOBIA

heights: ACROPHOBIA

ideas: IDEOPHOBIA

infinity: APEIROPHOBIA

lice: PEDICULOPHOBIA

marriage: GAMOPHOBIA

men: ANDROPHOBIA

mice: MUSOPHOBIA

missiles: BALLISTOPHOBIA

movement: KINESOPHOBIA

night: NYCTOPHOBIA

noise: PHONOPHOBIA

novelty: NEOPHOBIA

number 13: TRISKAIDEKAPHOBIA

ocean: THALASSOPHOBIA

open spaces: AGORAPHOBIA

pain: ALGOPHOBIA

poison: TOXICOPHOBIA

red: ERYTHROPHOBIA

reptiles: OPHIDIOPHOBIA

sharp objects: AICHINOPHOBIA

sleep: HYPNOPHOBIA

snow: CHIONOPHOBIA

solitude: AUTOPHOBIA

speaking: LALOPHOBIA

stars: ASTROPHOBIA
thunderstorms: ASTRAPHOBIA
women: GYNOPHOBIA
phonograph record collector or connoisseur: DISCOPHILE
phonograph records catalogued: DISCOGRAPHY
photograph improvement through handwork to remove blemishes or add details: RETOUCHING
photographs attractively: PHOTOGENIC
phrase, clause or word inserted in a sentence to add explanation or comment: PARENTHESIS
phrase or put into words: COUCH
phrase or watchword of a group: SHIBBOLETH
phraseology verbal expression: LOCUTION
phraseology peculiar to a language or region and accepted though it may differ from the normal pattern: IDIOM
physically strong: POTENT
physically suitable for marriage: NUBILE
physician's training period at a hospital: RESIDENCY
piano-like instrument: CLAVICHORD
pick, sort out, select: CULL
pickle in a spicy, vinegary solution: MARINATE
picnic, pleasure trip, feast, banquet: JUNKET
picture, image, likeness, usually an object of veneration: ICON
picture or symbol representing a word, sound or object: HIEROGLYPHIC
picture painted on transparent curtains: DIORAMA
picture printed from engraving made with hard needle: DRY POINT
picture produced by superimposing different pictorial elements to make a single composition: MONTAGE
picturelike scene represented by silent and motionless persons: TABLEAU VIVANT
picturesque, pleasant: IDYLLIC
pie that is custard-like and made of cheese, bacon, etc., and served hot: QUICHE LORRAINE
piece cut or broken off: CANTLE
piece out, supplement: EKE
pier or wharf to protect a harbor or beach: JETTY
pierce through, impale: TRANSFIX
pigeon, especially when an unfledged nestling: SQUAB

pig-headed, stubborn, unyielding: OBSTINATE
piglike, swinish, hoggish: PORCINE
pigmentation deficiency: ALBINISM
pile of wood, etc., for burning a dead body: PYRE
pillage during a search: RANSACK
piles: HEMORRHOIDS
pilfer: FILCH
pillage, plunder, prey upon: DEPREDATE
pillage, ruin, wreck: RAVAGE
pillar in shape of a male figure: TELAMON
pimp: PANDER
pin someone or something with a sharp stake: IMPALE
pincers of small size: TWEEZERS
pincers or small tongs: FORCEPS
pine, weaken, droop gradually: LANGUISH
pink-eyed and white-skinned person: ALBINO
pinkie: LITTLE FINGER
pins, ribbons and other small miscellaneous articles for sale: NOTIONS
pinwheel-like firework: CATHERINE WHEEL
pipe with a tube passing through water to cool the smoke: HOOKAH
pirate: PICAROON
pirate or appropriate the ideas, writings, music, etc., of another: PLAGIARIZE
pit of the stomach: SOLAR PLEXUS
pitcher or jug with wide mouth: EWER
pitchers' practice area: BULLPEN
pithy saying: APOTHEGM
pitiable, inferior, paltry: SORRY
pitiful, causing sorrow, sad: PATHETIC
pitiless, hardhearted, stubborn: OBDURATE
pitiless, harsh: RELENTLESS
pivot about: SLUE
pivotal or pivoting on its own axis: TROCHOID
place for storing goods: REPOSITORY
place in a female mammal where young are generated and developed: WOMB
place name, or name derived from a place: TOPONYM
place of rest or shelter: HOSPICE
place or install in office formally: INVEST
place or position forces according to a plan: DEPLOY
place to stand on: POU STO
place where a crime is committed or a trial is to be held: VENUE
place where criminals, addicts, etc., are

helped to readjust to society: HALF-WAY HOUSE

plaid or checkered pattern of dark lines on a light ground: TATTERSALL

plain: UNVARNISHED

plain, clear, obvious, evident: MANIFEST

plain, direct: FLAT-FOOTED

plain, simple, rough: RUSTIC

plain devoid of forest, especially one of the extensive plains in Russia: STEPPE

plain of Arctic regions, treeless and vast: TUNDRA

plain or rolling tract of open land: WOLD

plait: PLEACH

plan, proposal, undertaking: PROJECT

plan of top priority to meet an emergency: CRASH PROGRAM

plane designed for short takeoffs and landings: STOL

plane designed for vertical takeoffs and landings: VTOL

planets shown as models or images on a circular dome: PLANETARIUM

planing tool having a blade set between two handles: SPOKESHAVE

planned deliberately, premeditated: STUDIED

planning for the future, prudence: PROVIDENCE

plant adapted to extreme changes of weather: TROPOPHYTE

plant and animal periodicity, as a study: PHENOLOGY

plant and animal structures, as a study, apart from function: MORPHOLOGY

plant eating, feeding on vegetables: HERBIVOROUS

plant growing in nutrient mineral solutions rather than in soil: HYDROPONICS

plant or animal selected as representative of a new species: HOLOTYPE

plant or animal series of changes in formation: SERE

plant or animal surviving from an earlier period or type: RELICT

plants growing in a given region: FLORA

plaster of Paris and glue mixed as a base for painting or for making of bas-reliefs: GESSO

plaster or a like wall coating: PARGET

platform, low and wheeled: DOLLY

platform or porch with steps at the entrance to a house: STOOP

platform that an orchestra conductor or a speaker stands on: PODIUM

platform that is raised and on which guests of honor or speakers are seated: DAIS

platitude: BROMIDE

plausible, but not certain: SPECIOUS

play rehearsal, usually the final one, performed exactly as play will be on opening night: DRESS REHEARSAL

play side by side: COLLOCATE

play written for reading rather than performance: CLOSET DRAMA

player in sports who is not on the regular team: SCRUB

playful, jesting: JOCOSE

playful conversation: BANTER

playful or lively movement in music: SCHERZO

playful teasing: BADINAGE

playfully leap about: CAPER

playfulness, fun, quip: JEST

plead against, disapprove: DEPRECATE

plead in protest or opposition: REMONSTRATE

pleasant tasting, savory: SAPID

pleasantness: AMENITY

please, if you please: S'IL VOUS PLAÎT

please reply: RÉPONEZ S'IL VOUS PLAÎT

pleasing: PREPOSSESSING

pleasing, attractive: WINSOME

pleasing in sound, harmonious, smooth: EUPHONIOUS

pleasurable and unpleasurable states, as a psychologic study: HEDONICS

pleasurably excited: TITILLATED

pleasure as the only good and proper goal or moral behavior: HEDONISM

pleasure at one's own suffering or pain: MASOCHISM

pleasure-loving and luxury-loving person: SYBARITE

pleasure or self-indulgence as a way of life: PRIMROSE PATH

pleasure-seeking and pain-avoiding drive of the ego: PLEASURE PRINCIPLE

pleasure trip, banquet, picnic, feast: JUNKET

pleated or plaited, as a fan: PLICATED

pleats that resemble bellows folds of an accordion: ACCORDION PLEATS

pledge, security, challenge: GAGE

pledge of securities or property as collateral for a loan: HYPOTHECATION

pledge property set aside by a borrower to insure repayment of a loan: COLLATERAL

plentiful: BOUNTEOUS

plentiful, abundant: RIFE
pliable: PLASTIC
pliable, flexible: MALLEABLE
pliant, supple, agile, lithe: LISSOME
plod, as through mud: SLOG
plot, conspiracy, secret and underhanded activity: INTRIGUE
plot to foil another: COUNTERMINE
pluck, spirit, courage: METTLE
plucking instrument's strings: PIZZICATO
plucking out, extracting forcibly, uprooting: EVULSION
plug or seal edges or crevices: CAULK
plump, rounded out: ROTUND
plume on a helmet; dash, verve: PANACHE
plunder: PILLAGE
plunder, invade for booty, raid: MARAUD
plunder, pillage, prey upon: DEPREDATE
plunder, pillage, raid: FORAY
plunder, during a search: RANSACK
plunder or destroy a city: RAPE
plunge straight down: PLUMMET
pod, husk, or shell: SHUCK
poem in which one poet mourns the death of another: MONODY
poem of a short, pastoral nature: ECLOGUE
poem of eight lines and two rhymes with two of the lines repeated: TRIOLET
poem of ten or thirteen lines with two rhymes: RONDEAU
poem of three stanzas and an envoy, the last lines of which are the same: BALLADE
poem or arrangement of words in which certain letters of each line spell a word: ACROSTIC
poem or composition in which the end letters of successive lines form a word: TELESTICH
poem or composition in which the middle letters of successive lines form a word: MESOSTICH
poem or stanza of four lines: QUATRAIN
poem retracting something stated in an earlier one: PALINODE
poem that is metrically complete: ACATALECTIC
poem usually of fourteen lines in rhymed iambic pentameter: SONNET
poet: BARD
poet without much talent: POETASTER
poetic forms, as a study: PROSODY

poetic metrical foot consisting of three syllables, the first accented, the others not: DACTYL
poetic metrical foot consisting of two equally accented syllables: SPONDEE
poetic metrical foot consisting of two syllables, the first accented: TROCHEE
poetical metrical foot consisting of two syllables, the first unaccented and the second accented: IAMB or IAMBUS
poetic metrical foot consisting of two unaccented syllables followed by one accented: ANAPEST
poetic pair of rhymed lines in iambic pentameter: HEROIC COUPLET
poetry with final lines usually in the form of a dedication: ENVOY
poetry free of conventional meter and rhyme: FREE VERSE
point made by showing contrary to be absurd: APAGOGE
point of view from which facts or matters are seen or judged: PERSPECTIVE
points on sole of shoe to prevent slipping: CALK
point or rod on which something rotates: PIVOT
point out, signify, indicate: DENOTE
pointed, sharp-edged: CULTRATE
pointless, silly, empty-headed: INANE
pointless or merely hypothetical: ACADEMIC
poison: ENVENOM
poisonous: TOXIC
poker bet made on a hand having only four cards of a suit: FOUR-FLUSH
poker game in which the first card is dealt face down, the four others face up: STUD POKER
poker hand made up of three of a kind and a pair: FULL HOUSE
poker hand of cards all of one suit: FLUSH
poker term for demanding a show of hands: CALL
police officer on a naval vessel: MASTER-AT-ARMS
police surveillance of a suspect or suspected place: STAKEOUT
polish or burnish: FURBISH
polite, good-natured remark: PLEASANTRY
polite, suave, refined: URBANE
polite behavior: AMENITIES
political candidate unexpectedly nominated: DARK HORSE

political device of altering a voting area to promote the interests of one political party: GERRYMANDER

political disorder: ANARCHY

political or governmental organization: POLITY

political party chief: SACHEM

political party meeting to select candidates, plan campaign: CAUCUS

political power to appoint to offices: PATRONAGE

politician from outside who is resented: CARPETBAGGER

politician who appeals to prejudices and passions: DEMAGOGUE

politicians' practice of trading votes and influence: LOGROLLING

politician's route in campaigning: HUSTINGS

politicking in rural districts: BARNSTORMING

politics of power: REALPOLITIK

poll tax: CAPITATION

pollens and spores, as a study: PALYNOLOGY

pollute, desecrate: PROFANE

polo time period: CHUKKER

polysyllabic, as of words: SESQUIPEDALIAN

pompous, artificially formal: STILTED

pompous, bombastic: FUSTIAN

pompous, bombastic style of speaking: GRANDILOQUENT

pompous, dogmatic, arrogant, haughty: PONTIFICAL

pompous, inflated: TUMID

pompous in speech: OROTUND

pompous person: BASHAW

pompously conceited: VAINGLORIOUS

ponder or meditate upon: RUMINATE

poor, also stingy: PENURIOUS

poor, penniless: IMPECUNIOUS

poor judgment shown: INJUDICIOUS

poor person, charity case: PAUPER

poorly made, cheap, shoddy: SLEAZY

poorly made, underdone: SLACK-BAKED

Pope's ambassador to a foreign government: NUNCIO

popular: DEMOTIC

popular, accepted, everyday speech: VULGATE

popular but incorrect idea of the origin of a word: FOLK ETYMOLOGY

populated densely, crowded: IMPACTED

population science: DEMOGRAPHY

porcelain or china that is very thin and delicate: EGGSHELL CHINA

porch or platform with steps at the entrance to a house: STOOP

porch with room held up by columns: PORTICO

pores admit fluids, air or light: POROUS

pornography: SMUT

pornography, as a study: COPROLOGY

port side of a ship: LARBOARD

portent, omen: AUGURY

portent, omen, warning: PRESAGE

portion, share, half: MOIETY

portion or serving: DOLLOP

portray, trace out, outline: DELINEATE

posing under a false name or character: IMPOSTURE

position or office that pays, but involves few or no duties: SINECURE

position specially suited to a person: NICHE

positive, arrogant assertion of opinion: DOGMATIC

positive, final, decisive, absolute: PEREMPTORY

positive, with no qualifications: CATEGORICAL

positive declaration: ASSEVERATION

possessive case in grammar: GENITIVE

possible, imaginable, secular: EARTHLY

possible but not in existence: POTENTIAL

possible or liable: CONTINGENT

possible outcome: EVENTUALITY

possession that is more trouble than it's worth: WHITE ELEPHANT

post at end of handrail of a staircase: NEWEL

postage stamp sold at an advanced price, the excess going to a charity or public service: SEMIPOSTAL

poster: PLACARD

poster or large sheet of paper with a printed message: BROADSIDE

postpone or forgo a right: WAIVE

postpone or put off habitually: PROCRASTINATE

postpone punishment or pain: REPRIEVE

posts supporting a handrail: BALUSTER

posture: STANCE

postponement, delay, interval of relief or rest: RESPITE

pot, small and made of earthenware: PIPKIN

pot or jar, broad-mouthed and of earthenware: OLLA

pot that is airtight and cooks food quickly under pressure: PRESSURE COOKER

potatoes prepared with finely sliced fried onions: LYONNAISE

potency, efficacy: VIRTUE

potential for development: SEMINAL

pottery, glazed, usually blue and white: DELFT

pottery of a very hard variety: STONE-WARE

pouchlike receptacle on the abdomen of female marsupials for carrying the young: MARSUPIUM

pour or spread out in all directions: DIF-FUSE

pour off a liquid without disturbing its sediment: DECANT

pouting facial expression: MOUE

poverty: INDIGENCE

powdered, demolished: PULVERIZED

powdery, dusty: PULVERULENT

power equal to a thousand watts: KILO-WATT

power of great proportions, gigantic: HERCULEAN

power of thought or feeling: INTENSITY

power that is absolute: DESPOTISM

powerful, mighty: PUISSANT

powerful appearing but really ineffective: PAPER TIGER

powerful or wealthy man: NABOB

powerless: IMPUISSANT

powerless, incapable of producing the effect desired: INEFFECTUAL

powerless, worthless: NUGATORY

powerless to act or accomplish anything: IMPOTENT

practicable, workable: VIABLE

practical, not theoretical: PRAGMATIC

practical, obstinate, shrewd: HARD-HEADED

practical, suitable: FEASIBLE

practical rather than scientific measure: RULE OF THUMB

practical saying: APOTHEGM

practice rather than theory: PRAXIS

praise: LAUD

praise, especially when formal and delivered publicly: EULOGY

praise extravagantly: ADULATE

praise for an achievement: KUDOS

praise in the highest terms, exalt, laud: EXTOL

praise or eulogy formally delivered: EN-COMIUM

praise that is elaborate, laudation: PAN-EGYRIC

prance or caper about: TITTUP

prance or frisk about: CAVORT

prank, spree, fling, reckless behavior: ES-CAPADE

pray earnestly for something, ask for humbly: SUPPLICATE

pray for or call down a calamity or a curse: IMPRECATE

prayer, short and suitable to an occasion: COLLECT

prayer at the opening of a ceremony: IN-VOCATION

prayer consisting of a long list of supplications, with a fixed response after each: LITANY

prayer or entreaty in behalf of others: IN-TERCESSION

prayer shawl worn by Orthodox and Conservative Jewish men: TALLITH

prayer stand with a shelf for a book: PRIE-DIEU

prayer stool, usually folding and cushioned: FALDSTOOL

prayer that is brief: EJACULATION

prayers made on nine days: NOVENA

prayers or services in the evening: VES-PERS

precarious position: SWORD OF DAMOCLES

preceding: PREVENIENT

precipice that extends a distance: PALI-SADES

precise, accurate, exact: NICE

precise, overly fastidious, fussy, exacting: FINICKY

pre-Christmas season: ADVENT

preconceived judgment: PARTI PRIS

predecessor, forerunner, something in advance: PRECURSOR

predetermination: FATALISM

predicament: QUANDARY

predicament, complicated situation: PLIGHT

predicament entailing a choice between two undesirable alternatives: DI-LEMMA

prediction, forecast: PROGNOSIS

predictor of the future: SOOTHSAYER

predisposition to certain forms of disease: DIATHESIS

preempt or appoint: CO-OPT

preface, introductory remark: PROLEGOM-ENON

preface, introductory statement: PROEM

preference preconceived: PREDILECTION

preferred stock on which unpaid dividends do not accrue: NONCUMULATIVE

preferred stock that is entitled to dividends beyond those stated: PARTICIPATING PREFERRED

pregnancy: GESTATION

pregnant: ENCEINTE

pregnant: GRAVID

pregnant for the first time or the mother of just one: PRIMIPARA

prejudice, bias: PRECONCEPTION

prejudiced, biased, favoring one party: PARTIAL

prejudicial appeal: AD HOMINEM

prelate, high priest: HIERARCH

prelate with highest rank in the country: PRIMATE

preliminary work for a project: SPADE-WORK

prematurely born animal, especially a calf: SLINK

prematurely bring forth young: ABORT

prematurely developed: PRECOCIOUS

premeditated, deliberately designed: STUDIED

precise about details, overly painstaking: METICULOUS

preoccupation with a thought or feeling that is compulsive and excessive: OBSESSION

preoccupied: BEMUSED

preparatory work for a project: SPADE-WORK

prerequisite: POSTULATE

present everywhere at once: UBIQUITOUS

present period or occasion: NONCE

present tense used to narrate a past event: HISTORICAL PRESENT

preside over, as a meeting: MODERATE

press a debtor for payment: DUN

press food, drinks, etc., on a person: PLY

pretend, dissemble, conceal: DISSIMULATE

pretend, feign: SIMULATE

pretend not to see wrongdoing: CONNIVE

pretended, deceptive, sham: FEIGNED

pretended blow or deception meant to distract: FEINT

pretending to be someone else in order to deceive: IMPOSTURE

pretending to be what one is not or better than one is, pretending to be virtuous or good: HYPOCRISY

pretense, false appearance: GUISE

pretentious, inflated: OVERBLOWN

pretentious, ostentatious or hypocritical ceremony: MUMMERY

pretentious, overdignified, self-important: POMPOUS

pretentious behavior: AFFECTATION

pretentious boasting: BRAGGADOCIO

pretentious language: CLAPTRAP

pretentious official: PANJANDRUM

pretentious or extremist person: HIGHFLIER

pretentiously grand, imposing: GRANDIOSE

pretentiousness, windy promposity: FLAT-ULENCE

prevalent, dominant: REGNANT

prevent, avert: OBVIATE

prevent, guard against or hinder in advance: FORESTALL

prevent, render impossible, exclude: PRE-CLUDE

preventing sleep: AGRYPNOTIC

preventive treatment against disease: PRO-PHYLAXIS

previous to examination: A PRIORI

previously, before now: HERETOFORE

prey, game: QUARRY

prey upon, pillage, plunder: DEPREDATE

price at which a bond may be redeemed before it reaches maturity: REDEMP-TION PRICE

price at which a person is ready to buy a security: BID

price at which a person is ready to sell a security: OFFER

price changes that can be absorbed by the market in a particular security: LIQUIDITY

price fall caused by decrease of money in circulation: DEFLATION

price last reported at which security was sold: MARKET PRICE

price level reduced to increase purchasing power but avoid deflation: DISINFLA-TION

price of a stock transaction higher than the preceding transaction: UP TICK, PLUS-TICK

price range of buyer and seller of a given stock at a given time: QUOTATION

price rise and fall in value of money: IN-FLATION

price that is the lowest at which something will be sold at an auction: UPSET PRICE

priceless: INESTIMABLE

priceless: INVALUABLE

prickly: SPINOUS

prickly heat: MILIARIA

pride, especially in someone else (Yiddish): NACHUS

priestly: SACERDOTAL

priest's forgiveness of sin, in confession: ABSOLUTION

priests or clergy in charge of government: HIEROCRACY

prima donna, female operatic singer: DIVA

primary in which people rather than delegates select candidates: DIRECT PRIMARY

primitive: ABORIGINAL

primitive, pure: PRISTINE

primitive state, reversion to: ATAVISM

primp, dress showily: PREEN

principle, belief or doctrine maintained as true by a person or a group: TENET

principal, original, first: PRIMAL

principal commodity, regularly in demand: STAPLE

print a line, paragraph, etc., in from the margin: INDENT

printed character containing two or more letters joined together: LIGATURE

printed sheets, loosely bound together: CAHIER

printer's shallow tray for holding type before it is put into a form: GALLEY

printer's term for an opening cut in a plate for the insertion of type: MORTISE

printing type group containing all the characters in one size and style: FONT

printing even with the outside margin: FLUSH

printing from a flat stone or metal plate on which the material to be printed is treated with grease that absorbs ink: LITHOGRAPHY

printing from raised surfaces: LETTER PRESS

printing machines that cast type in single characters: MONOTYPE

printing or writing with flowing lines: CURSIVE

printing ornament or symbol: DINGBAT

printing press that prints both sides of a sheet simultaneously: PERFECTING PRESS

printing press that uses webs, or rolls of paper, rather than separate sheets: WEB PRESS

printing press using curved plates and rolls of paper: ROTARY PRESS

printing process in which subjects are reproduced by photography on plates in relief: PHOTOENGRAVING

printing process in which the impression is transferred to a rubber roller and then to the paper: OFFSET

printing, receptacle for broken or battered type: HELLBOX

printing sign (☞) to direct attention: INDEX or FIST

printing term for a blurred impression: MACKLE

printing term for part of a letter that extends downward: DESCENDER

printing term for part of a letter that extends upward: ASCENDER

printing term for thinnest of metal spaces separating letters or words: HAIR SPACE

printing type characteristic consisting of a fine line that finishes off a stroke: SERIF

printing type jumble: PI

printing type set in excess of the space available: OVERSET

printing type that is bold and somewhat fancy: OLD ENGLISH

printing type with thin light lines: LIGHTFACE

prints transferred from specially prepared paper to glass, wood: DECALCOMANIA

prisoner of captors setting terms for his release: HOSTAGE

prisoner surrendered or delivered up to the jurisdiction of another state or country: EXTRADITION

private, isolated room: SANCTUM

private or confidential, as a conversation: TÊTE-À-TÊTE

privately said, undertone: SOTTO VOCE

privilege extended to stockholders ahead of others, to buy new issues, usually at lower than market price: RIGHTS

privilege or benefit owed because of status: PERQUISITE

privilege or exemption as in right to send mail without charge: FRANK

prize that is the biggest one possible to win: JACKPOT

problem of choosing between unpleasant alternatives: DILEMMA

problem that is complicated: GORDIAN KNOT

problems pile up; solution of one raises another and leads back to the original one: VICIOUS CIRCLE proclamation, public declaration: PRO-NUNCIAMENTO

prod or incite: GOAD

produce, beget: PROCREATE

produce, perform or invent without previous thought or preparation: IMPROVISE

producing many or much: PROLIFIC

producing or capable of producing a desired effect: EFFICACIOUS

production of goods and services by a nation: GROSS NATIONAL PRODUCT (G.N.P.)

productive, inventive, fruitful: PREGNANT

productive, potential, germinal: SEMINAL

productive equipment owned by businesses: CAPITAL GOODS

profane or use sacrilegiously: DESECRATE

profaning or violation of anything sacred: SACRILEGE

professional or clerical worker: WHITE COLLAR

profile or dark shape with a light background: SILHOUETTE

profit anticipated but not yet realized on a security still held: PAPER PROFIT

profit from sale of assets: CAPITAL GAIN

profitable: LUCRATIVE

profitable: REMUNERATIVE

profitable source: PAY DIRT

profound, hidden: RECONDITE

progress resulting from planning: TELESIS

progression by a constant quantity: ARITHMETIC PROGRESSION

progression or arrangement that is orderly or gradual: GRADATION

prohibit, debar, forbid a person to have or do something: INTERDICT

prohibit, outlaw, condemn: PROSCRIBE

prohibited, unlawful: ILLICIT

prohibited by convention or tradition: TABOO

prohibition: INJUNCTION

project on the basis of facts already known, infer from evidence at hand: EXTRAPOLATE

projecting part of a battle line: SALIENT

projecting structure supported at only one end: CANTILEVER

proliferate, sprout: BURGEON

prolific, fruitful, fertile: FECUND

prolific or fond of children: PHILOPROGENITIVE

prologue: PROLUSION

prolonged or held, in music: SOSTENUTO

promenade or strut: CAKEWALK

prominent or memorable object in the landscape: LANDMARK

promiscuous woman, slut: SLATTERN

promise, guarantee: STIPULATE

promotion awarded on the battlefield: BREVET

promptness, speed: DISPATCH

pronounce with a sound omitted: ELIDE

pronounced without stress when in combination with a preceding word: ENCLITIC

pronunciation standards: ORTHOEPY

pronouncing "r" as "l" or vice versa: LALLATION

proof of a crime: CORPUS DELICTI

proof of the genuineness of a document such as a will: PROBATE

proof of printed matter used for making corrections: GALLEY

proof or safe against attack: UNASSAILABLE

propensity: APPETENCE

proper, advisable, suitable: EXPEDIENT

proper, conventional: ORTHODOX

proper, seemly in behavior: DECOROUS

proper or customary act or procedure: FORMALITY

properness, conformity with accepted usage: PROPRIETY

property improvements: CAPITAL EXPENDITURE

property ownership as the key to political power: TIMOCRACY

property reverting to government in absence of legal heirs: ESCHEAT

property seizure in legal proceeding: ATTACHMENT

property transfer: CONVEYANCE

prophesying, foretelling the future: DIVINATION

prophet or messiah in Islam: MAHDI

prophetess of doom whose prophecies go unheeded: CASSANDRA

prophetic, enigmatic: ORACULAR

prophetic, having divinatory power: MANTIC

prophetic, inspired: PYTHONIC

prophetic, oracular: VATIC

proportionate: COMMENSURATE

proposal in outline form for a written work or business project: PROSPECTUS

propose, suggest: PROPOUND

proposition that is demonstrably true, as in geometry: THEOREM

propriety or aptness of behavior: CONVENANCE

prosaic, dull, mediocre: PEDESTRIAN

prose that is long and tiresome: SCREED

prosperity, as a mark of the times for instance: FLUSH

prosperous or successful period: FLORESCENCE

prostitute: COCOTTE

prostitute: HARLOT

prostitute: HOOKER

prostitute: TROLLOP

prostitute catering to men of wealth or high rank: COURTESAN

prostitute who works in response to telephone calls: CALL GIRL

prostitute's agent: PIMP

prostitutes as a group: DEMIMONDE

prostitution, as of talent or office, for gain: VENALITY

protect against loss or damage: INDEMNIFY

protected against malfunctioning: FAILSAFE

protected legally by patent or copyright, owned by a proprietor: PROPRIETARY

protection against disease: PROPHYLAXIS

protective influence: AEGIS

protector of the people: TRIBUNE

protest or oppose by pleading: REMONSTRATE

protoplasm building and breaking down as continuous bodily processes: METABOLISM

prototype: ARCHETYPE

protruding: EXSERTILE

protuberance, swelling: TUBEROSITY

prove false or contradict: BELIE

prove someone or something wrong: CONFUTE

proverb: ADAGE

proverb: APHORISM

provincial, limited, narrow: PAROCHIAL

provincial, limited in outlook: INSULAR

provisions for a journey: VIATICUM

provoker of punishable acts: AGENT PROVOCATEUR

provoking, annoying person: GADFLY

provoking anger or resentment by being unjustly discriminating: INVIDIOUS

prudence: CALCULATION

prudent, diplomatic, wise: POLITIC

prudent, tactful, careful about what one says: DISCREET

prudent, wary: CANNY

prudish editing: BOWDLERIZATION

prudish, shocked or nauseated easily: SQUEAMISH

pry or break open as with a crowbar: JIMMY

prying or offensively curious: INQUISITORIAL

psychiatric disorder marked by separation of thought from emotions: SCHIZOPHRENIA

psychoanalysis patient: ANALYSAND

psychoanalyst, psychiatrist: SHRINK

psychoanalytical arrested development: FIXATION

public attention or notice: LIMELIGHT

public brawl: AFFRAY

public display: BLAZON

public forum place: AGORA

public good as the objective: PRO BONO PUBLICO

public offices offered as rewards of partisan service: SPOILS SYSTEM

public sale or auction: VENDUE

publicize officially, put into effect: PROMULGATE

publicizer of real or alleged corruption: MUCKRAKER

publisher of books at the author's expense: VANITY PRESS

publisher's trademark: COLOPHON

puckish, gay, strange: FEY

pudding baked under a roast to catch the drippings: YORKSHIRE PUDDING

puff, blow in gusts: WHIFFLE

pugnacious in a disagreeable way: TRUCULENT

pull or force away by violent twist: WREST

pulsatory: SPHYGMIC

pulsing, throbbing: VIBRANT

pulverize: COMMINUTE

pulverize: TRITURATE

pulverize to fine powder: LEVIGATE

pun: PARONOMASIA

pun, double meaning: PLAY UPON WORDS

punch holes into: PERFORATE

pungent: ACRID

punish, beat or thrash severely: TROUNCE

punish, discipline: FERULE

punish by arbitrary fine: AMERCE

punishment for evil: RETRIBUTION

punishment that corresponds to the nature of the crime: TALION

punitive, avenging: VINDICATORY

punning: PARONOMASIA

pupil absent from school without permission: TRUANT

purchasing power of individuals: REAL INCOME

pure, primitive: PRISTINE

pure essential part: QUINTESSENCE

purging or purifying of emotions: CATHARSIS

purify by a sacrifice or ceremony: LUSTRATE

purify by exposure to air: AERATE

purify by washing and straining or decanting: ELUTRIATE

purify or refine: RAREFY

purifying: DEPURATIVE

purplish red: MURREY

purpose, aim, goal: INTENT

purposeful: TELIC

purposeless, haphazard: RANDOM

pursue an undertaking: PROSECUTE

pursuit, search, adventure: QUEST

push down, thrust away from: DETRUDE

push or crowd roughly, shake up, elbow, shove: JOSTLE

push out, make protrude: EXSERT

pushy, nosy, obtrusive, forward: OFFICIOUS

put down, belittle: DISPARAGE

put down, suppress forcibly: QUASH

put down by force, allay: QUELL

put in gradually by drops: INSTILL

put in or inject a comment or digression in a speech or argument: INTERPOSE

put in prison: INCARCERATE

put into words, phrase: COUCH

put off or postpone habitually: PROCRASTINATE

put out of consciousness unacceptable memories, desires and impulses: REPRESSION

putting into effect, carrying through: IMPLEMENTATION

puzzle in which the sound of a word or phrase is represented by letters, numerals, pictures: REBUS

puzzle out, interpret, understand: FATHOM

puzzled, uncertain, bewildered: PERPLEXED

puzzling, complicated, involved: INTRICATE

puzzling, secret, hidden, occult, mystifying: CRYPTIC

pyramid or cone with top sliced off: FRUSTUM

Pyrrhic victory: CADMEAN VICTORY

Q

quack medicine, cure-all, medicine of one's own invention: NOSTRUM

quack-medicine vendor, charlatan: MOUNTEBANK

quadrangular: TETRAGONAL

quail, tremble or crouch as in fear: COWER

quaint, fanciful, as in a literary work: WHIMSY

quality, goodness, moral excellence: VIRTUE

qualm, doubt, apprehension: MISGIVING

quantity that a container lacks of being full: ULLAGE

quantity that is specified: QUANTUM

quarrel: ALTERCATION

quarrel, difference of opinion, discord: DISSENSION

quarrel, wrangling: JANGLE

quarrel or argue noisily: WRANGLE

quarreling, inability to agree: AT LOGGERHEADS

quarrelsome: BELLICOSE

quarrelsome: CANTANKEROUS

quarrelsome: CONTENTIOUS

quarrelsome: DISSENTIOUS

quarrelsome: LITIGIOUS

quarrelsome: PUGNACIOUS

quarrelsome, vixenish: TERMAGANT

queenly: REGINAL

queer, eccentric: CRANKY

quench or satisfy, as a thirst: SLAKE

question, examine: INTERROGATE

question a person insistently: PLY

question and answer method of instruction: SOCRATIC METHOD

question and answer method of teaching: CATECHISM

question asked for effect and not calling for an answer: RHETORICAL QUESTION

question searchingly and at length: CATECHIZE

questionable, difficult to solve: PROBLEMATIC

questionable or suspicious: EQUIVOCAL

questionable or uncertain: DUBIOUS

questioning existence of God: AGNOSTICISM

questioning or prying characterized by harshness: INQUISITION

quibble: CAVIL

quibble, lie: PALTER

quibbler over small matters: PETTIFOGGER

quibbling: CAPTIOUS

quick disposal of a matter, as of a piece of business: DISPATCH OR WITH DISPATCH

quick efficiency: DISPATCH

quick or ready in performance, easily achieved: FACILE

quick tempo, rapidly, swiftly, in music: VELOCE

quickly, briskly, lively, in music: VIVACE

quickly or suddenly, in music: SUBITO

quickness of mind: ACUMEN

quick-tempered, irritable: IRASCIBLE

quiet, abate, calm: SUBSIDE

quiet, reserved, reluctant to speak: RETICENT

quiet consent: ACQUIESCENCE

quiet down, soothe, mitigate, pacify: MOLLIFY

quiet, make peaceful: PACIFY

quiet, serene, calm: TRANQUIL

quilt made of irregularly shaped pieces of variously colored and patterned fabric: CRAZY QUILT

quip: SALLY

quip, fun, playfulness: JEST

quirk, habit, mannerism peculiar to an individual: IDIOSYNCRASY

quiver, flutter, beat rapidly: PALPITATE

quota for a race or class in admission to an
academic   institution: NUMERUS
CLAUSUS

quotation or motto prefixed to a book:
EPIGRAPH

quoting a person without using his exact
words: INDIRECT DISCOURSE

R

"r" pronounced like "l" or "l" pronounced like "r" or "w": LALLATION

rabbit dwelling: WARREN

rabbit fur: LAPIN

rabbit stew as prepared in Germany: HASENPFEFFER

rabies: HYDROPHOBIA

race course's section farthest from spectators: BACK STRETCH

race course's straight portion forming the final approach to the finish: HOME STRETCH

race improvement study or science: EUGENICS

race on horseback along a course containing obstacles: STEEPLECHASE

races and ethnic groups, as subjects of study: ETHNOLOGY

racial and ethnic groups brought together in legal and social equality: INTEGRATION

racial equalizing: DESEGREGATION

racial segregation in South Africa: APARTHEID

racing finish so close that a camera is needed to decide the winner: PHOTO FINISH

racing gambling system in which those backing the winners share in the total wagered: PARIMUTUEL

racing gambling system in which winnings of a previous race are placed on a later one: PARLAY

rack or frame on which to dry fish, cheese, bricks, etc.: HACK

rack or platform for drying food: FLAKE

racketeers' money collector: BAGMAN

racy, stimulating: PIQUANT

radar warning system in North America: DEW LINE

radiance, splendor: EFFULGENCE

radiance, brilliance: REFULGENCE

radiance enveloping a sanctified being: AUREOLE

radiant, transparent: LUCENT

radiate, diffuse: EXUDE

radiating, star-shaped: STELLATE

radical or liberal political figure: LEFTIST

radical or liberal political position: LEFT

radio announcer who conducts a program of recorded music: DISC JOCKEY

radio or television station code letters: CALL LETTERS

radioactivity duration measure: HALF-LIFE

radio-reflecting layer of the ionosphere: HEAVISIDE LAYER

ragamuffin: TATTERDEMALION

ragged edge of handmade paper: DECKLE EDGE

raggedly dressed person, usually a child: RAGAMUFFIN

raging, fanatical: RABID

raging, frenzied: MADDING

raid, invasion: INCURSION

raid, lay waste, pillage: HARRY

raid, plunder, invade for booty: MARAUD

raid, plunder, pillage: FORAY

raiding force or member of one: COMMANDO

rail at, berate, find fault abusively: VITUPERATE

railroad building for repairing and switching locomotives: ROUNDHOUSE

railroad signal to go ahead: HIGHBALL

railway with a single track: MONORAIL

rainbow-like colors that shift: IRIDESCENCE

rainbow trout along the Pacific coast: STEELHEAD

rainfall study: HYETOGRAPHY

rainy: PLUVIOUS

rainy season that comes with the summer

wind along the Asian coast of the Pacific: MONSOON

raise trivial objections, or carp: CAVIL

raise with a rope: TRICE

raised figures worked on a surface as decoration: EMBOSSED

raised platform on which guests of honor or speakers are seated: DAIS

raised sculpture in which figures project slightly: BAS-RELIEF

rake, profligate: LIBERTINE

rake, sensualist: ROUÉ

raking gunfire: ENFILADE

rakish, vulgar: RAFFISH

ram that has been castrated: WETHER

ramble, wander from main subject: DIGRESS

rambling, aimless wandering: MEANDERING

rambling, confused: INCOHERENT

rambling, discursive, digressive: EXCURSIVE

rambling and wordy talk: GARRULITY

ramp or incline: GRADIENT

ramp with curving or spiral passageway: HELICLINE

ram's horn of ancient times still used in synagogues: SHOFAR

rancorous, bitter: VIRULENT

random, accidental: HAPHAZARD

random, confused: INDISCRIMINATE

random shot or criticism: POT SHOT

range, extent, scope: PURVIEW

range, scope: LATITUDE

range in its entirety: GAMUT

range or limit, as of power or action: TETHER

rank, spoiled-smelling: RANCID

rank formation as with troops, fleets, airplanes: ECHELON

rank in society, organization, business, etc.: PECKING ORDER

rankle, irritate, cause bitterness: FESTER

ransack and rob: RIFLE

rapid, swift: TANTIVY

rapidly, swiftly, quick tempo, in music: VELOCE

rapture or emotion that is overpowering: ECSTASY

rare person or thing: RARA AVIS

rare-book dealer: BIBLIOPOLE

rascal, rogue: RAPSCALLION

rash: BRASH

rash, hasty, impulsive: IMPETUOUS

rash, incautious, thriftless: IMPROVIDENT

rash, reckless: TEMERARIOUS

rashly, recklessly: HEADLONG

ratify, approve, permit: SANCTION

rational, clear, easily understood, bright, shining: LUCID

rationalization of matters of morals and ethics: CASUISTRY

rattle, crackle: CREPITATE

rattling or clattering noise: BRATTLE

rattle that is gourd-shaped and used to sound a rhythm: MARACA

rave, speak violently: RANT

raw cane sugar: MUSCOVADO

raw material: STAPLE

reach or arrive at a port: FETCH

react: REDOUND

reaction developed by training: CONDITIONED REFLEX

reaction in exaggerated form to a psychological defect: OVERCOMPENSATION

reaction in exaggerated form to a situation or subject: COMPLEX

reaction of a violent nature: BACKLASH

read intently or study with care: PORE

read or examine thoroughly, scrutinize: PERUSE

read or glance over hastily: SKIM

read quickly, glance at: SCAN

readily, willingly: LIEF

readiness to comply, pliancy: FACILITY

reading ability impairment: DYSLEXIA

reading ability is beyond this person: FUNCTIONAL ILLITERATE

reading ability lost: ALEXIA

reading of a word or sentence is the same backward as forward: PALINDROME

ready, easy-going, agreeable: FACILE

ready to be put into use: OPERATIONAL

real, actual: SUBSTANTIVE

real, material, having definite shape: TANGIBLE

real existence of something in the mind, actual being: ENTITY

realistic to the point of looking real, as in art or decoration: TROMPE L'OEIL

reality studied as a philosophical theory: ONTOLOGY

realization or accomplishment of things worked for: FRUITION

reappearance or fresh outbreak: RECRUDESCENCE

rear, feed, support, raise: NURTURE

rear car of freight train: CABOOSE

rear end of a boat: STERN

rear, toward the stern, on a boat: AFT

reason, think: INTELLECTUALIZE
reason by logical methods: RATIOCINATE
reason or justification for being: RAISON D'ETRE
reason earnestly with someone, remonstrate: EXPOSTULATE
reasonable, apparently true, but open to doubt: PLAUSIBLE
reasonable, practicable, suitable: FEASIBLE
reasoned, sensible: RATIONAL
reasoning as opposed to intuition in reaching conclusions: DISCURSIVE
reasoning from general to particular: DEDUCTION
reasoning that is clever but unsound: SOPHISTRY
reasoning that is faulty or illogical: PARALOGISM
reasons underlying something: RATIONALE
rebellious: INSUBORDINATE
rebellious: INSURGENT
rebellious, insolent: CONTUMACIOUS
rebellious, irritable, unruly, cranky: FRACTIOUS
rebirth, restoration, reconstitution: REGENERATION
rebound or skip of a bullet or stone after it hits a surface at an angle: RICOCHET
rebuff, reject, repel: REPULSE
rebuke, castigate, rake over the coals: KEELHAUL
rebuke, censure, blame for a fault: REPROACH
rebuke, disapproval, censure: REPROOF
rebuke, criticize, find fault with, blame: REPREHEND
rebuke or censure severely: REPRIMAND
rebuke or chastise severely: CASTIGATE
rebuke sharply, upbraid, berate: OBJURGATE
recall, cancel, rescind, annul: REVOKE
recall to mind, remember: RETRIEVE
recalling or telling of past events: REMINISCENCE
recalling past occurrences, remembering: RETROSPECTION
recalling to mind: ANAMNESIS
recant: ABJURE
recapitulation of an oration: PERORATION
receptive: HOSPITABLE
recess, time between parts of a performance or between events or activities: INTERMISSION
recess period in work: COFFEE BREAK

recipient of benefits or favors: BENEFICIARY
reckless, careless: DEVIL-MAY-CARE
reckless, careless, weak: FECKLESS
reckless, rash: TEMERARIOUS
reckless dealing: PLAY DUCKS AND DRAKES WITH
reckless ride in a stolen vehicle, ride for pleasure: JOY RIDE
recklessly, rashly: HEADLONG
reclining, leaning, lying down: RECUMBENT
recluse: ANCHORITE
recluse: TROGLODYTE
recognize as different, perceive: DISCERN
recoil: BACKLASH
recoil, resume original shape after being stretched: RESILE
recollection: ANAMNESIS
reconcile and blend, as various philosophies: SYNCRETIZE
record of happenings worth remembering: MEMORABILIA
recover: RECUPERATE
recover, pay off: REDEEM
recover, remedy the consequences of, regain, make up for: RETRIEVE
recovery of property pending a court test: REPLEVIN
rectify, compensate: REDRESS
rectum and its diseases, as a branch of medicine: PROCTOLOGY
recurrence in the mind of the same thought, experience, etc.: PERSEVERATION
recurrent: CHRONIC
recurring at regular intervals, intermittent: PERIODIC
red, especially in heraldry: GULES
red color that is dull: STAMMEL
red tape in government: BUREAUCRACY
reddening: RUBESCENT
redemption price of a bond, if it is higher than the face value: PREMIUM
red-handed: IN FLAGRANTE DELICTO
redistrict a voting area so as to advance the interests of a political party: GERRYMANDER
reduce expenses: RETRENCH
reduce in quantity or force: ABATE
reduce in rank or position: ABASE
reduce in size, lessen, belittle: MINIFY
reduce to smallest possible amount or degree: MINIMIZE
reduction of debt or liability, done gradu-

ally as by installment payments:
AMORTIZATION

reduction of personnel through retirement,
death, etc.: ATTRITION

redundancy: TAUTOLOGY

redundancy, use of excess words: PLEO-
NASM

refine or purify: RAREFY

refine, purify, clear of waste matter: DEF-
ECATE

refined, polite, suave: URBANE

refined or delicate to an extreme: FASTIDI-
OUS

refined to excess: RECHERCHÉ

refinement, well-bred in one's ways:
GENTILITY

reflect, think about, consider carefully:
PONDER

reflecting light, shining back, bright: RE-
LUCENT

reflective, serious, often melancholy:
PENSIVE

refrain from: ABSTAIN

refreshments: COLLATION

refusal given bluntly: REBUFF

refuse, scorn, reject: SPURN

refuse, waste matter: DROSS

refuse scornfully, treat with contempt:
DISDAIN

refuse to accept, disown, reject: REPUDI-
ATE

refuse to deal with so as to punish: BOY-
COTT

refuse to go forward, balk: JIB

refutation in syllogistic form: ELENCHUS

regain, as for a loss: RECOUP

regain, recover, make up for, remedy the
consequences of: RETRIEVE

register or enroll in a college or university
as a candidate for a degree: MATRIC-
ULATE

register of deeds, etc.: CARTULARY

regret an action, feel contrite: REPENT

regret extremely: RUE

regret, plead against: DEPRECATE

regular fixed-dollar amount method of
purchasing securities: MONTHLY IN-
VESTMENT PLAN

regular repetition: CONTINUAL

regularly recurring, intermittent: PERIODIC

regulate, adjust, temper or soften: MODU-
LATE

rehearsal: DRY RUN

reimburse: RECOUP

rein thirty or more feet long at the end of

which the horse moves for training
and exercise: LONGE

reinvigorating: ANALEPTIC

reject, rebuff, repel: REPULSE

reject, drive back: REPEL

reject, refuse, scorn: SPURN

reject, refuse to accept, disown: REPUDI-
ATE

reject with contempt, refuse scornfully:
DISDAIN

rejection of customary belief, immortality
and institutions: NIHILISM

rejoice greatly: EXULT

related on the male or father's side: AG-
NATE

related or alike in meaning, significance or
effect: SYNONYMOUS

related or similar in structure, position,
value: HOMOLOGOUS

related superficially: TANGENTIAL

related to a subject, relevant: PERTINENT

related to what is being discussed, relevant, pertinent: GERMANE

relationship that is close: AFFINITY

relationships within a group, as a study:
SOCIOMETRY

relaxant, sleep-producing medicine:
OPIATE

release from care and pain, bliss: NIRVANA

release of repressed emotion by reliving or
talking about original situation:
ABREACTION

relentless: INEXORABLE

relevant, pertinent, related to what is
being discussed: GERMANE

relevant, related to a subject: PERTINENT

relevant only in part: TANGENTIAL

relief design, as in metal: REPOUSSÉ

relieving irritation, soothing: DEMULCENT

religious belief rejected: ATHEISM

religious devotion: PIETY

religious ecstasy: THEOPATHY

religious literature, traditions, etc.:
HIEROLOGY

religious movement based on literal accep-
tance of everything in the Bible:
FUNDAMENTALISM

religious offering: OBLATION

religious ritual: LITURGY

religious washing of hands: ABLUTION

relinquish, give up, forgo: WAIVE

reliquary: FERETORY

reliving a traumatic situation for release
from it: ABREACTION

reluctant, unwilling: LOATH

remainder, leftover part: RESIDUE

remainder after deducting all allowances: NET

remark made in passing, comment that is not binding: OBITER DICTUM

remark or observation that is brief, clever and pointed: EPIGRAM

remarkable, strange, extraordinary: UNACCOUNTABLE

remarriage after death or divorce of first spouse: DIGAMY

remedy: TREACLE

remedy for all ailments, cure-all: PANACEA

remedy or cure for all ills: CATHOLICON

remedy that one swears by, medicine of one's own invention, quack medicine, cure-all: NOSTRUM

remedy the consequences of, get back, regain: RETRIEVE

remember, recall to mind: RETRIEVE

remembering: RETROSPECTION

remembering in complete detail: TOTAL RECALL

remind one of a mistake or fault in order to taunt or annoy: TWIT

remission of sin: ABSOLUTION

remorse: COMPUNCTION

remove, take off, as clothing: DOFF

remove attention from: PRESCIND

remove obscene or otherwise objectionable material: EXPURGATE

remove or dissociate from former habits: WEAN

remove or drive away, as by scattering: DISPEL

remove property to a distance or beyond a jurisdiction: ELOIGN

removing by surgery: ABSCISSION

renaming a parent after his or her child: TEKNONYMY

render null and void: INVALIDATE

renew, repair: RENOVATE

renew, restore to perfection: REDINTEGRATE

renounce: ABJURE

renounce: ABNEGATION

renounce, give up: RELINQUISH

renounce claim to right or power: ABDICATE

renounce or abandon emphatically: FORSWEAR

renovate, make over: REVAMP

renown or splendor of reputation: ECLAT

renowned, distinguished: ILLUSTRIOUS

renowned, important: PRESTIGIOUS

repay evil in kind, take revenge: RETALIATE

repay in kind, compensate: REQUITE

repay or pay, make up for, as a loss: RECOMPENSE

repeal: ABROGATE

repeal, revoke, abrogate: RESCIND

repeat: ITERATE

repeat, say or do over and over: REITERATE

repeat meaningless words over and over, babble: VERBIGERATE

repeated: CONTINUAL

repeated song or phrase in music: REPRISE

repeatedly appearing: RECURRENT

repel: REBUFF

repel, reject, rebuff: REPULSE

repent: RUE

repetition needlessly in different words: TAUTOLOGY

repetition of an initial sound in a series of words: ALLITERATION

repetition of last word of one sentence at beginning of next sentence or clause: ANADIPLOSIS

repetition of word or phrase: ANAPHORA

repetition of someone's words in senseless fashion: ECHOLALIA

repetition of written letters or words done unintentionally: DITTOGRAPHY

replace, supplant: SUPERSEDE

replies that are quick and witty: REPARTEE

reply, please: RÉPONDEZ S'IL VOUS PLAÎT (R.S.V.P.)

reply proving someone or something wrong: CONFUTE

reply sharply: RETORT

report of proceedings: CAHIER

reporting official for a conference or committee: RAPPORTEUR

representative of a government, as a civil magistrate or officer: SYNDIC

representative of a special interest group who tries to influence legislation: LOBBYIST

representative or symbol of something, as of a doctrine or a cause: EXPONENT

reprimand, scolding: RATING

reproach, scold, censure: UPBRAID

reproach sarcastically: TAUNT

reproduction or imitation of the original: ECTYPE

reprove mildly: ADMONISH

reptiles and amphibians, as a study: HERPETOLOGY

repudiate: ABJURE
repudiate, contradict, deny: DISAFFIRM
repudiate a former belief: RECANT
repugnant, disgusting, offensive, hateful: ODIOUS
repulsive: LOATHSOME
repulsive, evil, flagrantly bad: VILE
repulsive appearance: EYESORE
reputed, usually considered: PUTATIVE
request or entreaty that succeeds: IMPE-TRATION
require, claim: POSTULATE
require as a matter of justice, demand rigorously: EXACT
required, indispensable: REQUISITE
required, obligatory: MANDATORY
required by long use or custom: PRE-SCRIPTIVE
required earlier than something that follows: PREREQUISITE
resemblance in certain aspects of otherwise dissimilar things: ANALOGY
resembling another closely: COUNTER-PART
resent another's possessions or enjoyment: BEGRUDGE
resentful, angry: IN HIGH DUDGEON
resentfully morose, glum: SULLEN
resentment, anger: DUDGEON
resentment, injured feeling: UMBRAGE
resentment, offended pride: PIQUE
reservation, excuse: SALVO
reserve accumulation of goods: STOCKPILE
reserve of unfilled orders: BACKLOG
reserved, close-mouthed: TACITURN
reserved, coy, shy, modest: DEMURE
reserved, reluctant to speak, quiet: RETI-CENT
residence: ABODE
resignation or giving up an office: DEMIS-SION
resiliency of market in a particular security in the face of changing prices: LIQUIDITY
resistance to established government: IN-SURRECTION
resistance to harmful influence or disease, exemption from obligation or penalty: IMMUNITY
resistant, immune: INSUSCEPTIBLE
resistant, not yielding to treatment, as a disease: REFRACTORY
resistant, unyielding: IMPREGNABLE
resistant to change, cautious, moderate: CONSERVATIVE

resisting, doubting, ignoring attitude: NEGATIVISM
resolved, unflinching, determined: RESO-LUTE
resonant: SONOROUS
resounding loudly: REBOANT
resounding or echoing: RESONANT
respect, reverence or homage: OBEISANCE
respect deeply: VENERATE
respect demanded, criticism forbidden for such a person or idea: SACRED COW
respectable: SAVORY
respects paid to a dignitary such as a king: DEVOIRS
responding involuntarily to a stimulus, as an organism does: TROPISM
response developed by training: CONDI-TIONED REFLEX
response, echo: REPLICATION
responsibility for all one's acts (Buddhism and Hinduism): KARMA
responsive to persuasion or change: AMENABLE
responsive to persuasion or entreaty: EX-ORABLE
rest in peace: REQUIESCAT IN PACE
rest interval, postponement, delay: RE-SPITE
restaurant or bar that is small: BISTRO
restaurant or cafe that provides entertainment: CABARET
resting, leaning or weighing upon something: INCUMBENT
resting, nonactive: STATIC
resting place for travelers or pilgrims: HOSPICE
restless, superficial, frivolous: YEASTY
restless, unruly, fidgety: RESTIVE
restless or nervous movements: FIDGET
restlessness, anxiety: DISQUIETUDE
restlessness, uneasiness: INQUIETUDE
restoration, compensation, amends: REP-ARATION
restore friendship: RECONCILE
restore to perfection, renew: REDIN-TEGRATE
restore to rank, position, or state of health: REHABILITATE
restore youthful feeling or vigor: REJUVE-NATE
restrain or check, as an impulse: INHIBIT
restrained, moderate: TEMPERATE
restraint in sexual activity; moderation: CONTINENCE
restrict to a scanty amount: STINT

restriction, boundary: PALE

restriction on freight transportation: EMBARGO

result: AFTERMATH

result, effect: RAMIFICATION

result or consequence that is normal: COROLLARY

resuscitation: ANABIOSIS

retaining wall: REVETMENT

retaliation: REPRISAL

retentive, as memory: TENACIOUS

retinue, train of attendants: CORTEGE

retire, make oneself inconspicuous: EFFACE

retired from active service, but retained in honorary position: EMERITUS

retired on account of age: SUPERANNUATED

retort that is sharp and swift: RIPOSTE

retract: ABJURE

retraction: PALINODE

retreat to an earlier or worse condition: RETROGRESS

retroactive: EX POST FACTO

return by an offender to criminal acts or antisocial behavior: RECIDIVISM

return in kind or amount: RECIPROCATE

return like for like, repay evil with evil, revenge: RETALIATE

return of part of the output of a system into the input: FEEDBACK

return to a former place, position or condition: REVERT

return to normal condition or better: RALLY

reveal, bring to light, disclose: EXHUME

reveal, give vent to: UNBOSOM

reveal, tell, as a secret: DIVULGE

revelry, usually lasting for a special season or period: SATURNALIA

revenge sought by a country at the cost of war or violence: REVANCHISM

revengeful, spiteful: VINDICTIVE

reverberation, aftereffect: REPERCUSSION

revere: VENERATE

reverence, homage, respect: OBEISANCE

reverie: BROWN STUDY

reversal of opinion: ABOUT-FACE

reversal of opinion: FLIP-FLOP

reverse counting of time: COUNTDOWN

reverse of a proposition in logic: OBVERSE

reverse of truth thought of as if it were truth: DOUBLETHINK

reverse of phraseology in second of two parallel expressions: CHIASMUS

reverse reading of a word or sentence is the same as forward reading: PALINDROME

reverse side of a phonograph record: FLIP SIDE

reverse vision, as when objects are seen as in a mirror: STREPHOSYMBOLIA

reversed or opposite in order or effect: INVERSE

reversed order of things or events, used as a figure of speech: HYSTERON PROTERON

reversion, backward movement: REGRESSION

reversion to a more primitive type: ATAVISM

reversion to an earlier form or condition: THROWBACK

reviewing past occurrences, remembering: RETROSPECTION

revise, renovate: REVAMP

revise or vary, restrict or limit: MODIFY

revival, new birth: RENASCENCE

revive, bring or come back to life: RESUSCITATE

revive, refresh, renew: RENOVATE

revoke, abrogate, repeal: RESCIND

revoke a legacy: ADEEM

revoke or reverse a command: COUNTERMAND

revolve or rotate, usually around a fixed point: GYRATE

revolting, detestable, abominable: EXECRABLE

revolving, whirling or circular motion: GYRAL

rewarding partisan service with public offices: SPOILS SYSTEM

rewording of a statement with the original meaning retained: PARAPHRASE

reworked literary material, rehash: RECHAUFFÉ

rhyme composed of words similar in spelling but not in sound: EYE RHYME

rhyme in which stress falls on next to the last syllable: FEMININE RHYME

rhyme scheme in which a word within the line of verse rhymes with the final word of the line: LEONINE RHYME

rhyming game in which a rhyme must be given for word or line given by another: CRAMBO

rhythmic or measured flow: CADENCE

rhythmic placement of a tone so that its

accent does not coincide with the metric accent: SYNCOPATION

rib or ridge, as on fabric: WALE

ribbon cluster or rosette worn as a badge: COCKADE

ribbon worn as an insignia of honor or rank: CORDON

ribbons and pins in a store: NOTIONS

rice cooked in broth: RISOTTO

rich and resonant, as a tone: VIBRANT

rich man: CROESUS

rich or influential man: NABOB

rich person who has become so only recently: NOUVEAU RICHE

riches, wealth: OPULENCE

rickety: RAMSHACKLE

rid oneself of: SLOUGH

riddle, involving a pun: CONUNDRUM

riddle, puzzle, obscure or ambiguous saying: ENIGMA

ride for pleasure, reckless ride in a stolen vehicle: JOY RIDE

ridge around hatchway or skylight to keep out water: COAMING

ridge or rib, as on fabric: WALE

ridges fixed across the fingerboard of a guitar or other stringed instrument: FRETS

ridicule or scorn publicly: PILLORY

ridicule or treat with scornful mirth: DERIDE

ridicule or wit used to attack vices or follies: SATIRE

ridiculous, absurd: LUDICROUS

ridiculous or ludicrous situation: FARCE

riding the crest of a wave toward shore on a surfboard: SURFING

rifle with short barrel: CARBINE

right a wrong, make compensation: REDRESS

right- and left-handed: AMBIDEXTROUS

right angle position of a line or place to another: PERPENDICULAR

right-angled triangle's side that is opposite the right angle: HYPOTENUSE

right of feudal lords to first night with a bride: DROIT DU SEIGNEUR

right of the state to take over private property for public use: EMINENT DOMAIN

right or claim that is legal: DROIT

right or left part of something, side: FLANK

right side as opposed to the left side: DEXTER

right that is exclusive or a privilege: PREROGATIVE

right to left, a word or sentence reads the same as left to right: PALINDROME

right word or expression: MOT JUSTE

righteousness or holiness pretended: SANCTIMONIOUS

rigid, enlarged condition of the penis: ERECTION

rigid, inflexible: HARD-SHELL

rigid, severe: STRINGENT

rigidity of the muscles after death: RIGOR MORTIS

rigmarole: AMPHIGORY

ring, as for the finger, made up of two interlocked circlets: GIMMAL

ring for attaching a leash, as to a dog's collar: TERRET

ring or disk used to make a connection watertight or gastight: GASKET

ring in the ears: TINNITUS

ringing of bells: TINTINNABULATION

ringing or tinkling sound: JINGLE

ring-shaped hard breadroll: BAGEL

Rio de Janeiro resident: CARIOCA

riot, civil or political disturbance: DISTEMPER

riotous, wild: TURBULENT

rip apart forcibly: REND

ripen: MATURATE

ripple, bubble, heave: POPPLE

rise above: TRANSCEND

rise and float in the air: LEVITATE

rise or overflow of a stream occurring suddenly: FRESHET

rise somewhat from the water when moving at high speed: PLANE

rising again: RESURGENT

rising and falling gently, wavy in appearance: UNDULATING

rising and setting of a star: ACRONICAL

rising market: BULL MARKET

rising up in insurrection: INSURGENCE

risks taken to achieve some end: BRINKMANSHIP

risky: SPECULATIVE

risky, uncertain: TOUCH-AND-GO

risqué, indecent: SCABROUS

risqué, suggestive: RACY

rite considered ordained by Jesus as a means of grace: SACRAMENT

ritual of public religious worship: LITURGY

rival or vie with successfully: EMULATE

rivalry or competition: CONTENTION

river bank area: RIPARIAN

river embankment built to prevent flooding: LEVEE

river mouth where the stream's current meets the sea, an inlet of the sea: ESTUARY

river of oblivion, forgetfulness: LETHE

river of woe: ACHERON

river's head or supply of water: WATERSHED

road ascending a steep incline in a zigzag pattern: SWITCHBACK

road raised over marshy land: CAUSEWAY

road repairing utilizing forced labor: CORVEE

roam about in search of diversion, gad about: GALLIVANT

roaming, homeless: NOMADIC

rob, strip, deprive of: DESPOIL

rob a truck or seize a plane in transit: HIJACK

robber or bandit, usually one of a group: BRIGAND

robber who assaults victim from behind: MUGGER

robber who smuggles goods out of an open store: SHOPLIFTER

robe or undercoat, long sleeved and sashed: CAFTAN

robust, sound and vigorous health: HALE

robust, tough: HARDY

rock projecting and isolated: SCAR

rocket-firing schedule measured in records in reverse order: COUNTDOWN

rocket's forward separable section designed to stand intense heat: NOSE CONE

rocket's head containing explosive: WARHEAD

rocks and their characteristics, as a study: PETROLOGY

rocks' structure and composition as a scientific study: LITHOLOGY

rocky cliff that extends a distance: PALISADES

rococo: BAROQUE

rod that holds meat together for cooking: SKEWER

rod that is pointed and is used for cooking meat over a fire: SPIT

rod that is symbol of royalty: SCEPTER

rogue, rascal: RAPSCALLION

roll in shape of a crescent: CROISSANT

roll of film or magnetic tape in a case: CASSETTE

roll of hard bread that is ring-shaped: BAGEL

roll of sliced meat filled with minced meat: ROULADE

roll of minced meat or fish in a thin pastry: RISSOLE

roll or move tumultuously: WELTER

rolled up, spirally curling: VOLUTE

rollicking type of square dance: HOEDOWN

romantic in intentions but impractical: QUIXOTIC

roof that is rounded, dome: CUPOLA

roof tile with an unbalanced S shape: PANTILE

roof with single slope and its upper edge abutting a wall: LEAN-TO

roof with two slopes on each side: MANSARD

roof with two slopes on each side, the lower having a steeper pitch: GAMBREL ROOF

room or territory for expansion: LEBENSRAUM

roomy: CAPACIOUS

rooster that is castrated to make the meat better for eating: CAPON

root out, destroy wholly: EXTIRPATE

rootlike: RHIZOID

rope, cable or wire used to steady or secure something: GUY

rope or cable for mooring or towing: HAWSER

rosette or ribbon badge: COCKADE

rosy: RUBICUND

rotary combustion engine for automobiles: WANKEL ENGINE

rotate or revolve, usually around a fixed point: GYRATE

rotation force: TORQUE

rotten: CARIOUS

rotten, corrupt: PUTRID

rotten or dead flesh: CARRION

rough, crude, unrefined: UNCOUTH

rough, plain, simple: RUSTIC

rough-and-tumble clash, fracas: SCRIMMAGE

roughly handle, manhandle, abuse: MAUL

roughness: ASPERITY

round building or hall: ROTUNDA

round up: CORRAL

roundabout: AMBIGUOUS

roundabout or indirect: CIRCUITOUS

roundabout talk: CIRCUMLOCUTION

rounded, full, clear voice: OROTUND

rounded, spherical: ORBICULAR

rounded mass: GLOMERATION
rounded out, plump: ROTUND
roundness: SPHERICITY
rouse to action, stimulate, arouse: GALVANIZE
route followed in traveling: ITINERARY
routine, commonplace, ordinary: MUNDANE
routinely performed without interest: PERFUNCTORY
roving, wandering, straying, itinerant: ERRANT
royalty symbol in the form of a rod: SCEPTER
rub away: ABRADE
rub out, erase, cancel, obliterate: EFFACE
rub the body with oil: EMBROCATE
rubbing off or wearing off of particles: DETRITION
rubbish, nonsense, worthless: TRUMPERY
rubbish, refuse, leavings: OFFAL
ruddy: SANGUINE
ruddy, flushed: FLORID
rude, disorderly, boisterous: RAMBUNCTIOUS
rude, sullen: SURLY
rude or discourteous manner: INCIVILITY
rude or ill-natured person: CHURL
rudeness, insolence: IMPERTINENCE
rudeness in speech that is insulting and scornful: CONTUMELY
rudimentary: ABECEDARIAN
ruffle at the neckline or front of a bodice or shirt: JABOT
ruffle on a blouse or coat at the waist: PEPLUM
ruffle or upset the balance: DISTEMPER
ruffled or pleated strip of fabric worn about the neck or wrists of a woman's costume: RUCHE
rugged and weather-beaten: GNARLED
ruin, destruction: HAVOC
ruin, rout, sudden and ruinous breakdown or collapse: DEBACLE
ruin, wreck, pillage: RAVAGE
rule, moral guide, maxim: PRECEPT
rule by the best: ARISTOCRACY
rule of principle that is established: CANON
rule or standard by which a judgment can be made: CRITERION
rule or treat with cruel power: TYRANNIZE
ruler who governs in place of a sovereign: REGENT
ruler of a people or province: ETHNARCH

ruler or similar instrument used to punish children: FERULE
ruler who is supreme: SOVEREIGN
rulers or sovereigns reigning in succession in one line of descent: DYNASTY
rules or directions printed for use in religious services: RUBRIC
Rumanian and Israeli folk dance in which dancers lock arms in a circle: HORA
rum drink that includes lemon or lime juice and sugar: PLANTER'S PUNCH
rummage about for something: FOSSICK
rumor, gossip, the lowdown: SCUTTLEBUTT
rumor that is false: CANARD
rumpled, untidy, unkempt, tousled: DISHEVELED
rumbling noise, move with rumbling noise: LUMBER
run, go in a hurry: SCAMPER
run away to escape law: ABSCOND
run with steady swinging stride: LOPE
run-down, neglected, fallen into ruin or decay: DILAPIDATED
runners fastened to shoes for gliding over snow: SKIS
running at a slow, jolting pace: JOG
running together of final and initial sounds of two adjacent words: SANDHI
rural: AGRESTIC
rural life portrayed as peaceful and idyllic: PASTORAL
rural or farming affairs: GEORGIC
rush forward: SALLY
rush headlong: HURTLE
rush wildly: CAREEN
ruthlessly compelling conformity: PROCRUSTEAN
Russian country home: DACHA
Russian dance in which a squatting man kicks each leg out alternately: KAZATSKY
Russian for comrade: TOVARICH
Russian title equivalent to Mr.: GOSPODIN
Russian triangular shaped stringed instrument: BALALAIKA
Russian vehicle drawn by three horses abreast: TROIKA
rustic or pastoral: BUCOLIC
rustling, whispering, softly murmuring: SUSURRANT
rustling as of silk, swish, fanciness: FROUFROU
rye or bourbon cocktail made with vermouth: MANHATTAN

S

"s" shaped: SIGMATE

sable fur: ZIBELINE

sack of canvas or duck used for carrying personal possessions: DUFFLE BAG or DUFFEL BAG

sacred books of any sect or religion: CANON

sacredness maintained, unbroken: INVIOLATE

sacrificial offering, wholly consumed by fire: HOLOCAUST

saddened, dejected, gloomy: DISCONSOLATE

sad, mournful, painful: DOLOROUS

sad, pitiful, causing sorrow: PATHETIC

sad or mournful, especially in a ludicrous manner: LUGUBRIOUS

saddened or desolate through loss: BEREAVED

saddle, the hind part of which projects upward: CANTLE

sadism or masochism: ALGOLAGNIA

safe or proof against attack: UNASSAILABLE

said or done for effect or as a formality: GESTURE

sail of triangular shape ahead of the foremast: JIB

sailboat with a single mast and fore and aft rigging: SLOOP

sailboat's mast or boom: SPAR

sailing close to the wind: LUFF

sailor ranking below an able-bodied seaman: ORDINARY SEAMAN

sailor who is a veteran, old salt: SHELLBACK

sailor's bag for belongings: DITTY BAG

sailors' rhythmical working song: CHANTEY

St. Vitus dance: CHOREA

sainted: CANONIZED

salary, pension, allowance: STIPEND

salary or fee for a service: EMOLUMENT

sale item priced near or below cost to promote sale of others: LOSS LEADER

sales force manager in a store: FLOORWALKER

saliva, spittle: SPUTUM

salmon before it enters the ocean: PARR

salmon of a salty, smoked variety: LOX

salmon that has returned for the first time from the sea to fresh water: GRILSE

salty: SALINE

salty, briny: BRACKISH

salvage something usable from refuse: SCAVENGE

same: DITTO

same as previous reference: IBID

same kind of person or thing: CONGENER

sameness in style, tone, expression, color: MONOTONE

sample strip of fabric: SWATCH

sanctimonious: PHARISAIC

sandals with uppers made of straps: HUARACHES

sandstone used to scour the wooden decks of a ship: HOLYSTONE

sandwich with three slices of bread and two layers of filling: DOUBLE-DECKER

sandy grittiness: SABULOUS

sarcastic: ACRIMONIOUS

sarcastic, caustic, cutting: MORDANT

sarcastic or biting: CAUSTIC

sarcastic or humorous speech in which opposite of what is said is meant: IRONY

sardinelike fish: SPRAT

sarong style loincloth worn by Samoan natives: LAVA-LAVA

sash, usually wide, worn as a waistband: CUMMERBUND

sassy: CHEEKY

151

sassy young woman: BAGGAGE
satanic: CLOVEN-HOOFED
sated, full, amply supplied: REPLETE
satire that is sarcastic or coarse and is posted publicly: PASQUINADE
satirize or abuse in humorous prose or verse: LAMPOON
satisfy or quench, as a thirst: SLAKE
saturate, permeate, fertilize: IMPREGNATE
sauce, as for fish, made of mayonnaise and chopped pickles, capers, etc.: TARTAR SAUCE
sauce made with mayonnaise and spices: RÉMOULADE
sauce of onions, butter and white sauce: SOUBISE
sauce thickened with fat and flour: ROUX
sauciness, impertinence: FLIPPANCY
saucy, brazen, shameless, bold: IMPUDENT
saucy, lively: PERT
sausage-shaped: ALLANTOID
savage, fierce, bloodthirsty, cruel: FEROCIOUS
savage, wild: FERAL
save from destruction: SALVAGE
saved material after a wreck, fire, etc.: SALVAGE
savory, pleasant tasting: SAPID
say or do over and over, repeat: REITERATE
saying long in use: ADAGE
saying something that one suggests is too obvious to say: PARALEIPSIS
sayings ascribed to Jesus but not found in Bible: AGRAPHA
scale ramparts by ladders: ESCALADE
scaly: SQUAMOUS
scanty: SKIMPY
scanty, inadequate, thin: MEAGER
scanty, small, diminutive: EXIGUOUS
scanty, stingy: NIGGARDLY
scar or scarlike marking: CICATRIX
scarcity, lack, famine: DEARTH
scarf, long and made of fur or fabric, worn over a woman's shoulders: STOLE
scarf, necktie: CRAVAT
scarf, often of lace, worn over head and shoulders by Spanish women: MANTILLA
scarf worn about the head and shoulders by Spanish and Latin American women: REBOZO
scarf worn on the head by women: BABUSHKA

scatter, drive away, dispel: DISPERSE
scatter among other things, set here and there: INTERSPERSE
scatter or diffuse, as if by sowing: DISSEMINATE
scattered, not concentrated: SPARSE
scattered, wasted: DISSIPATED
schedule or select: SLATE
scheme or plot: MACHINATE
scheming person (a derogatory term): JESUIT
schizophrenia, usually associated with puberty, characterized by unsystematic behavior, exaggerated mannerisms: HEBEPHRENIA
scholarly, learned: ERUDITE
scholarly life: ACADEME
scholarly person: SAVANT
scholarship displayed in an undiscriminating way: PEDANTRY
science of bullets, missiles, rockets, etc.: BALLISTICS
science of soil: AGROLOGY
science that treats of earth's surface and its physical, political and social characteristics: GEOGRAPHY
scientific husbandry: AGRONOMY
scoff: JEER
scold, censure, reproach: UPBRAID
scold, rake over the coals, reprove severely: KEELHAUL
scold, sharp-tongued woman: VIRAGO
scold severely, upbraid, berate: OBJURGATE
scolding: ABUSIVE
scolding, harsh reprimand: RATING
scolding and abusive woman, shrew: TERMAGANT
scope: AMBIT
scope, range, extent: PURVIEW
scorched, hot: TORRID
scorched, or colored as if by scorching: USTULATE
scorn, despise: CONTEMN
scorn, reject, refuse: SPURN
scorn or ridicule publicly: PILLORY
scornful, sneering, cynical: SARDONIC
scornful rudeness in speech: CONTUMELY
Scotch whisky and vermouth cocktail: ROB ROY
Scottish cap with a tight headband and a wide, flat top: TAM-O'SHANTER
Scottish dish containing animal's insides boiled in its stomach: HAGGIS
scoundrel: CAITIFF

scowl, look angry or sullen: LOWER
scowl sullenly: GLOWER
scrap, do away with: SCUTTLE
scrap, fragment: SNIPPET
scrape, paw or scratch: SCRABBLE
scrape away: ABRADE
scrape or grind harshly, cut, pierce: GRIDE
scratch, cut: SCOTCH
scratch, scrape or paw: SCRABBLE
scream, bawl, cry loudly: SQUALL
screen behind an altar: REREDOS
screen or shutter of overlapping horizontal
    slats: JALOUSIE
screw or nail inserted so that it lies flush
    with or below surface: COUNTERSINK
scribble: SCRABBLE
scribble or draw aimlessly: DOODLE
scribblings or drawings on wall: GRAFFITI
scruffy, uneven: SCRAGGLY
scrutinize, examine or read thoroughly:
    PERUSE
scrutinize, look at closely: SCAN
sculpture in which figures project slightly:
    BAS-RELIEF
sculptured basket of fruit: CORBEIL
scum, froth, foam: SPUME
sea arm, long and narrow path and be-
    tween high banks: FIORD
sea-green or yellowish-green color:
    GLAUCOUS
sea spray: SPINDRIFT
sea with numerous islands: ARCHIPELAGO
seal or plug edges or crevices: CAULK
seal rings, as a subject of study:
    SPHRAGISTICS
seamen's short coat of heavy woolen fab-
    ric: PEA JACKET
sear: CAUTERIZE
search, pursuit, adventure: QUEST
search, scour, move rapidly: SKIRR
search for food or supplies: FORAGE
search for gold in abandoned mines: FOS-
    SICK
search for information, investigate: DELVE
search out by careful investigation: FER-
    RET
search thoroughly: RANSACK
search through: ROOT
search through refuse, as for food: SCAV-
    ENGE
seas, lakes, rivers, etc., studied to deter-
    mine their use for navigation: HY-
    DROGRAPHY
season of warm, hazy weather in late au-
    tumn: INDIAN SUMMER

seat behind the saddle on a horse or mo-
    torcycle: PILLION
seat for riders on an elephant or a camel:
    HOWDAH
seat or small stool, usually without arms
    or back: TABORET
seat or step in a series that rises: GRADIN
seated a great part of the time, settled,
    inactive: SEDENTARY
seaward current of water beneath the sur-
    face: UNDERCURRENT
seaweed or other marine vegetation cast
    ashore: WRACK
secluded: CLOISTRAL
secluded: SEQUESTERED
secluded, solitary person: RECLUSE
secluded garden for quiet pleasure:
    PLEASANCE
secluded or inactive for a period, espe-
    cially winter: HIBERNATING
second experience imagined when it is ac-
    tually only the first: DÉJÀ VU
second marriage: DEUTEROGAMY
second marriage: DIGAMY
second seat on a motorcycle: PILLION
second self: ALTER EGO
second sight: CLAIRVOYANCE
secondary, casual, minor: INCIDENTAL
secondary phenomenon occurring with an-
    other but having no power to produce
    effects: EPIPHENOMENON
secret, abstruse, unknown except by an
    inner few: ESOTERIC
secret, as of a meeting or plan, kept hid-
    den for an illicit purpose: CLANDES-
    TINE
secret, hidden, puzzling, occult, mystify-
    ing: CRYPTIC
secret, sheltered: COVERT
secret agreement, usually to defraud
    someone: COLLUSION
secret group joined in intrigue: CABAL
secret jargon, especially of thieves,
    beggars, etc.: CANT
secret meeting: CONCLAVE
secret meeting: EXECUTIVE SESSION
secret meeting, as of lovers: ASSIGNATION
secret or closed session: IN CAMERA
secret or hidden: ARCANE
secret or mystic system: CABALA
secret or private things: PENETRALIA
secret or unofficial means of relaying in-
    formation, usually from person to
    person: GRAPEVINE
secretary: AMANUENSIS

secretly: SUB ROSA
secretly depart, to escape law: ABSCOND
secretly informed: PRIVY
section of a city in which a minority lives: GHETTO
secularize: LAICIZE
securities bought over a period, by the dollars' worth rather than by number of shares: DOLLAR COST AVERAGING
securities list: PORTFOLIO
securities pledged as collateral for a loan: HYPOTHECATION
security, pledge, challenge: GAGE
security for discharge of an obligation: COLLATERAL
security selling that is not done on the floor of a stock exchange: OVER-THE-COUNTER
security that is transferable by delivery: NEGOTIABLE
sedate, steady, sober: STAID
sedative, sleep-producing medicine: OPIATE
seduce, corrupt, deprave: DEBAUCH
see (reference in a book): VIDE
see before: VIDE ANTE
see below: VIDE INFRA
seed bearing: SEMINIFEROUS
seed-bearing part of flowering plants: PISTIL
seeing into the future: PRESCIENT
seeing or knowing: COGNITION
seeing things that are not visible: CLAIRVOYANCE
seeming, apparent: OSTENSIBLE
seemly, proper: DECOROUS
see-through fabric: DIAPHANOUS
segment: CANTLE
seize, capture or secure: CORRAL
seize, grip tightly, struggle or contend with: GRAPPLE
seize and place in legal custody: IMPOUND
seize by legal means: SEQUESTER
seize by violence: WREST
seize or appropriate: CONFISCATE
seize or appropriate beforehand: PREEMPT
seize or stop on the way, prevent from reaching the destination: INTERCEPT
seizure of property in legal proceeding: ATTACHMENT
select, pick out, sort: CULL
select, schedule: SLATE
selecting from diverse sources: ECLECTIC
selections or fragments from literary works: ANALECTS

self, the part of the psyche that organizes thought and governs action: EGO
self held to be the only thing really existent: SOLIPSISM
self-assertive, bold, indecent: IMMODEST
self-assurance: COCKINESS
self-assurance, composure, serenity: POISE
self-centered: EGOCENTRIC
self-confidence: APLOMB
self-confident, lively, brisk, dashing: JAUNTY
self-confident to an extreme: COCKSURE
self-contradictory, false or ridiculous statement: PARADOX
self-denial: ABNEGATION
self-determination: AUTONOMY
self-evident statement: AXIOM
self-examination: INTROSPECTION
self-governing: AUTONOMOUS
self-important, overdignified, pretentious: POMPOUS
self-important, petulant: HOITY-TOITY
self-interested person: INTROVERT
selfish person: EGOIST
selflessness: ALTRUISM
self-love: NARCISSISM
self-mortification: ASCETICISM
self-protective reaction of an organism: DEFENSE MECHANISM
self-reproach, guilt feeling: REMORSE
self-satisfaction: COMPLACENCY
self-satisfied, complacent: SMUG
self-service meal: BUFFET
self-supporting, as a country: SUBSTANTIVE
self-styled: SOI-DISANT
sell goods in the street, peddle: HAWK
sell property for profit: REALIZE
selling by quiet persuasion rather than high pressure tactics: SOFT SELL
semicircle: HEMICYCLE
semifluid, sticky, honeylike consistency: VISCOUS
seminar or group of people who study together some subject or topic: WORKSHOP
semiskilled worker: BLUE COLLAR
semitransparent: TRANSLUCENT
send back to one's own country: REPATRIATE
send forth or give off as light or heat: EMIT
send from one place to another: TRANSMIT
send or order back: REMAND
senility: CADUCITY

senility: DOTAGE

senior or eldest member of a group: DOYEN

senseless, absurd: IRRATIONAL

senseless or foolish talk: DRIVEL

senses as source of pleasure: SENSUOUS

sensibility, perception: ESTHESIA

sensible, reasoned: RATIONAL

sensitive: SUSCEPTIBLE

sensitivity in extreme to touch, heat, pain, etc.: HYPERESTHESIA

sensitivity to heat and cold: THERMESTHESIA

sensual, carnal, worldly: FLESHLY

sensual, especially concerning food: EPICUREAN

sensualist: VOLUPTUARY

sensualist, rake: ROUÉ

sentence analysis that gives the form, function and syntactical relationship of its words: PARSE

sentence in which sense and structure are not completed until the end: PERIODIC SENTENCE

sentence in which the main clause appears at the beginning and less important matter follows: LOOSE SENTENCE

sentence or word that reads the same backward as forward: PALINDROME

sentence within which one grammatical construction changes to another: ANACOLUTHON

sentimental features incorporated in a play or story to evoke emotional response: HOKUM

sentimental or emotional, tearfully so: MAUDLIN

sentimentality that is false: MAWKISHNESS

sentimentality to excess: SCHMALTZ

sentimentally pensive: LANGUISHING

sentimentality: BATHOS

separate, as the good from the bad: WINNOW

separate, disconnected: DISCRETE

separate, mark out boundaries of limits: DEMARCATE

separate, part, divide: DISSEVER

separate, set apart: SEQUESTER

separate a group into small dissenting factions: BALKANIZE

separate from, break away: DISSOCIATE

separate into opposing groups or views: POLARIZE

separate into parts: DIFFRACT

separate into two parts: DICHOTOMIZE

separate or break up into parts, analyze: RESOLVE

separated, set apart: ISOLATED

sepulchral: FERAL

sequence in logic or grammar: CONSECUTION

serene, calm, quiet: TRANQUIL

serene, calm, unmoved: IMPASSIVE

series, succession: CONSECUTION

series of reactions or events in which results become causes: CHAIN REACTION

serious, reflective, often melancholy: PENSIVE

sermon, especially one based on a biblical text: HOMILY

sermon writing and delivery, as a study: HOMILETICS

sermonize, lecture: PRELECT

serpent, reputed to be hatched from a cock's egg: COCKATRICE

serpent in the headdress of Egyptian kings: URAEUS

servant: RETAINER

servant or assistant as of a magician or scholar: FAMULUS

servant or low person: MENIAL

servile, compliant, slavish: SEQUACIOUS

servile, fawning follower: MINION

servile, fawning person: TOADY

servile, obsequious: SUBSERVIENT

servile, overly obedient, fawning: OBSEQUIOUS

servile follower, toady: LACKEY

servile or lickspittle attitude: KOWTOW

servilely flatter: ADULATE

serving or portion: DOLLOP

servitude, slavery: THRALLDOM

set, surroundings, environment, as of a play: MISE EN SCÈNE

set apart, separate: SEQUESTER

set aside, as money for a special purpose: EARMARK

set here and there, scatter among other things: INTERSPERSE

set in from the margin as the first line of a paragraph: INDENT

set of concurrent symptoms indicating a specific disease or condition: SYNDROME

set speech or recitation: DECLAMATION

set straight, undeceive: DISABUSE

set up, establish: INSTITUTE

settle one's debts: LIQUIDATE

settlement of a dispute that is advanced by

friendly intervention of a conciliator:
MEDIATION
settlement of a dispute by the decision of a
person or body chosen with the consent of both sides: ARBITRATION
settler on public or unoccupied land without permission: SQUATTER
seven, or seven things: HEPTAD
seven days, a week: HEBDOMAD
sevenfold: SEPTUPLE
seventh year, in ancient Jewish system:
SABBATICAL YEAR
seven-year recurrences: SEPTENNIAL
several, various: DIVERS
severance of relations: RUPTURE
severe, allowing no letup: EXACTING
severe, rigid: STRINGENT
severe, stormy: INCLEMENT
severe, strict, grim: STARK
sew loosely: BASTE
sewage: SULLAGE
sewer: KENNEL
sewing together of the edges of a wound
in a surgical operation: SUTURE
sex bias against females: SEXISM
sex differentiation absent, as in clothes,
hair styles, etc.: UNISEX
sex glands in the male: TESTICLES
sexless: ANAPHRODISIA
sexless, asexual: NEUTER
sexless, effeminate: EPICENE
sexual, cheap: RAUNCHY
sexual abstinence: CELIBACY
sexual activity involving licking of female
genitals: CUNNILINGUS
sexual activity involving licking of male
genitals: FELLATIO
sexual characteristics of both sexes: AN-
DROGYNOUS
sexual climax in intercourse: ORGASM
sexual coupling: INTERCOURSE
sexual desire for a member of the same
sex: HOMOEROTICISM
sexual desire in women that is uncontrollable: NYMPHOMANIA
sexual desire lacking: ANAPHRODISIS
sexual desire or impulse: LIBIDO
sexual desire or lust: CONCUPISCENCE
sexual desire reducer: ANTAPHRODISIAC
sexual desire that is abnormally strong:
EROTOMANIA
sexual frenzy in a male elephant: MUST
sexual go-between: PANDER
sexual intercourse: COITUS
sexual intercourse: CONGRESS

sexual intercourse: COPULATION
sexual intercourse between persons so
closely related that marriage is forbidden them: INCEST
sexual intercourse forced on a woman:
RAPE
sexual intercourse that is illegal: FOR-
NICATION
sexual organ of male animals: PENIS
sexual organs: GENITALS
sexual organs of female animals: VULVA,
CLITORIS
sexual pervert, or to turn away from
straight course: DEVIATE
sexual pleasure resulting from pain:
ALGOLAGNIA
sexual potency of a man: VIRILITY
sexual practices between males, especially
between men and boys: PEDERASTY
sexual restraint; moderation: CONTINENCE
sexual stimulant: APHRODISIAC
sexually abandoned, lewd: LICENTIOUS
sexually arousing: EROGENOUS
sexual arousing, pertaining to the body:
SENSUAL
sexually attracted to persons of the opposite sex: HETEROSEXUAL
sexually capable at this period: PUBERTY
sexually desirous regarding those of the
same sex: HOMOSEXUAL
sexually preoccupied: CARNAL
sexually stimulating: EROTIC
sexually stimulating object that in itself is
not erotic, such as a shoe: FETISH
sexually unrestrained: INCONTINENT
sexually wanton man: SATYR
shabby, decayed, neglected: DILAPIDATED
shabby, decrepit: FLEA-BITTEN
shabby, dirty: DISREPUTABLE
shabby, drab: DOWDY
shackle, handcuff, fetter: MANACLE
shading, as in a picture, done with crossed
lines: CROSSHATCH
shading with close parallel or crossed
lines: HATCH
shadow pantomime in miniature: GA-
LANTY SHOW
shadow that does not completely cut off
light: PENUMBRA
shadows falling to north or south depend-
ing on season: AMPHISCIANS
shady: ADUMBRAL
shady or providing shade: UMBRAGEOUS
shake slightly: JOGGLE
shake suddenly or forcibly: SUCCUSS

shake up, elbow, push or crowd roughly, shove: JOSTLE

shake up and down, bounce, jolt: JOUNCE

shaking or shivering motion: TREMOR

shaky, loose: RAMSHACKLE

shallow, cursory, limited to the surface: SUPERFICIAL

sham: SIMULACRUM

sham, deceptive, pretended: FEIGNED

shameful: IGNOMINIOUS

shameful: OPPROBRIOUS

shameless: BRAZEN

shamelessness: IMPUDICITY

shank, part of leg between knee and ankle: CRUS

shape, outline, form: FIGURATION

shape distortion: ANAMORPHISM

shape or design that doesn't adhere to any rigid pattern: FREE-FORM

shapeless: AMORPHOUS

shapely buttocks: CALLIPYGIAN

share, portion, half: MOIETY

sharer of secrets: CONFIDANT

sharing the sensations of another as if one were participating in the action: VICARIOUS

sharp: ACERB

sharp: ACUATE

sharp, abrupt emphasis: STACCATO

sharp, keen, cutting, biting: INCISIVE

sharp answer or reply: RETORT

sharp but pleasant tasting, tart: PIQUANT

sharp taste, manner, speech, nature: ACRID

sharp tasting or smelling: PUNGENT

sharp-edged and pointed: CULTRATE

sharpen, as a razor, on a hone: HONE

sharpen, excite, stimulate: WHET

sharply affecting the mind: PUNGENT

sharp-tongued woman, a scold: VIRAGO

shatter, splinter into fragments: SHIVER

shattering effect of an explosion: BRISANCE

shave or pare the surface, as leather: SKIVE

shaving of the crown of the head: TONSURE

shed, get rid of: SLOUGH

shedding, or falling off, as of petals, leaves, fruit: DECIDUOUS

sheep or goat newly born: YEANLING

sheeplike: OVINE

sheepskin coat worn by Spanish shepherds: ZAMARRA

sheer or transparent: DIAPHANOUS

sheet carrying advertising or propaganda: BROADSIDE

sheet folded once and forming four pages: FOLIO

shelf above a fireplace: MANTEL

shelf above the back of an altar to hold ornaments, candles, lights: RETABLE

shelf for holding small ornamental items: WHATNOT

shell, pod or husk: SHUCK

shell containing baked minced food: COQUILLE

shell lined with mother-of-pearl: ABALONE

shell study: CONCHOLOGY

shelter or disguise: COVERTURE

sheltered, secret or concealed: COVERT

sheriff's office, term or jurisdiction: SHRIEVALTY

shield division in heraldry: CANTON

shield-shaped: SCUTIFORM

shield-shaped surface with armorial bearings: ESCUTCHEON

shift position or direction: VEER

shifting of a disease from one part of the body to another: METASTASIS

shifty, elusive: LUBRICOUS

shinbone: TIBIA

shingle knife: FROE

shining: IRRADIANT

shining, illustrious: SPLENDENT

shining back, reflecting light, bright: RELUCENT

shining with brilliance, dazzling, vividly bright: RESPLENDENT

ship opening in floor or deck giving access to area beneath: HATCH

ship portion above the main deck: TOPSIDE

ship so far away that the hull is hidden below the horizon: HULL DOWN

ship space where cargo is stored: HOLD

ship that is large: ARGOSY

ship with two or more masts, rigged fore and aft: SCHOONER

shipboard drinking fountain: SCUTTLEBUTT

ship's backbone: KEEL

ship's kitchen: GALLEY

ship's left side as one faces forward: PORT

ship's length: FORE AND AFT

ship's officer ranking next below the captain: FIRST MATE

ship's or plane's position checked by radio signals from known stations: LORAN

ship's or plane's right-hand side as one faces forward: STARBOARD

ship's permission to enter port: PRATIQUE

ship's sailing close to the wind: LUFF

ship's small boat: JOLLY BOAT
ship's upper front part: FORECASTLE
shivering or shaking motion: TREMOR
shock to the body or system, caused by an injury: TRAUMA
shocked or nauseated easily, prudish: SQUEAMISH
shocking, vivid, sensational: LURID
shoddy, poorly made, cheap: SLEAZY
shoe that is heavy and coarse: BROGAN
shoe's upper front part: VAMP
shoot (a liquid) in by mechanical or physical means: INJECT
shoot from a hiding place: SNIPE
shoot out copiously, as a liquid: SPOUT
shop that has long hours, insufficient pay, and poor conditions: SWEAT SHOP
shop that is small and fashionable: BOUTIQUE
shore or beach: STRAND
shore or coastal region: LITTORAL
shore uncovered by low tide: FORESHORE
short distance: STONE'S THROW
short fingers or toes: BRACHYDACTYLIC
short of breath: PURSY
shortage, scarcity: PAUCITY
shorten: ABBREVIATE
shorten: ABRIDGE
shortened: ELLIPTIC
shortened: TRUNCATED
shortening of a syllable that is naturally or by position long: SYSTOLE
shorthand, especially in ancient times: TACHYGRAPHY
short-lived, of short duration: TRANSIENT
short-lived, transitory, fleeting: EPHEMERAL
short takeoff and landing plane: STOL
shoulder bag, especially as used by soldiers: MUSETTE BAG
shoulder ornament, especially on the uniforms of military and naval officers: EPAULET
shout, bawl, exclaim loudly: VOCIFERATE
shout, violent denunciation: FULMINATE
shove, shake up, elbow, push or crowd roughly: JOSTLE
show clearly, manifest, demonstrate convincingly: EVINCE
show consisting of skits, songs, and dances: REVUE
showcase of glass, for displaying art objects: VITRINE
shower, scatter, sprinkle: SPARGE

showiness: OSTENTATION
showoff tendency: EXHIBITIONISM
showy, bombastic, florid: FLAMBOYANT
showy, excessively ornamented: ORNATE
showy, useless ornaments: FURBELOWS
showy and cheap: TAWDRY
showy but valueless: TRUMPERY
showy but without substance: SPECIOUS
shrew: VIXEN
shrew: XANTHIPPE
shrew, scolding and abusive woman: TERMAGANT
shrewd, practical, obstinate: HARD-HEADED
shrewd, wise: SAGACIOUS
shrewish old woman: GRIMALKIN
shrill, grating: STRIDENT
shrink or crouch in servility: CRINGE
shriveled, shrunken, withered: WIZENED
shrubs or trees cut and arranged in fantastic shapes: TOPIARY
shrunken, withered, shriveled: WIZENED
shuffle cards by bending up corners of two parts of the pack and letting cards slip together: RIFFLE
shun as unworthy: ESCHEW
shut, block or close off: OCCLUDE
shut one's eyes to wrongdoing: CONNIVE
shut out, exclude: OSTRACIZE
shut out, exclude, render impossible: PRECLUDE
shutter or screen of overlapping horizontal slats: JALOUSIE
shy, inept person (Yiddish): NEBBISH
shy, jumpy: SKITTISH
shy, meek, apologetic person: MILQUETOAST
shyly embarrassed: SHEEPISH
shyness: DIFFIDENCE
shyness, timidity, lack of confidence in self: DIFFIDENCE
sick: NAUSEATED
sick-making: NAUSEOUS
sickening to an extreme: AD NAUSEAM
sickening or insipid: MAWKISH
sickle or scythe shaped: FALCATE
sickness caused by eating or drinking too much: CRAPULENCE
sickness pretended to avoid work: MALINGER
side, right or left part of something: FLANK
side by side: ABREAST
side by side: CHEEK BY JOWL
side by side: JUXTAPOSITION

side or sides of a main thing: LATERAL

side sheltered from the wind: LEEWARD

side to side: ATHWART

side to side lurch or twist: CAREEN

side to side measurement: BREADTH

side track connecting with the main track of a railroad: SPUR TRACK

sideboard or buffet, usually without legs: CREDENZA

sideburns: BURNSIDES

sidepiece in a door or window sash: STILE

sides touching: ABUTTING

sidewise glance: ASKANCE

sievelike: CRIBRIFORM

sift, examine or analyze minutely: WINNOW

sift through a coarse sieve: RIDDLE

sighing sound, as of the wind: SOUGH

sight loss without organic defect: AMAUROSIS

sight or eye: OCULAR

sighting land: LANDFALL

sight marred by specks or threads seeming to float before the eyes: MUSCAE VOLITANTES

sign language, deaf-mute alphabet: DACTYLOLOGY

sign of a solemn pledge: SACRAMENT

sign or abbreviation representing a word, as the dollar sign: LOGOGRAM

sign or dedicate a book for presentation: INSCRIBE

sign or mark supposed to exercise occult power: SIGIL

sign or trace of something absent: VESTIGE

signal for parley, made by drum or trumpet: CHAMADE

signal for pillage and destruction: CRY HAVOC

signature, especially of a sovereign: SIGN MANUAL

signature appendage, such as a flourish or a mark: RUBRIC

signature ending made with a flourish: PARAPH

signature that authenticates another signature: COUNTERSIGNATURE

silence, subdue utterly, crush: SQUELCH

signify, hint at: IMPLY

signify, point out, indicate: DENOTE

silence, in music: TACET

silence or feigned ignorance as of a wrongdoing: CONNIVANCE

silencing or putting down, as a rumor: QUIETUS

silent, unspoken: TACIT

silk-screen process used by artist: SERIGRAPHY

silky: SERICEOUS

silky, light and fluffy: FLOSSY

silly, empty talk: TWADDLE

silly, fickle: FRIVOLOUS

silly, pointless, empty-headed: INANE

silly, vain, foppish behavior: COXCOMBRY

silver or bronze gilt: VERMEIL

silver or white in armorial bearings (heraldry): ARGENT

similar: AGNATE

similar, like, same composition throughout, uniform: HOMOGENEOUS

similar or related in structure, position, value: HOMOLOGOUS

similar thing: ANALOGUE

similarity in form: HOMOMORPHISM

similarity in sound: ASSONANCE

similarity without identity: ANALOGY

simmer: CODDLE

simple, candid, artless, unaffected: NAIVE

simple, frank, innocent, naive, straightforward: INGENUOUS

simple, rough, plain: RUSTIC

simple, sincere: UNAFFECTED

simple, unaffected, in music: SEMPLICE

simplicity, innocence and peace, portrayed as associated with rural life: PASTORAL

simultaneous: CONCURRENT

simultaneousness: SYNCHRONISM

sin, wrongful act, unjust thing or deed: INIQUITY

sincere, candid, artless: GUILELESS

sincere, real: UNAFFECTED

sinful, at fault: PECCANT

sinful, obstinate: UNREGENERATE

sing a tune heartily: TROLL

sing with trills, as a bird does: WARBLE

singing leader in church: PRECENTOR

singing that alternates falsetto and normal chest tones: YODEL

singing that is akin to ordinary speech: RECITATIVE

singing without accompaniment: A CAPPELLA

single file: INDIAN FILE

single file, one behind the other: TANDEM

single piece of stone, used in architecture or sculpture: MONOLITH

single woman: FEME SOLE

single word applied to two thoughts, each

of which gives it a different meaning: SYLLEPSIS

single word applied to two thoughts, with the linkage to one of them incorrect: ZEUGMA

single-colored: MONOCHROME

singled out for special honor because of excellence in one's achievements: LAUREATE

sink, collapse, fail: FOUNDER

sink a ship by cutting holes in the bottom of it: SCUTTLE

sink in mud, bog down: MIRE

sinuous: ANFRACTUOUS

sinuous, gliding motion: UNDULATION

sister killer: SORORICIDE

sisterhood, female student organization: SORORITY

sit and hatch eggs, develop: INCUBATE

six: HEXAD

six units: SENARY

sixfold: SEXTUPLICATE

six-ounce bottle of a beverage: SPLIT

size or extent: MAGNITUDE

skeptic: DOUBTING THOMAS

skeptical, disbelieving: INCREDULOUS

sketch of a character or a drawing of a side view: PROFILE

sketchily outline: ADUMBRATE

skewer for broiling meat: BROCHETTE

ski down a straight, steep slope: SCHUSS

skiing cross-country run: LANGLAUF

skiing jump made from a crouching position: GELÄNDESPRUNG

skiing over ice or snow in tow of a horse or motor vehicle: SKIJORING

skiing race over a winding downhill course laid out between posts: SLALOM

skiing term for a pit in the snow left by a skier who has fallen backward: SITZMARK

skill, ability: PROWESS

skill, knowledge: EXPERTISE

skill, style, technical mastery, as of an art: VIRTUOSITY

skill at a particular thing: KNACK

skill in avoiding giving offense: TACT

skill or dexterity in manipulation: SLEIGHT

skilled craftsman: ARTIFICER

skillful, adroit: DEXTEROUS

skillful, inventive, clever: INGENIOUS

skillful in use of bodily or mental powers: ADROIT

skillfully done: WORKMANLIKE

skin, remove impurities from: DESPUMATE

skim over water, glide: SKITTER

skin and its diseases, as a study: DERMATOLOGY

skin disease: ECZEMA

skin hanging loosely from neck or throat, as on turkeys: WATTLE

skin markings made by pricking with a needle and inserting indelible colors: TATTOO

skin's outer layer: EPIDERMIS

skip or rebound of a projectile after it hits a surface: RICOCHET

skirt that is full and has a gathered waist: DIRNDL

skirtlike garment worn by both sexes in the Malay Archipelago: SARONG

skip about playfully: CAPER

skip or bounce over water: DAP

skip or leap about, frolic: GAMBOL

skull: CRANIUM

skull conformations as indicating degree of development of mental facilities: PHRENOLOGY

skull study: CRANIOLOGY

skullcap worn by Orthodox and Conservative Jewish men: YARMULKE

skullcap worn by Roman Catholic clergymen: ZUCCHETTO

sky, heavens: FIRMAMENT

slake thirst: QUENCH

slander: ASPERSE

slander: CALUMNIATE

slander, calumny, curse against someone: MALEDICTION

slander, speak evil of: MALIGN

slander, mock: TRADUCE

slander, defame: VILIFY

slanted, indirect: OBLIQUE

slanting diagonal: BIAS

slanting kind of type, usually used for emphasis: ITALIC

slanting line in printing or writing: VIRGULE

slash mark in printing or writing: VIRGULE

slaughter or massacre: CARNAGE

slaughterhouse: ABATTOIR

slaughterhouse: SHAMBLES

slavery's end in U.S.: ABOLITION

Slavic alphabet: CYRILLIC

Slavic folk dance performed by a male and marked by the prisiadka step in which from a squatting position each leg is kicked out alternately: KAZATSKY

slavish, servile, compliant: SEQUACIOUS
slavish, submissive: SERVILE
sleep, desire for, which is uncontrollable: NARCOLEPSY
sleep deterrent: AGRYPNOTIC
sleep producing, narcotic: SOMNIFEROUS
sleep that is unusually deep: SOPOR
sleep-inducing medicine, relaxant: OPIATE
sleep-inducing or soothing sounds or motions: LULL
sleepiness or yawning: OSCITANCY
sleeping car on a European railroad: WAGON-LIT
sleeping sickness: ENCEPHALITIS LETHARGICA
sleepless period, as in keeping vigil: WATCH
sleeplessness or the chronic inability to sleep: INSOMNIA
sleep-producing: HYPNAGOGIC
sleep-producing medicine: SOPORIFIC
sleepwalking, somnambulism: NOCTAMBULATION
sleepy: SOMNOLENT
sleepy, drowsy: SOPORIFIC
sleeveless Arabian garment: ABA
sleight of hand: PRESTIDIGITATION
sleight of hand, trickery, hocus-pocus: LEGERDEMAIN
slender, graceful young woman: SYLPH
slender, slim, willowy: SVELTE
slender, wandlike, straight: VIRGATE
slice thinly, as leather: SKIVE
slide or glide, as a snake: SLITHER
sliding skillfully down a slope of ice or snow as in mountain-climbing: GLISSADE
slight, gracefully slender: GRACILE
slight suggestion, vague idea, notion, hint: INKLING
slighting: DISPARAGING
slightly, in music: POCO
slim, tall figure: ASTHENIC
slim, willowy, slender: SVELTE
sling for lifting or lowering a heavy object: PARBUCKLE
slink: SKULK
slip, error or fault: LAPSE
slip by, pass away (said of time): ELAPSE
slip-like undergarment: CHEMISE
slippery feeling, greasy: UNCTUOUS
slogan, rallying cry, password: WATCHWORD
slope, especially a defensive slope in front of a fortification: GLACIS

slope, incline, ramp: GRADIENT
slope, tilt: CANT
slope linking different levels: RAMP
slope or inclination of countryside: VERSANT
slope that is steep: ESCARPMENT
slope along a plateau's rim: SCARP
sloping edge: BEVEL
sloping steeply: DECLIVITOUS
slouching, awkward movement: LOP
slovenly in appearance: BLOWZY
slow, delay, hinder: RETARD
slow, dignified dance or music for such a dance: PAVANE
slow, straggler falling behind: LAGGARD
slow down: DECELERATE
slow movement, as in music: ADAGIO
slow tempo: LARGO
sluggish: INERT
sluggish, dull, inactive: TORPID
sluggish, lacking in energy: LYMPHATIC
sluggish, uninterested: STAGNANT
sluggishness, dullness, apathy: LETHARGY
slur over in pronunciation: ELIDE
sly, stealthy: FURTIVE
sly look: LEER
sly or indirect intimation, hint: INSINUATION
small: PETITE
small, cramped: INCOMMODIOUS
small, fashionable shop: BOUTIQUE
small, insignificant, trifling: MINUTE
small, scanty, diminutive: EXIGUOUS
small, stunted, as an imperfectly developed fruit or ear of corn: NUBBIN
small, trifling: NOMINAL
small, trifling work: OPUSCULE
small country that depends on a great power: SATELLITE
small decorative object: BIBELOT
small letters of the alphabet used in printing: LOWER CASE
small or insignificant amount: IOTA
small portable stove: CHAUFFER
small portion or piece: COLLOP
small quantity: MODICUM
small quantity, insufficiency: PAUCITY
small space, crack: INTERSTICE
small space between library stacks for private study: CARREL
small sum of money: PITTANCE
small to the point of being incalculable, microscopic: INFINITESIMAL
smallness of the head, to an abnormal degree: MICROCEPHALY

smallness so extreme that a thing cannot be easily seen: IMPERCEPTIBLE
smallpox: VARIOLA
smartness, style, dash: PIZZAZZ
smelling disagreeably: MALODOROUS
smelling good: ODORIFEROUS
smelling sense: OLFACTORY
smile in a silly, self-satisfied way: SMIRK
smile or smirk self-consciously: SIMPER
smoky or sooty: FULIGINOUS
smooth, flowing, graceful, expressive: FLUENT
smooth, glossy, well-groomed: SLEEK
smooth or toughen metal: PLANISH
smooth the way, as for a project or piece of work: EXPEDITE
smooth to an excess, oily-tongued: UNCTUOUS
smoothness, tact, highly refined skill: FINESSE
smug: SELF-RIGHTEOUS
smug, overexacting person: PRIG
smuggling: CONTRABAND
snake worship: OPHIOLATRY
snakelike, cunning: SERPENTINE
snake-shaped: ANGUIFORM
snap back, resume original shape after being stretched: RESILE
sneak, coward: DASTARD
sneaking, stealthy: SLINKY
sneaky, degraded, skulking: HANGDOG
sneer, laugh coarsely, jeer, deride: FLEER
sneering, ironical, taunting language: SARCASM
sneering, scornful, cynical: SARDONIC
sneeze or noise produced by it: STERNUTATION
sneeze-producing substance, snuff: ERRHINE
sniff, smell: SNUFF
snobbish person: BRAHMIN
snoring sound: STERTOROUS
snow that is coarse and granular: CORN SNOW
snowy: NIVEOUS
snub: REBUFF
snub or deliberate slight: COLD SHOULDER
snuggle for comfort, cuddle: NESTLE
so much the better: TANT MIEUX
so much the worse: TANT PIS
soak in a liquid: STEEP
soapy: SAPONACEOUS
sober, sedate, steady: STAID
soccer ball as it is moved by successive kicks: DRIBBLE

sociable: CONVIVIAL
sociable, associating habitually with others: GREGARIOUS
social only, meaningless, as applied to talk: PHATIC
social meal based on early Christian love feast: AGAPE
social status lowered: DÉCLASSÉ
society containing mixture of ethnic, racial, religious, or cultural groups: PLURALISM
Socratic method: MAIEUTIC
sodomy, sexual relations between males: PEDERASTY
sofa or bench with high back: SETTEE
sofa or couch with low cushioned seat and with arm rests or back: DIVAN
soft, rich, as certain soils: UNCTUOUS
soft spot, vulnerable point: ACHILLES' HEEL
soften, regulate, adjust or temper: MODULATE
soften by soaking in liquid: MACERATE
soften in temper, yield: RELENT
softening: MOLLESCENT
softening, soothing, relaxing especially to the skin: EMOLLIENT
softening colors or lines in a painting or drawing: SCUMBLE
softly performed in music: PIANISSIMO
soil, besmirch, defile: SULLY
soil, discolor: SMIRCH
soil deposited by water: ALLUVIUM
soil rather than climate as an affective factor: EDAPHIC
soil science: AGROLOGY
soil study: PEDOLOGY
soiled or untidy: BEDRAGGLED
soils that are soft and rich: UNCTUOUS
solar or sun: HELIACAL
soldier doing extra duty work for an officer: STRIKER
sole of the foot, palm of the hand: VOLAR
solemn declaration: ASSEVERATION
solicit for sexual purpose: ACCOST
solicit votes by going about a region: CANVASS
solid, forthright, firm: FOURSQUARE
solid, packed with meaning, terse: PITHY
solid earth: TERRA FIRMA
solidifying: CONCRETION
solitary, secluded person: RECLUSE
solo melody in opera: ARIA
solution, usually in alcohol, of a substance, used in medicine: TINCTURE

solution or final unraveling in a plot: DE-NOUEMENT

solve a complicated problem: CUT THE GORDIAN KNOT

something in return for something else: QUID PRO QUO

song, often contrapuntal: MADRIGAL

song for several male voices with no accompaniment: GLEE

song of triumph or joy: PAEAN

song of unhappy love: TORCH SONG

song performed by a lover under his sweetheart's window: SERENADE

song that is short and simple: DITTY

songlike: ARIOSE

sonorous: ROTUND

soothe, pacify: SALVE

soothe, put to sleep or calm through soothing sounds or motions: LULL

soothe, quiet down, mitigate, pacify: MOLLIFY

soothing: LENITIVE

soothing, melodious, pleasant: DULCET

soothing, relieving irritation: DEMULCENT

soothing, softening or relaxing, especially to the skin: EMOLLIENT

soothing agent: ABIRRITANT

soothing pain reliever: ANODYNE

soporific, sleep producing: SOMNIFEROUS

sorceress, fortuneteller: SIBYL

sorcery: DIABLERIE

sorcery, fortune telling, black magic: NEC-ROMANCY

sorcery or witchcraft practiced in the South, Africa and West Indies: OBEAH, OBI

sordid, low: GROVELING

sordid or worst aspect of something: SEAMY SIDE

sore, inflamed: IRRITATED

sorrow, sympathy-evoking: PATHOS

sorrow or grief, to cause: AGGRIEVE

sorrowful, mournful: PLAINTIVE

sorrowful, mournful: WOEBEGONE

sort, class, kind: ILK

sort out, pick, select: CULL

sorting of casualties to fix priorities for treatment: TRIAGE

soul: ANIMA

soul, spirit: PNEUMA

sound, pertaining to: ACOUSTIC

sound and scene reproduction: AUDIOVISUAL

sound imitated by a word: ECHOIC

sound in speech involving chiefly lips, teeth or tongue: CONSONANT

sound like cat's cries at rutting time: CATERWAUL

sound of sighing or murmuring, as made by the wind: SOUGH

sound or letter inserted into a word: EPENTHESIS

sound or vibration caused by the hitting of one body against another: PERCUSSION

sound producing or conducting: SONIFEROUS

sound reproduction: AUDIO

sound reproduction using two or more loudspeakers: STEREOPHONIC

sound with a plumb to test the depth of water: PLUMB

soundproof: ANACOUSTIC

sound-reflecting structure: SOUNDING BOARD

sound-related: SONIC

sounds in opposition in music: ANTIPHONY

sounds of speech, as a study: PHONETICS

sounds or tones in mutliplicity: POLYPHONIC

sounds repeated at the beginnings of words or in accented syllables: ALLITERATION

sound-track change from original language to another: DUBBING

sound-transmitting apparatus used under water: SONAR

sound-wave or light-wave change that seems to accompany change in distance between source and observer: DOPPLER EFFECT

soup, thick and creamy: BISQUE

soup that is clear: CONSOMMÉ

soup ingredients of dough casings filled with ground meat: KREPLACH

soup made with strained vegetables or a dish containing such vegetables or fruit: PURÉE

soup of cream and potatoes usually served cold: VICHYSSOISE

sour: ACERB

sour, fermented cabbage in shredded form: SAUERKRAUT

sour, spoiled-smelling: RANCID

sour juice of green fruit: VERJUICE

source: SPRINGHEAD

source of something: PROVENIENCE

source or forefather: PROGENITOR

source or potential for development: SEM-
INAL
souring: ACESCENT
sourness or sharpness of disposition: VER-
JUICE
South African grassland: VELDT
South African racial segregation:
APARTHEID
South African speech, based on Dutch:
AFRIKAANS
souvenir: MEMENTO
sovereign control over a locally autonomous region: SUZERAINTY
sovereigns or rulers in one line of descent reigning in succession: DYNASTY
Soviet Union collective farm: KOLKHOZ
Soviet Union's equivalent of a Cabinet:
PRESIDIUM
space for freedom of action, latitude:
LEEWAY
space from which something is missing or
has been omitted: LACUNA
space near the altar of a church: CHANCEL
spacecraft landing on water: SPLASHDOWN
spadelike tool for removing the roots of
weeds: SPUD
spangle or small metal disk: PAILLETTE
Spanish American, West Indian or Gulf
State inhabitant of European descent:
CREOLE
Spanish dialect with Hebrew elements:
LADINO
Spanish diacritical mark, as over the n in
señor: TILDE
Spanish for good day: BUENOS DIAS
Spanish for thank you: GRACIAS
sparing in eating and drinking: AB-
STEMIOUS
spark, trace: SCINTILLA
sparkle, gaiety, vivacity, lively spirits:
EFFERVESCENCE
sparkle, glitter, flash: SCINTILLATE
sparkle, glitter, shine: CORUSCATE
sparkle in intellect or action: SCINTILLATE
sparkling object: SPANGLE
spasm in a muscle: CLONUS
spasms of pain: THROES
spasm of the muscle: HYPERKINESIA
spat or trivial quarrel: TIFF
spatter, shower, pelt: PEPPER
speak at great length: PERORATE
speak dogmatically: PONTIFICATE
speak loudly or rhetorically: DECLAIM
speak or write more fully, elaborate: EX-
PATIATE

speak violently, rave: RANT
speak with clarity and exactness: ENUN-
CIATE
speaker who influences audience by his el-
oquence: SPELLBINDER
speaker's stand on which books or notes
may be placed: LECTERN
speaking fluently, glib, talkative: VOLU-
BLE
speaking impairment, or difficulty in understanding speech: DYSPHASIA
speaking in a bombastic or pompous style:
GRANDILOQUENT
speaking or writing with ease: FLUENT
speaking style, language, idiom: PAR-
LANCE
speaking trick that makes the voice seem
to come from source other than the
speaker: VENTRILOQUISM
special application, not general: AD HOC
specialty or strong point of a person:
FORTE
specific purpose and specific situation
committee: AD HOC COMMITTEE
specify: STIPULATE
specify exactly: CONCRETIZE
speck or particle: MOTE
speckled or spotted as if by drops: GUT-
TATE
specks or threads appearing to float before the eyes: MUSCAE VOLITANTES
spectacular exhibition or parade: PAGEANT
spectacular theater production: EXTRAVA-
GANZA
spectator who gives unwanted advice to
card players: KIBITZER
speculative: ACADEMIC
spectra, imiginary appearance: PHANTASM
speech constituting a bitter verbal oath:
PHILIPPIC
speech delivered simply to obstruct action:
FILIBUSTER
speech given at a formal event: ORATION
speech manner: LOCUTION
speech mechanism positions represented
by phonetic symbols: VISIBLE SPEECH
speech of fiery denunciation: TIRADE
speech or essay that is highly emotional:
DITHYRAMB
speech or sales talk: SPIEL
speech pattern: INTONATION
speech peculiar to a locality or group:
DIALECT
speech sound involving chiefly lips, teeth
or tongue: CONSONANT

speech sound that is the smallest unit of its kind and distinctive from others: PHONEME

speech sounds, as a study: PHONETICS

speech that is bombastic or flowery: RHETORIC

speech that is glib and swift: PATTER

speech that is lengthy, loud and vehement: HARANGUE

speech that is long and tiresome: SCREED

speech that is short and witty or satirical: SQUIB

speechlike sounds that are unintelligible: GLOSSOLALIA

speed: VELOCITY

speed, full speed: CAREEN

speed, promptness: DISPATCH

speed rate in music: TEMPO

speed that is dangerous: BREAKNECK

speed up, quicken, facilitate: EXPEDITE

spelling in which a letter represents different sounds in different words: HETEROGRAPHY

spelling or handwriting that is bad: CACOGRAPHY

spelling that conforms to accepted usage: ORTHOGRAPHY

spelling that varies from accepted standard usage: HETEROGRAPHY

spend wastefully, squander: DISSIPATE

spending or giving generously: LAVISH

spending to impress: CONSPICUOUS CONSUMPTION

spendthrift: WASTREL

sperm duct removal: VASECTOMY

sphere of action: AMBIT

sphere of authority: BAILIWICK

spherical, rounded: ORBICULAR

sphinxlike in having human head and animal body: ANDROCEPHALOUS

spiked wheel at the end of a spur: ROWEL

spinal column creatures: VERTEBRATES

spindle-shaped: FUSIFORM

spineless: INVERTEBRATE

spinning, whirling, dizzy: VERTIGINOUS

spinning like a top, or top-shaped: TURBINATE

spiral: HELIX

spiral coil: HELICOID

spirally curling, rolled up: VOLUTE

spire: FLÈCHE

spirit, soul: PNEUMA

spirit, wit: ESPRIT

spirit ancestors, among Pueblo Indians: KACHINA

spirit regarded as distinct from matter: ANIMISM

spirited, vital, joyful, vigorous: EXUBERANT

spiritless, not alive: INANIMATE

spiritlessness, weakness, fatigue, dreaminess, dullness, stagnation: LANGUOR

spirits or health: FETTLE

spiritual, insubstantial, nonmaterial: INCORPOREAL

spiritual, light, airy: ETHEREAL

spiritual sloth: ACEDIA

spiritual teacher or guide: GURU

spit: EXPECTORATE

spit or skewer used in broiling, usually small: BROCHETTE

spiteful, deliberately mischievous: MALICIOUS

spiteful, revengeful: VINDICTIVE

spitefulness, enmity: RANCOR

spitefulness, peevishness, ill temper: SPLEEN

splash, flounder: SLOSH

splashing or sucking noise, as when one walks in deep mud: SQUELCH

splendor, brilliance, radiance: REFULGENCE

splendor, radiance: EFFULGENCE

splinter: SLIVER

splinter into fragments, shatter: SHIVER

splinters: FLINDERS

split into factions in a church or other organization: SCHISM

split or cut into long thin pieces: SLIVER

splitting, cutting: SCISSION

splitting or breaking apart: FISSION

spoil, impair: VITIATE

spoil by indulgence: COCKER

spoil someone, pamper or pet: COSSET

spoiled-smelling: RANCID

spoiling for a fight: PUGNACIOUS

spoils, booty: PILLAGE

spoken, oral: VIVA VOCE

spoken error thought to disclose a person's true thinking: FREUDIAN SLIP

spoken in an undertone, privately: SOTTO VOCE

spoken statement of a false or defamatory nature: SLANDER

spokesman: PROLOCUTOR

sponsor: AEGIS

sponsorship, support: PATRONAGE

spontaneous, unprepared: IMPROMPTU

spontaneous talk by a patient in psychoanalysis: FREE ASSOCIATION sports, a player in the front line of attack or defense: FORWARD

sports feat that is highly unusual: HAT TRICK

sports term for an extra period in a tied game during which the first side to score wins: SUDDEN DEATH

spot, streak, blotch: MOTTLE

spot or blemish, blurred impression in printing: MACKLE

spotted, especially in white and black: PIEBALD

spotted horse or pony: PINTO

spotted or speckled as if by drops: GUTTATE

spotted or variegated: DAPPLED

spotting on animals or plants: MACULATION

spouse: CONSORT

spouse murder: MARITICIDE

spread, as information: DISSEMINATE

spread, pour or send out in all directions: DIFFUSE

spread, publicize, disseminate: PROPAGATE

spread about loosely for drying, as mown hay: TED

spread apart or branch out at a wide angle, diverge: DIVARICATE

spread false charges: ASPERSE

spread in all directions, circulate: DIFFUSE

spread or branch out, diverge: DIVARICATE

spread out, extend: SPLAY

spread out into divisions, divide: RAMIFY

spread the word far and wide: DISSEMINATE

spread thinly: SPARSE

spread through: PERVADE

spread through completely, penetrate: PERMEATE

spreading of a disease from one part of the body to another: METASTASIS

spree, fling, prank, reckless behavior: ESCAPADE

spring back, snap back, recoil, resume original shape after being stretched: RESILE

springlike, youthful, fresh: VERNAL

sprinkle: ASPERSE

sprinkle, shower, scatter: SPARGE

sprinkle, suffuse or cover with a liquid or color: PERFUSE

sprout, breed rapidly, swarm: PULLULATE

sprout, proliferate: BURGEON

spur into action, urge on, stir up: INCITE

spur of the moment, offhand: IMPROMPTU

spur on, goad, incite, foment, provoke to some drastic action: INSTIGATE

spurious: APOCRYPHAL

spurt or gush of liquid from a narrow orifice: JET

spy who infiltrates opposing espionage system to betray it: DOUBLE AGENT

squabble, heated argument: HASSLE

squall, brief windstorm: FLAW

squander, spend wastefully: DISSIPATE

squander or deal recklessly with: PLAY DUCKS AND DRAKES WITH

square dance of a rollicking kind: HOEDOWN

square dancing term for a change of step or figure: CALL

square surrounded by buildings: PIAZZA

squatting Slavic dance step in which a man kicks out each leg alternately: PRISIADKA

squeamish: QUEASY

squint: SKEW

squirm in agony: WRITHE

squirt, gush forth: SPURT

stab, pierce or tear painfully: LANCINATE

stable adjunct, enclosure for exercising horses: PADDOCK

stage curtain that can be raised and lowered: DROP CURTAIN

stage fabric, light and sheer, used as a backdrop: SCRIM

stage front: DOWNSTAGE

stage of a theater including its arch: PROSCENIUM

stage performer without speaking part, as in a mob scene: SUPERNUMERARY

stage scenery, flat, on side of stage: COULISSE

stage surrounded by seats: ARENA THEATER

stagnation, weakness, fatigue, dreaminess, dullness, spiritlessness: LANGUOR

stain or drench especially with blood: IMBRUE

stale joke: CHESTNUT

stall for time: TEMPORIZE

stamp collecting: PHILATELY

stamp out, stifle: SCOTCH

stamped or hammered, as the figure or design on a coin: INCUSE

stand on the hind legs and stretch out the forelegs: RAMP

stand on which a speaker may place notes or books: LECTERN

stand with shelves, usually ornamental: ÉTAGÈRE

standard of quality: BENCH MARK

standard or criterion for testing the qualities of something: TOUCHSTONE

standard or rule by which a judgment can be made: CRITERION

standards of polite society: THE PROPRIETIES

standing out, striking, conspicuous: SALIENT

standstill because of disagreement by two forces: DEADLOCK

star grouping: GALAXY

star mapping: URANOGRAPHY

star that suddenly becomes brilliant then fades: NOVA

star with six points and composed of two equilateral triangles: STAR OF DAVID

star used as guide in navigation; guiding principle or example: LODESTAR

stare at, make eyes at suggestively: OGLE

stare stupidly, gape: GAWK

stare with an angry frown: GLOWER

staring eyes, as in a fish: WALLEYED

starlike symbol in printing (*): ASTERISK

starlike very distant object that emits strong radio waves: QUASAR

stars, of and pertaining to: SIDEREAL

star's rising and setting, said of: ACRONICAL

star-shaped: ASTEROID

star-shaped, radiating: STELLATE

start, beginning: INCEPTION

start a discussion: BROACH

start of something: CONCEPTION

starting existence, newly conceived: NASCENT

starting point: JUMPING-OFF PLACE

startle, thrill, arouse: ELECTRIFY

state, declare, detail: EXPOUND

state or affirm something on basis of known facts or conditions: PREDICATE

state positively: ASSEVERATE

stately, impressive, grand: IMPOSING

stately beauty: JUNOESQUE

stately passage or movement of music: MAESTOSO

statement that decides the matter: CLINCHER

state's right to take over private property for public use: EMINENT DOMAIN

stationary, resting: STATIC

statistician dealing with vital statistics, as of births, deaths, disease: DEMOGRAPHER

status of holding one's position on an enduring basis: TENURE

statute, especially of a municipal body: ORDINANCE

staunch, brave: YEOMANLY

staves ready for assembling into barrels or boxes: SHOOK

stay or dwell temporarily: SOJOURN

steadfast, brave: UNFLINCHING

steadfast, firmly directed, unwavering: INTENT

steadily at work, diligent: SEDULOUS

steady, sober, sedate: STAID

steady stream, as of people or things: INFLUX

steal: PURLOIN

steal, take by fraud: EMBEZZLE

steal funds, especially public funds, embezzle: PECULATE

steal in a petty way: PILFER

steal slyly in small amounts: FILCH

stealthily approach game: STALK

stealthily move about: SKULK

stealthy, sly: FURTIVE

stealthy, sneaking: SLINKY

steam-bath room: SAUNA

steam-whistle organ: CALLIOPE

steep: PRECIPITOUS

steep downward slope: DECLIVITY

steep slope: ESCARPMENT

steep slope: SCARP

steering instrument: RUDDER

stench: MEPHITIS

stencil process that forces ink through open meshes of a silk screen: SILK-SCREEN PROCESS

steps at the entrance to a house: STOOP

step recorder to measure walking distance: PEDOMETER

sterile, barren, fruitless: INFECUND

stern, gloomy, morose, ill-tempered: DOUR

stern, rear, toward the stern on a boat: ABAFT

stern, toward the stern on a boat: AFT

stew of meat and vegetables well seasoned: RAGOUT

stick for stirring drinks: MUDDLER

sticking together: COHERENT

sticky, adhesive: VISCID

sticky, honeylike, semifluid: VISCOUS

stifle, stamp out, suppress: SCOTCH

stigmatize: BRAND
still, placid: QUIESCENT
stimulate, enliven, arouse: QUICKEN
stimulate, excite, raise the spirits of: ELATE
stimulate, excite, rouse to action: GALVANIZE
stimulate, push or touch with a slight jar, shake lightly: JOG
stimulate, sharpen, excite: WHET
stimulating, arousing: PROVOCATIVE
stimulating, racy: PIQUANT
stimulus, incentive: FILLIP
stimulus that hastens a result: CATALYST
stimulus to action: INCENTIVE
stinginess: PARSIMONY
stingy, also poor: PENURIOUS
stingy, scanty: NIGGARDLY
stingy or mean practice: CHEESE-PARING
stinking: MALODOROUS
stinking, offensive, disgusting, noxious: NOISOME
stinking or foul odor: FETID
stipulation or condition: PROVISO
stir or cut up the surface, as of topsoil: SCARIFY
stir up, instigate, incite: FOMENT
stir up, spur into action, urge on: INCITE
stirring stick used for mixed drinks: MUDDLER
stitch used in surgery: SUTURE
stitching that is loose and temporary: BASTING
stock bought in order to repay stock previously borrowed, a short sale operation: SHORT COVERING
stock bought in such quantity as to give the buyer control over the price: CORNER
Stock Exchange, New York: BIG BOARD
stock in a corporation that entitles the owner of the shares to dividends after other obligations have been met: COMMON STOCK
stock issued but reacquired by a company: TREASURY STOCK
stock market on the decline: BEAR MARKET
stock market on the rise: BULL MARKET
stock of a company known for its quality and, therefore, for its ability to make money for investors: BLUE CHIP
stock of a company with good prospects for future earnings: GROWTH STOCK
stock of goods of a business listed: INVENTORY

stock on which dividends must be paid ahead of those on common stock: PREFERRED STOCK
stock on which omitted dividends must be paid before dividends are paid on common stock: CUMULATIVE PREFERRED
stock options to sell a fixed number of shares at a specified price within a certain period or to buy a fixed number of shares at a specified price within a certain period of time: PUTS or CALLS
stock or bond sales that are not made on the floor of a stock exchange: OVER-THE-COUNTER
stock phrases: CANT
stock purchaser does not receive recent dividend: EX-DIVIDEND
stock purchase at one broker and equivalent sale at another to make trading seem active: WASH SALE
stock that is high-priced and good: BLUE CHIP
stock that is traded on a securities exchange: LISTED STOCK
stock trading of fewer than the established 100-share unit: ODD-LOT
stock's market price divided by earnings per share for a 12-month period: PRICE-EARNINGS RATIO
stocks selling at less that $1 a share: PENNY STOCKS
stocky, fleshy: PYKNIC
stomach ache resulting from muscular spasms: COLIC
stomach inflammation: GASTRITIS
stomach pit: SOLAR PLEXUS
stone for sharpening knives: WHETSTONE
stone or block on which a column or statue stands: PLINTH
stone shaft that tapers to a pyramidal top: OBELISK
stone slab carrying an inscription or design: STELE
stone to death: LAPIDATE
stone used to scour the wooden deck of a ship: HOLYSTONE
stones set up as marker or memorial: CAIRN
stony, hard: PETROUS
stony, stonelike: LITHOID
stool or small seat, usually without arms or back: TABORET

stoop to an action or person, condescend: DEIGN

stop, impede, block, hinder: OBSTRUCT

stop, keep back, suppress: STIFLE

stop or check the flow of: STANCH

stop or pause at intervals or temporarily: INTERMIT

stop or seize on the way, prevent from reaching the destination: INTERCEPT

stop someone or something from all activity: IMMOBILIZE

stoppage in the flow of any bodily fluid: STASIS

stoppage of growth: ATROPHY

storage place for goods: REPOSITORY

store carrying general merchandise: EMPORIUM

store as in a granary, gather, accumulate: GARNER

storm characterized by sudden burst of wind, usually with rain or snow: SQUALL

storm consisting of a whirling column of air: TORNADO

stormy, severe: INCLEMENT

stormy, violent: TEMPESTUOUS

story, always long, sometimes poetic, chronicling adventure or heroic acts: SAGA

story between two main floors, a partial balcony: MEZZANINE

story or statement issued to news media: HANDOUT

story that is highly improbable: COCK-AND-BULL STORY

story with a moral: PARABLE

story with hidden or symbolic meanings: ALLEGORY

storyteller of great skill: RACONTEUR

stout: PORTLY

stove of cast-iron, open-faced and resembling a fireplace: FRANKLIN STOVE

stove that is small and portable: CHAUFFER

straggler, slow, falling behind: LAGGARD

straight, slender, wandlike: VIRGATE

straight line over a vowel indicating long sound: MACRON

straightforward, frank, innocent, simple, naive: INGENUOUS

strain, stretch, irritate: RACK

strained, done with great effort: LABORED

strained, forced: FAR-FETCHED

strained as in aiming at effect: AGONISTIC

strange, extraordinary, remarkable: UNACCOUNTABLE

strange, freakish: OUTLANDISH

strange, weird, unnatural, eerie: UNCANNY

strangle: GARROTE

strap encircling the body of a horse: SURCINGLE

strap passing across the forehead that helps to support a load carried on the back: TUMPLINE

stratagem or tactic to outwit someone: PLOY

strategies in games, economics, warfare: GAME THEORY

stratagem that is a sudden, telling blow: COUP

stratagem to avoid unpleasantness, dodge: SUBTERFUGE

straw bed that lies on the floor: PALLET

straw mattress: PALLIASSE

stray: WAIF

stray animal enclosure: PINFOLD

stray from script: AD LIB

stray or wander aimlessly: DIVAGATE

straying from the right course: ERRANT

streak, blotch, spot: MOTTLE

stream or bay leading into the land from a larger body of water: INLET

stream or creek: KILL

street, usually narrow, lined with dwellings that were formerly stables: MEWS

street for pedestrians, with stores on each side: MALL

street show, peep show: RAREE SHOW

strength, vigor: STAMINA

strength or degree of some quality, feeling, action: INTENSITY

stretch out, swell, expand: DISTEND

stretchable, capable of being drawn out: TENSILE

strict: EXACTING

strict, grim, severe: STARK

strict, tightly enforced: STRINGENT

strict disciplinarian: MARTINET

strict in religious or moral matters: PURITANICAL

strictness, exactness: RIGOR

stride that is steady and swinging: LOPE

strike against, bump: JAR

strike against, fall upon: IMPINGE

strike hard: SLOG

strike in which workers stay in plant but refuse to work: SIT-DOWN

string looped over the fingers into intricate arrangements: CAT'S CRADLE

stringed instrument used in Hindu music: SITAR

strip, deprive, as of possessions: DIVEST
strip, deprive of, rob: DESPOIL
strip, edging or selvage, as of cloth: LIST
strip as of clothes, deprive as of rights or possessions: DIVEST
strip blubber or skin from a whale or seal: FLENSE
strip of leaves: DEFOLIATE
strip of material sewn to a seam: WELT
strip of ornamentation as along the top of a wall: FRIEZE
strip or row of cut grass or grain: SWATH
striped, grooved: STRIATED
strips of meat or vegetables cut very thin: JULIENNE
stripteaser: ECDYSIAST
striving: CONATION
stroll, walk leisurely: SAUNTER
strong: PUISSANT
strong, determined, brave: STALWART
strong, sturdy, masculine: VIRILE
strong and dark in color, said of cigars: MADURO
strong physically: POTENT
strong point of a person: FORTE
stronghold: REDOUBT
structural unit used in planning or building: MODULE
structure, framework: FABRIC
structure or outline of something: CONFORMATION
structure that projects and is supported at only one end: CANTILEVER
struggle clumsily, move awkwardly, stumble: FLOUNDER
struggle of people that is confused and noisy: MELEE
struggle or contend with: GRAPPLE
strut, bluster: SWAGGER
strut or promenade: CAKEWALK
stubborn, cantankerous: CROTCHETY
stubborn, cranky: PERVERSE
stubborn, determined: HEADSTRONG
stubborn, obstinate: PERTINACIOUS
stubborn, unmanageable: REFRACTORY
stubborn, persevering: INDOMITABLE
stubborn, persistent, tough: TENACIOUS
stubborn, pitiless, hardhearted: OBDURATE
stubborn, rebellious, disobedient: RECALCITRANT
stubborn, unruly, difficult: INTRACTABLE
stubborn, unyielding: INFLEXIBLE
stubborn, unyielding, pig-headed: OBSTINATE
studio: ATELIER

study intensively for an examination: CRAM
study of insects: ENTOMOLOGY
study or read intently: PORE
study or write laboriously: LUCUBRATE
study space between library stacks: CARREL
stumble or move clumsily: FLOUNDER
stun, amaze, bewilder: STUPEFY
stunted, small, as an imperfectly developed fruit or ear of corn: NUBBIN
stupid: ADDLED, ADDLEBRAINED, ADDLEHEADED, ADDLEPATED
stupid, foolish, unmoved, brutish: INSENSATE
stupid, foolish person: SCHMO
stupid, graceless fellow: LOUT
stupid, idiotic, inane: FATUOUS
stupid, senseless: VACUOUS
stupid, ungainly individual: GAWK
stupid in a gross way: CRASS
stupid person: CLODPATE, CLODPOLL
stupid person: IGNORAMUS
stupid person, blockhead, dunce: DOLT
stupor, apathy: TORPOR
stupor, muscular rigidity and occasional mental agitation: CATATONIA
sturdy, athletic physical structure: MESOMORPHIC
sturdy, strong, masculine: VIRILE
style, skill, technical mastery, as of an art: VIRTUOSITY
style, smartness, dash: PIZZAZZ
style of great brilliance: BRAVURA
style of speech or writing that is artificially elegant: DUPHUISM
style that is spirited, dash: PANACHE
suave, refined, polite: URBANE
subconscious mind exhibited in art and literature: SURREALISM
subdue or suppress by force, allay: QUELL
subdue utterly, silence, crush: SQUELCH
subject to the law or rule of another: HETERONOMOUS
subjective aspect of an emotion: AFFECT
sublime, celestial, superior, fiery: EMPYREAL
submerge, engulf, overpower: WHELM
submissive: AMENABLE
submissive, slavish: SERVILE
submission to or respectful regard for the wishes or opinions of another: DEFERENCE
subsidiary business on certain premises: CONCESSION

subsidy to support a study or institution: SUBVENTION

substance produced chemically: SYNTHETIC

substitute: SURROGATE

substitute: VICAR

substitute, deputy: ALTER EGO

substitute, especially for an actor or actress: UNDERSTUDY

substitute, usually inferior: ERSATZ

substitute for or authority to act for another: PROXY

substitute goals or abilities to make up for personal lack: COMPENSATION

substitutes on an athletic team: BENCH

substituting a roundabout word for another to avoid giving pain or offense: EUPHEMISM

substitution of title or epithet for proper name: ANTONOMASIA

subtle: FINE-DRAWN

subtle, as a distinction made: NICE

subtle, vague: INDEFINABLE

subtle and gradual introduction: INSINUATION

subtle or fine variation or gradation: NUANCE

subtraction term for the number from which the subtrahend is to be deducted: MINUEND

subverting person or group that undermines from within: TROJAN HORSE

success that comes unexpectedly to this venture or person: SLEEPER

success that is sudden and removes an obstacle to progress: BREAKTHROUGH

successful or prosperous period: FLORESCENCE

succor, aid: SUBVENTION

sudden, abrupt: PRECIPITATE

sudden and overwhelming: FOUDROYANT

sudden and turbulent outburst: PAROXYSM

sudden burst of activity or energy: SPURT

sudden change of mind without adequate motive: CAPRICE

sudden impulse: IMPETUOSITY

sudden inspiration: BRAINSTORM

sudden sharp twist: QUIRK

sudden start: SALLY

sudden success that removes an obstacle to progress: BREAKTHROUGH

suffering, capable of feeling: PASSIBLE

suffering, distress, pain, anguish: TRAVAIL

suffering that affords pleasure: MASOCHISM

sufficient grounds for, justify: WARRANT

suffocating someone to death: BURKE

suffocation: ASPHYXIATION

suffuse or cover with a liquid or color: PERFUSE

sugar raw in the cane: MUSCOVADO

sugared or candied, iced, frozen: GLACÉ

suggest, imply: CONNOTE

suggest, propose: PROPOUND

suggest or mention for the first time: BROACH

suggestive, off-color: RISQUÉ

suggestive, risqué: RACY

suggestive in a delicate way: SUBTLE

suggestive of something, fragrant: REDOLENT

suicidal Japanese air attack: KAMIKAZE

suicide: FELO-DE-SE

suicide by disembowelment as a Japanese ritual: HARA-KIRI

suitable: APROPOS

suitable, advisable, proper: EXPEDIENT

suitable, practicable: FEASIBLE

sulkily pugnacious: TRUCULENT

sullen, stern, gloomy, morose: DOUR

sullen or angry look, scowl: LOWER

sum of the squares of the two legs of a right-angle triangle equals the square of the hypotenuse: PYTHAGOREAN THEOREM

summarize: RECAPITULATE

summary: PROSPECTUS

summary: RÉSUMÉ

summary, diagram, or synopsis as of a process: SCHEMA

summary, digest: CONSPECTUS

summary, general view of a subject: SYNOPSIS

summary in concise form, abstract: PRECIS

summary of a document: ABSTRACT

summary of the main points of a course of study: SYLLABUS

summary or synopsis of the plot of a dramatic work: SCENARIO

summary that is brief but comprehensive: COMPENDIUM

summation of an oration: PERORATION

summer, to pass the: ESTIVATE

summer and that which pertains to it: ESTIVAL

summer home, Russian: DACHA

summerhouse or similar structure: GAZEBO

summerhouse, tent or canopy: PAVILION

summer's beginning when the sun is farthest north of the Equator, about June 22: SUMMER SOLSTICE

summon, draw or call forth: EVOKE

summons or formal demand: REQUISITION
sun, solar: HELIACAL
sun as the center: HELIOCENTRIC
sun at its greatest distance north or south
of the equator: SOLSTICE
sunroom: SOLARIUM
sun-dried brick: ADOBE
sunken design, incised carving: INTAGLIO
sunset occurrence: ACRONICAL
superficial: FACILE
superficial follower of an art or science:
DILETTANTE
superficial or little knowledge: SMATTER-
ING
superfluous: DE TROP
superfluous: EXCRESCENT
superfluous, extraneous: SUPEREROGATORY
superfluous, redundant word or phrase:
PLEONASM
superintendence or management: INTEND-
ANCE
superior to all others: SUPERLATIVE
superiority in weight, influence: PREPON-
DERANT
superiority worshiper who shows contempt for supposed inferiors: SNOB
superstition or story passed on from generation to generation: OLD WIVES' TALE
superstitious regard for an object thought
to have magical powers: FETISHISM
supplant, replace: SUPERSEDE
supple, agile, lithe, pliant: LISSOME
supplement, piece out: EKE
supply or feed to excess: SURFEIT
support: ABET
support: ADMINICLE
support, approval, encouraging look:
COUNTENANCE
support, sponsorship: PATRONAGE
support for wood in a fireplace: ANDIRON
support of wood or metal to keep a broken
bone in place: SPLINT
support or advocacy, as of a cause: ES-
POUSAL
support or aid as an auxiliary: ANCIL-
LARY
supporter or originator of a cause: PROPO-
NENT
supporters or voters: CONSTITUENCY
suppose or conclude from incomplete evidence: CONJECTURE
suppress, keep back: STIFLE
suppress, keep secret: HUGGER-MUGGER
suppress, stamp out, stifle: SCOTCH
suppress or put down forcibly: QUASH

suppression of truth to procure some favor
or reward: SUBREPTION
suppressing or silencing, as a rumor:
QUIETUS
supreme and independent authority: SOV-
EREIGN
supreme command, absolute power: IM-
PERIUM
supreme or highest good: SUMMUM BONUM
sureness: CERTITUDE
surface elegance: VENEER
surfeit, glut: SATIATE
surgery on living animals for medical re-
search purposes: VIVISECTION
surmountable, conquerable: SUPERABLE
surname: COGNOMEN
surname: PATRONYMIC
surpass, excel, beat: TRUMP
surpassing others: PREEMINENT
surprise attack: AMBUSH
surrender of a prerogative: ABDICATE
surround, beset: BELEAGUER
surrounded by land: LANDLOCKED
surroundings: AMBIENCE
surroundings, environment, set, as of a
play: MISE EN SCÈNE
surroundings, setting, environment: MILIEU
survey of a subject: CONSPECTUS
survey or map used for taxation basis:
CADASTER
survey to gain information: RECONNAIS-
SANCE
survive, pass through, as a crisis:
WEATHER
surviving, existing: EXTANT
susceptibility or tendency to: PREDISPOSI-
TION
suspend, supplant, annul: SUPERSEDE
suspend temporarily punishment or pain:
REPRIEVE
suspense or state of anxiety: ON TEN-
TERHOOKS
suspenseful story: CLIFF-HANGER
suspension of action: ABEYANCE
suspicious, cautious, wary: LEERY
suspicious, questionable: EQUIVOCAL
sustained or held, in music: TENUTO
sustenance: ALIMENT
swagger, bluster: FANFARONADE
swaggering self-assurance: COCKINESS
swallow food: INGEST
swallow up, overwhelm: ENGULF
swallowing difficulty: DYSPHAGIA
swampy body of water: BAYOU
swarm, teem, breed rapidly: PULLULATE

sway, totter, waver: VACILLATE
swayback: LORDOSIS
swear falsely, perjure oneself, renounce: FORSWEAR
sweat: SUDOR
sweater, knitted, collarless and long-sleeved that opens down front: CARDIGAN
sweating in excessive or abnormal manner: SUDATION
sweating that is excessive: HIDROSIS
sweet or rich in excess, cloying: LUSCIOUS
sweet sounding: MELLIFLUOUS
sweet-sounding, melodious, pleasant: DULCET
sweet to excess: SACCHARINE
swell, expand, widen: DILATE
swell, stretch out, expand: DISTEND
swelling: INTUMESCENCE
swelling, knot or knob: NODE
swelling, protuberance: TUBEROSITY
swelling, puffiness: TUMEFACTION
swelling in the body: EDEMA
swelling or tumor formed by an effusion of blood: HEMATOMA
swerve: SKEW
swift, dashing, large, vigorous: SPANKING
swift, dazzling, brilliant: METEORIC
swift, rapid, galloping: TANTIVY
swimmer's breathing tube that projects above water's surface: SNORKEL
swimming kick in which both legs are parted and bent at the knees, then thrust backward together: SCISSORS KICK
swimming pool: NATATORIUM
swimming under water with equipment such as flippers, scuba apparatus, etc.: SKIN DIVING
swindle: BUNCO
swindle: SKIN GAME
swindle, cheat: ROOK
swindle after the victim's confidence has been won: CONFIDENCE GAME
swine castrated after maturity: STAG
swing around: SLUE
swing to and fro, fluctuate: OSCILLATE
swirling motion of air, water, or gas, etc.: TURBULENCE
swish, fanciness, rustling as of silk: FROUFROU
switch from the lofty to the commonplace: BATHOS
switching of letters or sounds that changes a word: METATHESIS

swollen: BULBOUS
swollen: TUMESCENT
swollen: TUMID
swollen, distended: TURGID
swollen, bulging: VENTRICULAR
sword, short and curved: SCIMITAR
sword without cutting edge used in dueling: EPEE
swordlike in shape: XIPHOID
swordlike knife: SNICKERSNEE
sword-shaped: GLADIATE
sworn, written statement: AFFIDAVIT
syllable or letter appended to a word: PARAGOGE
syllable or syllabes placed at the beginning of a word: PREFIX
syllable or syllables placed at the end of a word: SUFFIX
syllable shortened although it is naturally or by position long: SYSTOLE
syllable third from last in a word: ANTEPENULT
syllables, used in music, as do, re, mi, etc.: SOLMIZATION
symbol for "and" (&): AMPERSAND
symbol of fruitfulness: CALATHUS
symbol or emblem by a publisher, used on title page of a book: COLOPHON
symbol or picture representing a word, sound or object: HIEROGLYPHIC
symbol or representative of something, as of a doctrine or a cause: EXPONENT
symbols devised to represent phonetically the positions of the speech mechanism: VISIBLE SPEECH
sympathize or grieve with someone: CONDOLE
sympathy-evoking, sorrow: PATHOS
symptom of an approaching disease: PRODROME
symptoms indicating a disease or condition: SYNDROME
synonyms and antonyms arranged in categories, in a book: THESAURUS
synopsis, summary or diagram as of a process: SCHEMA
synopsis or summary of the plot of a dramatic work: SCENARIO
syntax: COLLOCATION
synthesis of separate elements of emotion or experience that constitutes more than the mechanical sum of the parts: GESTALT
syphilis: LUES
systematized course of living: REGIMEN

T

table companion: COMMENSAL

table for holding a tea service: TEAPOY

table or its uses: MENSAL

table supported wholly or in part by brackets: CONSOLE TABLE

table wine: VIN ORDINAIRE

table with swinging legs that support drop leaves: GATE-LEG TABLE

tablet on a wall for decoration or to mark an event: PLAQUE

tableware: FLATWARE

tact, knowledge of the right thing to say or do: SAVOIR-FAIRE

tact, smoothness, highly refined skill: FINESSE

tactic or stratagem to outwit someone: PLOY

tactlessness: GAUCHERIE

tadpole: POLLIWOG

tail part that is fleshy, in animals: DOCK

tailless: ACAUDAL

take apart: DISMANTLE

take attention away from: PRESCIND

take away a legacy: ADEEM

take away from, detract: DEROGATE

take back, recant: RETRACT

take exception to, hesitate, object: DEMUR

take note: COGNIZANCE

take off, remove: DOFF

take over property from the owner, usually for public use: EXPROPRIATE

take place, happen: SUPERVENE

take the place of: SUPERSEDE

take parts from one piece of equipment to use in another: CANNIBALIZE

taking risks to achieve some end: BRINKMANSHIP

talisman or charm: GRIGRI

talk, conference of opposing sides: PARLEY

talk about publicly: BRUIT

talk boastfully: COCKALORUM

talk down or against something: DEPRECATE

talk foolishly: TWADDLE

talk in a wandering, incoherent manner: MAUNDER

talk quickly or incoherently: GABBLE

talk or chatter that is rapid, nonsensical or unintelligible: JABBER

talk rapidly and incoherently: GIBBER

talk senselessly, chatter: PRATE

talk that is foolish or senseless: DRIVEL

talk that is idle, also a discussion: PALAVER

talk that sounds important but isn't: BOMBAST

talk to oneself: SOLILOQUIZE

talkative: LOQUACIOUS

talkative, foolish person: BLATHERSKITE

talkative, glib, speaking fluently: VOLUBLE

talkativeness: GARRULITY

talkativeness to an abnormal degree: LOGORRHEA

talked-about object: CONVERSATION PIECE

talking about a traumatic situation for release from it: ABREACTION

talking foolishly: BLITHERING

talks learnedly in table conversation: DEIPNOSOPHIST

tall, lean, often awkward: LANKY

tall, slender figure: ASTHENIC

tall building: HIGH-RISE

tall story: COCK-AND-BULL STORY

Talmudic literature devoted to legal elements: HALAKHA

Talmudic stories and account of the Exodus read at Seder service: HAGGADAH tangible, touchable: TACTILE

tangle or make intricate: INVOLVE

tangle: RETICULAR

tantrum: CONNIPTION

tap dancing without metal taps: SOFT SHOE

tap firmly: PERCUSS

tap or drum monotonously: THRUM

tart or pleasantly sharp taste: PIQUANT

taste, flavor: SAPOR

taste or flavor that is sickeningly sentimental: MAWKISH

taste that is saline and distasteful: BRACKISH

tasteless, flat, bland, dull: INSIPID

tasting, taste: GUSTATION

tasty, appetizing: SAVORY

tasty, savory: SAPID

taunt, gibe: GIRD

taunt, jeer: GIBE

taunt or annoy by reminding of a fault: TWIT

taunting, sneering, ironical language: SARCASM

tautological, wordy: REDUNDANT

tax: IMPOST

tax of one tenth: TITHE

teacher: PRECEPTOR

teacher, lecturer, tutor without faculty rank: DOCENT

teacher or guide, in the East, especially in spiritual matters: GURU

teaching or learning through discovery and investigation: HEURISTICS

teacher who is narrow-minded, pedantic: PEDAGOGUE

tear, chafe, or burn away strips of: EXCORIATE

tear apart, as in searching for plunder: RANSACK

tear apart forcibly: REND

tear raggedly, mangle: LACERATE

tear to pieces: DILACERATE

tearful: LACHRYMOSE

tearfully emotional or sentimental: MAUDLIN

tearing away: AVULSION

tease or disappoint by repeated frustration of expectations: TANTALIZE

teasing talk, jesting: RAILLERY

teasing that is playful: BADINAGE

technical mastery, skill, style, as of an art: VIRTUOSITY

technicians as rulers: TECHNOCRACY

tedious, boring: WEARISOME

tedious, troublesome, tiresome: IRKSOME

teething, cutting teeth: DENTITION

telepathy, clairvoyance: CRYPTESTHESIA

telephone transactions in unlisted stocks: OVER-THE-COUNTER

television: VIDEO

television magnetic tape on which the video and audio parts of a program can be recorded: VIDEO TAPE

television or radio melodramatic series: SOAP OPERA

television's picture as distinguished from its sound, or audio: VIDEO

television's sound as distinguished from its picture, or video: AUDIO

tell, disclose, reveal: DIVULGE

temperate in eating and drinking: ABSTEMIOUS

temperature sense lacking, unable to recognize heat or cold: THERM-ANESTHESIA

temperature standard used to estimate fuel requirements for heating of buildings: DEGREE DAY

tempo and expression of music at performer's pleasure: A CAPRICCIO

temporary: INTERIM

temporary, brief: TRANSIENT

temporary buildings for housing troops: CANTONMENT

temporary camp, usually without shelter: BIVOUAC

temporary inaction: ABEYANCE

temporary or makeshift, as applied to a ship's rigging: JURY RIGGED

temporary residence or stay: SOJOURN

temporary stitching: BASTING

tendency, bent: PROPENSITY

tendency, trend, liking, leaning or bent: INCLINATION

tendency or drift that is hidden: UNDERCURRENT

tendency or inclination: BENT

tendency or way of reacting: DISPOSITION

tendency or inclination, usually toward something objectionable: PROCLIVITY

tendency or susceptibility to: PREDISPOSITION

tendency that is inborn: INSTINCT

tender, emotional, sometimes mawkish: SENTIMENTAL

tender part of a loin of meat: TENDERLOIN

tending to a particular point of view: TENDENTIOUS

tendon at the back of the human knee: HAMSTRING

Ten Commandments: DECALOGUE
ten-year anniversary: DECENNIAL
ten-year period, decade: DECENNARY
tennis: SPHAIRISTIKE
tennis ball returned before it hits the ground: VOLLEY
tennis court's screened gallery for spectators, especially in court tennis: DEDANS
tennis return in which softly stroked ball barely clears the net: DROP SHOT
tennis rule violation of failing to keep both feet behind the base line when serving: FOOT FAULT
tennis set in which the winner wins every game: LOVE SET
tennis stroke in which the ball is arched high into the air: LOB
tennis stroke in which the hand holding the racket hits the ball from the opposite side of the body: BACKHAND
tennis stroke made on the same side of the body as that of the hand wielding the racket: FOREHAND
tense, bewildered, agitated, worried: DISTRAUGHT
tenth part of anything: TITHE
terminology, names: NOMENCLATURE
territory surrounded by that of another country or class: ENCLAVE
terse, concise, brief and meaningful: SUCCINCT
terse, pithy, axiomatic: SENTENTIOUS
terse, solid, packed with meaning: PITHY
test for diphtheria: SCHICK TEST
test for uterine cancer: PAP TEST
test or gauge the weight of by lifting: HEFT
test the depth of water: SOUND
test word, password: SHIBBOLETH
textiles, also perishable goods: SOFT GOODS
ticket selling above regular rates: SCALPING
tickle or excite pleasurably: TITILLATE
tidal wave: TSUNAMI
tide occurring at or shortly after the new or full moon: SPRING TIDE
tide when rise and fall show least change: NEAP TIDE
tides in conflict producing turbulent water: RIP TIDE
tidy: KEMPT
tie, a race in which two competitors finish together: DEAD HEAT

tie or draw, as in a game: STANDOFF
tie or fasten together: COLLIGATE
tie that connects, bond: LIGAMENT
tie together the four feet, or the feet and hands: HOG-TIE
tight spot, predicament: QUANDARY
tighten up or make concise: CONDENSE
tight-rope walker: FUNAMBULIST
tilelike, either in shape or arrangement: TEGULAR
tilt or slope: CANT
timber driven into the earth to support a building or pier: PILE
timber in a stand: STUMPAGE
time between periods or events, meantime: INTERIM
time counted in reverse, as in rocket launching: COUNTDOWN
time flies: TEMPUS FUGIT
time, in addition to length, width and thickness: FOURTH DIMENSION
time erroneously associated with an event or a thing: ANACHRONISM
time nature of a verb form: TENSE
time or rate agreement arranged: SYNCHRONIZED
time out from work, for a short period: COFFEE BREAK
time period memorable for important events or influence: EPOCH
time to be off the streets: CURFEW
time-consuming tactics to obstruct action: FILIBUSTER
time-honored, venerable, classic: VINTAGE
time-measuring science: CHRONOLOGY
timepiece: HOROLOGE
time-to-get-up signal on bugle or drum: REVEILLE
timid: PIGEON-HEARTED
timid, fearful: TIMOROUS
timid or cowardly: CHICKEN-HEARTED or CHICKEN-LIVERED
timid or fearful, trembling: TREMULOUS
timidity, shyness, lack of confidence: DIFFIDENCE
tin mine region: STANNARY
tinder of decayed wood: PUNK
tint, light color: TINCTURE
tiny: IOTA
tiny, very small: MINUSCULE
tiny person: HOP-O'-MY-THUMB
tiny quantity: SOUPÇON
tip: POURBOIRE
tip, gift of money: GRATUITY
tirade: HARANGUE

tireless, unflagging: INDEFATIGABLE

tiresome, tedious, troublesome: IRKSOME

tissue and tissue structure, as a biological study: HISTOLOGY

tissue growing abnormally, as a tumor: NEOPLASM

tissue removed from living organism for examination: BIOPSY

title or epithet substituted for proper name: ANTONOMASIA

title or heading of a section in a law: RUBRIC

that's life: C'EST LA VIE

theater bulletin board: CALLBOARD

theater fabric, light and sheer, used as a backdrop: SCRIM

theater space above the stage containing drop curtain and lighting: FLY

theater waiting room for performers when they are off-stage: GREEN ROOM

theater with stage surrounded by seats: ARENA THEATER

theaters, tents, modified barns, usually in resort areas, for plays, concerts: STRAW-HAT CIRCUIT

theatrical, overly emotional: HISTRIONIC

theatrical collection of works prepared for production: REPERTORY

theatrical stage objects: PROPS

theft: LARCENY

theme used throughout a work of art to indicate a certain person, event or idea: LEITMOTIF

theoretical, as opposed to practical: ACADEMIC

theoretical, not concrete: ABSTRACT

theological branch dealing with facts and proofs concerning Christianity: APOLOGETICS

theoretical or conjectural: SPECULATIVE

theory or supposition used as basis for further investigation: HYPOTHESIS

therapy using doses of medicines that produce symptoms of the disease treated: HOMEOPATHY

thesis established by showing its opposite to be absurd: APAGOGE

thick and dense, as heavy smoke: TURBID

thicken: INCRASSATE

thicken as by evaporation: INSPISSATE

thickening of artery walls: ATHEROSCLEROSIS

thief: GONIF or GANEF

thin, flimsy, delicate: TENUOUS

thin, lean: SPARE

thin, scanty, inadequate: MEAGER

thin and pale: PEAKED

thin biscuit or cooky: WAFER

thin down, emaciate: MACERATE

thin sheets of fabric, wood, etc., bonded together: LAMINATED

thing that goes into a mixture: INGREDIENT

think, reason: INTELLECTUALIZE

think about, reflect, consider carefully: PONDER

think of separately: PRESCIND

think out carefully, devise: EXCOGITATE

thinker, clever man: SOPHIST

thinking, using the intellect: INTELLECTION

thinly diffused: SPARSE

third anniversary: TRIENNIAL

third syllable from end in a word: ANTEPENULT

thirst-causing, dry up: PARCH

thirteen: BAKER'S DOZEN

this side of the Atlantic: CISATLANTIC

thorough, thorough-going: INGRAINED

thoroughfare or open space for crowds: CONCOURSE

thought, idea: INTELLECTION

thought apart from matter: ABSTRACT

thoughtful, serious, often melancholy: PENSIVE

thoughtless, unthinking: INCOGITANT

thousand, as by the thousand: PER MILL

thousand, or thousand years: CHILIAD

thousand tons: KILOTON

thousand year period: MILLENARY

thrash severely, punish or beat: TROUNCE

threat or denunciation, especially from a divine source: COMMINATION

threaten: IMPEND

threatening, menacing: MINACIOUS, MINATORY

threatening and dark, as the weather: LOWERING

. . . (three dots) indicating the omission of words in a sentence: ELISION

three in a governing group: TROIKA

three miles: LEAGUE

three persons or things: TRIAD

three rhyming lines: TERCET

three separate but related literary or dramatic works: TRILOGY

three spots, as on a card or domino: TREY

three-figure design, with branches, arms, or legs coming from a common center: TRISKELION

threes, grouped in threes: TERNARY

thrift or economy in managing: HUS-
BANDRY
thriftless, rash, incautious: IMPROVIDENT
thrifty: FRUGAL
thrifty, careful: CANNY
thrill, arouse, startle: ELECTRIFY
throat irritation often causing loss of
voice: LARYNGITIS
throb regularly, vibrate: PULSATE
throbbing, pulsing: VIBRANT
throw forth or forward: PROJECT
throw goods or cargo overboard: JETTISON
throw in or introduce abruptly: INJECT
throw things at: PELT
throwing out of a window: DEFENESTRA-
TION
thrust away from, push down: DETRUDE
thumb: POLLEX
thumb one's nose: SNOOK
thumb rapidly through a book's pages:
RIFFLE
thus passes away worldly glory: SIC
TRANSIT GLORIA MUNDI
to the point: APROPOS
toady, cringe fondly: FAWN
toady, servile follower: LACKEY
toast or bread, in small pieces, dipped in
gravy or sauce: SIPPET
toasted slices of bread that has been baked
yellow: ZWIEBACK
tobacco ash left in pipe after smoking:
DOTTLE
tobacco grown in Louisiana, dark and
strong: PERIQUE
toe with joint bent downward: HAMMER-
TOE
toeless: ADACTYLOUS
toes linked by membrane: WEB-FOOTED
together: IN CONCERT
together, cooperative: SYNERGETIC
toilet bowl for bathing genitals: BIDET
toilet for numbers of people, as in a camp:
LATRINE
toilet in nautical language: HEAD
token of a solemn pledge: SACRAMENT
token or counter: JETON
tolerate by use or exercise, accustom:
INURE
tomato juice mixed with vodka as a cocktail: BLOODY MARY
tomato juice served as if it were a cocktail: VIRGIN MARY
tomboy: HOYDEN
tombstone inscription: EPITAPH

tomcat: GIB
tomorrow (Spanish): MAÑANA
tone color, as of a voice or an instrument:
TIMBRE
tongue lashing: EXCORIATION
tonguelike: LANGUET
tonguelike or pertaining to language:
LINGUAL
too glib, facile: PAT
too great or too numerous to be determined: INCALCULABLE
too much, in music: TANTO
too much sweetness: CLOYING
tooth cleanser: DENTIFRICE
tooth extraction: EXODONTIA
tooth that is broken or projects: SNAGGLE-
TOOTH
tooth with two points: BICUSPID
toothache: ODONTALGIA
toothless: EDENTATE
tooth-gnashing: BRUXISM
top, apex: VERTEX
top course of a wall or roof: COPING
top grade or quality: FIRST WATER
top having four, lettered sides, used in a
gambling game: TEETOTUM
topmost point, acme: PINNACLE
top-shaped, or spinning like a top: TUR-
BINATE
top rank: PREEMINENT
torch, candlestick that is large and decorated: FLAMBEAU
torment, tease, rant, browbeat, bluster:
HECTOR
tornado: TWISTER
torpor: ACEDIA
Torrid Zone inhabitants whose shadows
fall according to season: AMPHISCIAN
tortoiselike: TESTUDINAL
tortuous: ANFRACTUOUS
tossing or twitching to an abnormal degree: JACTITATION
total, end-to-end: OVERALL
touch at sides or ends: ABUT
touch or meet lightly: KISS
touch or push with a slight jar, shake
lightly, stimulate: JOG
touchable: TANGIBLE
touchable, perceptible: PALPABLE
touchable, tangible: TACTILE
touching: TANGENT
touching, emotionally moving: POIGNANT
tough, robust: HARDY
tough, unyielding: HARD-BITTEN

toughen or smooth metal: PLANISH

tour rural districts: BARNSTORM

tournament: JOUSTS

tournament in which each player engages every other player: ROUND ROBIN

tousled, untidy, unkempt: DISHEVELED

toward the center: CENTRIPETAL

toward the stern on a boat: ABAFT

tower or keep of a castle: DONJON

tower that tapers to a point: SPIRE

trace, sign of something absent: VESTIGE

trace, slight hint: SOUPÇON

trace, spark: SCINTILLA

trace out, portray verbally, describe: DELINEATE

track, trail, footprint or other trace of a wild animal: SPOOR

track and field event in which an athlete uses a long pole to leap over a high horizontal bar: POLE VAULT

track or trail behind any moving thing, such as a ship: WAKE

tractable, yielding: PLAINT

trademark of a publishing house: COLOPHON

trader: CHANDLER

trader or dealer: MONGER

trading of votes and influence between politicians: LOGROLLING

trading unit on a stock exchange, usually 100 shares: ROUND LOT

tragic muse: MELPOMENE

trail, track, footprint or other trace of a wild animal: SPOOR

train of persons or animals fastened together as for marching: COFFLE

train to a behavior pattern: CONDITION

training of employes to develop skills, etc.: IN-SERVICE COURSES

traitor: RECREANT

traitor, deserter: RENEGADE

traitor, renegade: TURNCOAT

tramp, wanderer: VAGABOND

tranquil, calm, untroubled: SERENE

tranquil, serene, uniform: EQUABLE

tranquillity: ATARAXIA

transaction conditionally authorized when, as, and if a security is issued: WHEN ISSUED

transference of an emotion to something other than the original object: DISPLACEMENT

transform: TRANSMOGRIFY

transform, convert: RESOLVE

transformation: PERMUTATION

transformation of form, character, or appearance: METAMORPHOSIS

transient, fickle, unstable, fleeting: VOLATILE

transitional form: INTERGRADE

transitory, fleeting: FUGACIOUS

transitory, lasting a short time, fleeting, of short life or duration: EPHEMERAL

transitory or passing: CADUCITY

translation literally of a word or construction from one language to another: LOAN TRANSLATION

translation word for word: METAPHRASE

translucent, limpid: PELLUCID

transmit to another: BEQUEATH

transmutation process: ALCHEMY

transparent, lucid, pure, clear: LIMPID

transparent, radiant: LUCENT

transparent or translucent, as a cloth: DIAPHANOUS

transposing letters of a word to form another: ANAGRAM

transposition of letters or sounds that changes a word: METATHESIS

transposition of sounds or of parts of words unintentionally: SPOONERISM

trap, situation with no escape: CUL DE SAC

trapeze acrobat: AERIALIST

trashy art or literature: KITSCH

travel a route: PEREGRINATE

travel urge: WANDERLUST

traveler, wayfarer: VIATOR

travelers moving in a group: CARAVAN

traveling or going from place to place: ITINERANT

traveling salesman who sells or gives away religious books: COLPORTEUR

tray: SALVER

treacherous: PERFIDIOUS

treacherous woman: DELILAH

treacherous, wily, cunning: INSIDIOUS

treason, offense against sovereign authority: LESE MAJESTY

treasurer: BURSAR

treatise: DISSERTATION

treatise, formal discourse: DISQUISITION

treatise or pamphlet usually on a political or religious subject: TRACT

treatment of disease by manipulation of joints: CHIROPRACTIC

treatment of disease by producing incompatible conditions: ALLOPATHY

treaty, contract, agreement: PACT

tree grown from seed: STAND

tree rings used to estimate dates of past events: DENDROCHRONOLOGY

tree with its top cut to cause growth of shoots: POLLARD

trees, like or living in: ARBOREAL

trees as studied in botany and forestry: DENDROLOGY

trees or shrubs cut and arranged in fantastic shapes: TOPIARY

trembling paralysis: PALSY

trench mouth: VINCENT'S ANGINA

trespass, intrude, advance beyond proper limit: ENCROACH

trespass for hunting or fishing: POACH

triangle with two equal sides: ISOSCELES

triangles and the relationship of their sides and angles, as a study: TRIGONOMETRY

triangular jet aircraft: DELTA WING

triangular or wedge-shaped piece of fabric set into a garment to provide greater fullness: GORE

triangular roof feature: GABLE

triangular stringed instrument (Russian): BALALAIKA

tribute, elaborate praise: PANEGYRIC

trick, cajole, entice by flattery or guile: INVEIGLE

trick, cheat, deceive: FINAGLE

trick, maneuver, device for obtaining advantage: STRATAGEM

trick or cheat: HOODWINK

trick or deceive someone: BAMBOOZLE

trickery: CHICANERY

trickery, deceitfulness, double-dealing: DUPLICITY

trickery, deception: HOCUS-POCUS

trickery, hocus-pocus, sleight of hand: LEGERDEMAIN

trickery, rascality, deceitfulness: KNAVERY

trickery, underhandedness: SKULDUGGERY

tricky or fraudulent action: JOCKEYING

tricky or lewd: LUBRICOUS

trifle: BAGATELLE

trifle, little something: QUELQUE CHOSE

trifle with or flirt: COQUET

trifles, unimportant details: MINUTIAE

trifling, small work: OPUSCULE

trifling or insignificant size or amount: NEGLIGIBLE

trifling, small: NOMINAL

trifling, unimportant, frivolous: FRIBBLE

trifling, unimportant, insignificant: PETTY

trilling sound, as that of grasshoppers or birds: CHIRR

trim or cut the branches as from a tree: LOP

trimming for women's gowns, as beaded lace or braid: PASSEMENTERIE

trimming on edges or seams of material: PIPING

trinket: BIBELOT

trinket: GEWGAW

trinket or ornament either gaudy or trifling: FALLAL

triplicate: TERNATE

trite, commonplace, banal remark: PLATITUDE

trite, commonplace, worn out by overuse (as a phrase): HACKNEYED

trite expression: BROMIDE

trite or hackneyed: HACK

trite, worn-out, overused expression: CLICHÉ

trite story, song, saying: CHESTNUT

triumphant, joyful: JUBILANT

trivial, of small importance: FEATHERWEIGHT

trivial, petty: INSIGNIFICANT

trivial, petty: PICAYUNE

trivial, petty, contemptible: PALTRY

trivial, silly, unimportant: FRIVOLOUS

trivial, unimportant: INCONSEQUENTIAL

trivial or worthless matter: CHAFF

trolley in parallelogram shape that draws current for an electric locomotive: PANTOGRAPH

troop call for service, review, etc.: MUSTER

trouble: TSOORIS

trouble, bother, inconvenience: DISCOMMODE

trouble, torment relentlessly: HARASS

trouble with persistent demands: IMPORTUNE

trouble-free state: ATARAXIA

troublemaker: ENFANT TERRIBLE

trouble-making: PESTILENT

troublesome, tiresome, tedious: IRKSOME

trousers of women resembling a skirt: CULOTTE

trudge laboriously: PLOD

true apparently but open to doubt: PLAUSIBLE

truism: PLATITUDE

truly so: VERITABLE

trumpet mute: SOURDINE

trumpet or drum signal for a parley: CHA-MADE

trustee, guardian: FIDUCIARY

truthful, accurate: VERACIOUS

truthful appearing: VERISIMILITUDE

tub for boiling and bleaching fabrics: KIER

tube between mouth and stomach: GULLET

tube of small size, often graduated: PIPETTE

tuck made in a garment to achieve good fit: DART

tuft of ribbons, yarn, feathers: POMPON

tuft or clump, as of grass or hair: TUSSOCK

tumbler, vaulter: VOLTIGEUR

tumor that is malignant: SARCOMA

tumult, confusion: TURMOIL

tune an instrument: TEMPER

turbulent, dangerous condition or place: MAELSTROM

Turkish confection: HALVAH

Turkish title of respect (formerly): EFFENDI

turmoil, confusion: HURLY-BURLY

turmoil, haste, excitement: HECTIC

turn, as the hand, so that the palm is upward or forward: SUPINATE

turn, rotate or swing, as on a pivot: PIVOT

turn aside: SHUNT

turn aside, deflect, distract, amuse, entertain: DIVERT

turn aside, swerve: SKEW

turn aside, wander from the main subject: DIGRESS

turn aside, ward off, avoid: PARRY

turn away from straight course, or sexual pervert: DEVIATE

turn or go back to a former place, position or condition: REVERT

turn out finally, result ultimately: EVENTUATE

turn outward or inside out: EVERT

turned up at the tip: RETROUSSÉ

turncoat, traitor: RENEGADE

turning of one's interest inward upon oneself: INTROVERSION

turning point in action, belief, etc.: WATERSHED

turreted like a castle: CASTELLATED

tutor, teacher, lecturer, without faculty rank: DOCENT

tuxedo, semiformal attire: BLACK TIE

twelve or twelfths: DUODECIMAL

twentieth: VIGESIMAL

twenty-one, a card game: VINGT-ET-UN

twenty-year period: VICENNIAL

twice a week: SEMIWEEKLY

twice a year: BIANNUAL

twilight, dusk: GLOAMING

twilight dimness, obscure: CREPUSCULAR

twin-bearing: BIPAROUS

twinge of fear: QUALM

twist, bend, contort: WRITHE

twist, bend, misrepresent: DISTORT

twist or bend out of shape: DISTORT

twist or lurch from side to side: CAREEN

twist or pull away: WREST

twisted cord used for ornamentation: TORSADE

twisting or being twisted: TORSION

twitching or tossing to an abnormal degree: JACTITATION

two, double or paired: BINARY

two bids made simultaneously are decided by a flip of a coin: MATCHED AND LOST

two dancers in a ballet figure: PAS DE DEUX

two dots over a Germanic vowel to indicate sound change (ü): UMLAUT

two dots over second of two consecutive vowels to indicate different pronunciation: DIERISIS

two equally accented syllables making up a poetic metrical foot: SPONDEE

two meanings in a phrase, one of them risqué: DOUBLE ENTENDRE

two months apart: BIMONTHLY

two months duration: BIMESTRIAL

two names or two terms: BINOMIAL

two negatives in a single sentence ("I don't have no pencil"): DOUBLE NEGATIVE

two or more husbands at once: POLYANDRY

two or more wives at once: POLYGYNY

two persons sharing ruling power: DIARCHY

two prosecutions for the same offense: DOUBLE JEOPARDY

two sections or two opposed parts: DICHOTOMY

two-sided: BILATERAL

two loudspeakers for stereophonic effect: BINAURAL

two tickets for the price of one: TWOFER

two tones rapidly alternated, in music: TRILL

two vowel sounds that blend into one syllable: DIPHTHONG

two years apart: BIENNIAL

two-colored: DICHROMATIC

two-edged battle ax: TWIBIL

two-footed animal: BIPED

two-god theology: DITHEISM

two-handed: BIMANOUS

two-part division of groups or classes that are often opposed: DICHOTOMY

tying up or binding together; also two or more letters united in print: LIGATURE

type assortment of all the characters in one size and style: FONT

type in which the letters slant, usually to denote emphasis: ITALIC

type or kind, as in art or literature: GENRE

type measure equal to square of the type body: EM

type measure half the width of an em: EN

type plate containing company's distinctive form of name, trademark, newspaper nameplate, etc.: LOGOTYPE

type set by printers that exceeds the space available: OVERSET

type that is heavy and black: BOLDFACE

type that looks like handwriting: CURSIVE

type 12 points high used as a unit of measurement in printing: PICA

typesetter: COMPOSITOR

typewriter operated by telephone: TELEX

typify: PERSONIFY

typical example, model, pattern: EXEMPLAR

typical or specific language, style, etc, as in art, literature: IDIOM

typographical error: TYPO

typographical ornament or symbol: DINGBAT

typographical term for part of a letter that extends below the line: DESCENDER

typographical term for part of a letter that extends upward: ASCENDER

typographical unit of measurement, 12 points: PICA

tyrant: DESPOT

tyrannical subordinate official: SATRAP

U

U-shaped piece of metal with pointed ends used as a fastener: STAPLE

ugly, unpleasant in appearance, disagreeable: ILL-FAVORED

ugly and malicious old woman: BELDAM

umpire: ARBITER

unable to produce the desired effect: INEFFECTUAL

unable to survive: INVIABLE

unable to swallow: APHAGIA

unabridged: IN EXTENSO

unacceptable, unwelcome person: PERSONA NON GRATA

unaccompanied singing: A CAPPELLA

unadorned, as speech or writing: LITERAL

unaffected, simple, candid, artless: NAIVE

unaffected by pain or pleasure: STOICAL

unalike, varied: DIVERSE

unalive, spiritless: INANIMATE

unambiguous: UNEQUIVOCAL

unattractive, dingy: SNUFFY

unavoidable, authoritative, urgently necessary: IMPERATIVE

unavoidable, certain: INEVITABLE

unavoidable, inevitable: INELUCTABLE

unaware, unmindful: OBLIVIOUS

unbearable: INSUFFERABLE

unbeliever: INFIDEL

unbelieving, irreligious: HEATHEN

unbending: INTRANSIGENT

unbiased: INDIFFERENT

unbiased, impartial: DISPASSIONATE

unbiased, objective, impartial: DISPASSIONATE

unbreakable: INFRANGIBLE

unbreakable: IRREFRANGIBLE

unbiased, detached: OBJECTIVE

uncalled for: GRATUITOUS

unceasing: INCESSANT

uncertain: AMBIVALENT

uncertain: VACILLATING

uncertain, risky: TOUCH-AND-GO

uncertain or unforeseen but possible event: CONTINGENCY

unchangeable: IMMUTABLE

unchangeable: INVARIABLE

unchangeable, fixed: INFLEXIBLE

unchanged, undamaged, whole: INTACT

unchaste, morally unrestrained: LIBERTINE

unchecked, wild: RAMPANT

unclean: UNSAVORY

unclear: AMBIGUOUS

unclear, hazy, misty, vague: NEBULOUS

uncle-like: AVUNCULAR

uncomfortably small, cramped: INCOMMODIOUS

uncommunicative: TACITURN

uncommunicative, quiet, reserved: RETICENT

unconcealed: ABOVEBOARD

unconcealed, open, evident: OVERT

unconcerned, apathetic: INDIFFERENT

unconcerned, lighthearted, carefree: INSOUCIANT

unconquerable: INEXPUGNABLE

unconquerable, not capable of being injured: INVULNERABLE

unconscious, lethargic, torpid: COMATOSE

unconscious part of the psyche regarded as source of instinctual drives: ID

unconscious perception: SUBLIMINAL

unconsciousness caused by injury or disease: COMA

unconsciousness caused by too little oxygen: ASPHYXIA

uncontrolled response by a patient in psychoanalysis to a given stimulus: FREE ASSOCIATION

unconventional, odd: OUTRÉ

unconvincing, inadequate, fragile: FLIMSY

uncultivated, unseeded: FALLOW
undamaged, whole, unchanged: INTACT
undeceive, free from false or mistaken ideas: DISABUSE
undecided, wavering: IRRESOLUTE
undeniable: INCONTROVERTIBLE
undependable person in a group: WEAK SISTER
underdeveloped countries, especially in Asia and Africa: THIRD WORLD
underdone, poorly made: SLACK-BAKED
underground structure or vault: HYPOGEUM
underhanded and secret activity, plot: INTRIGUE
underhanded or shady dealing: CHICANERY
underhandedness, trickery: SKULDUGGERY
undermine the morale, corrupt: SUBVERT
understand, interpret, puzzle out: FATHOM
understandable, clear: PELLUCID
understandable with ease, rational, clear, bright, shining: LUCID
understanding, compatible: SIMPATICO
understanding, knowledge, or grasp of ideas or things: PERCEPTION
understanding or agreement: ENTENTE
understatement for effect, a form of litotes: MEIOSIS
understood, implied: IMPLICIT
understood only by an inner group: ESOTERIC
undertone: SOTTO VOCE
underwater breathing apparatus: SCUBA
underwater work chamber: CAISSON
underworld vocabulary: ARGOT
undeveloped: LATENT
undisclosed, beyond what is spoken of: ULTERIOR
undiscovered, unused, untrod hitherto: VIRGIN
undo, void: NULLIFY
uneasiness, anxieties, restlessness: INQUIETUDE
uneasiness, misgiving: QUALM
uneasy: QUEASY
uneatable: INEDIBLE
uneducated, illiterate: UNLETTERED
unemployed people or vagrants: FLOTSAM
unending: AD INFINITUM
unequal: DISPARATE
unequaled: PEERLESS
unequaled, matchless: NONPAREIL
unequaled: SANS PAREIL

unerring: IMPECCABLE
unerring: INFALLIBLE
unessential: UNIMPORTANT
unethical clash of public duty and self-interest: CONFLICT OF INTEREST
unexplored land or area: TERRA INCOGNITA
unexpected, without warning: UNAWARES
unexpressed, unspoken: INARTICULATE
unfair: INEQUITABLE
unfaithful, cowardly: RECREANT
unfavorable, inauspicious: UNTOWARD
unfeeling, hardened: INDURATE
unfeeling, impassive: STOLID
unfeeling, invulnerable: IMPASSIBLE
unfeeling, stupid, foolish: INSENSATE
unfilled orders: BACKLOG
unflagging, tireless: INDEFATIGABLE
unflinching, resolved, determined: RESOLUTE
unfortunate: STAR-CROSSED
unfortunate, unlucky: HAPLESS
unfriendly: DISAFFECTED
unfriendly: ILL-DISPOSED
unfriendly: INIMICAL
unfruitful, barren: STERILE
ungodliness, lack of reverence: IMPIETY
ungrateful person: INGRATE
unified: INDISCRETE
uniform, similar, like, same composition throughout: HOMOGENEOUS
uniform worn by male household servants or employes: LIVERY
unify, bring together into a whole, fit together: INTEGRATE
unimaginative: LITERAL
unimportant, frivolous, trifling,: FRIBBLE
unimportant, trivial: INCONSEQUENTIAL
unimportant, trivial, petty: FRIVOLOUS
unimportant or small details, trifles: MINUTIAE
unimportant person or thing: CIPHER
unimportant person or thing: NONENTITY
uninjured, whole, untaxed: SCOT-FREE
unintelligible: INCOMPREHENSIBLE
unintelligible speech or sounds: GLOSSOLALIA
unintentional: INADVERTENT
uninterested: APATHETIC
uninterrupted or extended: CONTINUOUS
union man who represents fellow workers: SHOP STEWARD
union members alone allowed to be employed: CLOSED SHOP

union membership not required for employment: OPEN SHOP

union membership required after employment: UNION SHOP

unique, one of a kind: SUI GENERIS

unit of trading on a stock exchange, usually 100 shares: ROUND LOT

unit that is indivisible: MONAD

united: IN CONCERT

united in opinion, all assenting: UNANIMOUS

United States and Soviet Union: SUPERPOWERS

uniting of atomic nuclei into one of heavier mass: NUCLEAR FUSION

unity of purpose, relations or interests: SOLIDARITY

universal, all-embracing knowledge: PANSOPHY

universal, widespread, also general epidemic: PANDEMIC

universal, world-wide, general, especially concerning the church: ECUMENICAL

universe, especially when viewed as a unity: MACROCOSM

universe, theories of its creation, structure, etc.: COSMOLOGY, COSMOGONY

universe in miniature: MICROCOSM

unjust: INIQUITOUS

unjustifiable: INSUPPORTABLE

unjustifiable, unprincipled: UNCONSCIONABLE

unjustly: UNDULY

unkempt, tousled, rumpled, untidy: DISHEVELED

unknowable through physical perception: NOUMENON

unknown except by a few specially instructed individuals; secret, abstruse: ESOTERIC

unknown or hidden difficulty: JOKER

unlawful, unauthorized: ILLICIT

unlawful dispossession: DISSEIZIN

unlawful manner of performing a lawful act: MISFEASANCE

unlike, dissimilar, unequal: DISPARATE

unlike, dissimilar, unrelated: HETEROGENEOUS

unlikeness: DISSIMILITUDE

unlikeness, inequality: DISPARITY

unlimited as to subject, duration, etc., or, in an investment company, as to number of shares: OPEN-ENDED

unlimited authority in a government: ABSOLUTISM

unlimited money or authority made available: BLANK CHECK

unlucky: ILL-STARRED

unlucky, unfortunate: HAPLESS

unmanly, womanlike, weak, soft: EFFEMINATE

unmarried, abstaining from sexual congress: CELIBATE

unmindful, unaware: OBLIVIOUS

unmoved, calm, serene: IMPASSIVE

unnatural or disfiguring outgrowth, such as a wart: EXCRESCENCE

unoccupied, idle: VACUOUS

unorganized: AMORPHOUS

unorthodox: HETERODOX

unorthodox in his attitudes: MAVERICK

unorthodox or liberal in attitudes or beliefs: LATITUDINARIAN

unpardonable: IRREMISSIBLE

unperceivable by the sense of touch: IMPALPABLE

unperceptive: PURBLIND

unpleasant appearance: EYESORE

unpleasant in appearance, ugly, disagreeable: ILL-FAVORED

unplowed land near fence or at end of furrows: HEADLAND

unpolished, crude: INURBANE

unpolished, uncouth: AGRESTIC

unpractical, though romantic in intentions: QUIXOTIC

unpredictable, uncertain: INCALCULABLE

unpremeditated: EXTEMPORANEOUS

unpremeditated: SPONTANEOUS

unpremeditated homicide in a sudden fight: CHANCE-MEDLEY

unprepared, spontaneous: IMPROMPTU

unprincipled, unjustifiable: UNCONSCIONABLE

unprovoked, unjust, malicious: WANTON

unquestionable: VERITABLE

unquestionable, certain: INDUBITABLE

unquestionable, unassailable: INCONTESTABLE

unreadable: INDECIPHERABLE

unreal, false, artificially invented: FICTITIOUS

unreasonable: ABSONANT

unreasoning: IRRATIONAL

unreasoning devotion to one's race country, etc.: CHAUVINISM

unreasoning passion, foolish love: INFATUATION

unreceptive, not open: IMPERVIOUS

unrefined, coarse, natural: EARTHY

unrefined, rough, crude: UNCOUTH
unrelated, unlike, dissimilar: HETEROGE-
NEOUS
unrelated to the matter at hand, coming
from without: EXTRANEOUS
unrelenting, merciless: IMPLACABLE
unreliable: IRRESPONSIBLE
unreliable: SKITTISH
unreserved, absolute: IMPLICIT
unresolved: PENDENT
unrestrained: IMMODERATE
unrestrained, excessive: WANTON
unrestrained, unchecked: INCONTINENT
unrestrained as in speech or action: IN-
TEMPERATE
unrestricted authority: CARTE BLANCHE
unrivaled: INAPPROACHABLE
unruffled, calm: IMPERTURBABLE
unruly, boisterous: OBSTREPEROUS
unruly, difficult, stubborn,: INTRACTABLE
unruly, fidgety, restless: RESTIVE
unruly, loud: RAUCOUS
unruly, malicious, fierce: VICIOUS
unruly, rebellious, irritable, cranky:
FRACTIOUS
usage-based law, rather than legislation:
UNWRITTEN LAW
unscrupulous: UNCONSCIONABLE
unseeable because of smallness: IMPER-
CEPTIBLE
unseeded, uncultivated: FALLOW
unseemly: INDECOROUS
unselfish devotion to others: ALTRUISM
unserviceable: IMPRACTICABLE
unsettled, difficult to solve: PROBLEMATIC
unsettled, vague: INDETERMINATE
unskilled or inexperienced: FRESH-WATER
unskilled worker: BLUE COLLAR
unsociable, fierce, wild: FAROUCHE
unsophisticated, artless, unaffected, unin-
structed, simple: NAIVE
unsophisticated, narrow: PROVINCIAL
unspoken, unexpressed: INARTICULATE
unspoken, silent: TACIT
unstable, changeable: LABILE
unstable, fleeting, transient, fickle: VOLA-
TILE
unsteady, wavering: FLUCTUATING
unsteady or irregular movement at sea:
YAW
unsubstantial, flimsy, weak: TENUOUS
unsuccessful, fruitless: INEFFECTUAL
unsuccessful, futile: UNAVAILING
unsuccessful, short of goal: MANQUÉ
unsuccessfully conclude a project: ABORT

unsuitability: INAPTITUDE
unsuitable, inappropriate, at odds with:
INCONGRUOUS
unsuitable, untimely: INOPPORTUNE
unsure, risky,: PRECARIOUS
unsurmountable: INSUPERABLE
untanned skin of a calf or lamb: KIP
untaxed, uninjured, whole: SCOT-FREE
unthinking, thoughtless: INCOGITANT
untidy, slovenly: UNKEMPT
untidy, unkempt, tousled, rumpled: DI-
SHEVELED
untidy in appearance: BLOWZY
untidy or careless person: SLOVEN
untidy or soiled: BEDRAGGLED
untidy or slovenly woman: SLATTERN
untimely, unsuitable: INOPPORTUNE
untruthful: MENDACIOUS
unusable: IMPRACTICABLE
unused, brand new, original condition:
MINT CONDITION
unused condition, neglected: DESUETUDE
unusual happening: PHENOMENON
unutterable: INEFFABLE
unwavering, firmly faithful: STEADFAST
unwavering, steadfast, firmly directed:
INTENT
unwelcome or unacceptable person: PER-
SONA NON GRATA
unwholesome, noxious atmosphere, influence, effect, etc.: MIASMA
unwieldly, ponderous, enormous: ELE-
PHANTINE
unwilling, reluctant: LOATH
unwise: INADVISABLE
unwise, imprudent: INDISCREET
unyielding: ADAMANT
unyielding: INDUCTILE
unyielding, aggressive: TRUCULENT
unyielding, resistant: IMPREGNABLE
unyielding, refusing to compromise or
come to terms: INTRANSIGENT
unyielding, stubborn: INFLEXIBLE
up for consideration: ON THE TAPIS
up to date: AU COURANT
upbraid or denounce scathingly: EX-
CORIATE
upheaval that is violent: CATACLYSM
upholstery or drapery fabric with varicolored stripes of satin or moiré: TAB-
ARET
uplift, enlighten, benefit: EDIFY
upper class, aristocrat: PATRICIAN
upper class rule: ARISTOCRACY
upright, honest: INCORRUPT

uprightness, correctness of judgment: RECTITUDE

uproar: BALLYHOO

uproar: BROUHAHA

uproar, brawl, conflict, fight: FRAY

uproar, confused sound: HUBBUB

uproar of a crowd: TUMULT

uproot, eradicate, dislocate, extirpate: DERACINATE

uproot, pull up by the roots, destroy utterly, erase: ERADICATE

uprooting, extracting forcibly: EVULSION

upset, confuse, frustrate: DISCONCERT

upset, disturb, alarm: PERTURB

upset or irritate: RUFFLE

upstart: JACKANAPES

upstart, newly rich or influential: PARVENU

upward leap, made by a trained horse: CAPRIOLE

upward stroke of a small letter (typography): ASCENDER

urban complex: CONURBATION

urbane, cheerful, lively: DEBONAIR

urbane, gracious: SUAVE

urge on, drive or force to action: IMPEL

urge on, stir up, spur into action: INCITE

urge by earnest appeal, recommend strongly, advise: EXHORT

urgent: IMPERIOUS

urgent, demanding immediate action: EXIGENT

urgently necessary, unavoidable, authoritative: IMPERATIVE

urinary system, as a branch of medicine: UROLOGY

urinate: MICTURATE

urination that is excessive: DIURESIS

urination that is involuntary: ENURESIS

urine-increasing substance: DIURETIC

urine of cattle or horses: STALE

urn of metal for heating water for tea: SAMOVAR

used to or accustomed to, habituated: WONT

useless: INUTILE

useless, ineffectual: OTIOSE

useless person or thing: DEADWOOD

useless work: BOONDOGGLE

usurp: ARROGATE

utensils and serving dishes that are concave: HOLLOWWARE

uterine cancer test: PAP TEST

uterus surgery: HYSTERECTOMY

V

"v" shaped insignia: CHEVRON

vacation for one year, or less, originally granted every seven years: SABBATICAL YEAR

vacillate, veer, shift about: WHIFFLE

vagrant on beach living off what he can find: BEACHCOMBER

vagrants or unattached persons: FLOTSAM

vague: AMBIGUOUS

vague, confused: HAZY

vague, subtle: INDEFINABLE

vague, unclear, hazy, misty: NEBULOUS

vague, unsettled: INDETERMINATE

vague concept, general idea: NOTION

vague idea, notion, slight suggestion, hint: INKLING

vague or indefinite: INTANGIBLE

vague state between two others: LIMBO

vain, silly, foppish behavior: COXCOMBRY

valiant, courageous: METTLESOME

valley or mountain pass that is narrow: DEFILE

value, in proportion to: AD VALOREM

value of a business in excess of liabilities: EQUITY

value of a bond, as it appears on the security: FACE VALUE

value of a nation's annual output of goods and services before any deductions: GROSS NATIONAL PRODUCT

value per share, calculated by totaling market price and deducting all liabilities: NET ASSET VALUE

valueless: TINKER'S DAMN

valueless though showy: TRUMPERY

valve or faucet used to drain off water or air: PETCOCK

vanish gradually, disappear by degrees: EVANESCE

vanquish, as in battle, or defeat the purposes of: DISCOMFIT

variation or inflection of words: ACCIDENCE

variations or changes occurring irregularly, as of fortune: VICISSITUDES

varied, diverse to a great degree: MULTIFARIOUS

varied, unalike: DIVERSE

varied with many forms: MANIFOLD

varied without limit: OMNIFARIOUS

variegated in color or other elements: MOTLEY

variegated or spotted: DAPPLED

various, several, many: DIVERS

vary or change often and in irregular manner: FLUCTUATE

vary or diversify by interjecting something different: INTERLARD

vary or revise, restrict or limit: MODIFY

vary the products of a business so as to expand it: DIVERSIFY

vary the tone or pitch of the voice, modulate: INFLECT

vast indefinite number, innumerable: MYRIAD

vast or limitless: INFINITE

vat used by brewers for fermenting: TUN

veal cutlet breaded and garnished: WIENER SCHNITZEL

veal thin-sliced and sautéed: SCALOPPINE

veer, vacillate, shift about: WHIFFLE

vegetate, become dull or inert: STAGNATE

vehemently censure: INVEIGH

vehicle that carries passengers for a small fee: JITNEY

vehicle with three wheels moved by pedaling: PEDICAB

vehicles traveling together: CARAVAN

velvety, covered with soft hairs: VELU-TINOUS

venerable, classic, time-honored: VINTAGE

vengeance or just retribution as identified with an antagonist or thing: NEMESIS

verb form that relates to time of action: TENSE

verb mood used to express hypothesis, possibility, or nonfactual condition: SUBJUNCTIVE

verb of weak form that links subject and predicate: COPULA

verb that forms its past tense by internal vowel change, as "swim": STRONG VERB

verb that is a copula, serving mainly as a connection between subject and predicate: LINKING VERB

verbal contention, or argument about words: LOGOMACHY

verbal noun: GERUND

verbose: PROLIX

verbose: REDUNDANT

verbose, wordy: DIFFUSE

verse containing eight lines and two rhymes (a-b-a-a-a-b-a-b) with the first line repeated as the fourth and seventh, and the second as the eighth: TRIOLET

verse, humorous and often bawdy, containing five lines with the rhyme scheme a-a-b-b-a: LIMERICK

verse free of conventional meter and rhyme: FREE VERSE

verse in praise of wine and sensual pleasures: ANACREONTIC

verse of three stanzas and an envoy, with last line of each the same: BALLADE

verse rhythm analysis: SCANSION

verse that is trivial and awkwardly written: DOGGEREL

verse that is humorous, metrical and usually rhymed: LIGHT VERSE

verse that ends with a lack of a syllable in its final foot: CATALECTIC

verse with two feet to the line: DIMETER

verse's feet analyzed: SCANNED

vertical: PERPENDICULAR

vertical sidepiece in a door or a window sash: STILE

vertical takeoff and landing plane: VTOL

very much: BEAUCOUP

vessel that services another at sea: TENDER

veto performed by the U.S. President by not signing a bill by the time Congress adjourns: POCKET VETO

vex, annoy, weary: IRK

vibrate, throb regularly: PULSATE

vibrating effect produced on a stringed instrument or with the voice: TREMOLO

vibration or sound caused by the hitting of one body against another: PERCUSSION

vicarious sharing of another's emotions or feelings: EMPATHY

vice-ridden and corruption-ridden area of a city: TENDERLOIN

vicious, inhuman, cruel: FELL

victimized or injured by one's plans to injure another: HOIST BY ONE'S OWN PETARD

victims of poverty or discrimination: UNDERPRIVILEGED

victory at great cost, Pyrrhic victory: CADMEAN VICTORY

vie with or rival successfully: EMULATE

view in all directions: PANORAMA

view of the proportional relation of parts to the whole: PERSPECTIVE

vigilant, watchful: JEALOUS

vigor, dash: VERVE

vigor, strength, endurance: STAMINA

vigor or youthful feeling restored: REJUVENATION

vigorous, interesting: SUCCULENT

vigorous, large, shift, dashing: SPANKING

vigorous, lively: VIBRANT

vile, base, degraded: SORDID

vile, contemptible: DESPICABLE

vile, evil: NEFARIOUS

vileness, depravity, baseness: TURPITUDE

vilify, abuse: REVILE

village: HAMLET

vinegary: ACETOUS

violation of a law or a pledge: INFRACTION

violation of conventional language usage: SOLECISM

violation or profaning of anything sacred: SACRILEGE

violent, impetuous, ardent: VEHEMENT

violent, intermittent: SPASMODIC

violent, stormy: TEMPESTUOUS

violent, sudden outburst: PAROXYSM

violent and loud denunciation: FULMINATION

violent disturbance: CATACLYSM

violent outbreak: RAMPAGE

violent reaction: BACKLASH

violently destructive: BERSERK

violinist who leads his section of an orchestra: CONCERT MASTER

violin-like instrument, but slightly larger and tuned lower: VIOLA

virgin, woman of pure character: VESTAL

visible or observable occurrence or experience: PHENOMENON

visible to the naked eye: MACROSCOPIC

vision blurring or temporary loss caused by oxygen deficiency, experienced especially by pilots: GRAYOUT

vision defect in which specks or threads appear to float before the eyes: MUSCAE VOLITANTES

vision, dimmed: PURBLIND

vision less distinct by day than by night, day blindness: HEMERALOPIA

vision of something not actually present: HALLUCINATION

vision or discernment faulty: MYOPIA

vision that is distorted: ASTIGMATISM

vision that is normal at 20 feet: 20-20 VISION

visionary or dreamer: FANTAST

visionary or imaginary semblance: SIMULACRUM

visit frequently or habitually: RESORT

visitor who frequents a place: HABITUÉ

visual arts involving the use of lines or strokes on a flat surface, as painting or drawing: GRAPHIC ARTS

visual defects treated by exercises: ORTHOPTICS

visualizing objects previously seen: EIDETIC IMAGERY

vital principle: ANIMA

vital statistics as of births, deaths, disease: DEMOGRAPHY

vivacity, enthusiasm, dash: ÉLAN

vivacity, lively spirits, gaiety, sparkle: EFFERVESCENCE

vivid: GRAPHIC

vivid, sensational, shocking, violent: LURID

vividly bright, shining with brilliance, dazzling: RESPLENDENT

vocabulary of a class or group: ARGOT

vocabulary or jargon of a profession or class: LINGO

vocabularly that is specialized or technical and used by members of a particular group: JARGON

vocal quality that is dry and rough or coarse: HUSKY

vocalist's runs and trills: COLORATURA

vodka and tomato juice cocktail: BLOODY MARY

vodka and orange juice cocktail: SCREWDRIVER

voice of a male higher than a tenor: COUNTERTENOR

voice of the people: VOX POPULI

voice on television commenting on the picture or narrating: VOICE-OVER

voice tone or pitch variations or modulations: INFLECTION

voice-affecting throat irritation: LARYNGITIS

void, undo: NULLIFY

voiding, nullifying: DEFEASANCE

voiding, nullifying: DIRIMENT

volatile, lively, changeable: MERCURIAL

volume of bids and offers on stocks is relatively low: THIN MARKET

vomit: REGURGITATE

vomit-causing medicine: EMETIC

vomiting: EMESIS

vomiting action causing strain: RETCH

vote against: BLACKBALL

vote to obtain the people's will on an issue: PLEBISCITE

vote that is unofficial and used to determine group opinion: STRAW VOTE

voters or supporters: CONSTITUENCY

votes and influence traded between politicians: LOGROLLING

votes for a candidate in excess of the number cast for his nearest opponent: PLURALITY

vowel for changed tense, etc.: ABLAUT

vowel inserted into word: ANAPTYXIS

vowel lost at beginning of a word (alone, lone): APHESIS

vowel marking (straight line) over vowel to indicate long sound: MACRON

vowel that is neutral, occurring in unstressed syllables in English: SCHWA

vulgar, common: PLEBEIAN

vulgar, disreputable, tawdry: RAFFISH

vulgar, obscene: FESCENNINE

vulgar language or behavior: BAWDRY

vulgar or coarse joking: RIBALD

vulgar, sexual, cheap: RAUNCHY

vulgar talk: BILLINGSGATE

vulnerable: PREGNABLE

vulnerable point: ACHILLES' HEEL

W

wad of compressed cotton or lint used for a wound: PLEDGET

wages remaining after payroll deductions: TAKE-HOME PAY

wagon maker: WAINWRIGHT

wagon without sides: LORRY

wail, howl, hoot: ULULATE

wail, whimper, cry: PULE

wailing lament for the deceased: KEEN

waist measure: GIRTH

waistband that is broad and worn with men's formal clothes: CUMMERBUND

wait for and accost: WAYLAY

waiter or waitress at a drive-in restaurant: CARHOP

waiting room in theater used by performers when they are off-stage: GREEN ROOM

walk, able to: AMBULATORY

walk about idly or aimlessly, gad about: TRAIPSE

walk around something: CIRCUMAMBULATE

walk clumsily with short steps, swaying from side to side: WADDLE

walk heavily: CLUMP

walk laboriously, trudge: PLOD

walk leisurely: AMBLE

walk leisurely, stroll: SAUNTER

walk with a latticework roof, arbor: PERGOLA

walker: PEDESTRIAN

walking or moving about, itinerant: PERIPATETIC

walking space that is narrow and elevated: CATWALK

walking with short, dainty steps: MINCING

wall bracket that holds candles or lights: SCONCE

wall hanging attached to a roller devised by Japanese: KAKEMONO

wall of stone, cement, etc., for protective purposes: REVETMENT

wall painting by an artist: MURAL

wall paneling or wood or marble: WAINSCOT

wall scribblings or drawings: GRAFFITI

wan, colorless: PALLID

wand or staff of Mercury, symbol of medical profession: CADUCEUS

wander from main subject: DIGRESS

wander idly or without plan: MEANDER

wander or stray aimlessly, digress: DIVAGATE

wander or turn aside from main subject: DIGRESS

wanderer, tramp: VAGABOND

wanderer without a permanent home: NOMAD

wandering, roving, straying, itinerant: ERRANT

wandering away from the right way: ABERRANCE

wandering from the point, passing quickly from one subject to another: DISCURSIVE

wanting one's own way: WAYWARD

wanton or lewd: CYPRIAN

ward off: STAVE OFF

ward off, avoid, turn aside: PARRY

ward off, drive back: REPEL

warding off, preventing: PREVENTIVE

wardrobe with drawers on one side: CHIFFOROBE

warhead of a missile: PAYLOAD

warlike, brave, disciplined: SPARTAN

warm, glowing, earnest: FERVENT

warmth, or increasing warmth: CALESCENCE

warn, presage, foreshadow: PORTEND

warning: CAVEAT

warning, danger sign, especially in zoology: SEMATIC

warning notice: MONITION

warning, omen, portent: PRESAGE

warning system by radar in North America: DEW LINE

war-provoking event: CASUS BELLI

wart or other skin growth: KERATOSIS

washing the body: ABLUTION

wasps or a wasp colony: VESPIARY

waste matter, refuse: DROSS

waste matter from the bowels, feces: EXCREMENT

waste matter removal, as by kidneys or intestines: EMUNCTORY

waste or entrails of a butchered animal: OFFAL

waste time, dawdle, loiter: DILLY-DALLY

waste time, dwadle: PIDDLE

waste time, loiter: DAWDLE

wasted, scattered: DISSIPATED

wasteful, extravagant, lavish: PRODIGAL

wasting away: TABESCENT

wasting or withering away: ATROPHY

watch kept over one: SURVEILLANCE

watch kept, usually at night: VIGIL

watchful, alert: VIGILANT

watchful, suspicious: JEALOUS

watching and guarding carefully: WARY

watchman, keeper, guard: WARDER

water channel made with a gate to regulate the flow: SLUICE

water craft with winglike structures that lift the hull above water at certain speeds: HYDROFOIL

water cure: HYDROPATHY

water nymph: NAIAD

water nymph of folklore, who could obtain a soul by marrying a human and bearing his child: UNDINE

water of the soil not available to plants: ECHARD

water or land vehicle or creature: AMPHIBIAN

water search with a divining rod: DOWSE

water signs as a means of divination: HYDROMANCY

water tower: STANDPIPE

waterfront or river vessels laborer: ROUSTABOUT

waterproof hat: SOUTHWESTER

waters of the earth, as a study: HYDROLOGY

waters under the jurisdiction of a state: TERRITORIAL WATERS

watertight chamber for construction in a body of water: COFFERDAM

watery: AQUEOUS

wave or flood: SPRING TIDE

wave that breaks on reef, rock or shore: BREAKER

wavelike or watered appearance, as in fabrics: MOIRÉ

waver, sway, totter: VACILLATE

wavering, undecided: IRRESOLUTE

wavering, unsteady: FLUCTUATING

waving motion: WAFTURE

wavy, winding: SINUOUS

wavy in appearance or motion: UNDULATING

way of entry: ACCESS

wayfarer, traveler: VIATOR

waylay: AMBUSH

weak: ANILE

weak, barren: EFFETE

weak, careless, reckless: FECKLESS

weak, cowardly: PUSILLANIMOUS

weak, emaciated condition: CACHEXIA

weak, flimsy, unsubstantial: TENUOUS

weak, ineffective: IMPOTENT

weak, listless, lacking animation: LANGUID

weak, loose: SLACK

weak, self-indulgent: EFFEMINATE

weak, unconvincing, fragile: FLIMSY

weaken, destroy the affection of: DISAFFECT

weaken, hang down: FLAG

weaken, make feeble or languid: DEBILITATE

weaken, pine, droop gradually: LANGUISH

weaken, sap the strength of, devitalize: ENERVATE

weaken by degrees, impair secretly: UNDERMINE

weakness, fatigue, spiritlessness, dreaminess, dullness, stagnation: LANGUOR

weakness or failing in one's character: FOIBLE

wealth, riches: OPULENCE

wealthy, fashionable people: JET SET

wealthy, powerful industrialist: TYCOON

wealthy man: CROESUS

wealthy person who has become so only recently: NOUVEAU RICHE

wear away by friction: ABRADE

wearied, exhausted, sated, worn-out, dulled from overindulgence: JADED wearing away or eating away of a substance: CORROSION

wearing off or rubbing off of particles: DETRITION

wearisome, boring: TEDIOUS

weary, vex, annoy: IRK

weather that is dark and threatening: LOWERING

weather and atmospheric conditions, as a science: METEOROLOGY

weather-beaten and rugged: GNARLED

weave together, combine, blend: INTERLACE

webfooted: SYNDACTYL

wedding song or poem: HYMENEAL

wedged or packed firmly: IMPACTED

wedge-shaped especially as used in ancient writing: CUNEAL, CUNEIFORM

weed killer: HERBICIDE

weeping or grief that is false: CROCODILE TEARS

weigh down, burden, hamper: CUMBER

weighing, resting, leaning upon something: INCUMBENT

weight: HEFT

weight a missile can lift and carry to a target: THROW-WEIGHT

weight lost, abnormally lean: EMACIATED

weight of container deducted to find weight of contents: TARE

weight unit for gems: CARAT

weightlessness, in space: ZERO GRAVITY

weird, ghostly: EERIE

weird, unnatural, eerie, strange: UNCANNY

welcome or acceptable person: PERSONA GRATA

welcome with an outburst of applause: OVATION

well-being, relaxation, happiness: EUPHORIA

well-being or happiness as found in a life of moderation: EUDEMONIA

well-bred, distinguished, dignified: DISTINGUÉ

well-bred in one's ways, refinement: GENTILITY

well-chosen, apt, agreeable in manner or style: FELICITOUS

well-groomed: SOIGNÉ

well-groomed, smooth, glossy: SLEEK

werewolf: LYCANTHROPE

West Indian, Spanish American or Gulf State inhabitant of European descent: CREOLE

western hemisphere: OCCIDENT

whale oil: TRAIN OIL

wharf for loading and unloading vessels: QUAY

wharf or pier to protect a harbor or beach: JETTY

wheedle: CAJOLE

wheedle or flatter: BLANDISH

wheel, spiked or toothed, at the end of a spur: ROWEL

wheel about: CARACOLE

wheel heavy enough to resist sudden changes of speed: FLYWHEEL

wheel on a fixed axis and containing seats hanging from frame: FERRIS WHEEL

wheel-shaped: ROTIFORM

wheels with the rims slanted in or out from the hub: DISHED

while away the time: BEGUILE

whim: CAPRICE

whimper, wail, cry: PULE

whining, complaining, fretful: QUERULOUS

whip or scourge: FLAGELLATE

whiplash-like, long, slender and flexible: FLAGELLIFORM

whirling, revolving or circular motion: GYRAL

whirling, rotating rapidly: VORTICOSE

whirling, spinning, dizzy: VERTIGINOUS

whirling on the toes in ballet dancing: PIROUETTE

whirlwind or whirlpool: VORTEX

whirlpool: MAELSTROM

whisky and vermouth cocktail: MANHATTAN

whisper intended to be overheard: STAGE WHISPER

whispering, rustling, softly murmuring: SUSURRANT

whistle or call derisively: CATCALL

white linen worn around the neck by a priest: AMICE

white- or gray-haired, ancient, venerable: HOARY

whiten or turn yellowish, as a plant does when kept from sunlight: ETIOLATE

whitening: ALBESCENT

white-skinned and pink-eyed person: ALBINO

who goes there?: QUI VIVE?

whole, unchanged, undamaged: INTACT

whole composed of originally separate parts: SYNTHESIS

whole number: INTEGER

whole, untaxed, uninjured: SCOT-FREE

whole that is uninterrupted: CONTINUUM
wholesaler: JOBBER
wholesome: SALUTARY
whore: HARLOT
whorehouse: BORDELLO
wicked: INIQUITOUS
wicked, atrocious: FLAGITIOUS
wicked, atrocious, odious: HEINOUS
wicked, erring: PERVERSE
wicked, ominous: SINISTER
wicked, vicious woman: JEZEBEL
wicked, vile: NEFARIOUS
wickedness, monstrous act: ENORMITY
wicker receptacle for documents or valuables: HANAPER
wide-awake, on the alert: ON THE QUI VIVE
widely practiced, common: PREVALENT
widen, swell, expand: DILATE
widespread: RAMPANT
widespread, prevalent: RIFE
widespread, universal, also general epidemic: PANDEMIC
wife: HELPMEET
wife or husband: CONSORT
wifely: UXORIAL
wig for a man: TOUPEE
wild: BERSERK
wild, irresponsible, reckless: HARUM-SCARUM
wild, riotous: TURBULENT
wild, savage: FERAL
wild, unchecked: RAMPANT
wild, unexpected action: VAGARY
wild or wanton revelry, drunken carousal, debauchment: ORGY
wild party: BACCHANAL
wild prank or escapade: CAPER
wild uproar: PANDEMONIUM
wildly excited: DELIRIOUS
will exercised: VOLITION
will maker, one who has left a will: TESTATOR
will rather than reason stressed as the active factor in man's role in a hostile world: EXISTENTIALISM
willful, capricious: WAYWARD
willing, desirous: SOLICITOUS
willingly, readily: LIEF
willingly or unwillingly: WILLY-NILLY
willingness that is cheerful: ALACRITY
will-o'-the-wisp, delusion: IGNIS FATUUS
willowy, slender, slim: SVELTE
willy-nilly: NOLENS VOLENS
wily, treacherous, cunning: INSIDIOUS

win by cleverness: OUTWIT
win over, appease: PROPITIATE
win the favor or confidence of others by deliberate effort: INGRATIATE
wind, cold and dry, that blows from the north through southern France: MISTRAL
wind, hot, dry, and full of sand, especially in deserts: SIMOOM
wind, hot and dusty, that blows from the African coast to Europe: SIROCCO
wind, soft and gentle: ZEPHYR
wind direction indicator consisting of a cone-spaced cloth bag, as at an airfield: WINDSOCK
wind from ahead blowing directly opposite to the course of a ship: HEAD WIND
wind from the east in Mediterranean regions: LEVANTER
wind from the Sahara that blows in the Middle East before the vernal equinox: KHAMSIN
wind in a sudden, violent burst, usually accompanied by rain or snow: SQUALL
wind in and out: SINUATE
wind is blowing toward this direction: LEEWARD
wind moving in a cold, sudden, violent blast down a mountain to the sea: WILLIWAW
wind of the Argentine pampas: PAMPERO
wind science: ANEMOLOGY
wind-driven rain or snow: SCUD
winding: TORTUOUS
winding and turning: ANFRACTUOUS
winding or bending, wavering, unsteady: FLEXUOUS
winding path: AMBAGE
window, a throw out of: DEFENESTRATION
window, balcony or porch with an excellent view, in Spanish architecture: MIRADOR
window division, a vertical dividing piece in the opening: MULLION
window frame: SASH
window in a spire: LUCARNE
window opening vertically in the middle as a double door does: FRENCH WINDOW
window or any small opening suggestive of a window: FENESTELLA
window or doorway covering that covers

only top half of opening: LAM-BREQUIN

window side post: JAMB

window slats, horizontal and overlapping: LOUVER BOARD

window that opens on hinges at the side: CASEMENT

window that projects from a sloping roof: DORMER

windstorm that is brief, gust of wind: FLAW

windy pomposity, pretentiousness: FLATULENCE

wine aroma: BOUQUET

wine bottle holding almost four quarts: JEROBOAM

wine bottle or large vessel with handle and spout used for serving liquids: FLAGON

wine bottle twice the ordinary size: MAGNUM

wine measure of about 18 wine gallons: RUNDLET

wine merchant: VINTNER

wine named for the principal grape from which it is made: VARIETAL

wine named for the region where its type originated: GENERIC WINE

wine of no distinction, cheap red wine: VIN ORDINAIRE

wine steward: SOMMELIER

wines and winemaking as a study: OENOLOGY

wing, PINION

wink: NICTITATE

winning of every event, as in a series: SWEEP

winter's beginning when the sun is farthest south of the Equator, about Dec. 21: WINTER SOLSTICE

wintry,: HIBERNAL

wintry: HIEMAL

wipe off or cleanse: DETERGE

wipe out: EXPUNGE

wipe out, destroy completely: OBLITERATE

wire, rope or cable used to steady or secure something: GUY

wisdom, discernment: SAGACITY

wise: SAPIENT

wise, prudent: JUDICIOUS

wise, prudent, diplomatic: POLITIC

wise, shrewd: SAGACIOUS

wise person, infallible authority: ORACLE

wise saying, maxim: GNOME

wise statement: APHORISM

wishful thinking modifying reality: AUTISM

witches' sabbath on April 30, the eve of May Day: WALPURGIS NIGHT

with reference to: APROPOS

withdraw, move backward: RECEDE

withdraw a contestant from a race, etc.: SCRATCH

withdraw formally from an organization: SECEDE

withdraw in fear, lose heart: QUAIL

withdraw or end by plan: PHASE OUT

withdraw or remove from former habits: WEAN

withered, shriveled, shrunken: WIZENED

withering or wasting away: ATROPHY

withering, mercilessly severe, harsh: SCATHING

within the same school, college, etc.: INTRAMURAL

without a center: ACENTRIC

without a date being set (for the next meeting): SINE DIE

without dividend: EX-DIVIDEND

without warning: UNAWARES

witness's sworn statements in court: TESTIMONY

witticism: SALLY

witty, characterized by higher and finer qualities of the mind: SPIRITUEL

witty, quick replies: REPARTEE

witty, short saying: MOT

witty, terse statement: EPIGRAM

witty remark: BON MOT

witty remark or gibe: QUIP

wizard, sorcerer: WARLOCK

woeful tale, complaint, lament: JEREMIAD

woman, elderly, dignified, wealthy: DOWAGER

woman, old and ugly: CRONE

woman adviser: EGERIA

woman beside herself with frenzy or excitement: MAENAD

woman hater: MISOGYNIST

woman hired to suckle a child of another: WET NURSE

woman living under canon law in a community, but not under vows: CANONESS

woman-man relationship without sexual activity: PLATONIC

woman or women forming the government: GYNARCHY

woman servant in Orient: AMAH

woman to whom a man is engaged: FIAN-CÉE

women who have lost social position and reputation because of promiscuity: DEMIMONDE

woman who is abusive and scolding, shrew: TERMAGANT

woman who is aggressive, domineering: BATTLE-AX

woman who is disreputable, ill-tempered, perverse: JADE

woman who is divorced, separated or lives apart from her husband: GRASS WIDOW

woman who is dowdy and sometimes also ill-tempered: FRUMP

woman who is homosexual: LESBIAN

woman who is sharp-tongued or a scold: VIRAGO

woman who is untidy or slovenly: SLATTERN

woman who is vicious or hateful: HARRIDAN

woman who is voluptuous but treacherous: DELILAH

woman who is wicked and vicious: JEZEBEL

woman who lives with a man though not married to him: CONCUBINE

woman whose allure leads to downfall of men: FEMME FATALE

womanhood, femininity: MULIEBRITY

womanlike, unmanly, weak, soft: EFFEMINATE

woman's dressing room: BOUDOIR

woman's legal status in marriage: COVERTURE

woman's paid escort: GIGOLO

woman's trousers that resemble a skirt: CULOTTE

woman's work and domain traditionally: DISTAFF

women in general: DISTAFF

wonderful or marvelous to tell: MIRABILE DICTU

wood from broad-leaved deciduous trees, as oak or maple: HARDWOOD

wood in a thin, broad piece, as that forming the back of a chair: SPLAT

wood in thin flexible strips, as used for basketmaking: SPLINT

wood layers glued together: PLYWOOD

wooded: ARBORACEOUS

wooden vessel for butter or lard: FIRKIN

woodworking knife with a handle at each end: DRAWKNIFE

woodworking training system: SLOYD

woolly or crispy hair: ULOTRICHOUS

word, phrase, or clause inserted into a sentence to add explanation or comment: PARENTHESIS

word adopted from another language and partly or completely naturalized: LOANWORD

word blindness: ALEXIA

word categories, of which there are eight in English: PARTS OF SPEECH

word choice and arrangement in speaking or writing: DICTION

word coined for a single or special occasion: NONCE WORD

word derived from the same root as another: PARONYM

word-for-word: TEXTUAL

word formed by combining parts of two words: PORTMANTEAU WORD, CENTAUR WORD, BLEND WORD

word formed by transposing letters of another: ANAGRAM

word formed from initial letters of lines: ACROSTIC

word formed from initial letters or syllables of series of words: ACRONYM

word game in which a rhyme must be given for word or line given by another: CRAMBO

word group between punctuation stops: SENTENCE

word hard to pronounce: JAWBREAKER

word having the same, similar, or equivalent meaning as another word: SYNONYM

word identical with another in spelling, but having different origin and meaning: HOMOGRAPH

word inflection: ACCIDENCE

word interpretation largely spiritual and mystical: ANAGOGE

word list, with definitions, of technical, obscure or foreign words of a work or field: GLOSSARY

word of more than three syllables: POLYSYLLABLE

word opposite in meaning to another word: ANTONYM

word or expression that is not standard: BARBARISM

word or phrase often repeated, as a slogan: CATCHWORD

word or phrase serving only to complete a rhythm or a pattern: EXPLETIVE

word or prhase that is an exclamation or obscene oath: EXPLETIVE

word or phrase that is substituted for another to avoid giving offense or pain: EUPHEMISM

word or saying that is familiar to most people: HOUSEHOLD WORD

word or sentence that reads the same backward as forward: PALINDROME

word order inverted: ANASTROPHE

word origin popularly conceived but erroneous: FOLK ETYMOLOGY

word origins and development, as a study: ETYMOLOGY

word puzzle, as an anagram: LOGOGRIPH

word selection and arrangement: PHRASEOLOGY

word spelled like another but having a different sound and meaning: HETERONYM

word spoken, considered only as sound: VOCABLE

word structure, as a study: MORPHOLOGY

word that has been coined or existing word that has been given a new meaning: NEOLOGISM

word that is a compound and is divided by an intervening word: TMESIS

word that makes a statement misleading or ambiguous: WEASEL WORD

word use that is effective: RHETORIC

word used humorously in two different meanings: PUN

word used in cabalistic charms: ABRACADABRA

word used in sense opposite to its meaning, ironically,: ANTIPHRASIS

word widely used without regard to its exact meaning: COUNTER WORD

word with no accent but pronounced as part of preceding word: ENCLITIC

word with several different meanings: POLYSEMY

word with the same sound as another but different meaning: HOMONYM

wordiness: VERBIAGE

wordiness, circumlocution: PERIPHRASIS

wordless drama played with gestures: PANTOMIME

word's alteration by shifting to its beginning the final consonant of a preceding word: PROVECTION

words altered by transposing sounds or parts unintentionally: SPOONERISM

words and word groups, their development and changes of meaning, as a subject of study: SEMANTICS

words in phrases, clauses and sentences in terms of their arrangement and interrelationship: SYNTAX

words in a series each having same initial sound: ALLITERATION

word's last syllable: ULTIMA

words of one language altered to resemble words in another, usually for humorous effect: MACARONIC

words of wisdom: APOTHEGM

words or book of an opera: LIBRETTO

words or expressions placed next to each other, the second explaining the first: APPOSITION

words that reflect natural sounds, or the use of such words: ONOMATOPOEIA

wordy, long-winded: DIFFUSE

wordy, superfluous: REDUNDANT

wordy, tedious: PROLIX

wordy, wearisome in conversation: VERBOSE

work at: PLY

work avoided by pretending of sickness: MALINGER

work clumsily: BUNGLE

work crew selection, especially among longshoremen: SHAPEUP

work expands to fill the time allotted to it: PARKINSON'S LAW

work for which one is particularly suited; forte: MÉTIER

work shift beginning at midnight: GRAVEYARD SHIFT

work shift usually from 4 p.m. until midnight: SWING SHIFT

work slowdown caused by employes' ostensibly following the rules closely: JOB ACTION

work tediously: PLOD

work that is dull and wearisome: DRUDGERY

workable, practicable: VIABLE

worker, clerical or professional: WHITE COLLAR

worker who is ultraconservative: HARD HAT

worker, unskilled or semiskilled: BLUE COLLAR

workers employed in excess of actual needs: FEATHERBEDDING

workers' organization in a single company and unaffiliated with other unions: COMPANY UNION

working class: PROLETARIAT

working independently, as a writer or artist, for instance, rather than for one employer: FREE LANCE

working on a job in addition to one's regular occupation: MOONLIGHTING

working or moving, effective: OPERATIVE

working with the hands, work done by hand: HANDICRAFT

workshop: ATELIER

world and life as viewed comprehensively: WELTANSCHAUUNG

world betterment: MELIORISM

worldly, as opposed to narrow or parochial: COSMOPOLITAN

worldly, sensual, carnal: FLESHLY

worldly as distinguished from spiritual or religious: SECULAR

worldly-wise: SOPHISTICATED

world-weariness: WELTSCHMERZ

world-wide, general, universal, especially concerning the church: ECUMENICAL

worn, gaunt, or wild look, as from fatigue, hunger or anxiety: HAGGARD

worn out, exhausted, sated, dulled from overindulgence: JADED

worn out or enfeebled by age or use: DECREPIT

worried, tense, bewildered, agitated, crazed: DISTRAUGHT

worry, harass: CHEVY

worry, harass: HARRY

worry, torment relentlessly: HARASS

worry-free, carefree: SANS SOUCI

worse, inferior, morally degraded: DEGENERATE

worsen as in quality or power: IMPAIR

worsening, declining, going backward: RETROGRADE

worship given properly only to God, in the Roman Catholic Church: LATRIA

worship of idols: IDOLATRY

worthless: CHEESE-PARING

worthless, meaningless: NUGATORY

worthless, rubbish, nonsense: TRUMPERY

worthlessness or futility imposed on something or someone: STULTIFIED

wounds that Christ received during the Passion and Crucifixion: STIGMATA

wrangle, bandy words: SPAR

wrangling, quarrel: JANGLE

wreck, pillage, ruin: RAVAGE

wreckage that is afloat or washed up on shore: FLOTSAM

wrestler or boxer over 175 pounds: HEAVYWEIGHT

wrestler or boxer weighing between 127 and 135 pounds: LIGHTWEIGHT

wrestler or boxer weighing between 136 and 147 pounds: WELTERWEIGHT

wrestler or boxer weighing between 147 and 160 pounds: MIDDLEWEIGHT

wrestler or boxer weighing between 161 and 175 pounds: LIGHT HEAVYWEIGHT

wrestler weighing up to 134 pounds or a boxer up to 126 pounds: FEATHERWEIGHT

wrestling hold in which an arm is passed under the opponent's armpit and the hand pressed against the back of his head: HALF NELSON

wrestling hold in which arms are under the opponent's armpits from the back and hands against his neck: FULL NELSON

wrestling hold in which opponent's arm is twisted behind his back and upward: HAMMERLOCK

wrestling hold in which the wrestler's head is gripped between his opponent's arm and body: HEADLOCK

wrestling term for head caught and held under opponent's arm: CHANCERY

wrestling throw: FLYING MARE

wretched, cheerless, abandoned, deserted: FORLORN

wrinkle or pucker: COCKLE

writ authorizing seizure of property: ATTACHMENT

writ ordering that a person be brought before a court: HABEAS CORPUS

write: INDITE

write, mark or engrave, especially for some solemn or public purpose: INSCRIBE

write or speak more fully, elaborate: EXPATIATE

write or study laboriously: LUCUBRATE

write out, compose or edit: REDACT

writer of articles, books, speeches for someone else to whom the authorship will be attributed: GHOSTWRITER

writer of polemical pamphlets: PAMPHLETEER

writers, scholars, men of letters: LITERATI

writer's assumed name: PEN NAME

writer's name at head of article: BYLINE

writing describing a pleasant, peaceful scene: IDYLL

writing desk: ESCRITOIRE

writing difficult to decipher: HIERO-GLYPHICS

writing in which lines alternately read left to right and right to left: BOU-STROPHEDON

writing of an ancient mode: PALEOGRAPHY

writing of words or phrases erroneously because of cerebral injury: PARA-GRAPHIA

writing or printing with flowing lines: CURSIVE

writing paper measuring about 13 by 16 inches: FOOLSCAP

writing prose in line lengths corresponding to the sense: STICHOMETRY

writing technique that records inner thoughts and feelings of characters: STREAM-OF-CONSCIOUSNESS

writing that is backward and readable in a mirror: MIRROR WRITING

writing that is long and tiresome: SCREED

written statement or graphic representation that is false or malicious and damaging to person's reputation: LIBEL

wrong; if anything can go wrong, it will: MURPHY'S LAW

wrong name: MISNOMER

wrongdoing, especially by a public official: MALFEASANCE

wrongdoing or guilt implied: INCRIMINA-TION

wrongful act, unjust thing or deed, sin: INIQUITY

wrongful act not involving breach of contract but a possible basis for a suit: TORT

wrongful use: ABUSE

Y

yarn length: SPINDLE
yarn length equaling 80 yards for wool, 120 for cotton, 300 for linen: LEA
yarn or thread wound in a coil: SKEIN
yawning or sleepiness: OSCITANCY
yearn, desire, crave: HANKER
year or period that is critical: CLIMACTERIC
year-old animal: YEARLING
yellow fever: VOMITO
yellowish complexion: SALLOW
yellowish-green color, sea-green: GLAUCOUS
yelp or bark: YAWP
yes, just so; used after a quoted word or phrase to indicate that it is accurate: SIC
yield to or gratify, as one's desires: INDULGE

yield weakly or with bad grace, cringe: TRUCKLE
yielding, persuadable: PLIANT
yielding courteously or respectfully to the wishes or opinions of another: DEFERENCE
yielding readily in an emotional way: SUSCEPTIBLE
young and innocent woman: INGÉNUE
young man, youth: SPRIG
young or becoming young: JUVENESCENCE
youthful, fresh, springlike: VERNAL
youthful days of freshness and inexperience: SALAD DAYS
youthful feeling or vigor restored: REJUVENATION
you've scored a point, you've got me: TOUCHÉ

Z

zeal that is extravagant or frenzied: FA-NATICISM

zenith, highest point of anything: MERID-IAN

zest, enthusiasm: GUSTO

zestless, dull: PERFUNCTORY

zigzag course in sailing: TACK

Index of Key Words

bumper 40, 73
bumpkin 12, 30, 36
bumptious 6, 33
bunco 28, 173
bungle 20, 30, 197
bunt 15
buoyant 28, 100
bureaucracy 75, 143
burgeon 136, 166
burke 171
burnoose 9, 82
burnsides 159
bursar 179
bursitis 124
busby 71
bush league 15, 109
busman's holiday 82
butterfingers 30, 70, 128
buttocks 16
by-election 55
byline 115, 198
byword 63, 128

cabal 91, 153
cabala 114, 120, 153
cabalistic 114
cabana 15
cabaret 24, 146
cacoethes 105
caboose 70, 142
cabriolet 25
cache 49, 81
cachet 106
cachexia 105, 192
cachinnate 98
cacography 13, 78, 165
cacophany 48, 79
cadaster 106, 172
cadaverous 43, 72, 124
cadence 58, 147
cadenza 87, 113
cadge 16, 73
Cadmean victory 44, 138, 189
cadre 36, 56, 117
caduceus 108, 191
caducity 120, 154, 179
caesarean section 13, 17
caesura 21
caftan 102, 149
cafe au lait 31
cafe noir 31
cahier 135, 145
cairene 24

cairn 106, 168
caisson 7, 184
caitiff 14, 152
cajole 30, 193
Cajun 102
cakes and ale 74
cakewalk 136, 170
calathus 173
calculation 69, 137
caldron 19
calefacient 80
calendar 74, 104
calescence 191
caliber 44, 128
calipers 47, 90
calisthenics 59, 77
calk 131
call 131, 166
callboard 22, 177
call girl 137
callable 19
calligraphy 127
calliope 122, 167
callipygian 15, 157
call letters 141
call loan 102
callosity 79
callow 86, 88
calorific 80
calorimetry 80
calumet 126
calumniate 4, 160
calvities 13
calypso 113
camaraderie 64
camarilla 5, 24, 30
Camelot 95
camera 94
camouflage 48, 81
campanile 16
campanology 16
camp follower 78
canalize 47
canapé 8
canard 63, 150
cancroid 37
candelabrum 24
canister 34
canker 36
cannibalize 22, 174
cannikin 24
canny 26, 137, 178
canon 58, 150, 151
canoness 195
canonized 151

canorous 108, 113
go to Canossa 50
cant 84, 90, 153, 161, 168, 176
Cantabrigian 24
cantankerous 13, 139
cantata 113
cantatrice 64
canticle 27
cantilever 136, 170
cantle 22, 129, 151, 154
canton 81, 157
cantonment 175
canvass 46, 59, 162
capacious 149
cap-a-pie 80
caparison 30
caper 130, 160, 194
capital expenditure 87, 136
capital gain 136
capital goods 136
capital loss 102
capitalization 36
capitation 132
capitulate 73
capon 26, 149
caprice 171, 193
capriole 187
capstone 81
captious 39, 63, 139
captive audience 127
caracole 78, 193
caraqueno 25
carat 72, 193
caravan 179, 188
caravansary 89
carbine 148
carcinogen 24
carcinoma 24
cardigan 173
cardinal virtues 94, 115
careen 103, 150, 159, 165, 181
caret 90, 91
carhop 191
carillon 16
carioca 148
carious 43, 149
carminative 66
carmine 44
carnage 18, 107, 160
carnal 19, 66, 156
carnivores 66
carom 17, 82
carp 32
carpetbagger 132
carrel 161, 170

carrion 43, 149
carte blanche 18, 186
cartography 106
cartulary 144
caryatid 31, 64
casbah 117
casement 195
cashier 49
cassandra 128, 136
cassette 149
castanets 30
caste 29
castellated 26, 181
castigate 28, 143
casting vote 43
castrate 56
casual 120
casuistry 142
casus belli 192
catachresis 110
cataclysm 48, 186, 189
catafalque 31
catalectic 189
catalepsy 112
catalyst 6, 168
catamite 21
catapult 83, 98
catastrophe 24
catatonia 112, 170
catcall 24, 193
catchall 35
catchpenny 28
catchword 197
catechesis 121
catechism 139
catechize 139
categorical 3, 117, 132
catena 27
catenate 34
cater-cornered 46
caterwaul 163
catharsis 48, 138
Catherine wheel 129
cathexis 33
catholic 22
catholicon 124, 145
cat's cradle 169
cat's-paw 53, 100
catwalk 115, 191
caucus 132
cauliflower ear 20, 54
caulk 131, 153
cause celèbre 87
causerie 28, 35
causeway 149